# Primer in Radical Criminology: Critical Perspectives on Crime, Power and Identity

## Fourth Edition

by

### Michael J. Lynch

and

### Raymond J. Michalowski

in memory of

### W. Byron Groves

Criminal Justice Press
Monsey, New York U.S.A.
2006

Printed in the United States of America. No part of this book may be reproduced in any manner whatsoever without written permission, except for brief quotations embodied in critical articles and reviews. For information, contact Criminal Justice Press, Willow Tree Press Inc., P.O. Box 249, Monsey, NY 10952 U.S.A.

ISBN 978-1-881798-64-4

Cover art by Vincent T. Lynch.

Graphics by Gojmerac Publishing, Land 'O Lakes, Florida.

# Contents

*continued*

# Contents

# PREFACE

When Casey Groves and I (Lynch) agreed to write the first edition of *Primer* in 1985, I didn't think about a second, let alone a fourth edition. I also didn't think that 20 years after we wrote the first edition, that there would be more editions to write. Perhaps if I had known this in advance, there would never have been a *Primer in Radical Criminology*, at least not one I had co-authored. Nor, at the time, could I have anticipated the events that would lead to writing new editions with a new coauthor. But, 20 years later, as I contemplated what to change about *Primer* to make a new edition actually *new*, I decided that it wasn't simply the changes that made *Primer* worthwhile, it was its very existence. On this both Ray and I agree. This statement requires some elaboration.

Radical, Marxist, socialist, critical – call it what you like – criminology emerged in the 1960s as an attempt to explain criminal behavior and criminal justice practices by taking class conflict as its starting point. That small, fledgling effort has now grown into a large and vibrant segment of contemporary criminology. *Primer's* continued existence and the growth in its size is testimony to the strength of radical thought in criminology.

As we make clear in this book, radical criminology's early focus on class conflict has grown to embrace the powerful, intersecting forces of race, gender and culture. This maturation of radical thought has had a significant impact on criminology. As compared to the past, today, many more criminologists recognize that it is *impossible* to explain criminal behavior or criminal justice processes without reference to class, race, gender and culture. In fact, let us be so **bold** as to state that *any theory that does not employ these ideas cannot adequately explain the making, breaking or enforcement of laws.* In our view, most theories of crime are, indeed, inadequate for understanding either crime or justice.

Of course, many – in fact, the majority of criminologists – will disagree with our interpretation of criminological theory. This is to be expected since most theories about crime and criminal justice still give little explicit consideration to class, race, gender or culture. When theories do address these factors, they usually do little more than acknowledge correlations between crime and class, race, gender or culture. What they do not explain is *why* these correlations exist. Asking what pathways connect race, class, gender, and culture with crime and justice raises a set of questions that we contend ought be fundamental to criminological inquiry. Specifically:

- Why are men more likely to commit crime than women?
- Why are minorities more prevalent among criminal populations?
- Why are the behaviors we label as crime more prominent among the lower classes?
- Why do societies criminalize some harmful behaviors and tolerate others?
- Why do laws and the practice of justice differ among societies?
- Why do some societies that punish less have less crime, and some that punish more have more crime?
- Why have societies invented separate mechanisms for controlling and responding to street, corporate and white collar crime?

This book is based on the proposition that these and similar questions must be central to any sociological effort to understand crime. Why? Because what we have learned from the nearly 240-year history of criminology (if we trace its roots to Beccaria) is that orthodox criminological theories do a poor job of explaining variations in crime across individuals (as well as across societies and cultures). Empirically, the explanatory schemas of orthodox criminology are weak for three reasons.

First, most orthodox theories of crime begin with the assumption that differences among individuals are, per se, the *most important*, if not the only factor that needs to be explained when it comes to understanding the causes of crime. To be sure, it is individuals who commit crime. However, criminological theories that accept the primacy of individual differences also (perhaps unwittingly) accept the proposition that human behavior is the product of free and unfettered choices. We reject this empirically untenable proposition. There is too much evidence that human behavior is fundamentally shaped in important ways by forces beyond individual control. Indeed, the core *social* science disciplines of anthropology and sociology are predicated on the idea that *something* beyond the control of individual actors shapes their behavior, or at the very least shapes the choices available to be made in the first place. To the extent that criminological theories look to individuals to explain crime, they are not only looking for truth in all the wrong places, they are surrendering much of their claim to being sociological.

Second, crime rates vary from nation to nation. This is a problem for orthodox criminology's assumption that crime results from differences among individuals. From an orthodox perspective, this would mean that individuals with criminogenic characteristics are clustered in larger proportions in some countries than in others. In other words, one would have to conclude, for instance, that the high rate of violence in the United States is a sign that it is populated by a higher proportion of dysfunctional human beings than, let's say, Canada. In keeping with a radical criminological perspective, we suggest, it makes far more sense to inquire how the economy, the social structure, and the culture of countries differ in ways that result in greater or lesser impulses to violate the laws of their society than to continue searching for differences among individuals.

Third, even criminologists that address social-structural forces often forget that there is a need to address the many interconnections among these forces. Take opportunity theory as an example. This theory suggests that the cause of crime resides in some generic concept called "opportunity." Of course, opportunity is conceived at such an abstract level, that it is bound to have some truth to it. For instance, a person cannot be a thief if there is nothing to steal. What the theory does not address is how variables such as class, race, gender and culture relate to both the production of desire and the distribution of opportunities to gratify those desires. These key factors, however, are expressions of the structural and cultural dynamics of different societies, including race, class and gender inequalities in the distribution of opportunities to satisfy socially-established desires.

Fourth, orthodox criminology treats the *idea* of crime as unproblematic. That is, orthodox criminology assumes that the only thing that needs explaining is why people commit crime. Orthodox theories do not ask why some harmful acts (e.g. robbery) are defined as crime while other acts that are equal or worse in their consequences (e.g. knowingly marketing a deadly substance such as tobacco) are not. Nor do they ask why some acts that cause relatively little harm (e.g. prostitution) are criminalized, while others that lead to thousands of deaths (e.g. violations of workplace safety regulations) are not. Orthodox criminological theories simply assume that crime is ontological, that is, that it has a concrete existence, rather than recognizing that the meaning of "crime" is socially constructed. While criminologists have generated a large volume of literature that claims to explain the basic human differences between those who would commit crimes and those who would not, the very core of their subject matter – criminality – is a variable social construct, rendering their theories as tenuous as morning fog.

Thus, the first element that makes *Primer* worthwhile is that it forces us and our readers to examine crime in a different way than is allowable under the assumptions imposed by orthodox theory. That difference rests with our attention to how economic, political, and cultural structures as well as the construction of race, class, and gender within them are central for understanding crime, criminal behavior, and the practices of justice deployed to control crime.

The second thing that makes *Primer* worthwhile, from our perspective, it that it allows us to demonstrate how class, race, gender and culture can be added to traditional theories of crime, making them better and more complete.

The third thing that makes *Primer* worthwhile is that it presents radical criminological approaches in a readable way. By placing ourselves in the position of our readers, particularly student readers, we have been forced to continually ask whether what we are describing can be understood by someone who is not already well versed in criminology. Our goal is to provide clear explanations of complex ideas without sacrificing explanatory rigor. Indeed, we often find that attempting to explain complex ideas in plain language helps sharpen, rather than dilute the power of key concepts.

The fourth thing that we feel makes *Primer* valuable is that it is not simply a textbook that assembles the ideas of others. While we relate what others have written, we have also added our own interpretations and sometimes elaborations of them. Thus, while we attempt to clearly explain what others have said, *Primer* is also an ongoing work of scholarship that we use to develop our own understanding of crime and justice. The addition of new chapters on environmental crime and state crime and terrorism are examples of the way *Primer* has become an expression of the ongoing development of our own thought, not just that of others.

Marx taught us that all labor is collective, and this book is particularly so. It began as a collaborative effort between Mike Lynch and W. Byron (Casey) Groves over 20 years ago. Although, the complexities of post-mortem publishing rights have resulted in the removal of Casey's name from this issue, we want to note that his intellectual influence remains a part of this book. This book would never have come into existence without his ideas and efforts in those early years. *Primer* has shouldered on and even grown with the benefit of a new collaboration between Mike Lynch and Ray Michalowski, again demonstrating the value of collaboration in a world that privileges private accomplishment. But it is not only our work that has brought this fourth edition of *Primer* to fruition. For that we also have to thank the many colleagues and intellectual compatriots who have contributed to expanding radical inquiry into crime and justice in the years between the third and fourth editions of this book. Their ideas, their writings, their criticisms, and most of all, their commitment to a world where justice will someday be a reality – not just a word – are the mainspring from which we draw the energy to write. So, to all of them – and you know who you are, and whether you are willing to admit it is another issue – thank you.

M.J.L. and R.M.

Fall 2005

# ACKNOWLEDGMENTS

**Michael J. Lynch**. Over the past few years, a number of people have made a significant contribution to the ideas developed in my work and which are now reflected in this book. In addition, I owe a debt of gratitude to those who have listened to or commented on my explanations of additions to this volume, or who have provided materials used in this edition. This list (alphabetically) includes: Bruce Arrigo, Keri Birchfield, Jana Bufkin, Ronald Burns, Elizabeth Cass, Thomas Castellano, Billy Close, John Cochran, Frank Cullen, Walter DeKeseredy, Melissa Fenwick, Nancy Frank, David Friedricks, James Garofalo, Vicki Gojmerac, Mike Hogan, Jeff Holcomb, Jackie Huey, Lenny Krzycki, Richard McCleary, Danielle McGurrin, Ray Michalowski, Richard Monk, Mahesh Nalla, Randy Nelson, Graeme Newman, Santiago Nunez, Ihekwoaba Onwudiwe, Emmanuel Onyeozili, Wilson Palacios, Britt Patterson, Herman Schwendinger, Julia Schwendinger, Chris Sellers, David Simon, Paul Stretesky, Lynne Veriatis, Michael Welch, Jennifer Wareham. Given my belief in the utility of structural explanations, any errors in thinking and logic in this text can somehow be traced to the influences provided by those named above, and to the conditions under which we have been forced to write this book (e.g., one stingy capitalist, namely Colin Heston; the nature of contemporary criminology; a distance of some 2500 miles; either too much sun or cold). Apologies to any omitted individuals (who may wish to step forward and claim their fair share of responsibility for errors in the text of this work).

Ray and I would also like to acknowledge three people who have made the publication of *Primer* possible and more accurate. First, we would like to thank Rich Allinson, owner and publisher of Willow Tree Press, for purchasing our contract from Harrow and Heston and saving us from having to look for a publisher. Rich has made the transition to Willow Tree easy, and we enjoyed working with him. Second, many thanks to Dr. Ellen Chayet and to Leslie Bachman who painstakingly edited and produced our manuscript, particularly with respect to in-text references and bibliographic citations. This is a thankless job which often goes unnoticed. But, anyone who uses the bibliography of *Primer* in their research should be grateful to Ellen and Leslie.

**Raymond J. Michalowski**. For their intellectual support, friendship and wisdom I would like to thank, my partner and quintessential anthropologist, Jill Dubisch, and the following friends and colleagues who helped grow me in a number of ways. In order of their appearance in my life they are: Stephen

Pfohl, Ronald Kramer, Margaret Zahn, Nancy Wonders, William Chambliss, Michael Pearson, Michael Sheely, James Livingston, Michael Fennell, Susan Caringella-MacDonald, James Messerschmidt, Drew Humphries, Susan Carlson, David Aday, Fred Solop, Susanna Maxwell, Larry Gould, John Hewitt, Alex Alvarez, Marianne Neilsen, Neil Websdale, Jeff Ferrell, Linda Robyn, Barbara Perry, Mark Hamm, Kenneth Tunnell, Dave Kauzlarich and Rick Matthews.

Finally, we would like to take this opportunity to thank Rich Allinson, the owner of Criminal Justice Press (CJP), our publisher, for needing a new edition of *Primer* to keep up with the rest of the publishing capitalists who use new editions to sell more books, and to suppress the second hand book market. Maybe someone can invent paper that disintegrates faster than the environmentally conscious paper stock CJP uses. Seriously, working with Rich on the past two editions has been a pleasure. Rich has allowed us great latitude in shaping *Primer* so that it serves, not just as a textbook conduit for the thinking of others, but as an outlet for our intellectual development and creative thought.

# AUTHOR BIOGRAPHIES

**Michael J. Lynch** is Professor in the Criminology Department at the University of South Florida. He received his Ph.D. from the State University of New York at Albany, School of Criminal Justice. His current research interests include: radical criminology, environmental justice, corporate crime, corporate regulation, racial bias in the criminal justice system, and theoretical criminology. His recent publications have appeared in *The Archives of Pediatric and Adolescent Medicine*; *The Journal of Health and Social Behavior*; *Society and Natural Resources*; *The Journal of Black Studies*; *The Social Science Journal*; *Social Science Quarterly*; *Sociological Quarterly*; *Mankind Quarterly*; *Theoretical Criminology*; and *Critical Criminology*. His most recent book is *Environmental Crime: A Sourcebook* (with Ronald G. Burns).

**Raymond Michalowski** is Arizona Regents Professor of Criminal Justice and Adjunct Professor of Sociology at Northern Arizona University. His published works include *State-Corporate Crime: Wrong-doing at the Intersection of Business and Politics* (Rutgers University Press); *Radikale Kriminologie* (AJZ Verlag), *Run for the Wall: Remembering Vietnam on a Motorcycle Pilgrimage* (Rutgers University Press); and *Order, Law and Crime* (Random House/McGraw-Hill). He had also published articles on a variety of topics including, the new-American imperialism, globalization and traffic in women, the political economy of crime and punishment, state-corporate crime, and law, lawyers and legal transformation in Cuba. His most current academic project focuses on the intersection of globalization, human rights, and immigration in the European Union and the United States.

# ONE.
# WHAT IS RADICAL CRIMINOLOGY?

Radical criminology is a way of doing criminology that frames the problem of crime in terms of the sociological forces of class, race, gender, culture and history. The radical criminological tradition, now more than 30 years old, has changed dramatically since its inception, and it is no easy task to summarize the issues that radical criminologists study. Further, any overview of radical criminology – including our own – will always be provisional due to the continuing development of radical thought in criminology. Our modest goal is to provide an overview of radical criminology's history, central themes, and potential directions.

During its initial stage of development, explanations of crime centering around political-economic and social class issues dominated radical criminology. Over the past decade and a half, however, the theoretical scope of radical criminology has expanded to include race, gender, culture, history, postmodernism and left-realism, among others. Our discussion of radical criminology examines each of these issues, and pays particular attention to how these explanations intersect with radical criminology's grounding concern with political economy and social class.

A complete understanding of radical criminology cannot be forged without relating its development to trends and practices taking place in orthodox criminology (sometimes called "mainstream" or "traditional" criminology), because radical criminology emerged as – and continues to be – an alternative to orthodox criminology. Thus, to orient our discussion of radical criminology, we begin with a brief overview of several general criminological themes.

## General Approaches to Doing Criminology

Criminology, the systematic study of crime and criminals, began in the last half of the 19th century. Since then, criminologists have offered a variety of explanations of the nature of crime, why people commit crime and what should be done to control crime. These theories have typically taken either a *behavioral* or a *definitional* approach to crime (Blum-West and Carter, 1983). Behavioral approaches focus on why people commit crimes, while definitional approaches examine how actions come to be labeled as criminal (Farrell and Morrione, 1978; Farrell and Swigert, 1978b). For instance, a researcher operating from a behavioral approach might ask: "What leads people to use marijuana?" In contrast, someone operating from a definitional approach would ask: "Why is getting high on marijuana illegal, while getting buzzed on beer is not?"

*Behavioral theories* look for answers to the question of why people commit crime in one of three areas: the individual, social groups or society as a whole. Individual-level explanations seek biological, mental or emotional defects that might explain criminal behavior. Group-oriented theories focus on how interpersonal relationships (in families, peer groups and middle-range social institutions such as schools and neighborhoods) increase or decrease the likelihood that someone will engage in crime. Both approaches stress the *development* of criminal tendencies when people are young, and tend to focus on juvenile delinquency rather than adult criminal behavior (see Sampson and Laub, 1993). In contrast, macro-level behavioral theories examine the crime-causing effects of sociological forces such as poverty, unemployment or inequality, and focus on how these forces are expressions of the overall structure of the society. This sociological approach is more typical of radical criminology than approaches focused on individuals or small groups.

*Definitional theories* focus on the political institutions that make and enforce laws (e.g., the state), the content of law and public perceptions of the "crime problem." When it comes to the character of the state and the content of law, definitional theories give particular attention to the role that powerful groups play in creating laws that reflect their interests, conflicts between more versus less powerful social groups, the correspondence between forms of law and types of states, and how stereotypes and structures related to gender, race and ethnicity influence lawmaking. For example, definitional studies might examine differences in the punishments provided for white collar crime and street crime (Friedrichs, 1996a, 1996b; Kauzlarich and Kramer, 1998; Michalowski and Kramer, 2005, Sutherland, 1983). Or they might examine how the portrayal of crime in news and entertainment media provides "information" and images that form the basis of people's understanding of crime and what they believe should be done about it (e.g., Cohen, 1972; Cohen and Young, 1973; Hall et al., 1978; Barak, 1994, 1988; Barlow et al., 1995a, 1995b; Brownstein, 1990; Baer and Chambliss, 1997; Ferrell, 1992, 1995; Huey and Lynch, 1996; Chiricos, 1996; Krzycki, 1996; Lynch and Krzycki, 1998; Lynch, Stretesky and Hammond, 2000).

Every school of criminology exhibits a preference for a particular style of explanation. This book details the kinds of explanations and preferences favored within *radical criminology*, and explores how these explanations and preferences have been applied to understand various problems of crime and justice.

For example, radical criminologists will be far more likely to base their behavioral or definitional analyses on theoretical perspectives that critique domination (e.g., Marxism, feminism or postmodernism), rather than on perspectives that accept status quo social arrangements and established definitions of crime. We begin by explaining in greater depth what we mean by the term "radical criminology."

## Beginning to Define Radical Criminology

It is no easy task to define radical criminology because it encompasses a variety of preferences regarding styles of explanation and variables to be analyzed (Lynch, 1997). In this section, we provide a history of radical criminology, and review various approaches to radical inquiry in criminology. We end by providing a definition of what we believe constitutes radical criminology today.

The term radical criminology was introduced in the 1970s by criminologists who sought to transcend individual-level and group-based behavioral explanations of crime. Prior to that time, most criminological inquiry was behavioral, devoted to identifying what was wrong with the "kinds of people" who commit crime or discovering what was amiss in the "kinds of communities or groups " that had high proportions of these people (e.g., Shaw and McKay, 1969; Cohen, 1955; Miller, 1958; Hirschi, 1969). This search for defective people and disorganized communities and social groups was, in turn, informed by the underlying tenets of what Kuhn (1970) termed "normal science." Key among these tenets were the beliefs that observable outcomes have knowable causes, that these causes are consistent over time and can be discovered through the application of value-free methods of scientific inquiry, and that once the causes are known, outcomes can be controlled. From its inception, criminology has been molded around these assumptions of the scientific model (Beirne, 1987a, 1987b, 1993; Lynch, 2000).

Radical criminologists questioned the normal-science approach on several accounts. First, they challenged the claim that the study of human life, particularly around a subject as politically-charged as crime and punishment, could be "value free." Radical criminologists argued that research designed to identify the defects within individuals that led them to commit crime was no less value-laden than research that sought to demonstrate how the definition and punishment of crime reflected the distribution of power characteristic of modern-day capitalist America (Schwendinger and Schwendinger, 1970).

Second, radical criminologists rejected the idea that the real causes of crime could be found in either defective individuals or disorganized communities. Instead, radicals argued that crime is a *sociologically situated* phenomenon and that patterns of crime and punishment in a society reflect its social-structural characteristics (Michalowski, 1977; Platt, 1974).

From this perspective, the behavior of individuals, groups and organizations must be understood in the context of their connection to broader economic, social, political, cultural and historical factors that provide the structures for social life. Thus, for example, insofar as American society is rooted in the social-structural features of capitalism, any search for the roots of crime in the United States must incorporate an analysis of capitalism (Quinney, 1974b).

Given the significance of capitalism in American society, early radical criminologists gravitated toward the most powerful existing critique of capitalism – Marxism. Informed by Marxist thought, radical criminologists sought to identify and critique the forms of domination, exploitation, inequality and class conflict characteristic of capitalist political economies, and to show how these social structures were related to the problem of crime (e.g., Balbus, 1973; Barak, 1974; Belknap, 1977; Harring and McMullin, 1975; Pfohl, 1979; Schwendinger and Schwendinger, 1977; Wright, 1973). Like other approaches to criminology, early radical criminology also generated a definitional and behavioral approach.

## Radical Criminology: Definitional and Behavioral Varieties

The *definitional* component of early radical criminology focused on how the distribution of political and economic power in capitalist society resulted in some harmful acts – typically those committed more often by the poor – being defined and treated as serious crime, while other equally harmful acts – typically those that could only be committed by people in positions of power – were often either not defined as criminal, or treated as minor technical offenses (Chambliss and Seidman, 1982; Chambliss and Mankoff, 1976; Harring, 1976, 1977, 1981; Kramer, 1984; Krisberg, 1975; Michalowski, 1979; Reiman, 1998; Tigar, 1971, 1977; Quinney, 1980; see also Frank and Lynch, 1992; Simon, 1999).

Radical criminologists operating within a *behavioral paradigm* sought to demonstrate how "street crimes" of theft and violence resulted from the distortions of human lives that arise from the oppressive and alienating experience of living with little in a land of plenty (Currie, 1985; Gordon, 1971, 1973; Michalowski, 1983; Wallace and Humphries, 1981; Blau and Blau, 1982). Specifically, radicals sought to identify the particular kinds of stresses experienced by people living in a capitalist society and how these stresses could produce deviant forms of behavior, including both street crime committed by the poor and white collar crime committed by the affluent (e.g., Quinney, 1980). Though different, behavioral and definitional approaches to radical criminology share a common theme: detailing the ways in which class relationships and class conflicts generated by a capitalist political economy affect the production of crime and punishment. Over time, these two approaches began to intermingle, so that today, most radical criminologists treat the behavioral and definitional aspects of crime and punishment as intersecting parts of the same problem.

Beyond the intellectual project of identifying political-economic forces that generated crime, early radical criminology was also a *criminology of resistance* (Michalowski and Bohlander, 1976; Platt, 1974; Schwendinger and Schwendinger, 1977; see also Cullen and Wozniak, 1982; Michalowski, 1996). By this we mean that radicals challenged the status quo distribution of wealth and power, and used this analysis to assist movements seeking to transform structural arrangements in ways that enabled the less powerful to gain greater control over their lives and destinies. This focus was derived from Marx's dictum that: "The philosophers have only *interpreted* the world in various ways; the point, however, *is to change it*" (Marx, 1967a:13). This attention to social change had two components. With respect to theory, radical criminologists constructed and communicated methods for transforming and transcending exploitative class relationships characteristic of life in capitalist society. In terms of policy (*praxis* in Marxian terminology), many radical criminologists became actively involved in movements representing oppressed social groups, including the poor, prisoners, people of color, gays and lesbians, women and blue-collar workers (see for example, Klein and Kress, 1976; Michalowski, 1975). By engaging in *praxis*, radical criminologists surrendered the value-free observer role promoted in orthodox criminology, and openly announced their partisanship with the disadvantaged by engaging in what eventually became a well-established movement in the social sciences (known as participatory research). Radical criminologists also argued that orthodox criminology, despite claims to the contrary, was not value neutral. Rather, by failing to question status-quo arrangements, orthodox criminology was itself expressing a *value preference,* in this case for keeping the dominant order in place.

## THE DEVELOPMENT OF RADICAL CRIMINOLOGY

Radical criminology cannot be defined without reference to the historical and political context within which it developed. In this section we review the social forces that led to increasing interest in Marxism and how these forces combined with criminological traditions to give rise to a Marxist criminology (for further discussion see Cardarelli and Hicks, 1993; Bohm, 1982b; Friedrichs, 1980b; Meier, 1976; Garofalo, 1978; Michalowski, 1996; Lynch, 1997; Schwendinger, Schwendinger, and Lynch, 2002).

## Social Conflict and the Rebirth of Radicalism

During the 1960s, scholars from several disciplines began to rediscover the works of Marx. The critique of capitalism and models of socialism contained in these works offered alternative explanations of the contemporary world as well as solutions to its problems. These approaches were grounded in the observation that history – the ongoing story of human society and struggle – is the record of how unequal power relations endemic to class-based societies are played out in arenas such as law, work, family and community. But what led to this rediscovery of Marxian analysis during the 1960s and 1970s?

First was the decline of McCarthyism. From the end of World War II through the late 1950s, the anti-communist fear fomented by Senator Joseph McCarthy (hence, McCarthyism), and promoted by a number of governmental, business and religious leaders, dominated the public world in the United States, including the world of American scholarship. Fear of being denounced as a "communist" and losing one's job or being blacklisted from future academic employment for holding a sympathetic stance toward Marxism dissuaded many from incorporating Marxist thought into their research and writing (Schrecker, 1998, 1994,; Caute, 1978; for a rare exception to this tendency, see the work of C. Wright Mills). After McCarthy was discredited and the era of blacklists came to an end, this fear began to wane and new opportunities were created to reconsider the utility of Marxist thought for analyzing capitalist societies.

Second, a central feature of American culture was the prominent belief that capitalism was an ideal form of social life, while socialism, as practiced in the Soviet Union, Eastern Europe and China, was the worst. Within this context there was little cultural space for discussions of the dark side of American capitalism such as poverty, inequality and racism. By the late 1960s, all this had changed. The civil rights movement, spearheaded by Martin Luther King Jr.'s highly visible and peaceful marches, forced Americans to confront the class and race biases they had previously ignored (Friedrichs, 1980a; King, 1987). This awareness was heightened by a number of highly publicized assaults against and the killing of activists who promoted basic civil rights for African Americans (Sitcoff, 1981).

At the same time the increasingly naked use of U.S. military power to force smaller nations to accommodate the interests of the American political economy contradicted claims about the benign character of American capitalism (Frank, 1975; Galeano, 1973; Williams, 1962). In the 1950s and 1960s, the destruction of the socialist democracy in Guatemala, sponsored by the U.S. Central Intelligence Agency; the failed, U.S.-sponsored invasion of Cuba; the U.S. invasion of the Dominican Republic; and the increasing escalation of the U.S. war in Vietnam; all tarnished the image of the United States as a benevolent, peace-loving nation that turned to war only as a last resort (Baritz, 1985). In the face of these events, Marxist critiques of the U.S. social system began to appear more reasonable, and a number of social movements began incorporating Marxist analyses into their challenges to existing distributions of wealth and power. Many opponents of the Vietnam War, for instance, viewed the war as an attempt to protect American corporate interests overseas and not as a "moral war" to protect Americans from communism (Stacewicz, 1997; Sykes, 1974; see also Baran and Sweezy, 1966). Black activists like Malcolm X and Stokely Carmichael, drawing on a long tradition of radical African-American thought (see Du Bois, 1968) utilized Marxism to analyze the link between racism and class domination within America (Carmichael and Hamilton, 1967; Malcolm X, 1965, 1966; see also, Gregory, 1971). Meanwhile, leaders of the Black Power Movement such as Eldridge Cleaver (1968) and George Jackson (1994) began to explore Marxist thought while in prison and used it to rally others to the cause of black liberation.

In addition to the civil rights and anti-war movements, the 1960s was characterized by an intensifying struggle for women's rights and feminism (Beauvoir, 1952; Friedan, 1963; Morgan, 1970). As women began to demand equal treatment in the workplace, on the street and in the home, their critique of gender relations added yet another dimension to the growing awareness of inequality in American society. While subsequent waves of feminists would part company with Marxism, during the 1960s and early 1970s many dissident women utilized writings by leftists such as Engels (1972) and Zaretsky (1976) to buttress their call for equality (Hartmann, 1981).

The social turmoil of the 1960s was not limited to the U.S., but rather constituted a "world historical movement," as students and leftists in Australia, Canada, Britain, France and elsewhere publicly protested policies in their countries, and demonstrated solidarity with the U.S. anti-war movement (Katsiaficas, 1987; Fanon, 1961). Because Marxist analysis had not been suppressed everywhere as it had in the U.S., in the 1970s American leftist scholars were often influenced by the works of British and European thinkers such as Louis Althusser (1972), Perry Anderson (1974), Jurgen Habermas (1975), Herbert Marcuse (1966) and Nicos Poulantzas (1978).

In the final analysis, the effect of political conflicts in the U.S. during the 1960s and early 1970s challenged the image of America as the land of freedom and equality for all (see Carnoy, 1994; Ryan, 1982). As a result, many Americans, even those who had been previously certain about the special quality of life in America, found themselves forced to confront issues of fairness, equality and justice.

## Radicalism Invades Academia

It was not long before this social turmoil began to influence the academic world. To be sure, sociologists such as C. Wright Mills (1940s-1960s) and, before him, Thorsten Veblen (1890s-1920s), and economists Paul Baran (1930-1960) and Paul Sweezy (1940-1990s), had incorporated Marxian thought into their critiques of American institutions (see also Beard, 1916). However, events of the 1960s led a number of young scholars whose political consciousness had been shaped by the turmoil of the 1960s to question widely used consensus models derived from the writings of Emile Durkheim (1966) and Talcott Parsons (1954). Such models appeared incapable of explaining the oppression, inequality and social struggle that seemed to be everywhere, and resulted in a search for new theories that would better explain social conflict. As it turned out, these "new" theories resembled a very old one – Marxism – and many American scholars began to read Marx for the first time.

Although the social and intellectual currents of the 1960s and early 1970s attracted many to a radical perspective, leftists remained a minority within U.S. academic circles. M-a-r-x remained a four-letter word to many Americans, and Marxism and socialism continued to serve as ideological targets for supporters of the status quo inequalities of wealth and power in the U.S. Marxian theories continued to be associated with political repression in self-proclaimed communist nations such as China, Cuba and the Soviet Union, or with caricatured versions of Marxism spread by right-wing propagandists from Joseph McCarthy to Ronald Reagan. Nevertheless, with English translations of many of Marx's work more readily available, Marx and his intellectual followers could now be read and evaluated on their own terms. Consequently, Marx's historical materialism became increasingly influential as a *method of inquiry*, even for many who were critical of repressive (and very un-Marxist) communist governments. As more U.S. scholars and activists began to read Marx, he came to be viewed as a humanistic scholar par excellence, and even his critics, such as Karl Popper (1957), acknowledged his passionate commitment to equal justice and an enhanced quality of life for all. By the mid-1970s American universities introduced Marxist studies programs and an academic rebirth of American Marxism was at hand.

## Marxist Criminology Emerges

Observing the struggles for social justice being waged around them, some criminologists were influenced by the academic turn toward Marxism. Though Marx wrote little about crime, law and justice (Engels wrote much more on these issues, see chapter 5; see also, Hirst, 1972), radical criminologists extended Marx's theories to discussions of these topics. A primary interest was developing a critique of existing criminology that demonstrated its neglect of the role that inequality and exploitation played in the formation of crime, law and punishment and that exposed the class bias of criminology. Although early radicals found Marx's writings useful, they also drew upon domestic strains of radicalism embedded in long-standing American traditions and struggles for social justice and equality (Weinstein, 2003; Zinn, 1995). This tradition, evident in the abolitionist movement, the nineteenth century battle for women's rights and a century-old labor movement, had its roots not in Marxism, but in the Declaration of Independence and the Bill of Rights as idealized liberal expressions of a society of human equals – idealized expressions that Marx recognized as crucial to the creation of a just world (Beard, 1916; Cain and Hunt, 1979; Ishay, 2004).

At the same time, radical criminologists were also influenced by several well-established criminological traditions. In particular, Robert Merton and Edwin Sutherland had a far-reaching impact on the formation of radical criminology (although they are typically characterized as representing orthodox criminological thought). Merton and Sutherland made their main contributions to criminology during the Great Depression of the 1930s, challenging the prevalent emphasis on individualism and the individual as the source of crime (on individualism in the U.S., see Bowles and Gintis, 1976; O'Connor, 1985). Merton and Sutherland articulated what, for their time, was the radical hypotheses that crime resulted from *social* rather than individual problems. Merton (1979) proposed that crime results when *societies* create gaps between their culturally approved goals and the distribution of means available to achieve those goals, creating strains for people. In other words, some individuals lacked access to culturally prescribed means for success even in democratic (i.e., egalitarian) nations such as the U.S. Radical criminologists, who located the cause of "street" crime in the poverty and inequality of the lowest segments of the working class, owe a theoretical debt to the work of Robert Merton.

For his part, Sutherland (1939, 1949) contended that those who broke the law *learned* to engage in law-violating behavior through *normal processes* of social interaction. According to Sutherland, the likelihood of becoming a criminal or a conformist was a consequence of social surroundings. Sutherland's theory, known as differential association, delivered a serious challenge to the then-dominant view that the majority of criminals suffered from defective personalities and/or were motivated by abnormal "drives." Sutherland's view of lawbreakers as normal individuals who learned deviant patterns of behavior is an often unrecognized cornerstone of later radical contentions that changing the character of social environments could reduce rates of crime.

Radical criminology was also influenced by the work of social-psychologist Edwin Lemert (1951) on the construction of social identities. Lemert suggested that the label of "deviant" or "criminal" is more likely to be applied to the powerless than powerful, and that being officially labeled propels deviants into further violations of law as they and others come to believe that they *are* "deviant" (as they adopt a deviant identity). Lemert's work also advanced the idea that crime control strategies may result in more rather than less crime (see also Lynch et al.,1993; Matza, 1968).

The emergence of Marxist criminology was also influenced by radical intellectual developments within sociology and non-U.S criminology (Meier, 1976; Beirne, 1979; Schichor, 1980b). The emergence of conflict theory within sociology (Coser, 1956; Dahrendorff, 1968), the growing influence of symbolic interactionism (Mead 1962; Blumer, 1969), and the development of labeling theories in the study of deviance (Becker, 1963; Rubington and Weinberg, 1987), all contributed additional intellectual impetus to radical criminology. The newly translated Marxist analysis of crime, *Crime and Economic Conditions*, by Dutch criminologist Willem Bonger (1969), and the publication of *The New Criminology* by British criminologists Ian Taylor et al. (1973), provided additional intellectual momentum.

In sum, as the social turbulence and heightened academic awareness of Marxist thought found its way into criminology, a radical approach emerged. Radicals began to explore how the political economy of American capitalism influenced the definition, commission and punishment of crime. At this time, the School of Criminology at the University of California, Berkeley became one of the earliest and most important American sites for radical criminology. A number of influential radical scholars, including Tony Platt, Herman Schwendinger, Julia Schwendinger and Paul Takagi, all taught at Berkeley, and a number of their students including – Gregg Barak, Elliot Currie, Drew Humphries and Dorie Klein – continue to develop criminologies of resistance today. Berkeley's radical criminologists also played an important role in founding the first journal of radical criminology, *Crime and Social Justice* (now titled *Social Justice*). This journal enabled radical criminologists to share their ideas with one another, and provided an important forum where interested scholars and activists could encounter the emerging world of radical criminology.

In short, a Marxist movement was born in criminology as theorists turned to Marxism to explain the link between social injustice and crime. Within criminology, Marxism emerged as a powerful tool for understanding: (1) why certain harmful behaviors came to be defined as crime while others were ignored; (2) why certain social groups were more likely to exhibit higher rates of "street crime" than others; and (3) why most strategies for crime control and punishment focused on crimes committed by the poor and by racial and ethnic minorities, rather than on those committed by the more affluent Euro-American sectors of the population.

It should be noted that as it began to develop, radical criminology was subject to considerable criticism and debate (see generally Inciardi, 1980; Greenberg, 1975; Akers, 1979; Klockars, 1979; Huff, 1980; Mankoff, 1980; Pepinsky, 1980; Schichor, 1980a, 1980b; Sparks, 1980; Toby, 1980). Some critics focused on radical criminologists' failure to maintain "scientific objectivity," and their presumed affinity with repressive communist nations. Sometimes these critiques generated uncivil character debates between radical and non-radical criminologists (see open letters, *Social Justice*). Others questioned whether labor and civil rights legislation that seemed to promote the interests of less powerful groups disproved "instrumentalist" Marxist theories that claimed that law was little more than a tool of the ruling class. Despite these criticisms, and sometimes because of them, radical criminology developed theoretically, incorporating a variety of emerging radical approaches such as structuralism, post-structuralism, feminism and post-modernism. Since the 1980s, the number of criminologists engaged in radical inquiry has grown, and the influence and acceptability of radical criminology have expanded. Today, a criminologist cannot claim to have a well-rounded education, or to "understand" the broad sociological characteristics of crime and justice, without possessing a basic understanding of radical criminology.

## 21st Century Radicals

Since the 1970s, radical criminology has been modified in response to criticism that political-economic and social class explanations needed to be broadened. The horizons of radical criminology have been substantially expanded by works that focus on gender (Danner, 1996; Chesney-Lind, 1996; Caufield and Wonders, 1994; Cain, 1990; Caringella-MacDonald, 1988; Daly and Chesney-Lind, 1988; Smart, 1987; Wonders, 1996), race and ethnicity (Bourgois, 1996; Hawkins, 1983; Lynch, 1996; McLean and Milovanovic, 1990;

Mann; 1993; Mann and Zatz, 1998; Zatz, 1987a, 1978b) and cultural processes such as language, mass media, and style (Altheide, 2002; Barak, 1994, 1996; Cohen, 1972; Ferrell, 1992; Fishman and Cavender,1998; Hall et al., 1978; Henry and Milovanovic, 1996; Milovanovic, 1992, 1997; Pfohl, 1985; Arrigo, 1995, 1993; Arrigo, Milovanovic, and Schehr, 2005). These newer modes of explanation brought with them preferences concerning which topics to explore, and *how* they should be explored. In place of historical materialism or quantitative analysis, these newer approaches favor methodologies such as ethnography, biography, narrative analysis and deconstruction (for discussion, see Arrigo, 1995; Ferrell and Sanders, 1996; Pfhol and Gordon, 1986; Wonders, 1996). Many of these changes reflect the impact of two of the most sweeping and influential intellectual movements during the last part of the twentieth century – feminism and postmodernism – that we will explore in greater detail later. For now, we will note that radical inquiry in criminology has grown from its deep roots in Marxist political economy into a more eclectic intellectual movement that encompasses a variety of distinct criminologies based on resistance to numerous forms of structural inequalities.

In addition to the long-standing concerns with social class, race/ethnicity, gender issues, and cultural processes, radical criminology now has to confront two pressing challenges of the new 21st century: environmental degradation and a return to militarism.

Environmental issues, such as global warming, heavy reliance on fossil fuels, and toxic pollution, represent the greatest threat to human well-being ever created. These threats, however, cannot be controlled without widespread decentralization in the production of energy used to heat and cool homes, operate electrical equipment, and fuel vehicles. The movement to decentralized energy, however, would do more than help reduce global warming and environmental pollution: It would also make populations far less dependent on large corporations and foreign fuel suppliers as energy providers. Moves in this direction, however, threaten to make obsolete the fossil fuel corporations that have controlled fuel exploration, energy production and distribution, and much governmental policy for the last century.

Decentralizing the energy economy would require changing an energy industry that has little interest in changes that will reduce its power and profitability. Thus, limiting future environmental threats to human well-being will necessitate a new and stronger regulatory environment under federal and state laws. On the one hand, this can only come about if the U.S. government removes the extensive legal protections and financial support currently given to the fossil fuel and other technologically deficient industries. On the other hand, if political and corporate leaders continue to promote a political economy around today's energy monopolies, they will be guilty of one of the greatest crimes in the human habitation of the planet – widespread *avoidable* destruction of human, animal and plant life.

Current political policies point in the opposite direction. For example, the George W. Bush Administration has promoted older and more polluting technology; has opened the Artic to oil exploration; and has attempted to rewrite the Clean Air Act and to nullify other important environmental laws restricting toxic pollution, thereby increasing public exposure to toxins (see Burns and Lynch, 2004, and chapter 8). These policies will not eliminate the United States' dependence on foreign oil (Goodstein, 2004; Rifkin, 2002), will ensure the continued need to intervene in the Middle East, will escalate environmental health problems and environmental decay, and will strengthen the centralization rather the decentralization of energy production.

Another large-scale problem exists in the arena of militarism (see chapter 10). In 2002, U.S. President George Bush proclaimed what has become know as the "Bush doctrine," which grants the United States the right to engage in preemptive military attack against any nation it suspects of being a possible future threat to U.S. interests without submitting its claims to the judgment of international law (Kramer, Michalowski, and Rothe, 2005). This doctrine threatens to increase global instability by destroying the framework of international law that was established by the world community in response to the horrors of World War II.

The Bush doctrine was used to justify the invasion of Iraq even though claims that Iraq maintained close links to Al Qaeda and possessed weapons of mass destruction were false (Pitt, 2002; Rai, 2002; Ratner, Green and Olshansky, 2003; Solomon and Erlich, 2003). In the Middle East and in most places outside the United States, it is widely understood that this invasion is closely linked to America's insatiable need for petroleum to fuel its economy (Everrest, 2004). Nevertheless, by 2005, the U.S. coalition forces operating in Iraq had killed between 30,000 and 100,000 innocent civilians, according to medical researchers at Johns Hopkins University (Roberts et al., 2004). To the extent that this war violated international law, these deaths are not just collateral damage, they are *murders*. The impunity with which a global power such as the United States can take the lives and destroy or expropriate the property of other countries undercuts the possibility of a world organized according to the rule of law (Chambers, 2004). Furthermore, insofar as a dominant global power has now declared unilateral war to be an acceptable way to get what it wants, we stand on the brink of a great undoing of international law and a return to a world in which war becomes, once again, the dominant mechanism for resolving international conflicts.

The point is that there is a very complicated story that needs to be told about global warming, toxic pollution, the political-economy of oil and international relations, and their relationship to rules of law, existing power structures and economic and political interests that dominate the United States. One reason that this story is so important is that these events (global warming, toxic pollution, or war) can cause tremendous harm to the world as we know it. Consequently, these issues ought be central concerns for *criminologists,* especially at the beginning of the 21st century, while there is still time to react to these problems and address them.

## RADICAL CRIMINOLOGY AND CRITICAL CRIMINOLOGY

Taken as a whole, the contemporary criminologies of resistance discussed above are often called "critical criminology" (Michalowski, 1996; Thomas and O'Maolchatha, 1989; Schwartz, 1989), and many of its practitioners are members of the Division on Critical Criminology within the American Society of Criminology, and the Critical Criminology Section of the Academy of Criminal Justice Sciences. Thus, a thoughtful reader might ask: "Why isn't this book entitled *A Primer in **Critical Criminology?**"* We could take the easy way out, noting that this is a fourth edition and as a consequence we are "stuck" with the term "radical criminology." This explanation, however, is neither adequate, useful nor truthful. Rather, we retained the term radical criminology because we felt that it more accurately characterizes those dimensions that different "critical" approaches to criminology share and that differentiate it from orthodox criminology.

First, from an etymological point of view, to think "radically" means to be concerned with finding the roots of things. This was the first purpose of radical criminology – to get to the root of what is behind and beneath the crime problem. The different criminologies of resistance that comprise "critical criminology" each have their own particular view on where to look for the roots of crime and how this search should be conducted. Feminists look to gender relations, critical-race theorists to race relations, political-economists to social class, and post-modernists to cultural processes. What these views share is a commitment to understanding the deeper social forces that shape the definition, commission and punishment of crime.

Second, contemporary critical criminologists, whatever their orientation, pose a radical challenge to the established definition of crime by emphasizing that crime is a *relational* rather than a fixed social phenomenon. Rather than treating crime as something with permanent and independent characteristics, critical criminologists generally take the much more radical position that the social reality of crime is a fluid one, arising from the interplay among social forces, particularly gender, class, race and culture (see Schwartz and Milovanovic, 1996).

To be sure, there is substantial debate among radicals regarding the relative importance and contributions of class, race, gender, and culture to the crime problem (Lynch, 1996). Nevertheless, the emerging radical position rejects the idea that any *one* of these variables can be the *sole* explanation for crime and the system that controls it. Instead, the relative utility of these factors depends on the question being asked. If the question involves addressing higher rates of homicide in poor communities compared with wealthier ones, issues of social class come to the fore. If the question is why men kill more often than women, or why domestic violence is treated as less serious than other forms of violence, gendered patterns of behavior become the more salient factor. If higher rates of homicide or higher rates of imprisonment among African Americans as compared with ("white") European Americans are at issue, questions regarding race and ethnicity become central. Similarly, should we want to know why mass media shape public consciousness of crime or how deviant subcultures operate, theories that focus on mass media and culture become particularly useful.

Although the relative utility of theories regarding class, gender, race/ethnicity and culture can shift according to the specific questions being researched, radical criminologists increasingly recognize the importance of exploring the *intersection* of these factors in shaping what we know as the crime problem (Schwartz and Milovanovic, 1996). Thus, while some radicals might, for example, focus on the relationship between social class and homicide, it is increasingly likely that they will also recognize that it is *poor men of color* living in a society that has a *cultural admiration* for violence, and all the social structures that these conditions entail, that need to be addressed if we want a fuller understanding of the problem (see, for example, Messerschmidt, 1997, 1993).

Radical criminologists are not the only ones to utilize variables such as class, gender, race/ethnicity and culture in their research, and analysts from a variety of criminological traditions have studied the relationship between poverty, inequality, gender, etc. and crime (see, for example, the critique by Groves and Corrado, 1983). What distinguishes radical from orthodox criminology, and what unites radical criminologists, is how these factors are understood. From a radical perspective, class, gender, race/ethnicity and culture are viewed as *social relationships* whose meaning arises within a sociological context, rather than as the personal characteristics of individuals (Lynch, 1996; Lynch and Patterson, 1996a). In other words, the meaning of being an African American in the U.S. is not the result of being born black; it is the consequence of the historic and contemporary relationship between African Americans and European Americans. Similarly, the poor exist only in relationship to the wealthy, and the meaning of being male or female comes not from being born with a particular chromosomal structure but from the way the roles played by males and females in the society are constructed.

Radical criminologists view class, gender, race/ethnicity and culture *as relational sociological and organizational phenomena*. For instance, the meaning of being male or female is more than just cultural: it is constructed and enforced, in part, by legal institutions (MacKinnon, 1989; Minnow, 1997). Consider, for example, how laws governing abortion, or prohibiting homosexual acts or same-sex marriages, shape the definition of what it means to be a man or a woman in the U.S. Similarly, the labor market and subsequent distribution of income ensures that the poor do not live in the same neighborhoods, frequent the same recreational areas or enjoy the same access to political power as middle-class or affluent European Americans (Szymanski, 1983). Structural factors such as these give shape to what it means both culturally and personally to be poor or affluent, or male or female in the U.S.

Radicals seek to get beyond the *appearances* of social characteristics in order to understand their *underlying sociological import*. It is one thing to ask why poor people commit more of a particular kind of crime; it is quite another to address what makes them poor in the first place or to ask how poverty and class are connected to differences in the way we define and punish crimes of the poor versus crimes of the powerful. It is one thing to ask why women commit less crime than men, but quite different to ask how cultural and organizational constructions of maleness and femaleness increase the likelihood that men will resort to violence (Messerschmidt, 1997, 1993). The various critical approaches to criminology all share this drive to identify the larger, more inclusive configurations and processes that shape crime and justice.

Third, as we noted earlier, radical approaches are all criminologies of *resistance*. Each recognizes that problems of crime and justice arise from arrangements in the existing social order and that these problems can only be addressed by changing social structures. Crime reduction strategies directed toward individuals or small groups alone will not suffice. In addition, criminologies of resistance contain an element of *praxis,* that is, a desire to transform theories about the criminogenic effects of class, gender, and racial and ethnic inequalities into public policies that would reduce or eliminate such inequalities. This means that radical criminologists argue for the reduction or elimination of class, race and gender inequalities.

Fourth, as Benjamin Ward (1979) argued, radicals share a commitment to the wretched of the earth (see also Fanon, 1961), that is, to underprivileged, deprived and exploited populations in the U.S. and around the world. For radical criminologists this orientation is closely linked to the issue of *praxis*. Radical criminologists tend to pursue theories, polices and social programs aimed at making lower classes less poor and less powerless; that enable women to be socially, politically and economically equal to men; and that erase disadvantages that keep racial and ethnic minorities subordinate to white America, or keep gays and lesbians second-class citizens. In this sense, radical criminologists, whatever their specific theoretical focus, share a commitment to a future where crime and its control are no longer expressions of a society organized around an elaborate system of power and privilege.

Finally, we argue that those who seek to change the world in radical ways, whether through reducing economic inequalities, creating true gender equality or defeating racism, should openly announce that their agenda is a radical one. In the 1980s and 1990s, scholars on the left were confronted by the collapse of socialism abroad, the decline of liberalism at home and an apparent rise of popular support for right-wing political strategies in the U.S. In this climate, many began to embrace both theories and labels that provided a degree of protective coloring that would enable them to pursue their agendas of resistance without being immediately identified as political dissidents (Gitlin, 1995). The term *critical* criminology is less politically challenging than the term *radical*. But the underlying reality remains the same: Most "critical criminologists" hope their work contributes to radical change in the social forces that currently produce high levels of crime and injustice. It is our personal view that criminologists committed to radical change should be proud of their commitment to social equality and publicly proclaim that they are, indeed, radicals.

In sum, the theoretical approaches we subsume under the term radical criminology are linked by: (1) a desire to develop useful understandings about the deep sociological and cultural roots of crime; (2) a posture of resistance to existing systems of domination; and (3) participation in social movements that confront social inequality and seek to liberate oppressed peoples.

## What Follows

The chapters that follow explore ways of constructing radical criminology. Throughout the book we examine how radical perspectives on class, race, gender and culture have been and can be used to understand crime and justice. Our treatment of many issues will be condensed for several reasons. First, the short compass of this book makes it difficult to explore all of the ramifications of each issue. Second, our discussion of the intersection of class, culture, gender and race will be unavoidably limited by the relative underdevelopment of these ideas within criminology as compared to areas such as anthropology, sociology, and gender and race studies. Radical criminologists have only recently begun to explore the ways that class, gender, race and culture intersect with one another to produce patterns of lawmaking, crime and punishment. Because so much remains to be done in this area, our goal is to provide a basic introduction to these issues that will enable others to pursue the questions of how class, race, gender and culture intersect in ways that shape the production of crime and punishment.

In taking up this task we begin with social class. We do so for several reasons. First, class analysis was the historical starting point for radical theorizing. Without the insights of Marx and his followers regarding the impact of class relations on social life, it is unlikely there would be a radical criminology today.

Second, we need to begin with social class in order to appreciate the relationship between radical criminology's early emphasis on social class and subsequent critiques of class as a central organizing principle for radical criminology.

Third, the world is in the midst of the most dramatic social reorganization since the Industrial Revolution of the eighteenth century. The process of *globalization* has unleashed a worldwide capitalist revolution that is reordering the social life of both rich and poor nations in very fundamental ways. As William Greider (1997:12) notes in *One World, Ready or Not: The Manic Logic of Global Capitalism:* "The great paradox of this economic revolution is that its new technologies enable people and nations to take sudden leaps into modernity, while at the same time they promote the renewal of once-forbidden barbarisms. Amid the newness of things, exploitation of the weak by the strong also flourishes again."

Whether it is the increasing economic divisions between rich and poor within the U.S.; the return to punishment-oriented prisons; the 1993 burning deaths of 188 women who worked in a Thailand toy factory where the emergency exits were locked; or efforts to privatize basic commodities such as water in ways that threaten the lives of poor people around the world; the emerging world order demands that we develop new understandings of how the wealthy increasingly dominate the poor and the middle class within a cultural climate that blames the oppressed for the social problems resulting from inequality. The global capitalist revolution now under way is remaking the class structure of the world and, in doing so, is forging new crimes for the twenty-first century. Although twentieth-century communism has failed everywhere, the inequalities that led to communist and socialist revolutions have not disappeared.

Moreover, there is a growing body of evidence that suggests that inequality and revolution will intensify rather than decline in the coming decades (Burbach et al., 1997; Korten, 1995; Latouche, 1993; Mander and Goldsmith, 1996). It is, therefore, especially important that we consider how class conflict, both nationally and internationally, will continue to play a major role in shaping social life and along with it the definition of crime and the production of criminal behaviors.

Finally, we contend that social class is currently the most radical of all political issues. Debates and conflicts over equalizing race and gender and democratizing the content of mass culture have become part of ordinary political discourse in the U.S. While many people may presently oppose affirmative action programs, we *have had* affirmative action programs. In 1997 then-President Bill Clinton inaugurated a national debate on race relations. Although the Christian Right and other politically conservative groups have mounted vigorous efforts to roll back the gains of feminism, it has become part of the political and academic discourse. Broad public discussions of social class relations, in contrast, are almost nonexistent. By the mid-1980s, even mild liberal criticisms of economic inequality were silenced with claims that the proponents were trying to incite "class warfare." Modest redistribution programs, such as progressive taxation designed to limit economic inequality, have all but disappeared from the American agenda, and are now treated as unacceptable attacks on the rights of individuals – i.e., the wealthy – to keep what they have "earned." Thus, at this moment in history, analyses and critiques of how social class arrangements affect the construction of crime and punishment in the U.S. are the most radical of the radical criminologies.

With these introductory words in mind, let us turn to an analysis of Marxist methods and concepts, for it is here that radical criminology began.

# TWO.
# MARXIST METHODS AND CONCEPTS IN CRIMINOLOGY

Above all, Marxism is a critique of capitalism. It begins with an examination of a society's economic system, and details the ways in which economic order relates to the organization of social and political life. For Marx, such an analysis could only be undertaken with reference to two concepts: history and social class. Each of these ideas is discussed below.

## History

For Marx, capitalism was an historically specific kind of society that emerged from pre-capitalist economic organization. These pre-capitalist systems (slave economies, feudalism and mercantilism) were connected to one another as well, and each generated the conditions that gave rise to the subsequent form of economic organization. For example, Marx argued that feudalism grew out of the decline of ancient Rome's slave economy; mercantilism (small-merchant and trade-based capitalism) emerged from the decay of feudalism; and modern machine capitalism was born out of mercantilism. This historic process of development, decay and replacement is linked to another important concept, the *dialectic,* which we shall review below.

Whether one agrees or disagrees with Marx's particular interpretation of history (often called *historicism*), it has had a dramatic impact on subsequent forms of thought that emphasize the importance of *history* for understanding social life. Central to Marx's analysis was the contention that social systems develop and change over time and that the present form of any social system emerged from an earlier one. Thus, from a Marxian perspective, those who wish to understand social life in the present must, first, understand the history of that social system. This emphasis on *historicism* distinguishes radical analysis from forms of social science that examine only the immediate manifestation of social phenomenon.

Marx was not the first to stress the importance of taking a historical perspective or placing societies into a historical context. He was, however, the first to examine history from the perspective of political-economic development:

that is, to see history as a process related to economic development and class relations.

## Social Class

Marx observed that pre-capitalist societies had something in common: a division of society into those who had a lot and those who had very little. In slave societies, such as ancient Rome, this division resulted in conflict between free citizens and slaves; in feudal England and Europe, between nobles and serfs; and in early mercantile society, between merchants and guild craftsmen. In Marx's view, this pattern of division into classes with different levels of economic and political power, and consequently different interests, was also characteristic of capitalism. In *capitalist* society, however, the division was between owners of the means of production, whom Marx termed the *bourgeoisie*, and workers, or *proletariat*.

Marx and Engels viewed history as a series of successive economic systems in which the interests of the rich opposed the interests of the poor. In the *Communist Manifesto*, Marx and Engels theorized that "the history of all hitherto existing society is the history of class struggle" (1955:9). Central to Marx's argument is the idea that social classes stood in an *antagonistic relationship* to one another. In other words, people could not simply be divided into rich and poor, powerful and powerless. Rather, rich and poor, powerful and powerless exist in a *relationship*. Thus, the rich create the poor by controlling a disproportionate share of society's wealth; the powerful create the powerless by maintaining systems that ensure that some groups will enjoy greater access to political power. In effect, the powerful seek to maintain relationships that will preserve their advantage, while the less powerful search for ways to resist and redress this imbalance of power. As a result, class struggle becomes an ongoing social process rather than something that takes place only during moments of revolutionary upheaval.

Marx's notion of class struggle was not limited to material elements, and he recognized that class struggles also involved a battle over ideas (beliefs and ideology). Here, the dominant classes attempt to gain *cultural hegemony* – the power to determine and define cultural norms and values. A hegemonic culture is one where the norms and values supportive of the status quo are taken for granted by the vast majority of people in society. This taken-for-granted quality has two key sources: lived experience and formal socialization. For instance, people who live in a society where individuals must compete with one another for their daily bread will come to accept competition as "normal," and thus "inevitable." Consequently, they will tend to accept values and norms associated with organizing society around a "survival of the fittest" model as reasonable. Societies also maintain institutions such as religion, education and entertainment that promote dominant cultural values. Thus, in capitalist societies, for instance, religions will reinforce the idea that wealth is a reward for behaving properly and therefore a sign of morality (Weber 1985).

Hegemonic cultures never achieve total dominance. Dominant ideas, however, become so pervasive that large majorities – even large majorities of those who are disadvantaged by the existing system – accept interpretations of reality that tend to favor the interests of the powerful (these people exhibited what Marx called "false-consciousness"; for a discussion, see Lukacs, 1985). There are also times when the hegemonic culture breaks down, as some members of subordinate classes succeed in resisting the messages and practices that define their lower status as their "fault" or their preferred cultural practices as deviant. These challenges to cultural hegemony, which typically begin as a struggle over ideas, may gain sufficient momentum to become struggles over political or even economic relationships.

In short, Marxists emphasize that social classes are involved in a continual tug-of-war over the distribution of economic, political and cultural power. Like *historicism*, Marx's conceptualization of social class as a *relationship* between classes distinguishes radical analysis from those that view social groups as categories that exist in and of themselves; that is, as *sociologically abstract* groups of people who exist independent of social, economic, political and cultural relationships with one another.

What lessons do these elements of Marxist methodology hold for criminologists?

## MARX, HISTORY AND CRIMINOLOGY

Marxist thought has influenced both definitional and behavioral approaches in radical criminology. From a definitional perspective, contemporary Marxists examine how law was and is used at different times and in different societies to both maintain class divisions and minimize the destructive consequences of these divisions. By focusing on the class dimension of social control, radicals call attention to a matter often left unaddressed by other criminologists: namely, that the social construction of crime in every society will reflect the nature of the society's economic and social structure. In short, different economic systems generate different class structures, different power relations and different systems of inequality, and, therefore, different methods for managing the consequences of unequal relationships, of which crime control is one (see, for example, Rusche and Kirchheimer, 1968, and chapters in this book on policing, courts and corrections). As a result, radical criminologists ask the following kinds of questions about law and the criminal justice system: "How does the creation and enforcement of law maintain the interests of one class over another?" "How does the creation and enforcement of laws maintain or minimize class conflict at different points in history or in different societies?"

The concern with historically-generated systems of inequality (i.e., class relations) affects how radicals address criminal behavior. For instance, a radical criminologist concerned with criminal behavior might ask: "Are certain types of class structures more likely to generate anti-social behavior than others?"; and "How do class-based cultural understandings in a society influence what people desire, and consequently the kinds of crimes they will commit?"; and "What kinds of motivational and opportunity structures conducive to crime are created by particular kinds of class societies?" (e.g., see, Groves and Corrado, 1983).

In short, Marxists make sense of crime and criminal justice by examining them within their specific social and historical context. This requires close attention to how class relationships within different historical periods influenced both the production of deviant behavior and the development of legal systems to control this behavior. Roman and feudal economic and social systems, for instance, could not and did not produce the same types of law or the same types of criminal behavior that we find in 21st century America. Similarly, contemporary forms of law and criminal justice do not develop under any other type of social system. Our present-day legal system is a response to a number of specific societal institutions, processes and structures, such as: industrialization, urbanization, bureaucratization, the emergence of a large sector of white collar workers, the decline of industrial workers and their replacement by a growing sector of service workers, and rapid technological changes, all occurring within the context of a capitalist market economy combined with a two-party system of electoral democracy (see Lynch and Groves, 1995). These changes have led to new forms of behaviors, laws and social control that interact to produce the legal invention of new crimes such as auto theft, computer crime, identity theft, white collar crime, and skyjacking.

Even traditional concepts such as theft take on a new meaning and significance as societies change. In capitalist societies, for example, private ownership and respect for private property are essential components of social organization. Therefore, the capitalist state will devote considerable energy to protecting property rights through criminal prosecution. This was not always the case. For instance, in *Theft, Law, and Society*, Hall (1952) demonstrated that it was only with the development of mercantile capitalism that theft became a criminal offense prosecutable by the state. Prior to that time, theft was treated as a a private, civil matter in which the state had no interest. In a similar vein, Commons (1957) detailed how "future interest," that is, potential profit, came to be recognized as a new form of property to be protected under U.S. law. More recently, the computer revolution has created a new form of property – *electronic property* – that has been protected through revisions of computer crime laws (Michalowski and Pfuhl, 1992). The variability of criminal definitions is mirrored in who the law treats as a "threat" to society. For instance, laws governing "vagrants" and "illegal immigrants" have typically reflected changing needs to increase or decrease the geographic mobility of labor (Calavita, 1993a, 1993b; Castles and Miller, 2003; Chambliss, 1964; Harring, 1977; Sassen, 2000; Wonders and Michalowski, 2003; see also Adler, 1989; Huggins, 1983). As Renee (1978) effectively demonstrated in *The Search for Criminal Man,* at every point in modern history, the definition of "dangerousness" has been focused on behaviors that threatened underlying elements of the political order.

In sum, Marxism is a historical account of how crime, law and social control develop within a wider social, economic and political context. A central argument of radical criminology is that we cannot fully appreciate issues related to crime and crime control without first locating them in their social and historical context. This assertion constitutes a central point of departure from other approaches to criminology.

## The Ahistorical Tradition in Criminology

Most theories of crime tend to be *ahistorical*. That is, they do not treat the question of how the material conditions of society and crime evolve together as relevant to the study of crime (Chambliss, 1974). From a Marxist perspective, this poses a problem because ahistorical theories fail to link the phenomenon under investigation – in this case, crime – to the broader contexts of history or class relations. Instead, most ahistorical theories in criminology focus on individual criminals or small groups in an effort to identify the "defects" that cause criminal behavior. Well-known examples include Lombroso's concept of the "born criminal" (Gibson, 2002; Lombroso-Ferrero, 1972); the contemporary preoccupation with the links among race, low I.Q. and crime (Fraser, 1995; Herrnstein, 1994), and theories of how maladaptive families produce criminal offspring (Gottfredson and Hirschi, 1990; Hirschi, 1969).

By removing the problem of crime from its historical context, ahistorical theories create the impression that crime is something that occurs outside of the normal evolution of social systems. From this vantage point, crime appears to be a defect of individuals or perhaps small groups, evident in "ineffective" families or decaying neighborhoods. In contrast, placing crime and criminal justice in their historic context foregrounds the relationship between crime and historically specific features of economic and social systems. In making this connection, radical criminologists call attention to the idea that trends and changes in crime can only be explained with reference to the changing nature of society. We will explore these ideas more extensively in chapter 5. For now, we simply want to establish the basic tenet that crime and justice can only be fully understood when analyzed with respect to the historical, social and political-economic context within which they occur. Two important implications follow from this proposition.

(1) each society produces specific types and amounts of crime; and,

(2) each society will have its own distinctive ways of dealing with criminal behavior.

In short, we could say that *every society gets the amount and type of crime it deserves*, or that each society has a different amount and type of crime depending on how it is organized socially, economically, culturally and politically.

These points lead radical criminology in very different policy directions from orthodox criminology. Because orthodox criminology is ahistorical and individual-centered, it advocates policies aimed at correcting these individuals' personal defects. Such policies include: (1) intervening in the lives of individual criminals (e.g., through imprisonment, rehabilitation, drug testing); (2) attempting to change groups presumed to carry on or condone criminal behavior (e.g., making welfare mothers work, promoting "family values," making parents responsible for the costs of crimes by their children); and (3) expanding the criminal justice system in ways that are assumed to keep people from breaking the law (e.g., passing mandatory sentencing laws, increasing the number of police, increasing the severity of criminal sanctions).

In contrast, radical criminologists begin with the proposition that crime is a *social* problem that can only be significantly improved by changing society since the roots of crime reach down to the political-economic, social and cultural organization of society. From this perspective, the only way to substantially reduce the level and/or change the character of crime is through policies that alter society's criminogenic characteristics. In particular, radicals favor policies that equalize economic relations (e.g., higher minimum wages, progressive taxation, laws protecting workers' rights, social welfare and urban development programs, socialized medicine, free education) and that reduce or eliminate inequality and subordination based on gender, race or ethnicity. In order to understand why radicals adopt this stance, let us take a closer look at

Marx's general view of how political economy shapes a social life, including crime and concepts and the practice of justice.

## The Concept of Historical Materialism

Marx's strategy for studying the evolution of societies is called *historical materialism*, a theory of history based on empirical "observations and an accurate description of real conditions" (Bottomore et al., 1983:206). Unlike the 19th century philosophers known as "idealists" – who viewed history as a succession of abstract ideas such as "the great chain of being," "Absolute Spirit," or "inalienable rights" – Marx described social change in terms of observable transformations in a society's economic structure. Marx used the term *mode of production* to describe a society's economic structure, and characterized a society's mode of production as its *principal defining characteristic*. Marx took the position that all other characteristics of society were shaped by its mode of production. Thus, the laws and culture found in a slave economy would be different than those found in a feudal or capitalist society since each is based on a different mode of production.

Economic systems also have different *means of production* and *relations of production*. The *means of production* includes the types of tools, machines and institutions and forms of labor found in a society. For example, in different historic periods, tools such as the plow, the steam engine, large-scale industrial machinery, or computers have been the central engines of production. Similarly, economic systems have organized their basic productive activities around the forced labor of slaves, the tribute labor of serfs, or the purchased labor of wage workers. Finally, every historic period has organized tools and workers into distinctive social systems to accomplish the tasks of production and distribution of goods and services. These different systems have included the feudal manor, the plantation, the private farm, the local factory and the global corporation. For example, if the mode of production is corporate capitalism, the *means* of production will be complex machines operated by wage laborers, supervised by salaried white collar employees, within the context of a hierarchical structure that produces profit for stockholders who are not a direct part of the production process.

Systems of production are also linked to specific strategies for distributing the goods and the wealth that is produced. For instance, industrial capitalism divides workers into hourly workers who do "manual" labor, salaried workers who do "mental" labor, and investors whose money "works" for them. In this system, the lowest incomes are reserved for those who labor with their bodies, higher incomes for those who labor with their minds, and the highest income for those who do not have to work because they can send their money out to work for them. This system of distribution links the means of production, as we discuss below, to a society's class structure. Marx contended that in order to appreciate the historically specific features of any society, we must understand both its mode and means of production. Once these are identified, according to Marx, it becomes possible to ascertain how the economic structure influences other aspects of social life such as religion, family, law or even crime.

As Marx conceptualized it, "mode of production" was a *totalizing* concept, meaning that understanding a society's mode of production would make it possible to explain just about every aspect of life in a given society (Jay, 1973). A number of analysts have criticized Marx's emphasis on the mode of production to the exclusion of other factors. These critics correctly suggest that a society's mode of production cannot explain all social life. Factors such as gender relations, racial politics and cultural belief systems also play important roles in shaping social life – including the particular way capitalism is practiced. If this were not the case, all capitalist societies would be identical. At the same time, social forces outside the sphere of production exist in relationship to a mode of production and cannot be expressed independently of that mode any more than the mode of production can function independently from existing gender relations, language or cultural beliefs.

Societies organized around capitalist modes of production often differ in very significant ways, highlighting the importance of non-economic factors in shaping social life. Capitalist societies also have a number of salient features in common such as labor markets, commodity markets and social class divisions based on access to capital that make them all recognizable as capitalist social systems. Thus, although understanding a society's mode of production does not provide *sufficient* information to explain all aspects of a society, it provides information that is *necessary* if we hope to understand anything about that society.

## Production, Social Class and Political Power

The third key concept Marx used was *relations of production,* which addressed how any person or group of persons *related* to the *means* of production found in a given *mode* of production. Did a certain group participate in the mode of production as masters or slaves, lords or serfs, owners or workers? Did they own the means of production, or did they own nothing? If the latter, they would have considerably less power and influence than those who owned the means of production. Marx used a group's relationship to the means of production as the basis for determining that group's *class affiliation*, and saw ownership and control of the means of production as measures of economic and political power. For Marx, the concept of social class came to mean much more than simply a location in society. It was a concept that encompassed an entire range of social relationships that determined who worked, how they worked and who received the benefits of work. Marx's departure from the more typical view of social class as simply an income category shaped an important distinction between orthodox criminology and radical criminology. Consequently, orthodox criminologists tend to measure social class by an individual's income, while radicals measure class by one's location in the relations of production (e.g., worker, manager, investor, dependent).

Consider, for example, the differing relations of production found in feudal and capitalist economies. Under the agrarian mode of production known as feudalism, land was the most important means of production, and was owned by a small group of lords and kings. Those who worked the land – the serfs – were prohibited by law from owning land. Thus, serfs related to the mode of production as non-owners, and as non-owners they were excluded from the primary basis of wealth, status and power. The *economic* relationship of lords and serfs to the feudal mode of production doubled as a *political* relationship of one class (lords) to another (serfs). Needless to say, this political relationship, which in Marx's model must always be seen against its economic background, allowed the dominant class to live off the labor and control the behavior of the subordinate class. This explains why Marx saw class conflict as an economically grounded phenomenon. Let us turn to contemporary capitalist society for another example of what Marx meant by the relations of production.

## Class in Capitalist Society

In the United States, the means of production (factories, joint-stock companies, financial corporations – in short, capital) are owned by a small investor class. Even though many middle class Americans "own" some corporate stock through pension plans or mutual funds, most corporate stock remains in the hands of just 2 percent of the population. (see chapter 5). Marx referred to this group as the capitalist class, or *bourgeoisie*. The members of this class relate to the production process as owners. The vast remainder of the population relate to the production process as self-employed workers, salaried employees, or hourly workers. Marx referred to those who worked in their own small businesses or who managed business for capitalists as the *petty bourgeoisie* (small capitalists). He employed the term *proletariat* to identify non-managerial wage workers. In addition, capitalist societies produce another group of people whose relationship to production is marginal or nonexistent. These are the underemployed and unemployed. Marx labeled groups that were not meaningfully incorporated into the economic system as *lumpen-proletariat,* a group that today is sometimes called *the underclass.*

Marx made these distinctions to show that the way the classes relate to the mode of production determines the way they will relate economically and politically to one another. For example, to relate as owner is to have command over the means of production, and since one component of the means of production is labor, to own the means of production is to command or control labor. By analyzing economic arrangements Marx was able to reveal how the relationship of owners to workers, of one class to another, was not only an economic relationship but a *political* one as well. By combining what people today typically see as separate spheres of activity – economics and politics – Marx demonstrated the economic character of political conflicts, and the political character of economic conflicts. In short, Marx made a powerful case for the idea that societies do not have political and economic spheres, they had *political-economies.*

Marx's focus on political economy explains why *class* is such an important category for Marxist analysis. If a Marxist wished to understand a specific group, the first questions posed would be: "In which mode of production did this group exist?" "To which social class did it belong?" Put in more general terms, if we want to understand why people in different social groups manifest different values and different behaviors, we must understand their historically generated relationship to other classes within the context of their historically specific mode of production. This is the essence of historical materialism, summarized by Marx and Engels (1970:42) as follows:

> "The mode of production... is a definite form of activity of these individuals, a definite form of expressing their life, a definite *mode of life* on their part. As individuals express their life, so they are. What they are, therefore, coincides with their production, both with *what* they produce and *how* they produce. The nature of individuals thus depends on the material conditions determining their production." [emphasis in original]

But how much of a *materialist* was Marx? This is a point of contention among Marxists and non-Marxists alike.

## Marx's Materialism

Marx believed that studying a society's economic system was quite important. But since the economy is only one aspect of a society, how does it relate to other significant social institutions? The following passage is indicative of Marx's response to this question. It is perhaps the most significant yet notoriously ambiguous statement in all of Marxism:

> ...the economic structure of society [is] the real foundation, on which rise legal and political superstructures and to which correspond definite forms of social consciousness. The mode of production in material life determines the general character of the social, political, and spiritual processes of life. It is not the consciousness of men that determines their existence, but, on the contrary, their social existence determines their consciousness. [Marx, 1982:20-21]

A small library could be filled with the commentaries and criticisms written about Marx's notions of *base* and *superstructure*. Marx's critics usually argue that this passage is too deterministic. They contend that a one-way causal relationship from the economic base to the legal, cultural and political superstructure is a form of economic reductionism that gives no independent role to forces other than the economy in shaping social life. Some turn Marx's own methods against him, arguing that such a unidirectional causal model undermines a "dialectical" interpretation of society, which emphasizes reciprocal effects and mutual interrelationships rather than one-way causal links between an economic base and the legal, cultural and political superstructure (see Wright, 1978).

Marx's supporters have responded to these criticisms in a number of ways. Some argue that Marx did not mean what his critics claim (Harrington, 1976). Others argue that if we read between the lines we will see that Marx was really advocating a dialectical, interactive position (Rader, 1979). Still others suggest that Marx was right – the legal, cultural and political life of a society *are* expressions of their economic base (Cornforth, 1977; Miliband, 1969). Even those who suggest that legal, cultural and political structures are partially autonomous from the economic base, such as the French social theorist Louis Althusser (1971), hold that "in the final instance" the economy is primary. What are the implications of this debate over the autonomy of non-economic components of *society,* especially with respect to concepts such as law and social control that are central to the radical perspective on crime and justice?

## The Concept of Superstructure

A central element of Marx's model of base and superstructure is the idea that every economic system will be supported by superstructural factors such as law, politics, religion, education and consciousness. For example, in a capitalist mode of production:

(1) laws will be created and enforced to protect private property;

(2) those holding economic power will be better able to promote and defend their interests by appropriating (or purchasing) political influence, either legally or illegally;

(3) society's educational system will be designed to reproduce values, skills and ways of behaving appropriate to the workers who will operate the machinery of production in a capitalist society; and,

(4) the consciousness of students will be shaped in a manner that is consistent with their class position, preparing the children of elite classes to accept "their right to manage and control others," and preparing children from middling and lower classes to accept a life of working for wages [Willis, 1981].

With reference to the construction of consciousness, Marx (Marx and Engels, 1955:62) notes that "ideas are themselves the outcome of bourgeois methods of production." For example, values such as individualism and the work ethic are congruent with the need to produce individuals who are suited to a society based on economic competition (Ryan, 1982; O'Connor, 1985). It should also be noted that societal values often have a plastic quality that enables them to adapt to changing conditions. Thus, "individualism" in the U.S. once meant the rugged individualism of the pioneers, sodbusters (farmers), miners and ranchers who provided the labor to build an agrarian capitalist economy on the North American landscape. With the rise of industrialization, "individualism" came to be characterized by the hard working, honest young man who moved from a lowly position to company president by "virtue of exceptional hard work and unswerving honesty" (MacLeod, 1980; see also MacLeod, 1975). Today, with the advent of consumer society, the concept of individualism has come to mean expressing one's uniqueness through the ownership and display of certain products, whether it is a Hummer, a jacket bearing the logo of some sports team, or t-shirts from the latest tour by one's favorite anarchist band (Ewen, 1988; Veblin, 1948; Henry, 1965). In each case, however, consciousness of one's identity and location in the society is framed by and against the underlying productive system.

Marx's ideas regarding the construction of consciousness suggest that non-economic (superstructural) institutions tend to present images and reward behaviors that do not challenge the class structure and economic relationships underpinning it. This does not mean that non-economic institutions simply reflect society's economic arrangements. Because they possess a degree of what has been termed *relative autonomy,* non-economic institutions can change without corresponding changes in the economy (Althusser, 1971, 1969; Poulantzas, 1975). But relative autonomy is not absolute autonomy. Public grammar schools, for instance, may begin teaching more about self-esteem and less about the work ethic than they once did, and they may do this independently of any need on the part of the economy to have workers full of self-esteem. It is highly unlikely, however, that these same schools could begin teaching that profit is theft and that capitalism is a system of exploitation without quickly being brought into line by the political-economic system.

The relationship between cultural systems and modes of production is never unidirectional. If America's capitalist class decided to break faith with evolving cultural standards of human rights by declaring that America can improve its economic productivity by turning half of the labor force into slaves, they would lose their cultural capital. Without it, they could not command the economic system despite their present ownership of the means of production. Every political-economic system must have a degree of *legitimacy* in the eyes of those it rules. Governments without legitimacy, as we discuss in chapter 3t, inspire revolt. Thus, it is not a question of whether economic institutions influence non-economic ones or vice versa. Rather it is a question of *how* and *in what ways* these institutions influence one another.

One of the more important interactions between economic and non-economic institutions with respect to crime is the relationship between law and political economy. The core of a capitalist legal system will support and buttress the economic arrangements necessary to ensure the reproduction of a capitalist society. The law will be used by those with economic and political power to augment or maintain their power and to minimize threats from those who would displace them. Except during revolutionary periods, law is rarely a progressive tool for changing social order. It is more typically a tool used to protect and reproduce the status quo (d'Enricco, 1984a).

As a general orientation, Marx's claims are hardly startling. What political-economic system does not use law to protect its interests, design education to recreate itself in the next generation, craft political decisions to uphold and strengthen the status quo and use ideas to integrate members into the socio-economic community? At the same time, different systems integrate themselves with varying degrees of effectiveness. Some societies, such as the United

States, have sufficiently integrated their economic, political and cultural institutions to create a degree of social stability. In contrast, some developing nations have been unable to blend capitalist markets, Cold War-equipped armies and traditional pre-capitalist values and institutions into a pattern for social stability.

If Marx actually meant to claim that superstructures were merely a passive reflection of its economic base, the contemporary world would make such a claim untenable. What Marx provided was a starting point, a general orientation toward analyzing social life (Sykes, 1974). Summarizing that orientation, Marx suggests that when analyzing a specific society we begin by looking at the way it is structured economically; that is, we look at its mode and means of production. This accomplished, we can then turn our attention to the relations of production in order to determine how different social classes relate to the system of production in question. At this point, economically generated class conflict, and differences in beliefs, values and behaviors among different social groups, become important explanatory factors in their own right. Put another way, beliefs or practices that may have had economic origins, once they are created, may continue to play a role in the life of the society long after the originating forces have changed or disappeared.

A case in point is the type of racism found in America. Many white Americans continue to view African-Americans citizens as less trustworthy and more dangerous than white citizens. For them, African Americans are "the other." These feelings are deeply rooted in the political-economic history of American slavery. And, while slavery was abolished in the United States over 140 years ago, few Euro-Americans can look at African Americans without registering that the difference in their heritage as marked by skin color is important, and that it is better to be white than black (Hacker, 1995). Thus, racism continues as an American problem even though the economic forces that brought Africans to this land have long since vanished. Or, said differently, the dead hand of the political-economic past weighs heavily on the cultural present.

Over all, a Marxist approach to the study of crime provides the intellectual tools to ask three questions:

(1) How has the socially and historically-specific class position of different social groups shaped the behaviors and beliefs they hold in common?

(2) In what ways do the institutions of law, culture and politics reflect and support the economic foundations of the political economy?

(3) In what ways do the institutions of law, culture, and politics pose challenges the economic foundations of the political economy?

Below, we examine another basic Marxist tool: the dialectic.

## The Dialectic

The term dialectic is a broad concept, interpreted in many ways by radicals. For example, in Marx's theory of history, the dialectic described a historical process of societal evolution that ended in a society of equals. An emerging consensus suggests that there is no simple dialectical formula that explains the movement of history. Nor is there a dialectical method, especially if method is defined as a precise, sequential set of procedures whose function is to test theory (Keats and Urry, 1975). But there is a dialectical perspective, with defining characteristics that comprise the dialectical imagination (Jay, 1973). We describe this use of dialectic below.

First, to think dialectically is to think comprehensively and contextually (Mills, 1977). The most comprehensive concepts social scientists have at their disposal are history and culture. One defining characteristic of dialectical imagination is that we place whatever we are trying to explain in its wider historical and cultural context. Second, to think dialectically is to think relationally (Ollman, 1978; Spitzer, 1980). In other words, one must think on a number of different analytical levels, and be able to specify relations between those levels (Groves and Lynch, 1990; Lynch and Groves, 1995).

For example, many have attempted to explain crime with reference to the presence or absence of broken homes. To think relationally, however, would demand that we situate the likelihood of family breakdown within a wider social and economic context, and also that we inquire into the cultural factors which give so-called "broken homes" their meaning. From the theorists of the Chicago school in the 1920s and 1930s, to the present, there is evidence that so-called "broken homes" are more abundant in "disorganized" communities; that is, communities with high rates of population turnover, unoccupied or non-residential buildings, unemployment, disease, mental illness and crime (Bursik, 1988, 1984; Shaw and McKay, 1969). Thinking relationally, we must raise our analytical sights and ask what causes this disorganization.

Communities do not become disorganized in a vacuum. Economic practices and political policies push some communities into disorganization while aiding others in becoming stable, affluent residential neighborhoods (Hagan, 1994). For instance, the investor class makes decisions to invest or not invest in communities. As early as the 1930s, agencies, banks and insurance companies were warning investors to avoid investing in urban neighborhoods with high percentages of minority residents (Massey and Denton, 1993). Therefore, economic decline in these communities was not simply the workings of the "invisible hand" of economics, it was based on the racist decisions of those in economically and politically powerful positions.

If we approach the question from a cultural angle, we would also want to know whose definition of "family" is in play when we talk about how certain arrangements increase the likelihood of crime. Whether it is the contemporary concern about "single mothers" or the nineteenth-century concern with broken homes, the dominant cultural stereotype of the family has been the European-American ideal of a mother, father and children operating as an independent social unit (Coontz, 1984). It is this kind of multi-layered analysis that comes from thinking dialectically.

A third characteristic of dialectical thinking is its interdisciplinary focus. Marx did not derive his explanations from a single discipline. As an economist, he was concerned with the way things were produced; as a political scientist, with how class was translated into political power; as a historian, with the emergence and evolution of socioeconomic formations; as an anthropologist, with how "human nature" responded to changes in the mode of production; and as a social psychologist, with the impact that class conflict had on crises in personal identity. With this in mind, Taylor et al. (1975:234) argue that false disciplinary distinctions should be "collapsed and their interpenetration revealed." No one discipline can explain all social phenomena, and a genuinely radical criminology must utilize the understandings derived from a variety of ways of studying social life.

A fourth and final characteristic of the dialectical imagination concerns the relationship of theory to practice (Platt, 1974; Taylor et al., 1975; Schichor, 1980b). In his 11th Thesis on Feuerbach, Marx noted that "the philosophers have only interpreted the world in various ways; *the point is to change it*" ([emphasis in original]; Marx and Engels, 1970:123). Crucial questions for the radical criminologist are: What do we change? How do we change it? Where do we intervene? Speaking to this issue, C. Wright Mills (1977:131) remarked that "any adequate answer to a problem will contain a view of the strategic points of intervention – of the levers by which the structure may be maintained or changed." In their own intervention strategies radicals have generally taken a macrosocial orientation, promoting policies that targeted large-scale forces such as inequality, discrimination or poverty, rather than more justice system-specific programs. This has led to the criticism that radical criminologists are utopian, offering wishful visions of a transformation of capitalism into some other type of social system (Sparks, 1980). This characterization, however, misrepresents the range of social changes advocated by radical criminologists (Currie, 1996; Barak, 1998; Lynch and Stretesky, 1998; Pepinsky and Quinney, 1991; Welch, 1996a; Young, 1996a, 1996b). Indeed, practitioners of radical criminology have a long history of working with social groups for small changes in a number of arenas (see chapters 1 and 13). The important point here is that dialectical thought requires that we connect with the world around us, that we come to understand it by our participation in it, not merely through our theorizing about it (Ferrell, 1997).

These four categories do not exhaust the meanings of "dialectic." For the Greeks, dialectic was the art of conversation; for certain philosophers of science dialectic is the opposite of formal, linear logic (Novack, 1971; Ball, 1979); for Sartre (1966) and for many Marxists, dialectic entails a totalizing or holistic orientation (Greenberg, 1981; Jay, 1973). Bertell Ollman (1978) describes dialectic as a philosophy of internal relations, and Michael Harrington (1976) uses the metaphor of complex interrelations within an organic whole. Others define dialectic as a law that guides historical movement (e.g., the frequently cited triad of Thesis-Antithesis-Synthesis) or a series of contradictory movements reconciled in a higher unity. The four-point summation provided here incorporates many of these ideas, but can scarcely do justice to them all. In contrast to those who would define dialectic as a rigid "law" or a definitive method, however, we emphasize that dialectic is a general intellectual orientation whose purpose is to assist in the selection of, and solution to, significant problems (Spitzer, 1980).

## MARXISM: LIVING AND DEAD

In 1974, Gresham Sykes (1974:213) claimed that radical criminology held "out the promise of having a profound impact on our thinking about crime and society." Others were less convinced of the utility of Marxian analyses of crime (Klockars, 1979; Inciardi, 1980). Still others suggested that there can be no such thing as a Marxist criminology (Hirst, 1979; Mugford, 1974). Paul Hirst (1979), a leading Marxist scholar, argues that any attempt to apply Marxist concepts to crime and criminology will reflect revisionist efforts that "modify and distort Marxist concepts..." The issues Hirst raises are important ones: How true to the "original" Marx was early Marxist criminology? Second, how true should it be? Third, what links exist between contemporary radical and early Marxist criminologies?

A short answer to these questions is that Marx is dead and things have changed. Marx valued the concept of historical specificity – the idea that each historical period must be assessed on its own terms. Thus, it should come as no surprise, especially with the tremendous changes in productive practices and social life during the 20th century, that history has moved beyond Marx. Thus, trying to capture current events by mechanically applying the concepts Marx developed makes little sense. This is not to say, however, that Marx's concepts belong in the "dustbin of history" – far from it. Many contemporary economists, political scientists, anthropologists and sociologists have adapted Marxist thought to the analysis of modern capitalism (see, for example, the journal *Review of Radical Political Economics*). As an example of the utility of Marxist thought, we will consider three influential scholars whose work would not have been possible without their Marxian heritage: Ralf Dahrendorf, C. Wright Mills and Max Weber.

Ralph Dahrendorf (1959), an early founder of "conflict theory" in sociology, began his classic study of *Class and Class Conflict in Industrial Society* with a chapter entitled "Changes Since Marx," in which he catalogues neo-Marxist developments in the institutionalization of class conflict. In *The Marxists,* C. Wright Mills (1974) sets forth his view of the errors, ambiguities and inadequacies of Marxism in a chapter entitled "Critical Observations," and Max Weber (1977) deepens Marxism by adding insightful and useful categories to make sense of social stratification. Bear in mind that each of these theorists acknowledged an explicit debt to Marx's model, with Weber remarking that we can assess a thinker's intellectual honesty in terms of his relation to Marx and Nietzsche.

In short, those who hope to utilize Marxist thought must adapt it to current realities. For instance, complex management structures and diffuse investment systems such as mutual funds and pensions make outdated a model of social class based exclusively on whether individuals are or are not owners of the means of production (Bernard, 1981). Early radical criminologists have been criticized for utilizing a two-class model that is ill-suited for analyzing the complexities of stratification in a post-industrial society (Sykes, 1974; Klockars, 1980). Indeed, if Marx was right about historical specificity, using concepts developed in the 1850s to analyze capitalism at the beginning of the twenty-first century will inevitably lead to the wrong conclusions. Marxist thought is one of the foundations of radical criminology. At the same time, Marx's words cannot be treated as sacred texts that can never be altered. Rather, Marxist thought is best appreciated as a set of intellectual tools for revealing the economic and political context of contemporary social life. C. Wright Mills (1974:11) said it best: "No one who does not come to grips with the ideas of Marxism can be an adequate social scientist...[but] no one who believes that Marxism contains the last word can be one either."

One example of the flexible character of Marxian thought is how contemporary radical analyses of capitalism have increasingly incorporated gender and race as important shapers of contemporary capitalist societies. In radical criminology, this tendency manifests itself in the increasing number of analyses that examine the role of gender,[1] race,[2] and race, class and gender intersections[3] in shaping both crime and crime control policy in capitalist America at the turn of the twenty-first century. In contrast, orthodox criminology has made little effort to give greater attention to issues of race and gender, especially as contextually and theoretically important concepts, identities, processes and structures.

As an approach to the study of crime, radical criminology has increasingly moved away from unidimensional economic models to broader race-class-gender models, about which we will have more to say in subsequent chapters. For now, it is important to emphasize that radical criminology owes an important intellectual debt to Marx and to suggest that it is important that we both remember and acknowledge that debt.

## In Sum

An important part of developing a theoretical framework is specifying the intellectual traditions from which it is derived. For radical criminology, this intellectual tradition is Marxism. Even radical criminologists whose work is not directly concerned with the political economy of crime either implicitly or explicitly accept a number of elements of Marxist thought. These include the view that history is essential to social analysis; that economic power and political power are closely linked; that social divisions along class, gender or race lines are *relationships* rather than static categories; and that social inequality generates social problems. Thus, in contrast to Hirst's (1979) assertion that radical criminologists "distort...Marxist concepts," we argue that radicals who accept the concept of historical specificity have and continue to modify Marxist concepts in ways that make them useful for understanding the contemporary world.

Our next step is to explore how Marxist analysis has been applied to criminology and criminal justice, and to consider how this has led to both developments and debates within radical criminology. We will begin with a review of Marxist perspectives on the state and law, for it is here that we find the first important theoretical debate within radical criminology.

## NOTES

1. See, for example: Danner, 1991, 1996; Messerschmidt, 1993; Daly, 1989; Welch, 1997; Arrigo, 1992; DeKeseredy, 1996b; DeKeseredy and Goff, 1992; DeKeseredy and Kelly, 1993; DeKeseredy and Schwartz, 1991.

2. See, for example: Welch, 1996b, 1996c; Platt, 1993a, 1993b, 1993c; Zatz, 1990, 1987a, 1987b; Chiricos, 1996; Lynch and Patterson, 1996a, 1996b, 1991a, 1991b, 1990; Patterson and Lynch, 1991, Lynch, 1990; Huey and Lynch, 1996.

3. See, for example: Messerschmidt, 1997; Daly, 1994a; Lynch, 1996; DeKeseredy, 1996a, 1996b; Arrigo, 1996; Barak, 1996; Friedrichs, 1996a; Caufield and Wonders, 1994; Wonders, 1996.

# THREE.
## STATE AND LAW: INSTRUMENTALISM, STRUCTURALISM AND DIFFERENCE

There are few issues as central to a radical analysis of crime and justice as the relationship between law and the political state. (By *political state* we mean not only governmental institutions for making and enforcing law, but also political *processes* such as lobbying that determine who gets what societal benefits, who will be valued and which groups will wield the most political power.) In orthodox criminology, research and theory focus primarily on behaviors that have been defined as crimes by the political state. Rather than ask why some kinds of trouble are defined as crime while other types are not, orthodox criminology typically takes existing definitions of crime for granted. In contrast, radical criminology *problematizes* the definition of crime, remaining sensitive to the underlying question: "Why are some harmful acts defined as serious crimes, some as minor crimes and others not defined as crimes at all?" Radical criminologists further develop this question by asking: "Who benefits from existing definitions of crime, and who is hurt by them?" Finding the answers to these questions requires studying how laws are made and implemented because it is at this point in the legal process that words about deeds (*laws*) are transformed into socially meaningful actions such as arresting, prosecuting and punishing people suspected of crime.

There is no firm consensus among radicals regarding the nature of state and law (Wonders and Solop, 1993), though there are some general points of agreement. Those operating from a political-economic standpoint — sometimes referred to as structuralists — emphasize the role of social class in determining how laws are made and enforced (Chambliss, 1994, 1993b; Currie, 1985; Greenberg, 1985; Michalowski, 1991, 1985; Sklar, 1988). In contrast, post-structuralists approach state and law as an expression of conflicts of interests whose outcomes are shaped by the interplay between a society's organizational and ideological characteristics (Althusser, 1996; Poulantzas, 1975). Meanwhile, post-modernists focus on how the cultural practices of everyday life – particularly language, symbolism and ritual – create the frameworks of consciousness which make laws appear as right and inevitable (Arrigo, Milovanovic, and Schehr, 2005; Foucault, 1972; Habermas, 1979, 1989; Henry and Milovanovic, 1991, 1996; Milovanovic, 1997; Pfohl, 1985). In order to take account of other relevant issues, researchers sometimes emphasize the powerful role played by gender (the division of society into males and females) in shaping the nature of the state (MacKinnon, 1989; Minow, 1997), while other researchers focus on other aspects of identity such as race and ethnicity (Hawkins, 1995; Mann, 1993; Mann and Zatz, 1998; Russell, 1998; Walker et al., 1996; Massey, 1995). Whatever the primary focus, however, radical approaches to state and law agree that laws are not simply codifications of popular consensus and that to understand crime we must first discern how a society's underlying social arrangements shape the character of the state and the laws it will create.

In this chapter we set forth the radical critique of a consensus model of law, and explore *instrumentalism*, *structuralism* and *difference* as distinct radical approaches to understanding the nature of state and law.

## The Radical Critique of Consensus Models of Lawmaking

Consensus models of law are among the earliest secular explanations of the nature of law. Prior to the development of consensus theories, law was typically viewed as an expression of divine will. The earliest formal consensus models were the "social contract" theories put forth in the eighteenth and nineteenth centuries. According to social contract theorists, law arises from a broadly shared desire for social order.

Thomas Hobbes, the preeminent social contract theorist, argued that humans are inherently selfish, pleasure-seeking creatures who, unless restrained by a state with the power to create and enforce rules, will pursue their self-interest regardless of the consequences for others. In a bit of fanciful anthropology, Hobbes described pre-state societies as a "war of everyone against every other" (Hobbes, 1968, part I, chapter 14) where life was "solitary, poor, nasty, brutish, and short" (part I, chapter 13). In a somewhat paradoxical formulation, Hobbes argued that humans escaped this natural condition by agreeing to surrender some of their freedom to a central authority that could maintain social order by restraining individuals whose pursuit of self-interest interfered with the freedom of others. In essence, Hobbes argued that by surrendering a portion of their freedom to a political state, humans *increased* their overall freedom by removing the burden of continually defending themselves against everyone else. Contrary to Hobbes's theory, the anthropological record indicates that life in societies without governments is relatively peaceful and cooperative (Binford, 1976; Hoebel, 1973; Mair, 1970; Middleton and Tait, 1967; for a somewhat different view see Changnon, 1977).

While Hobbesian theorizing about the state is inconsistent with what we know about the origins of states, the idea of a social contract to which all have agreed has remained the dominant description of, and justification for, secular states since the eighteenth century. Within criminology, this view is frequently associated with Emile Durkheim's (1963, 1951) writings on the concept of moral boundaries (see also, Erikson, 1966). Either explicitly or implicitly, orthodox criminology typically encompasses one or more of the following components of a consensus model of law:

(1) law arises from the need for social order;

(2) law reflects a consensus of values within the society;

(3) law is primarily a codification of preexisting "folkways";

(3) law serves to ensure the public good rather than to protect private interests; and,

(4) law serves as a neutral arena for the resolution of conflicts. (For extended critiques of the consensus perspective on lawmaking, see Chambliss, 1974; Michalowski, 1985; Quinney, 1970; and Vold and Bernard, 1979.)

As with any intellectual perspective, consensus theory has some utility. For example, laws against common crimes such as murder, assault, robbery and burglary have broad popular support, and reflect agreed-upon values regarding personal safety, private property and household security (Meier, 1976; Akers, 1980; Rossi et al., 1974; for critique, see Miethe, 1982). Some argue that this holds true even across cultures (Newman, 1976). However, Chambliss (1993a:37) has noted: "That most people… agree today that murder, rape, vagrancy, and theft constitute socially abhorrent behavior does not mean that the law making them crimes arose out of shared values."

The radical critique of consensus theory, originally founded in Marx's analysis of state and law, contends that consensus models seek to explain the nature of law in a wholly abstract manner; that is, without connecting it to the specific societies whose laws are being analyzed (for discussion, see Lynch, 1988b). Marx and Engels (1970:147), for example, noted that law is the "specific illusion of lawyers and politicians…," in order to highlight their point concerning the abstract nature of law. In the view of Marx and Engels, consensus theorists base their view of law on *ahistorical* assumptions about human nature. These assumptions include the supposition that humans are bundles of self-seeking appetites who seek pleasure and avoid pain (Bentham, 1995). In psychology, this view is reflected in Freud's (1961) view that individuals have a historically invariant reservoir of hostile and aggressive energy.

Neither of these views recognizes that human nature may be malleable, or that the content of psychological states such as "pleasure," "pain," or "aggression" is molded by historically specific economic and political conditions. Instead, propositions of the consensus theorists lead to the following tautological (circular) reasoning about the law and human nature:

1) all humans are self-seeking and will harm others unless restrained by external social control;

2) law is the primary tool for imposing external social control; and,

3) without law humans would simply prey on one another because

4) see item 1.

In contrast to consensus theorists, Marx took the position that human nature is variable across time and place (for criminological application see Grose and Groves, 1988). Specifically, he theorized that the nature of human beings "coincides with... production, both with what they produce and how they produce" (Marx, 1967a:142). The Marxist critique holds that consensus theory makes ahistorical assumptions about what humans might be "outside" of society, and, based on these assumptions, constructs an imaginary view of law as an expression of basic and unchanging human needs. The ahistorical approach of consensus theory ignores the basic anthropological fact that human beings have never lived in some natural state "outside" of human society without cultural rules and strategies for social control. Marx (1975:323) explicitly warned in the *Paris Manuscripts* that explanations based "on some imaginary primordial condition" should be avoided. He continued: "Such a condition explains nothing. It simply pushes the question into the grey and nebulous distance. It assumes as facts and events what it is supposed to deduce."

In keeping with Marx's insistence on historical specificity, radical approaches to state and law argue that conclusions about the consensual nature of law stem from the wrong questions. Consensus theorists frequently buttress their approach by asking questions such as: "Do people agree we should have the laws we do?" "Do people feel these laws are necessary to promote social order?" Questions such as these detach the issue of popular support for law from the historical contexts that led to the creation of both the social order that is being protected and the legal system designed to protect it. They also ignore the fact that individuals who have been socialized within a particular social order will tend to view both the general outlines of that social order, and its protective mechanisms, as normal and right. From a radical perspective, the more appropriate questions are: "Was there conflict or consensus over the law in question when it was created?"; "How did the mode of production, gender relations or racial contexts of the specific historical period in which the law was created shape its formulation?"; and, "Did the kind of social order the state promoted by creating some law benefit some more than others?" (For examples of research from this perspective see Calavita, 1993a, 1993b; Chambliss, 1993a, 1993b; McGarrell and Castellano, 1993; Michalowski, 1991; Zatz and McDonald, 1993.)

In contrast to the consensus approach, a radical perspective on state and law contends that social institutions do not have abstract characteristics that can be separated from the specific social and economic circumstances that brought them into being. There is, in other words, no such thing as abstract law. Rather, the origin and operation of specific legal systems must be analyzed in relation to their actual historical contexts. This distinction is of central importance for understanding the difference between radical and orthodox criminology: orthodox social inquiry typically searches for *time-invariant* rules for human behavior; that is, general principles that apply across time, different political-economic systems or even different cultures. (On general theories see Gottfredson and Hirschi, 1990; and Tittle, 1995; for critiques, see Lynch and Groves, 1995; Carlson and Michalowski, 1997.) In contrast, a radical perspective uses the Marxist method of historical materialism to identify and explain *historical contingency* – the idea that the social world is an ever-changing one, and that things happen for different reasons, in different ways and at different points in time (Carlson and Michalowski, 1998; Isaac and Griffin, 1989; Michalowski and Carlson, 1999). Thus, a radical perspective on state and law attempts to determine: (1) how these institutions operate in particular societies at particular points in time, and (2) whose interests were served by these institutions within specific historical contexts.

In sum, a radical approach to the questions of state and law examines how these institutions actually operate within a specific society and historical time periods, rather than generating an abstract view of law as a reflection of universal human needs. Even if we assume that people need some form of social control, it does not follow that law as we know it is the only way to achieve this control. Indeed, there is substantial evidence that informal social control is more effective than formal strategies such as law and criminal justice (Braithwaite, 1989). Many societies have relied on informal control strategies such as customs, traditions and folkways, rather than the law, to create relatively peaceful and functional social systems (see, for example, Dentan, 1968; Nader, 1990; Turnbull, 1965). Nor does it follow that legal systems necessarily represent the interests of all people equally, as claimed by social contract theory. Finally, we cannot assume that the relationship between law and some other social factor will remain constant over time. For instance, laws that served the interest of powerful classes at one time may not necessarily serve their interests at all times. Thus, the U.S. Constitution originally advantaged the propertied, white, English, Protestant, male elite of the original 13 colonies, while largely ignoring the interests of small farmers and entirely omitting political rights for women and people of African descent (Beard, 1916; Parenti, 1977; Zinn, 1980). In subsequent eras, however, this same document became an important tool for women, African Americans, the working class, and ethnic and religious minorities in their struggles for legal and social equality (Baer, 1983; Karst, 1989, 1993; Koppelman, 1996; MacKinnon, 1989). In the final analysis, a radical perspective demands that we avoid constructing ahistorical models of state and law typical of social contract and consensus approaches.

Having reviewed the radical critique of the consensus model, we now turn to an examination of two radical perspectives on state and law derived from Marx's analysis of political economy: instrumentalism and structuralism.

## POLITICAL ECONOMY, STATE AND LAW

Those who study state and law from a political-economic perspective take as their starting point Marx's claim that the central function of these institutions is to facilitate and legitimate the underlying economic structure of society. Attempts to verify this claim typically rely on either *instrumentalist* or *structuralist* approaches. Instrumentalist approaches hold that the state and law are tools used by powerful groups to secure and promote their political and economic concerns. This perspective reflects Marx's notion that the state is essentially an instrument for carrying out the will of the capitalist class (Marx and Engels, 1955). From a structuralist standpoint, state and law are an expression of the struggle between social classes – a struggle in which the powerful have an advantage, but also one where they cannot win every contest. These two views of the state are discussed more fully below.

### Instrumental Marxism

The instrumental Marxist perspective stems from claims made by Marx himself and from interpretations of Marx offered by various radical scholars. Recall Marx's argument that the economic structure is a primary determinant of social relationships, and that the basic function of legal and political structures is to promote and legitimate economic interests. In this view, state and law serve as an "instrument" of those who own and control the means of production (e.g., the bourgeoisie). With this in mind, Marx and Engels

(1955:11-12) claimed that "the executive of the modern state is but a committee for managing the common affairs of the whole bourgeoisie."

Within radical criminology the clearest example of an instrumental perspective is found in the early works of Richard Quinney. In *Critique of the Legal Order*, Quinney (1974b:16) asserted that the "criminal law is an instrument of the state and ruling class to maintain and perpetuate the existing social and economic order." In developing this position, Quinney argued that law is used to repress the poor so that the wealthy and the powerful can maintain their position of economic supremacy. By using the state to enforce its will on the rest of society, law is used by the ruling class as an *instrument* of class struggle. To provide evidence for these claims, Quinney analyzed the class composition of several crime commissions created in the 1960s including the President's Commission on Law Enforcement and Administration of Justice, the National Commission on the Causes and Prevention of Violence, and the National Advisory Commission on Civil Disorders. According to his analysis, "the ruling class is able to shape social policy to its own ends by participating in a variety of advisory organizations involved in the government decision-making process. These groups are composed, almost by definition, of the owners and managers of large corporations (Quinney, 1974:82). Based on this finding, Quinney (1974b:95) concluded, as have other instrumentalists, that "the ruling class through its use of the legal system is able to preserve a domestic order that allows the dominant economic interests to be maintained and promoted. The role of the state in capitalist society is to defend the interests of the ruling class."

In sum, for instrumentalists, the state, law, and the ruling class are one: the economic, social and political interests of the ruling class find expression in law, which is constructed and used by the ruling class to the advantage of that class and that class alone (see Chambliss, 1993c, for reviews and examples of other instrumentalist research).

Instrumentalist approaches have some utility. In some cases, such as the one cited by Quinney, or Sidney Harring's policing studies (see chapter 8 in this book), there is evidence of a clear link between elite interests and crime control policies. As a general model of the relationship between law and political economy, however, instrumentalism cannot explain the complex role of law in modern political states. Some have characterized instrumentalist models as crude versions of economic determinism (Greenberg, 1976; Collins, 1982; Meier, 1976), and even those who once advocated this position have revised their views (for example, see Quinney, 1980). A number of more specific criticisms have also been leveled at instrumentalist approaches to state and law.

First, instrumentalism exaggerates the cohesiveness of the ruling or capitalist class, as well as its ability to act in coordinated, singular fashion (Greenberg, 1981; Bernard, 1981; Chambliss and Seidman, 1982). We can find many historical instances when one group of capitalists – for instance, those representing big corporations – have come into conflict with other groups of capitalists, such as those representing self-employed entrepreneurs (Davis, 1986). There are some who argue that the American Civil War, for instance, was primarily a war between two groups of capitalists, those representing the agrarian, slave-holding interests in the South and those representing the urban, manufacturing interests of the North (Pollard, 1977). Furthermore, the simple division of society into a ruling class of capitalist and a working class of industrial laborers has been replaced by a far more complex division of labor that includes people who manage capital but do not necessarily own it, and a whole stratum of professional and technical workers who combine the characteristics of both the working class and the ruling class (Ehrenreich and Ehrenreich, 1979; Gorz, 1972; Walker, 1979; Wright, 1978).

Second, instrumental theory tends to be static and deterministic. In this it comes ironically close to espousing an ahistorical position where the economy is always and everywhere the prime determinant of state and law (Chambliss and Seidman, 1982). While the capitalist state may never be able to absolutely sever its dependence on the capitalist class, over time, structuralists argue, it has acquired an increasing degree of autonomy (Althusser, 1971; Block, 1977; Offe and Ronge, 1975). Thus, the instrumentalist perspective may be more useful for studying the relationship between ruling classes and the state during early periods of capitalist development than during subsequent eras.

Third, not *all* laws reflect the exclusive interests of the ruling class. Anti-trust laws, laws protecting labor unions, regulatory laws aimed at controlling corporate misbehavior, laws requiring corporations to limit environmental pollution, food and drug safety laws, worker safety laws and laws protecting the civil rights of women and minorities are often cited as examples of legislation enacted against the wishes of major segments of the capitalist class (Friedrichs, 1996b, 1980a; Frank and Lynch, 1992). During their creation, many of these laws faced stiff resistance from business and corporate leaders. As a result, their final form typically offered less protection for the working class than was originally proposed (Piven and Cloward, 1977). Nevertheless, the very fact of their passage reveals the importance of the state as a site where conflicts between unequal groups such as labor and capital, manufacturers and consumers, women and men, and industry and environmentalists, shape law. How and why capitalist states pass laws that appear to benefit the working classes rather than capitalists, or that benefit political minorities rather than political majorities, is a central theme of the structuralist approach, which we will detail in the next section.

Fourth, the instrumental perspective also ignores conflicts between the state and the capitalist class it presumably represents (Spitzer, 1980; Hagan and Leon, 1977). For instance, since the 1980s there has been a powerful movement backed by business interests to "shrink the size of government" (Edsall, 1984). Many of those who support this shrinkage do so because they would prefer the money spent by government be made available to private-sector financial, retail and manufacturing interests (Ackerman, 1982; Derber, 1998). Meanwhile, government bureaucracies that suffer from such funding declines attempt to maintain their budgets against the interests of capitalists.

Fifth, the state is no more monolithic than the capitalist class. Rather, the state has its own internal conflicts and therefore cannot be characterized as uniformly representing the interests of the capitalist class. For instance, during the U.S.-backed war against the leftist Sandinistas government of Nicaragua in the 1980s, one component of the U.S. government – the CIA – was helping finance the war by the illegal sale of missiles to Iran, while two other segments of the government – the State Department and the Department of Defense – were attempting to keep Iran from receiving such weapons (Marshall et al., 1987; Walsh, 1993). Similarly, in the 1990s, the Office of the Surgeon General and the Food and Drug Administration sought to limit the sale of cigarettes, while another part of the government – the Commerce Department – was helping cigarette manufacturers sell their products in developing nations (Glantz et al., 1996).

Finally, an instrumental perspective on law can easily lead to conspiracy explanations that imagine that capitalists and state managers frequently come together in secret to consciously manipulate law to their advantage. Certainly, these events occur sometimes. Conspiracy theories, however, contradict a central tenet of Marxist thought – the idea that individual actions are often the result of structural forces rather than the other way around (Marx, 1967a). From this perspective, conscious planning and control on the part of a capitalist class is not a sufficient explanation for state and law.

In sum, a number of criticisms have been raised regarding the instrumental perspective on state and law. Spitzer (1983:105) has suggested that reducing law to a reflex of economic interests of the capitalist class was "the greatest obstacle to the development of a Marxist sociology of law." Despite its various shortcomings, instrumentalist theories of law did make two important contributions to the development of radical criminology. First, instrumentalist critiques of state and law offered the first alternative to "legal fetishism," that is, the idea that law can be understood as a self-contained entity unaffected by wider economic, social and political contexts (Collins, 1982). Second, the instrumentalist perspective challenged the dominant consensus model that accepted law at face value and in doing so contributed to "piercing the veil of legitimacy that hangs over many of the specific institutions that systematically link the capitalist class to the state" (Gold et al., 1975a:34).

Faced with the limitations of instrumentalism, by the late 1970s many radical criminologists had gravitated toward a more "structural" understanding of state and law. It is to this perspective we now turn.

## Structural Marxism

During the 1970s and 1980s, "structuralism" received a great deal of attention, and a number of thinkers in a variety of fields were labeled "structuralists." What follows are some themes typical of many structural analyses.

The most basic element of structuralist analysis, and one that structuralism shares with many other sociological approaches, is the premise that observable social phenomenon reflect the operation of deeper and less immediately obvious social arrangements (Durkheim, 1938). An example would be Marx's claim that laws protecting property reflect the needs of an economic system based on private ownership of the means of production, instead of simply reflecting an abstract belief about the sanctity of property (DeGeorge and DeGeorge, 1972).

A second element of structuralism suggests that relations between component parts of a social system are more important than the individual elements making up that system (Ollman, 1978). These individual elements themselves "are comprised of sets of relations" (Keats and Urry, 1975:120), which gives rise to the idea that a social system may be greater than the sum of its parts (Lukacs, 1985). Thus, from a structuralist perspective, *how* workers and managers relate with one another in the production process is more important than the simple fact that some people belong to the category of workers and others to the category of managers. In other words, ordinary words such as "workers" or "managers" have a different meaning when employed as terms that describe class relations. In this view, for example, the term "worker" indicates subservience to a class of "managers" who control working conditions. Workers, therefore, must relate to manager as inferiors, and as exploited, low-level human machinery that provides labor power. The point is that for radicals, these words are not neutral, but contain within them a complex understanding of the economic and political relationship – of the unequal relations and forms of power – that exist between classes in society.

The third characteristic of structuralism suggests that any individual social phenomenon (e.g., law) must be considered in its wider context, with this context variously described as holistic (Greenberg, 1981) or a totality (Jay, 1973). The structural tradition has much in common with the dialectical approach outlined earlier and can be used in ways that bring it close to the more conservative structural-functionalist theories that dominated sociology in the 1950s (Keats and Urry, 1975). Beyond these general characteristics, what is a structural-Marxist approach to law and how does it overcome the limitations of instrumentalism?

For Marx, the political state was relatively unimportant since it was merely an "epiphenomenon," that is, an illusory form whose real meaning was to be found elsewhere. In Marx's words the state was little more than the "concentrated expression of economics," and within Marx's own writings there is no clear theory of the state, other than treating it as a committee for managing the interests of the bourgeoisie (Adoratsky, 1936). By the early 20th century, however, the modern republican state had become a far more complex structure than the one Marx experienced. Increasingly the state was required to take over the role of religion in providing an ideological justification for inequality, and to play a role in ameliorating those consequences of capitalism most likely to lead to social revolution (Isay, 2004:117-172). Responding to these changes, structural Marxists, moved beyond Marx's limited concern with the state and began theorizing the state as a distinct element of social organization, which, although linked to the interests of the ruling classes, is more than an extension of those interests. Structural Marxists characterize state and law as the outcome of the *contradictions* of capitalism (Gold et al., 1975a). This differs in several important ways from the instrumentalist position that law always and everywhere reflects the specific, conscious interests of the capitalist class. First, structuralism recognizes that capitalism is a *social system*. As such, it is more than the sum of the individual interests and actions that take place within its specific institutions. For instance, the capitalist business cycle is prone to periods of economic prosperity and periods of economic decline (Bowles et al., 1990). These periods of decline occur regardless of the desires and efforts of capitalists to continually grow profits, and may, in fact, occur *because of* their pursuit of profit.

Powerful interest groups may influence the direction of capitalist development within specific, limited arenas. For instance, laws that promoted the development of private automobiles and a national interstate highway system, rather than mass transit, as the basic mode of transportation in the U.S. were the product of conscious efforts by capitalists closely linked to the automobile, petroleum and tire industries (Halberstam, 1986; St. Clair, 1986). While the investment decisions and political strategies undertaken by capitalist interest groups in this case had a significant national impact, they did not determine the totality of American society. There is much more to the U.S. than its car-dependent character. Moreover, decisions made at one time may later have unplanned negative consequences. In this case, the automobile-dependent sub-urbanization of America led to costly air pollution and a relocation of well-paying jobs and their mostly white workforces to the suburban edges of older cities, leaving ethnic minorities clustered in decaying inner cities with declining job opportunities and rising crime and social pathology (Davis, 1990; Garreau, 1991; Wilson, 1996). This, in turn, led to increased government social expenditures for environmental cleanup, crime control and social welfare – monies that could have otherwise been used for social investments that would have benefited capitalist growth (O'Connor, 1973).

There is no better example of how the dynamics of capitalism can lead to outcomes that are beyond the control of any single group than the current process of economic *globalization*. Increasingly, corporations pursue profits by investing around the world in ways that are radically altering contemporary social life. Today the engineer, systems designer or mid-level manager, as well as the auto worker, key punch operator, or computer assembler in the U.S. is increasingly competing for jobs with lower-wage workers from around the world (Hira and Hira, 2004). While some U.S. industries and workers benefit from globalization, others – particularly manufacturing industries that historically generated the largest portion of well-paying, working-class jobs in the U.S. – suffer (Dobbs, 2005). Capitalism is currently undergoing a dramatic change in its form of organization, a change that is beyond the control of individual capitalists and that may be beyond the control of anyone. William Greider (1997:11) provides an ideal structuralist metaphor when he likens the process of globalization to a great machine that creates both enormous wealth and great human wreckage as it pursues its goals of expanding capitalist profits: "Now imagine that there are skillful hands on board, but no one is at the wheel. In fact, this machine has no wheel nor an internal governor to control the speed and direction. It is sustained by its own forward motion, guided mainly by its own appetites." As a theoretical framework, structuralism does not negate the importance of human decision making, but it views the consequences of the sum total of these decisions as something beyond the control (or even the intention) of individual actors. In this perspective, law can be the result of contradictions emerging from within a social system rather than as the direct will of a dominant capitalist class.

Another important contradiction within capitalist political economies (and possibly all modern political-economies) arises from the need for *legitimacy*.

Capitalist economies need political states to create the conditions for profit making. These include making and enforcing laws that protect the rights of capitalists to own the means of production and to exert control over laboring classes, creating and maintaining sound monetary systems and protecting capitalist enterprises at home and capitalist investment abroad from foreign enemies. Political states cannot secure these kinds of protection, however, unless they have a degree of public approval, i.e., legitimacy, in the eyes of their citizens. Without this legitimacy, both the power of the state and public acceptance of the economic system will erode (Weber, 1964). To preserve their legitimacy, states may sometimes act in ways that contradict the short-term goals of special-interests groups within the capitalist class (O'Connor, 1973).

No better example of this exists than the creation of the U.S. Bill of Rights. The framers of the U.S. Constitution were, to a *man*, major owners of the means of production, and they initially framed a constitution largely designed to meet their interests (Beard, 1916). In order to gain acceptance for the Constitution, however, they ultimately incorporated a Bill of Rights that addressed the interests of petit-bourgeoisie segments of colonial America without whose support more powerful elites could not build their new society (Amar and Amar, 2000). The right to vote reflected a similar compromise between those seeking to protect their propertied privilege to govern and those seeking a more democratic society. The original draft of the Constitution, for instance, granted all *free white* men the right to vote. This was anathema to the wealthy participants to the Constitutional Convention because it raised the specter of a society, as James Madison observed, where "the rights of property...may be overruled by a majority without property" (Beitzinger, 1972:295). The compromise solution was to extend voting rights to those with a total of 63 English pounds in real and personal property, or about *half* of all free white males (Zinn, 1980). A number of other examples exist in U.S. history. The passage of antitrust legislation at the end of the nineteenth century, the legalization of unions and the passage of minimum wage laws during the Great Depression of the 1930s and the passage of anti-discrimination, consumer protection and environmental protection laws are just some examples of how the U.S. political process struggled to preserve the legitimacy of America's capitalist democracy over the initial objections of many capitalists. As Chambliss and Seidman (1982:313) put it: "a great deal of state action concerns not the enhancement of profit for a particular fraction of the ruling class, but the maintenance of relations of production that make capitalism possible."

In one sense, structuralism is more consistent than instrumentalism with Marx and Engels' views about capitalism because it recognizes the role of *class struggle* in shaping society. From a structuralist perspective, the passage of laws that appear to benefit the working class rather than the capitalist class (e.g., minimum-wage laws, consumer-protection policies etc.) is the outcome of class struggle. Structuralists recognize that capitalists do not always win absolute victories, and that sometimes other classes are capable of rallying enough support behind their class interests that denying them would risk the legitimacy of the political-economic system. A structuralist analysis, however, is not the same as pluralist models of lawmaking that treat the state as a neutral entity within which fair contests are waged over who gets what. For example, workers' and poor peoples' movements must submit their demands for social change to a governmental process that is structured to preserve the belief that capitalism is a fair and equal means of distributing wealth (e.g., see Gordon et al., 1982; Piven and Cloward, 1977, 1997). In so doing, the state managers typically balance the need for state legitimacy against the interests of the capitalist sectors in order to determine how far that state can go to meet the demands of dissident groups or classes without suffering a backlash from capital (Offe, 1985; Wolfe, 1977). Sometimes the outcome is what has been termed "symbolic legislation" (Edleman, 1971); that is, laws that say: "We feel your pain," but that actually do very little to change the balance of power between capitalists and other social claimants. At other times, the outcome may result in very real gains in power for claimants outside the capitalist class. In either case, structuralism asks that we examine the *historical specifics* of lawmaking in order to determine how the state negotiated a path among the demands that it provide a climate conducive to capitalist profit making and popular acceptance of both the state and capitalism.

The structuralist approach also recognizes that, over time, states develop their own interests and then act to protect these interests (Wolfe, 1977). As previously mentioned, states may develop large and powerful bureaucracies that use this power to protect themselves against inroads by the capitalist class. In 1997, for instance, a number of conservative forces began to promote the idea of allowing workers to opt out of the Social Security system in favor of private investment programs. This would ensure that money that would otherwise go to the Social Security system would remain in the private sector where it could generate private profit for large-scale capitalist enterprises such as brokerage firms and banks. The Social Security Administration and the executive branch under Democratic President William Clinton moved quickly to oppose such plans, which, among other things, would seriously reduce the total financial resources available to pursue the kinds of social programs that are key to the maintenance of support for the Democratic Party among its political base (Steuerle, 1996; Tanner, 1996). In 2004, Republican President George W. Bush began a *Administration-initiated* campaign to use Social Security contributions in the form of "private investment accounts" to increase the stock of capital available to private investors, the key political base of the Republican party (Greenhouse, 2005)

The structural model outlined above is consistent with that posed by French structuralist Marxist, Louis Althusser. Althusser argued against the economic reductionism of instrumental Marxism, claiming instead that superstructural elements (e.g., law, ideology, the state, politics) have a degree of autonomy from the economic base. In Althusser's view, political, social and cultural forces can influence the direction of the economy, just as the economy exerts powerful influences over other aspects of social life. In Althusser's terms, law, ideology and politics have both a *specific effectivity* and *relative autonomy*, which means that superstructural elements (e.g., education, religion, law, popular culture) have some independence from the economy (relative autonomy). He also grants that non-economic institutions have some power to influence both the economy and other elements of the superstructure (specific effectivity). Thus, Althusser avoids one-way determinism and with it one major limitation of instrumentalism.

Althusser (1969, 1971) theorized that the state comes to enjoy a degree of "relative autonomy" from the desires of individuals in the ruling or capitalist class. While there has been considerable debate about just how autonomous this "relatively autonomous" state might be, it is clear that the modern capitalist state, while dependent upon capitalism and the capitalist classes for financial support and cultural validation, also frequently pursues agendas that are contrary to *some sectors* of the capitalist class (Livingston and Gregory, 1989; Offe, 1985; Sklar, 1988). Thus, the central tenet of a structuralist approach is that the state in capitalist society is not a simple instrument of the ruling class, but a semi-autonomous entity that operates to ensure the long-term continuation of the capitalist social system (Friedrichs, 1980a). This position loosens "the functional relationship between law and the economy" (Greenberg, 1976:617).

Instrumentalists such as Miliband (1969) question whether Althusser's stance undercuts the fundamental contribution of Marxism by giving equal time to the superstructural components of society. The concern is that structuralism replaced economic determinism with a confused model wherein everything causes everything else. To this Althusser (1969) responds as follows:

> Of course, these specific relations between structure and superstructure still deserve theoretical elaboration and investigation. However, Marx has at least given us "two ends of the chain" (i.e., base and superstructure), and has told us to find out what goes on between them; on the one hand, determination in the last instance by the

(economic) mode of production; on the other, the relative autonomy of the superstructures and their specific effectivity. [p. 111; see also Althusser and Balibar, 1977:42]

It is fair to ask whether Althusser, by divorcing law and other superstructural elements from the economy while simultaneously saying that "in the last instance" the economy will dominate, is seeking the best of both worlds. Spitzer (1983) argues as much, suggesting that Althusser's formulation is really a thinly disguised resurrection of economic reductionism. Despite these debates, many radical criminologists, either explicitly or implicitly, have come to accept Althusser's view that law enjoys a relative rather than absolute autonomy from economic forces, and his advice to examine the "two ends of the chain" (for present purposes, law and the economy) in order to assess the relation between them. Structuralists recognize that the relationship between law and the economy is dynamic and will change over time. However, the general rule of thumb within a structuralist model of law making is that all laws reflect some degree of economic interest, and many will have been significantly shaped by these interests. This approach is consistent with Marx's materialistic orientation and his preference for historically specific explanations.

While the view of increasing state autonomy is widespread among structural analysts, it has encountered a new challenge. Some contend that the twentieth-century pattern of expanding state autonomy is being reversed as political states become more dependent on global corporations and capitalist investors. These entities and people have the ability to extort states to meet their demands, threatening to relocate production facilities to more hospitable countries, or, in the case of major lenders such as the World Bank and the International Monetary Fund, refusing development loans unless conditions favorable to capital are met (Barnett, 1994; Kramer and Michalowski, 1995; Mann, 2003; Korten, 1995; Steiglitz, 2003; Verderey, 1996). How far this process continues depends on the political strategies developed with and across nation-states to challenge the growing power of international capital (Korten, 1998). Nevertheless, the current process of globalizing the economy reveals very real limits to state autonomy.

Structuralist theories of state and law exerted a significant impact on the development of radical approaches to both lawmaking and crime control policy. William Chambliss's (1993) structural-contradictions model of lawmaking provides an excellent example of the structuralist impact on radical thought in criminology. According to Chambliss (1993a:9), the process of lawmaking should be seen:

...as a process aimed at the resolution of contradictions, conflicts, and dilemmas that are historically grounded in time and space and inherent in the structure of a particular political, economic, and social structure. Every society, nation, economic system, and historical period contains contradictory elements which are moving forces behind social changes – including the creation of law ...[P]eople, not "society," "institutions," or "historical processes," make law.

Structuralist theories of the modern capitalist welfare state, such as Chambliss's, typically see law arising from the fundamental contradiction between the economic system's need for continual accumulation of capital (O'Connor, 1973) and the state's need for legitimacy (Wolfe, 1977). Accumulation is facilitated by shifting benefits from labor to capital through such things as regressive taxation, decreases in public expenditures by the state and limited state regulation of business. Popular legitimacy is facilitated by doing exactly the opposite. Because the state needs both legitimacy and the money that comes from taxing a growing capitalist economy, it can never move wholly to one side or the other. Instead, the state seesaws between competing sets of demands.

In recent years the issue of crime and crime control has come to play an important role in helping the state address contradictory pressures for legitimacy and accumulation. Beginning in the 1970s, public leaders increasingly began to treat street crime and violence as *the* most important political issue. From the 1970s through the present decade, federal and state governments have pursued war after war against crime and drugs – wars that enjoyed widespread popular support as media attention intensified public fear of crime (Altheide, 2002; Ferrrel and Websdale, 1999; Fishman and Cavender, 1998). At the same time that they were fighting crime, national and state leaders were engaged in a massive shift of resources away from labor and toward capital. Tax rates were adjusted in ways that increased the tax burdens on middle- and lower-income earners while reducing the burdens on the wealthy. In many jurisdictions, per-pupil public expenditures for education declined while expenditures for law enforcement and imprisonment rose. Funding for government agencies that regulate corporations and businesses declined, while funding for drug interdiction and similar crime-fighting measures increased. The popular support earned by governments through their wars on crime appear to have more than offset losses of legitimacy associated with what, under other circumstances, would be perceived as an unacceptable shift of national wealth away from the working class and toward capital. From an instrumentalist perspective, this shift of resources from labor to capital behind the banner of wars on crime would be seen as a deliberate strategy undertaken by capitalists' allies in government to hoodwink the population. A structuralist interpretation, however, suggests that politicians saw an opportunity to satisfy differing interests – the economic interests of capitalists and the safety interests of citizens – with little short-term cost to the state. Thus, from the later 1970s to the present, the state has been able to manage the contradiction between legitimacy and wealth accumulation by a two-pronged strategy, one aimed at bolstering legitimacy through fighting crime and the other promoting private accumulation of wealth by reducing state contributions to programs that benefit workers

## STATE, IDENTITY AND DIFFERENCE

In recent years theories regarding *identity and difference* have raised an important radical challenge to Marxist models of law making in two ways. First, radical criminologists have called attention to the ways in which law is not blind to identity. Instead they have demonstrated the many ways that law and legal processes disadvantage those whose identity lacks one or more of the key components of the ideologically dominant identity which is male, white, and heterosexual. While orthodox criminologists have a long history of examining racial disparities under the law, radical criminologists have brought new issues to the table. One was situating racial disparities within larger political-economic and cultural contexts. The other was to focus on legal disparities suffered by women, children, gays and lesbians. Second, radical criminologists have raised an important theoretical challenge to the idea that law merely *responds* to existing social difference by analyzing how law *creates* social difference. Thus, for instance, laws and social practices that prohibit gay marriage construct the meaning of "male" and "female" as beings who only engage in sex with their gender opposites.

By the late 1970s feminists, in particular, began to criticize Marxist theory for its failure to consider how the division of society into two sexes – male and female – shapes all other aspects of social life, including patterns of dominance and subordination. They also observed that men and women have experiences *as* men or women that will cut across class lines, contradicting the Marxist dictum that class position is the primary determinant of a person's identity and experience (Mitchell, 1971; Rubin, 1975). Feminists argued that men share common experiences that connect them with one another in ways they are not connected to women, regardless of their social class. Similarly, while the lives of working-class and upper-class women differ significantly, they share many experiences as women, including the experience of being subordinate to the men in their class (Cassell, 1977; Messerschmidt, 1986).

– 58 –

While Marxists typically contend that male dominance in modern societies is the result of capitalism, many feminists argue the opposite – that the modern state, whether capitalist or socialist, is an expression of male dominance, reflects a male-centered society, and could only have emerged by displacing women from central roles in society. From this perspective, the history, substance and form of the modern state are essentially male in character. Historically, the legal theories and political practices that became the basis of the modern state developed between the late middle ages and the beginning of the nineteenth century. During this crucial period of state development, women were excluded from political participation. In Europe and England, and later in the U.S., both law and religion held women subordinate to the authority of men in everyday life whether these men were their fathers, husbands or even grown sons. As a form of political rule developed with little or no participation from women, the modern state is, from this perspective, an expression of male experience and male perceptions of value and social order, not just a reflection of the interests of capitalists (Danner, 1996).

With respect to substantive law, feminist analysis contends that the legal codes of modern capitalist states treat the subjugation and abuse of women by men as normal (Coleman and Widom, 2004; DeKeseredy and Schwartz, 1996; Schur, 1984; Snider, 2003). As a result, the state intervenes to protect women from violence or mistreatment only when the acts are beyond what is accepted as normal. In the U.S., for instance, laws prohibiting rape have historically implied that the sexuality of wives or female date partners is the property of men, to be taken by force if desired (Bennice and Resick, 2003; Estrich, 1988). If this were not the case, rape laws would have criminalized forced sex by husbands the same way it criminalized forced sex by strangers. Only in recent years, and then only symbolically, have states begun to incorporate the concept of "marital rape" into law (Hasday, 2000). Other forms of violence against women similarly normalize high levels of brutality against women. For most of U.S. history, when men assaulted their wives, even if they caused grave injury, their behavior was either ignored by the justice system or treated as a lesser offense such as "assault on a female." For instance, the "rule of thumb" allowed husbands to beat their wives as long as they used a switch no wider than their thumb. Even though many states currently have enacted more stringent laws prohibiting spouse abuse, in many jurisdictions police continue to treat such assaults as less important than crimes with "innocent" victims (Websdale, 1997). In other words, the legal system's subtle endorsement of intimate violence against women remains a part of the patriarchal state (DeKeseredy and Hinch, 1991; Kantola and Dahal, 2005).

Some feminist theorists also contend that the very form of the state is male in character. For instance, MacKinnon (1989:170) writes: "The rule of law and the rule of men are one thing... State power embodied in law, exists throughout society as male power at the same time as the power of men over women is organized as the power of the state." The cornerstone of male power in law resides in the emphasis on juridical rather than substantive equality (Gilligan, 1982; MacKinnon, 1989; Young, 1990). Most Western legal systems are based on the liberal proposition that all people should be treated equally "in the eyes of the law." This proposition, in turn, rests on the assumption that if the law treats everyone identically, regardless of gender, skin color, income, and so forth, justice will result. But while people may be imagined as equal under law, it is the only place they are equal. The essence of modern social life is inequality on a number of dimensions. In substantive terms women are not equal to men. Women are typically paid less for their labor than men. Women, not men, are the primary targets of sexualized violence. Women are expected to bear, nurture and rear the next generation with relatively little assistance from men. When they speak, women are not believed as readily as men. Women are far less likely than men to be lawmakers, judges or heads of major businesses. Yet when men and women appear before the law, the notion of juridical equality requires that "blind" justice treat these differences as irrelevant, and treat women *as if* they are equal to men. Under this framework, a women who is raped by her husband presumably has the same opportunity to seek legal help as a women raped by a stranger. The realities of a male-dominated society, however, mean that it will be far more difficult for the victim of marital rape to be taken seriously by the justice system than the "innocent" women assaulted by a stranger.

Legal responses treat people as if they are equal. This assumption is problematic for women on a number of grounds, primarily because in modern societies women and men are not equal; power continues to reside mainly with men. Further, law doesn't really attempt to make people equal; rather, law is largely designed to help reproduce existing power relationships. Legal rules and procedures, for instance, are male-centered and reflect male experiences. Whether or not the "objective" moral reasoning of the state represents a uniquely "male" view of reality, it is clear that the modern state was historically created by men around so-called "objective" moral systems that have preserved the dominant role of men in society, culture and law. These clear gender relationships indicate that if we desire to understand the origins and operations of state and law, we must reach beyond social class to incorporate the fundamental impact that gender relations have on society and its system of justice.

Gender, however, is only one aspect of social identity that plays a role in the creation and implementation of law. Beginning in the 1990s, a number of other forms of *difference*, including race, sexual preference, age, religion, and ethnicity have joined class and gender as important factors in any analysis of lawmaking or law enforcement (Benhabib, 1996; Minow, 1990; Rich, 2004; Stein and Plummer, 1994; Young, 1990; Wonders, 1996). Increasingly, radical criminologists have come to view identity as multifaceted rather than mono-lithic (Arrigo, Milovanovic, and Schehr, 2005; O'Neil, 2003). No one is simply middle class, or Japanese American, or male. But someone might be a middle-class, Japanese-American male. Nor is identity fixed. In some situations, such as a locker room, gender may be the most salient aspect of a person's identity, while in another, a church for instance, a person's religious affiliation takes precedence. This requires that any radical analysis of state, law and crime be sensitive to the complex interactions that shape how both behaviors and people will or will not be defined as criminal in accordance with salient aspects of their identity.

## In Sum

Radical criminologists generally accept the proposition that law making and crime cannot be understood without reference to the political-economic environment within which they take place. At the same time, they also recognize that law and crime cannot be understood with reference *only* to political-economic forces. For radical criminology, analyses of state and law increasingly form around questions such as: "How has the interaction between the construction of social class and the construction of identity shaped a society's legal system?"; "How has a society's legal system shaped the construction of class and identity?"; "How do established cultural images of identity groups, such as the poor, the rich, gays, women, or African Americans influence what kinds of behaviors will be heavily controlled and what kinds will not?"; and, "How do people's compound identities affect how they will be treated when they enter the justice system as victims, offenders or workers?" These questions direct us to consider the complex interactions that shape state and law, while keeping a focus on the sociological processes underlying lawmaking and law enforcement.

In the next chapter we move from the radical analysis of the state to the radical concept of crime.

# FOUR.
# THE RADICAL CONCEPT OF CRIME

According to our system of laws, some behaviors (e.g., robbery, murder, rape, theft) are so harmful that they deserve the worst punishments society can offer, and those who commit these crimes are defined as deserving the worst punishments the law will allow. Yet, are these crimes really the greatest threat to our individual and collective well-being? Are the people who commit them the most callous of all criminals? Or is the law's focus on street crime the consequence of class biases inherent in a legal system that has been controlled largely by more privileged classes?

Regardless of the type of society, it is the least well off members of society who commit the majority of street crimes. Street crimes certainly impose real suffering, loss and pain on their victims. From a radical perspective, however, these crimes are far from the most serious threats to human welfare. Many callous actions committed by elite wrongdoers cause far more physical and financial harm than street crime. In cases such as environmental crime, exploitation of foreign labor, and war, the consequences of elite crimes reach well beyond the countries where the offenders reside. Nevertheless, as Ward and Green (2000:76) note, orthodox criminology is dominated by a "parochial obsession with the behavior of poor people in rich countries," while the harmful behaviors of elites either escape criminalization or are punished lightly (see Reiman, 1998; Simon, 1999; Frank and Lynch, 1992; Burns and Lynch, 2004, 2002; Sutherland, 1949).

Central to the radical approach to crime is the proposition that criminal law and justice helps reproduce or reinforce the established social order in several different but connected ways. First, the law criminalizes actions that threaten to disrupt the economic, racial, gender, political and cultural configurations of the existing order. Second, to uphold criminal law, the state creates agencies that are able to use physical force to control law violators. Third, legal rules and processes become ideological mechanisms for socializing citizens to accept prevailing economic, cultural, race, gender and political power relations as necessary and natural. Fourth, the system of criminal law has been created to allow for differential application of legal rules and justice processes so that the least powerful groups experience the greatest disadvantages in terms of surveillance, apprehension and punishment. Finally, because the system of law is not uniformly applied, it is able to turn a relative blind eye to harmful actions that contribute to the continuation of desired structures of power and privilege. In this chapter, we explore this idea here by examining the ways economic and political power shape the definition of crime.

## THE CONCEPT OF CRIME

Criminologists have long recognized that crime is a social construct. Echoing earlier theorists such as Becker (1963) and Lemert (1951), Gwynn Nettler (1984:16) argued that "crime is a word, not a deed." That is, crime is a label. When this label is attached to behavior, then and only then does that behavior become a crime. The operative term here is *becomes*: driving fast becomes an offense only when it is defined as speeding; killing becomes a crime only when it is labeled murder; certain forms of sexual contact become crimes only when they are defined as rape, sexual assault, or prostitution; and decisions by corporate executives to cooperate with one another in order to set prices at a certain level *become* crimes when defined as "price-fixing." In this view, regardless of how many people it harms, no behavior is criminal in itself until defined as such by law.

The radical concept of crime as a definition rather than a behavior has far-reaching implications. First, it suggests that viewing certain behaviors as criminal rests on a series of human decisions. The process of defining crime, which in modern states involves political legislation, is a social act laden with political and personal dynamics and is not the inevitable outcome of "natural laws" as conservatives often argue.

A second implication is that there are no self-evident criteria for deciding what will be considered crime. Sometimes the stated criterion is moral (e.g., prohibition, prostitution, gambling; see Gusfield, 1967; Helmer, 1975), or it involves identifying injury to a *specific* individual victim (e.g., rape, robbery, theft or murder). In other cases the criterion is the harm caused to people or society in general, as in the case of laws prohibiting price-fixing or environmental damage. And finally, behaviors are sometimes defined as offenses because they disrupt the smooth operation of complex activities, as in the case of traffic offenses.

A third implication is that definitions of crime are arbitrary. This does not mean that they are random or unimportant. Behaviors typically come to be defined as criminal because they violate the *subjective* values, beliefs or perceived interests of those with the power to win the political contests surrounding lawmaking (Chambliss and Seidman, 1982). Because these definitions are based on subjectively held visions, not immutable "facts," they could be otherwise. In this sense they are arbitrary. At the same time, the subjective values, beliefs and perceptions of interest used to define behaviors as criminal have often been a part of the dominant ideology in a society for so long that they appear to be "self-evident" and "natural." Thus, while it is theoretically possible to change the ideological basis on which behaviors are defined as crimes, making that change requires redefining what we take for granted.

In *The Social Reality of Crime*, Richard Quinney (1970:15) employed an instrumentalist position when he argued that "crime is a definition of human conduct that is created by authorized agents in a politically organized society." Quinney went on to argue that "authorized agents" (i.e., those holding political and economic power) shape criminal definitions, and impose those definitions on persons in positions of relative powerlessness, meaning that "the probability that criminal definitions will be applied varies according to the extent to which the behaviors of the powerless conflict with the interests of the powerful..." (1970:18).

Does this mean that definitions of crime always reflect the interests of those at the top of the political-economic pyramid? To this question, instrumentalists would answer "yes," but structuralist and agency theory approaches would say "no." Structuralists contend that lawmaking is the working out of sociological forces (particularly economic and political ones) over which neither the powerful nor the powerless have complete control. Meanwhile, agency theorists would contend that law results from purposeful human activity of individuals as they pursue ideologically and culturally understood goals. Thus, there is no clear agreement among radicals regarding the relative balance among underlying social forces, institutions and human agency in the construction of definitions of crime.

Whatever the specific model of explanation, all radical approaches to law contend that the behaviors encompassed by the word "crime" are not self-evident. Crimes are not necessarily those behaviors most harmful to society in some objective sense. Crime is a human construct, and "the social reality of crime is constantly being created" (Quinney, 1970:v). From a radical perspective the crucial questions are: who does the "creating," why and how?

Orthodox criminology defines crime as "behavior defined as criminal by law" (Tappan, 1947), and according to this definition, socially injurious behaviors that are not legally prohibited and prosecuted would not count as crimes. In contrast, radicals take law and definitions of crime as problematic, meaning that the process of law creation requires explanation. Because the definition of crime is treated as problematic, radical criminologists often look beyond law when studying crime. That is, they will sometimes study socially-injurious behaviors that the law omits as well as more traditional, legally defined crimes. For radicals, lawmaking is a selective process, and the process of selection reflects existing power relations and structures (e.g., class, race and gender relations). Tony Platt (1974:5) summarized this issue as follows: "...in the past, we have been constrained by a legal definition of crime which restricts us to studying and ultimately controlling only legally defined 'criminals.' We need a definition of crime which reflects the reality of a legal system based on power and privilege; to accept the legal definition of crime is to accept the fiction of neutral law."

Radicals are not alone in arguing against the constraints imposed by a legalistic definition of crime, and orthodox criminologists have also criticized criminology's reliance on legal definitions of crime (see especially, Sellin, 1938; Sutherland, 1949, 1945). Nor are radicals alone in exposing the socially injurious behaviors of elites. Many social movements (e.g., labor, civil rights movements, the environmental justice movement), journalists, and activists (e.g., Ralph Nader, Lois Gibbs, Robert Bullard) have taken up these issues. Thus, radical criminology is not the only voice arguing for an understanding of crime that goes beyond established definitions. Unlike social movements focused on very specific issues, however, radical criminology is concerned with developing an overall analysis of the definition of crime rather than being primarily concerned with any single issue.

## Orthodox Criminology and the Definition of Crime

The relationship between orthodox criminology and the definition of crime contains two contradictions. First, while orthodox criminology endorses a legalistic approach, it has never been interested in *all* behaviors defined as criminal by law but only those typically committed by the poor. For example, most published journal research in criminology focuses on the common street crimes typically associated with working-class and underclass segments of society (Lynch, McGurrin and Fenwick, 2005). Between 2000 and 2005, 93 percent of all articles published in the top three journals in criminology focused on street crime or systems designed to control street crime, 4 percent focused on non-criminal issues, and only 3 percent addressed crimes by the powerful (Michalowski and Kramer, 2005). Thus, the claim by orthodox criminologists that criminology is the study of behaviors defined as criminal by law is misleading. William Chambliss (1999:18) argues that orthodox criminology's emphasis on crimes of the poor reflects the field's inherent middle-class bias:

> Along with law enforcement agencies and politicians, middle class criminologists reflect the middle class bias of their own social backgrounds. Despite a preponderance of evidence of the frequency and

seriousness of white collar, corporate, and state crimes, middle class criminologists continue to believe that the "real crime problems" are the crimes that are disproportionately (though not exclusively) committed by members of the lower classes: Robbery, burglary, murder, rape, and theft.

The second contradiction results from the tendency within orthodox criminology to construct *general* theories from the study of crimes most likely to be committed by poor young men. Orthodox criminologists often speak and write as if theories based on street crime can explain *all* types of criminal and deviant behavior. For example, they suggest that factors such as age, poverty, inequality, dysfunctional and disrupted families, impulsiveness and inadequate socialization are highly correlated with crime (e.g. Gottfredson and Hirschi, 1990). These factors have been extracted by studying street crimes and criminals, and have little bearing on the causes of corporate and political crimes committed by society's most advantaged classes (Chambliss, 1999). At best, orthodox criminology has been characterized by theories of working-class and underclass crime, not the general theories of crime it purports to offer.

If criminologists truly accepted a legalistic approach to crime they would, at a minimum, see all forms of criminality as equally important for study, and confront the vast differences – including structural differences – between the kinds of crimes committed by the poor and the kinds of crimes committed by the rich and powerful. By excluding the crimes of the powerful from the equation, however, orthodox criminologists avoid considering how structural positioning shapes patterns of criminality. The real challenge is to develop a definition of crime that *accounts for* the variations in harmful behaviors across different social groups and strata, rather than obscuring these differences with a general theory of crime.

## Crime in the Radical View

In 1970, Herman Schwendinger and Julia Schwendinger addressed the contradiction of the orthodox definition of crime in a groundbreaking article, "Defenders of Order or Guardians of Human Rights?," challenging the dominant legalistic approach to criminology. Since that time radicals have explored an extensive list of socially injurious behaviors that have escaped criminalization including: violations of human rights due to racism, sexism and imperialism; unsafe working conditions; inadequate child care; inadequate opportunities for employment and education; substandard housing and medical care; crimes of economic and political domination; pollution of the environment;

price-fixing; police brutality; assassinations; war-making; violations of dignity; denial of physical needs and necessities; and impediments to self-determination, deprivation of adequate food and blocked opportunities to participate in relevant political decisions. Although some of these behaviors (e.g., price-fixing, police brutality, violations of workplace safety rules) are legally prohibited, the laws regulating these crimes are rarely enforced. Moreover, as radical criminologists have often noted, when they are, offenders are seldom subject to the kinds of punishments we accept as routine for street offenders (Groves and Newman, 1987).

The number of non-criminal yet harmful behaviors included as "crime" by radical criminologists has sparked criticism. Austin Turk (1975:41) refers to this as an "everything-but-the-kitchen-sink list" wherein crime is equated with "any evil perceived in human affairs." Robert Bohm (1982a:571) suggests that equating crime with any violation of human rights can be legitimately criticized as broad and vague. Green and Ward (2000:101) suggest that broad definitions of crime that move beyond legal prohibitions may "destroy what coherence criminology has as a distinct field of study."

One of the earliest challenges to expanding criminology beyond the legal definition of crime predates contemporary radical criminology, and came from Paul Tappan (1947), who opposed the emerging study of white collar wrongdoing as "crimes." Tappan was surely correct in claiming that expanding the definition of crime beyond the law reflects a subjective preference. As a human construction, however, "law itself reflects a set of subjectively held values" (Michalowski, 1985:317). Radical criminology does not challenge *objective* law with *subjective* values, as its critics have suggested. Rather it offers for consideration a set of subjective values that differs from the set of subjective values that dominate both law making and orthodox criminology. Additionally, as Taylor et al. (1974:462) note, allowing the presumably scientific study of crime to be determined by the *political* process of lawmaking "has been disastrous for criminology's claim to be scientific." Unless criminologists address why some harmful behaviors come to be defined as crimes while others do not, they can never fully understand the process of lawmaking (Michalowski, 1985). At the same time, those who wish to extend the definition of crime beyond the law must offer explicit theoretical models for doing so. This will enable others to determine whether they find a particular radical extension of the definition of crime to be useful.

The radical redefinition of "crime" contains another apparent contradiction: it would seem to promote *more* state control. Radical theory suggests that societies with high degrees of equality (i.e., those with few divisions along class, gender or race lines) would have fewer instances of antisocial behavior and equitable legal systems that play fewer favorites along class, race or gender lines. In contrast, societies with high degrees of inequality are likely to have high rates of antisocial behavior, and to have legal systems framed around class, gender and race inequalities that condemn the wrongdoings of the powerless and forgive those of the powerful. Most radical criminologists live in these latter types of societies. In order to call political attention to the legal distortions caused by social inequality, radical criminologists (with the exception of anarchists) typically argue that the state – which, by their own theory, is biased toward the interests of the powerful, be they capitalists, men, or whites – can promote greater justice by creating more laws to control the injurious behaviors of these powerful sectors of society. To some extent, this contradiction is the product of the political environment at the end of the twentieth century. Most political avenues to implementing the deepest implications of radical theory are, or at least appear to be, closed for the time being. Consequently, radical criminologists attempt to open small spaces for change by demanding that, at the very least, the criminality of powerful wrongdoers be punished according to the same rules applied to the less powerful.

In order to further explore our claim that the orthodox approach to defining crime overlooks significant forms of criminality, below we examine the costs of crimes by the powerful and offer some specific examples of these behaviors.

## Crimes of the Powerful

Although there have been some changes in recent years, media, public, and criminological attention remains focused largely on the common crimes found in the Federal Bureau of Investigation's (FBI) Uniform Crime Report (UCR) list of Part One, or "Index" offenses (i.e., murder, rape, robbery, burglary, assault, larceny, motor-vehicle theft and arson). Radicals argue that the selective attention generated by these sources of crime information shapes public perceptions of crime. Quinney (1974a) and Reiman (1998), for instance, claim that the focus on common crimes and common criminals serves ideological purposes that turn public attention away from crimes committed by the ruling class and toward crimes committed by the powerless. Michalowski (1985:216-165) suggests that the FBI's UCR performs important "culture work" by omitting comparable statistics on corporate crimes, thus diverting public attention away from large-scale corporate misbehavior and helping to reproduce the image of "real" crime as street crime committed by the poor. But what are these "crimes" of the powerful? And can we legitimately call them crimes?

Crimes of the powerful have been given a number of names: white collar crimes, elite deviance, corporate crimes, occupational crimes, political crimes, crimes of capital and suite crimes (e.g., see Ermann and Lundman, 1982; Simon, 1999; Friedrichs, 1996b). Each of these terms encompasses a slightly different assembly of wrongdoing (see especially, Frank and Lynch, 1992; Kramer, 1984; Michalowski, 1985; Lynch and Stretesky, 2003, 2001; Stretesky and Lynch, 1999a), and the offenses falling under each heading have been extensively catalogued in numerous research efforts (see, for instance, Clinard and Quinney, 1973; Brady, 1977, 1974; Stone, 1975; Krisberg, 1975; Reiman, 1998; Kramer, 1984; Michalowski, 1985; Ross, 2003; Burns and Lynch, 2004).

Michalowski (1985:314) characterizes many crimes of the powerful in modern state societies as *crimes of capital,* which include those "...socially injurious acts that arise from the ownership or management of capital or from occupancy of positions of trust in institutions designed to facilitate the accumulation of capital." This definition links wrongdoing in corporate, occupational, political and organized crime to access to capital or its institutions. Not all of the social injurious acts committed under the big tent of "crimes of capital" are defined as crimes by law. Michalowski (1985:317-318) suggests that by comparing those that have been criminalized with those that constitute "analogous social injuries" – that is, legal acts that cause harm equal to or greater than that caused by crimes – we can begin to understand the historical forces that have divided the world of harmful behaviors into those we condemn and those we tolerate.

## The Costs

In a 1992 report, the U.S. Department of Justice indicated that the cost of serious street crime was $17.6 billion (Klaus, 1994). This figure includes the value of stolen and damaged property, as well as medical expenses and lost income of victims of violent crime. Since then, the level of crime reported to police in the U.S. has declined about 25 percent, while average losses resulting from crime have increased by about 30 percent according to our estimates (see various *Crime in the U.S.* reports by the FBI: http://www.fbi.gov/-ucr/ucr.htm).

To be conservative, we round the losses to street crime upward to $20 billion a year. While $20 billion is a substantial loss, it is only a fraction of what white collar and corporate crime costs the public annually. According to the U.S. General Accounting Office (GAO), fraud and abuse account for 10 percent of all U.S. health care expenditures. Most of this fraud is committed not by health care users but by insurance companies and health care professionals and organizations. In 1995 the cost from this one area of fraud alone was estimated to be $100 billion, a figure which by itself is *five times greater* than the cost of all street crime (Davis, 1990; Thompson, 1992). According to the Association of Certified Fraud Examiners, the annual cost of all frauds within businesses in the United States is approximately $400 billion – *20 times higher* than the total cost of serious street crime. The total picture, however, is worse.

Consider this: you are probably aware that the U.S. has a serious deficit problem. But did you know that according to the GAO, 10 percent of our total federal budget goes to pay for fraud and abuse in spending? This figure – about $200 billion in 2004 (http://www.whitehouse.gov/omb/budget/fy2004-/hist.html) – is not just *ten times* the cost of street crime: It represents one-half the exceptionally high federal deficit under George W. Bush in 2004. From 1976 to 2002, the loss in revenue due to fraud and abuse against the government was equal to no less than two-thirds, and sometimes *all* of the Federal deficit during those years (calculated from http://www.littlepiggy.net/deficit-/index.php). Most of this loss is caused not by government officials or individual recipients of government money, such as welfare mothers, but by corporations and organizations that do business with the government. In 2005, George W. Bush sent Congress a federal budget in which the primary strategy proposed for addressing ballooning deficits was reducing funds for the kinds of government programs that assist the working class (Hulse, 2005). That is, the working class and the poor are being asked to bear the consequences of elite fraud and abuse against the government because the government leaders have little interest in declaring a "war" on elite criminals in the way they so readily declare wars against the crimes and drugs of the poor.

Fraud against government, however, is only part of the story. Losses to private-sector illegality exceed the tax dollars wasted on fraud and abuse in government. Corporate crime – which includes offenses such as illegal environmental pollution; bribery and kickbacks; price-fixing and other restraints of trade; marketing products known to be hazardous; violations of workplace safety laws; illegal anti-union activities; fraudulent schemes in real estate, financial, and insurance markets; and false advertising – make the economic costs of crimes in and against government seem paltry. Based on analysis of the Subcommittee on Antitrust and Monopoly of the U.S. Senate Judiciary Committee, Ronald Kramer (1984) estimated that corporate criminals cost society between $174 and $231 billion annually.

More recently, Reiman (1995) estimated the cost of corporate crime as closer to *$1 trillion* a year. While Reiman's estimate may be an accurate reflection of the average annual cost of corporate crime, it underestimates the cost of these crimes in specific cases. For instance, the collapse of many savings and loan banks in the United States in the 1980s due to questionable and often criminal practices by their executives imposed over $1 trillion of loss on America, consisting of at least $400 billion in asset losses and a $600 billion charge to U.S. taxpayers in the form of a bailout for the S&L industry (Calavita, Pontell, and Tillman, 1999). More recently, the United States experienced a wave of corporate collapses due to "pump and dump" schemes designed to inflate stock values in companies such as Enron, WorldCom, and Tyco (Tillman, 2005). Each of these schemes resulted in hundreds of millions of dollars of lost value to stockholders and employees, in many cases wiping out entire life savings and destroying people's hopes for their future.

If we take Kramer's conservative estimate, assume no increase in the rate of corporate crime, and calculate an average of 5 percent per year inflation, the current cost of corporate crime to the U.S. would be $400 to $500 billion. This is between *20 and 25 times* the cost of street crimes. If we combine the costs of private sector corporate crime with fraud and abuse in government spending, the costs of these upper world crimes are approximately *50 times* higher than those associated with street crime.

Over the years there have been many other estimates of the cost of white collar and corporate crimes. Conklin (1977), for example, concluded that white-collar crime cost $40 billion annually, while Messerschmidt (1986) estimated that a single form of corporate crime – price-fixing – cost $45 billion. In the early 1980s, the Environmental Protection Agency valued the combined cost of workplace illness due to toxins and the damage to buildings and clothes from pollution at $23 billion annually (Michalowski, 1985). Green and Berry (1985) estimated the cost of treating controllable toxic diseases caused by environmental hazards in the workplace to be $40 billion, and the tax loss due to corporate non-reporting of income to be $1.2 billion. The point is that each of these crimes, with the exception of corporate tax fraud losses, is greater than the economic losses due to street crimes.

Approaching the question of comparing economic losses from another direction, Wheeler and Rothman (1982) reported that the average loss from robbery, burglary and larceny in their study was $700 per offense, while the average amount stolen by white collar criminals (not corporations) was $387,274. According to their findings, a typical white collar crime will cost *550 times more* than a serious common felony offense. In sum, regardless of their focus, all of the studies and data reviewed above point toward substantially greater economic costs due to corporate crime than street crime.

The typical criticism directed against comparisons such as the ones made above are that although white collar and corporate crimes may cost more than street crime, they do not involve the same level of violence or injury, and this is the real source of our national concern with crime. Claims like this overlook the deaths, injuries and disease caused by corporate crimes in the workplace, the marketplace and against the environment. Nor do they take into account the real human suffering caused by things such as unaffordable health insurance, fraudulent investment schemes and raided pension funds. Each year, for example, between 9,000 and 11,000 people die from preventable work-related accidents. In addition, according to conservative estimates, between 50,000 and 70,000 other workers die from diseases contracted from exposure to toxins in the workplace (Langrin, 1988). Reiman (1998) places the total figure at 59,000 workplace deaths due to violation of law. Others have estimated the number of workplace deaths caused by violations of laws to be as high as 100,000 per year (Kramer, 1984). We term these deaths "workplace killings," because the victims are intentionally killed by purposeful violations of law. To be conservative, compare the lower estimate of 59,000 workplace killings with the 24,330 homicides reported by the FBI for 1990 – the *peak* year for homicide in the 1990s. The ratio indicates that *2.4 times as many* people were *killed by working* than were murdered at home or in the street. For the friends and relatives of those who killed as the result of workplace law violations, these deaths are very real and painful losses, made all the more so because, like homicide in the street or the home, they result from the criminal activity of others.

If we turn our attention to workplace injuries, we find a similar picture. According to the FBI, in 2001 the rate of violent crime in the U.S. was 504 per every 100,000 people (*Sourcebook*, 2003, Table 3.103). By comparison, the Occupational Health and Safety Administration (OSHA) estimated that there were roughly 6,800 non-fatal workplace injuries requiring medical care per 100,000 workers (U.S. OSHA, 1997). In other words, the odds of being the victim of an injury-causing workplace incident are nearly *13 times* greater than the risk of being the victim of a violent crime. These comparisons only touch on the ways corporate crime harm us in our everyday life.

The above estimates only approximate the death and injury caused by workplace killings and assaults as compared to street violence. Some categories of criminal violence, particularly domestic violence, are significantly underreported. At the same time, it should be kept in mind that the data used to estimate financial losses and deaths and injuries at work are also affected by underreporting (Leigh et al., 2000). Whatever inaccuracies are introduced by these hidden crimes, their inclusion would not significantly alter the stark fact that for many Americans, violations of workplace laws poses a far greater threat to life and limb than does violence by street criminals.

Our discussion so far has focused primarily on death and injury in the workplace. There are many other arenas in which crime and malfeasance by the powerful cause harm. In their pursuit of profit, for instance, medical practitioners are guilty of performing 3.2 million unnecessary surgeries annually – the majority on women. These surgeries, which, as Reiman (]1998) notes, also involve "cutting and stabbing," come with a price tag of $5 billion and result in an estimated 16,000 deaths annually, approximately the same as the number of deaths due to homicide. To this we can another 20,000 deaths estimated to result from inadequate emergency medical care (Reiman, 1998). Together, unwarranted surgeries and inadequate emergency medical care alone take almost *twice as many lives* as homicide. Nor have we detailed the extensive physical and economic costs resulting from the marketing of unsafe drugs, dangerous chemicals (especially herbicides and pesticides in common use), hazardous consumer products, corporate pollution of the environment (which causes illness, disease and death), the aggressive advertising of physically harmful pleasures such as alcohol and tobacco, or the many other ways the owners and managers of capital cause harm in the pursuit of profit (see, for examples, Karliner, 1997; Fagin et al., 1996; Gibbs, 1995; Friedrichs, 1996; Simon, 1999; Frank and Lynch, 1992; Lynch and Stretesky, 2001).

The above figures demonstrate that crimes of capital pose a far greater threat to our well-being than street crime. Another reason that upper-world wrongdoers are more dangerous than street criminals lies in the very nature of power. The essence of being powerful is the ability to make your will felt by others. The more powerful you are, the more people you can affect. Corporate officials who determine the safety budget for a workplace can affect the well-being of many people with the stroke of a pen. Health maintenance organization policy-makers who try to increase profitability by restricting access to medical services can impact the lives and health of thousands. A company that markets a product that is unsafe can place millions of people at risk. Street criminals lack this kind of institutionalized power. They affect people, for the most part, one at a time. While their deeds may be harmful, the scope of their harm is usually limited to the reach of their arms or occasionally the range of their guns. Consequently, as long as some sectors of society exert substantial power over others, the bulk of the harm produced in that society will come from those sectors.

While street criminals can strike at objects and people in their surrounding environment, elite wrongdoers can project harmful consequences across great distances, sometimes even around the globe. For instance, many U.S. corporations have relocated manufacturing facilities to other countries to escape what they consider to be burdensome safety regulations instituted by the U.S. Government (Frank and Lynch, 1992; Michalowski and Kramer, 1987). One example of this is provided by the chemical disaster in Bhopal, India. In

1984, 2,500 people died and upward of 200,000 were severely injured in the aftermath of a poisonous gas leak at a Union Carbide production facility. Safety equipment that could have prevented the leak had been shut down for repair, and, as a cost-saving measure, no backup equipment had been installed. Without the backup equipment in place, deadly gas escaped into the community surrounding the chemical plant – all because Union Carbide was more concerned with profit than people (Moro and Lapierre, 2002; Lynch et al., 1989).

As the process of globalization expands, corporations from the U.S. and other developed nations are increasingly enjoying – and helping promote – lax regulatory environments in Third World nations. This has led to the return of sweat shops, deadly fires in industrial plants and the repression of worker rights in a number of places (Greider, 1997). Meanwhile, corporations and investors are reaping substantial profits from the return to repressive labor policies and unsafe work practices. Few public leaders dare call it crime. Instead, the harmful consequences of globalization are treated as the natural outcome of the "invisible hand" of the marketplace, as if no one is making policy decisions that place profits ahead of the right of workers and people to lead safe and dignified lives.

Some of the harms described above — fraud, stock manipulation and prohibited workplace hazards — result from violations of existing law, and thus, constitute crimes. Others, such as unnecessary surgeries, pricing people out of the health insurance market, and exploitation of workers are allowable under U.S. law. Some might argue that insofar as these latter actions are legal, they cannot be considered crimes. . We would agree: under the existing legal system in the United States these harms do not constitute criminal acts. . We would also argue that these acts are excluded from the list of crimes because they are the domain of powerful social actors. Acts committed by individuals in positions of power that serve the individual and organizational interests of America's capitalist political economy, regardless of how harmful they may be, are far less likely to become the targets of legal control than less-harmful acts of social disruption emanating from weaker segments of the society. Law, in other words, defines behaviors differently depending on the status of those most likely to commit a given offense. Furthermore, law is also unevenly applied for the same reason. The inequalities that characterize law reflect the types of inequalities that characterize the broader inequalities found in society (e.g., race, class and gender). One of the important tasks of radical criminology is to examine this difference in order to better understand the origins, nature, and functioning of law in contemporary society.

## Guilty Minds

Not only are the social injuries caused by corporations widespread, they are often deliberate. That is, they are frequently committed with the same kinds of *mens rea* normally associated with street crime. For instance, in the late 1990s the U.S. tobacco industry came under investigation for hiding and lying about evidence that smoking is linked to cancer (see Glantz et al., 1996). Cigarette smoking kills more than 400,000 Americans every year – 20 times the homicide rate with which we are preoccupied. *As early as 1955*, research demonstrated high levels of toxicity associated with tobacco use . By the late 1950s, the tobacco industry *had produced enough evidence linking smoking and cancer* to create a code word for smoking-induced cancer: "zephyr" (Glantz et al., 1996:109). The industry began to search for a "safe cigarette" at the same time it stepped up the advertising campaign to sell more unsafe cigarettes. As Glantz et al. (1996) note, much of this deceit would have been impossible without the contribution of powerful law firms who helped the industry manage its damaging information.

At the same time that they *knew* their product caused life-threatening illness, tobacco executives mounted an aggressive defense against legal suits, claiming that because people choose to smoke, the tobacco companies bear no responsibility for the resulting cancers. In 1997, a class-action suit filed by airline flight attendants against several tobacco companies revealed the limits of this defense. The flight attendants alleged that they suffered elevated levels of smoking-related illnesses due to their exposure to secondhand smoke on airplanes before the ban on smoking was put into effect. The tobacco industry's traditional strategy was to deflect responsibility to smokers who, the industry claimed, choose to smoke. This strategy, however, lacked credibility in the case of secondhand smoke. In the middle of the trial, the defendant tobacco companies settled out of court, establishing their responsibility (though not admitting their guilt) for the harmful affects of tobacco smoke on non-smokers, and substantially weakening their claims regarding the harmlessness of tobacco smoke.

In a similar case, the Johns-Manville Company knew as early as the 1930s that the asbestos they produced was the origin of an ultimately fatal lung disease, *asbestosis*. Yet it hid this information from workers as well as the public that worked and lived in asbestos insulated houses for over 40 years. Lawsuits against the company in the late 1970s revealed the depth of the company's guilt. Faced with rising judgments against it, Johns-Manville declared bankruptcy, thus avoiding having to pay many of the claimants who had been harmed by its criminality (Broder, 1974).

## Regulatory Failure

Many corporate crimes occur not only because the businesses or industries involved are willing to put profits ahead of people, but also because the agencies designed to control such behavior are lax in enforcing the law.

In the late 1990s, for instance, the case of the drug Fen/Phen became public. Fen/Phen is a combination of two distinct drugs (fenfluramine and phentermine) approved for distribution by the U.S. Food and Drug Administration (FDA) as a short-term treatment for life-threatening obesity (defined as weighing 300 to 400 pounds). The drug, however, was widely used to promote weight loss. In the mid-1990s, approximately 18 million monthly prescriptions were written for Fen/Phen and its associated drugs. As the popularity of Fen/Phen grew, so did evidence of its harmful impacts.

In October of 1997, medical researchers reported 80 known cases of heart disease associated with Fen/Phen use as short as one month. It is likely that this figure substantially understates the extent of the problem, because the FDA (the agency that tracks drug-related illness, disease and other side effects) *stopped recording the number of illnesses* related to the use of Fen/Phen (personal telephone communication, September 1997). Nevertheless, the number of known cases continued to grow. The Mayo Clinic, for example, discovered a rare heart valve disease in 30 percent of women who took Fen/Phen, while other research indicates that between 1 and 28 people in a million who took Fen/Phen will develop primary pulmonary hypertension. Considering that approximately 6 million individuals have taken Fen/Phen, this disease rate translates into 1.8 million cases of heart disease. On the heels of this information, Florida became the first state to ban Fen/Phen during the summer of 1997. In September, 1997 the FDA requested that fenfluramine, the suspected culprit in the Fen/Phen combination (as well as dexfenfluramine), be voluntarily withdrawn from the marketplace. Because the withdrawal was voluntary, no official sanctions would be forthcoming.

Hidden behind the voluntary recall of Fen/Phen is the questionable behavior of executives at the pharmaceutical firm Wyeth-Ayerst, one of the two manufacturers of fenfluramine and the sole manufacturer of dexfenfluramine. Wyeth-Ayerst, a subsidiary of one of America's 100 largest corporations, American Home Products, had shown strong earnings increases after it introduced its Fen/Phen drug Redux, to the market in 1995. Spurred on by a $52 million dollar advertising campaign, sales of this "wonder" diet drug were high, and the *Wall Street Journal* estimated $1 billion in net sales over the next two years.

In the book *Dispensing with the Truth*, Alicia Mundy (2001) demonstrated that Wyeth-Ayerst executives knew about the health threats posed by its Fen/Phen drugs, Redux and Pondimin, since at least 1990, but hid this information from the public and the Food and Drug Administration. For example, Wyeth-Ayerst executives were aware that more than 100 people had died as a result of taking these drugs since the early 1990s. Not only that, they also knew that their products were not as effective as advertised, and were associated with an average weight loss of only three percent. Furthermore, the inclusion of phentermine – a stimulant – in the weight loss pill, promoted chemical dependency on Fen/Phen products.

The case of Fen/Phen reveals an important element in the definition of crime. While regulatory agencies such as the FDA were established to protect consumers from dangerous corporate practices, they were created in ways that still privileged the interests of corporate elites. Products such as Fen/Phen do not have to be *proven safe* in order to remain on the market. They have to be *proven harmful* in order to be removed from the market. Rather than requiring companies to stop marketing products where there is an emerging suspicion of danger until they can be proven safe, the regulatory system allows the company to continue marketing products unless they are proven dangerous. Moreover, the FDA relies primarily on research conducted or funded by the company requesting approval, rather than pursuing independent research. In a number of cases, data ultimately accepted by the FDA to declare drugs safe had been manipulated to obscure or remove indications of potential harm (Nolan, 2004).

Given the extensive amount of time necessary to *prove* beyond a doubt that a product is unsafe (and the scientific manipulation of evidence that accompanies this process; see Fagin et al., 1996), companies have sufficient time to continue making profits by continuing to market the drug, or at least to "dump" their products on unsuspecting markets elsewhere (Silverman et al., 1982). Those who decide to keep such products on the market or dump remaining supplies will never be defined as criminals under current regulatory schemas regardless of how many people sicken or are injured by the continued marketing of these products.

To the cases discussed above we could add many others: Lockheed Corporation offering millions of dollars in bribes to foreign purchasing agents (Ermann and Lundman, 1982); defense industry corporations charging the U.S. Government hundreds of dollars each for ashtrays and toilet seats; price-fixing conspiracies by electric companies; the poisoning of America by toxic waste dumps such as Love Canal in New York and Stringfellow in California (Brown, 1980); diseases related to silicon breast implants; questionable safety data about automobile crash-worthiness (Burns, 1997, 1999); placement of hazardous waste sites in minority communities (Stretesky, 1999, 1997a, 1997b, 1996; Stretesky and Hogan, 1998; Stretesky and Lynch, 1999a, 1999b, 2003; Lynch, Stretesky and Burns, 2004a, 2004b); the exploding Ford Pinto gas tank (Dowie, 1977; Cullen et al., 1984, 1987); the Dalkon Shield disasters (Frank, 1985); and many others. These cases and others like them, support the conclusion that "corporate crime represents the most widespread and costly form of crime in America" (Michalowski, 1985:325), while the regulatory system designed to control it remains more sensitive to the interests of corporate capital than to the people it is supposed to protect.

## Terrorism: A Case Study in Power and the Label of Crime

Another example of how definitions of behavior reflect power structures involve acts that are included and excluded under the heading "terrorism." We provide only a cursory summary of this issue here, since an extended analysis of terrorism is presented in chapter 9.

The word "terrorism," which conjures up images of fanatical rebels killing and injuring innocent civilians with homemade car bombs or pipe bombs, become more salient to Americans following the bombing during the 1990s of the World Trade Center in New York and the Murrah Building in Oklahoma City, and of two American embassies in Africa in 1998, and especially following the "9-11" attacks in 2001. What often escapes our view, however, is the way in which elites shape the definition of terrorism, and the ways in which the powerful also engage in terrorism and how this form of terrorism by the powerful increases the likelihood of terrorism by the powerless.

As is the case with common crimes, acts labeled as terrorism are committed by those who lack access to established institutions of power. A primary difference between common crime and terrorism is that terrorist acts are committed expressly against the powerful for overtly political reasons. As Herman (1987:1) notes, "…the powerful define terrorism, and the… media loyally follow [that definition]. The powerful naturally define terrorism to exclude their own acts and those of their friends and clients." Thus, terrorists are those who use force to challenge the legitimacy of a political or economic system – the very state and governmental arrangements that support the economic and political base of the powerful. At the same time, states never label as terrorism their own use of violence to suppress "oppositional" governments or politically dissident groups (see chapter nine).

The political nature of terrorism is evident when we realize that the U.S. has been quite outspoken in its criticism of governments it claims support terrorism when those nations are also defined as "unfriendly" (e.g., North Korea,

Libya, Iran, Cuba and Nicaragua). At the same time, the U.S. has failed to condemn as terrorism acts performed by "friendly" governments. The U.S. government has even promoted state terrorism among some of its allies by giving military aid to "freedom fighters" and training foreign police agencies in torture tactics. For example, 74 percent of the countries that employed systematic torture (a form of state terrorism) in the 1970s were U.S. client-states (Herman, 1987, 1982).

Like states, corporations could also be labeled as terrorists for they take part in supporting repressive governments and economic regimes. But the case in favor of labeling corporations as terrorist is not often made (see chapter 9).

Terrorism provides a clear example of how the label of "crime" is applied by the powerful to the behavior of the powerless. That does not mean, however, that the powerful are not involved in terrorism or crime; it means that their power allows them to escape negative labels.

## The Social Construction of Crime

If crimes by the powerful are so harmful, why do we hear so little about them in comparison to street crime? Why does orthodox criminology focus primarily on street crime? The underlying answer is that our *image* of crime is not the consequence of some formula that automatically totals measurable social injury and then tells us which behaviors are most harmful. Rather, it is *socially constructed* through the political processes of making and enforcing laws, and the public and private communicative processes by which we tell ourselves what the word "crime" means.

As an example of the socially constructed nature of crime, consider why we hear much more about muggings and murders than we do about workplace death, injury and illness even though the latter are far more damaging and widespread than the former. At the political level, it has never been in the interests of the owners of capital and managers of workplaces to promote policies that call attention to *their* wrongdoing. The owning/managing class historically has enjoyed sufficient political power to ensure that the law either does not criminalize its wrongdoings or that it directs it into regulatory procedures that "administratively segregate" it from both the image and the stigma of "crime" (Sutherland, 1949). Thus, we see few examples of "corporate killers" or "corporate thieves."

The ability of the powerful to influence the law, however, is not the only force at work. Within the world of mass communication, for instance, we find that most public opinion makers (e.g., politicians, media pundits, educators, academic researchers, ministers, etc.) do not live in a world where workplace hazards are part of their daily lives, as does the working class. Consequently, public policy crusades against street criminals come more easily to these middle-class public opinion leaders than does outrage directed at bosses and managers who violate workplace safety rules. In addition, because of their subordinated position within American society, many people in the working class finds it difficult to trust or believe in their own perceptions. As a result, their vision of what threatens their lives will often be influenced by the middle- and upper-class voices they have been socialized to respect, rather than trusting own experience.

Our culture teaches us, by example, what to believe about crime from the time we are children. We rarely hear of white-collar offenders being imprisoned for their crimes, but the media do regularly treat us to stories of lower-income street criminals being processed through the halls of justice (Barak, 1994; Ericson et al., 1991). Despite the occasional trial of some high-profile figure, such as WorldCom's former CEO Bernie Ebbers for stock manipulation or Martha Stewart for lying about stock transactions, street crime remains the dominant theme in crime news, particularly local crime news. Consequently, it is easier to believe that burglars, robbers, drug dealers and auto thieves pose a greater threat to our well-being than corporate criminals. When political leaders repeatedly denounce gangs as a fundamental threat to social order, but rarely, if ever, use their cultural authority to condemn corporate officials who deliberately poison and impoverish large segments of the world's population in pursuit of "economic growth," we are likely to believe that it is more important to control young men showing gang colors than those who believe profit justifies human suffering (Michalowski, 1998). The more the criminal justice system focuses on street criminals as the source of harm and danger, the more it appears as if they are the bulk, if not the totality, of the crime problem. Thus, the dominant understanding of what constitutes "crime" is not simply a statement of the obvious, it is an expression of living with a constant image of street crimes by poor young men as the essence of crime.

## In Sum

There are few topics more central to radical criminology than the definition of crime and how power shapes this definition. Law has created many crimes of the powerless and few crimes of the powerful. We draw several conclusions from our consideration of the link between power and law. First, behaviors not currently within the scope of the criminal law, but which pose a serious and measurable threat to our collective well-being, should be defined as crimes and be subject to sanctions of the criminal law. Second, corporate and political violations that currently fall within the scope of the criminal law should receive punishments and enforcement attention commensurate with the magnitude of social injury they inflict on society. Third, criminology should treat the social injuries committed by the powerful – whether or not they are defined as crimes – as equally important topics of study as the street crimes that currently dominate the field. To do anything less renders criminology yet another of the cultural tools through which the powerful obscure their harmfulness, rather than making it an independent, critical intellectual enterprise.

# FIVE.
# RADICAL THEORIES OF CRIME CAUSATION — PART I: INEQUALITY, CRIME AND CONTEXT

Historically, radical criminology has had an uneasy relationship with the question of crime causation. On one hand, Marx's view of the *lumpenproletariat* and the soul-destroying impact of a life dominated by alienated labor suggested that routine forms of crime would be most prevalent among the least well off in society. Many radical criminologists accept that high rates of street crime in the U.S. are one consequence of capitalism's inequalities, a view some say comes ironically close to orthodox perspectives on poverty.

On the other hand, Marx's political economy also suggests that the very definition of crime is tilted in such a way as to make it *appear* as if the poor are criminal and the rich law abiding (see Reiman, 1998). This aspect of Marxist political-economics offers a much different possibility – that all classes are equally likely to contain people willing to commit anti-social acts, and it is the inherent biases in lawmaking and law enforcement processes rather than the behavior of the poor that account for prisons being populated primarily by poor people of color. This assumption sets orthodox and radical criminology apart.

Early radical criminologists approached questions about crime causation gingerly or tended to avoid questions of causation. For example, early radicals often directed attention to the impact of formal criminal justice processes on the individual. Adopting a "labeling theory" approach, they argued that the stigma associated with formal labeling as a criminal altered the individual's self-image and was likely to lead that person down the path of secondary deviance and a life of crime. By taking this view, early radicals failed to develop a unique explanation of how a life of poverty, exploitation and hopelessness might magnify the propensity to commit crime. Criticism of early radical theories of crime causation soon emerged. Some argued that because they relied primarily on conflict and labeling theories, radical theories of crime treated criminality simply as the mirror image of social control, and ruled out questions of causation or succumbed to tautological reasoning where the only cause of crime is law (Spitzer, 1980:180; Akers, 1980; Quinney, 1974b:123). Others argued that radical theories of crime causation were limited to an oversimplified, "uni-causal" approach where the only source of crime was capitalism (Shichor, 1980b). Finally, it was also suggested that radicals proposed theories that were untestable (e.g., crime will end only when capitalism ends), and that radical criminology could not be subject to the kinds of empirical research that might support or validate its claims (Sparks, 1980; Shichor, 1980; Taylor et al., 1975).

By the mid-1980s radicals began to address these criticisms. Specifically, they expanded the insights drawn from conflict and labeling theories (Greenberg, 1981), qualified the depiction of capitalism as the "source of all evil" without deemphasizing the structuring power of capitalism's political economy (Mankoff, 1978), and began developing empirical strategies to test the relationships among social structure, crime and punishment (Carlson and Michalowski, 1997; Hochstetler and Shover, 1997; Lessan, 1991; Barlow et al., 1996; Barlow and Barlow, 1995; Lynch et al., 1994; Lizotte et al., 1982; Greenberg, 1981; Groves and Corrado 1983; Box and Hale, 1983a, 1983b; Lynch, 1988a; Lynch, Schwendinger and Schwendinger, 2004). To understand contemporary radical explanations of crime we must examine how these theories developed from and moved beyond purely Marxist models of crime.

## Origins of Marxist Models of Crime Causation

An underlying theme within radical criminology has been the role of capitalism as a "cause" of crime. Both Frederick Engels (1973, 1978, 1981, 1983) and Willem Bonger (1969), for instance, argued that individual manifestations of criminal behavior reflect the strains associated with life under capitalism. Engels's argument was twofold. First, every technological advancement associated with capitalist production freed workers from production, and generated unemployed populations who lived in "want, wretchedness, and crime" (1973:173). This theme reappears in the contemporary writings of Richard Quinney (1979, 1980) and David Gordon (1971, 1973), who suggest that crime is a rational response to systems of inequitable distribution that characterize capitalism. In a similar vein, Stephen Spitzer (1975) argues that capitalism excludes certain groups from meaningful attachment to economic and social institutions. These economically marginalized groups have a reduced stake in conformity and will, therefore, be more likely to engage in criminal behavior. Because capitalism's tendency to marginalize whole groups of people is unique in the history of economic systems, capitalism is thus seen as responsible for the resulting criminality.

Engels also argued that capitalism generated certain drives such as competitiveness that are simultaneously beneficial and harmful to society. While competition benefits capitalists by keeping wages low and productivity high, it erodes working-class solidarity. Workers must not only compete with the capitalist over working conditions, they must also compete with each other for a limited number of jobs. Consequently, Engels viewed crime as the result of competition over scarce resources, and saw competition engendered by capitalism as the cause of crime by the masses (1964; 1973), by businessmen (1964) and by the middle classes (1981).

In *Criminality and Economic Conditions*, Bonger (1969) made a similar argument. For Bonger, however, the competitiveness created by capitalism manifests itself in individuals as egoism, and it is egoism that generates crime among all classes. While Bonger believed that egoism was evenly distributed among all classes, he noted that the political strength of the ruling class enabled it to perform exploitative acts without having those acts treated as criminal behavior. This explains why more lower-class individuals are processed by the criminal justice system. For Bonger, egoism was a negative by-product of capitalism.

Engels (1964) and Marx (1981) even suggested that capitalism "creates a demand for crime which is met by a corresponding supply..." (Engels, 1964:224). Expanding on this theme, Colvin and Pauly (1983) and the Schwendingers (1976) suggest that forms of inequality and stratification that accompany capitalism affect educational opportunities, which, in turn, structure individuals' propensity to commit crime; Greenberg (1985) explains variations in delinquency rates in terms of the structural demands of capitalism; while Barnett (1981a) analyzes criminal opportunity as it relates to capital accumulation. Michalowski (1985) argues that the dynamics of capital accumulation generate two general categories of crime: those available to the working class, and crimes available to those who own or manage capital. Finally, Wallace and Humphries (1981) reinterpret the criminogenic effects of urbanization and industrialization by placing these processes within a broader Marxist perspective on investment and capital accumulation.

Over all, Marx and Engels's analyses of class conflict, materialism and the dialectic yield five propositions that can serve in developing theories of crime causation:

   (1) Within capitalist systems, the goal of generating the greatest possible profit for a dominant class that owns the means of production determines what goods will be produced and how they will be produced. As a consequence, capitalist systems are characterized by conflict between the owning/managing class and the la-

boring class because each group will favor decisions that would allocate more of the society's wealth in their direction.

(2) The structural inequality between labor and capital gives rise to a society that is stratified into social classes characterized by tremendous differences in wealth, status, prestige, power and authority. The division of society into haves and have-nots existed *before* capitalism, which is only one of a long sequence of historical systems based on inequalities between those who own and those who work. In each of these systems, both the definition and the production of crime was an expression of the particular inequalities of that system. Thus, while exploitation is not unique to capitalism, we cannot understand crime under capitalism without exploring how the particular characteristics of capitalism shape crime in *capitalist societies,* just as we need to understand the relationship between socialism and crime to comprehend crime in the former socialist states of Eastern Europe (Michalowski, 1998; Verderey, 1996).

(3) The differences in wealth, status and power shape – and are shaped by – other components of difference such as gender, race and ethnicity, further sharpening the criminogenic consequences of social differentiation.

(4) Taken together, these differences constitute variable material and social conditions that shape the life chances and life choices of people belonging to different economic and identity groupings.

(5) Among the differential opportunities provided by sociocultural systems is the chance or choice of becoming a criminal. Because of their particularly powerful impact on the material conditions of life, economic class and social identity are important explanatory factors because the differential distribution of chances and choices means a differential distribution of incentives and motivations for both criminal and non-criminal behavior (Groves and Frank, 1987; Lynch, 1993, 1996, 1997).

Understanding how the interplay among social class, gender, racial and ethnic experiences affects a person's life chances and life course is essential to understanding crime. The combination of these experiences is the basis on which people form their cultural understanding of human life and human purpose. These, in turn, frame how people define and pursue their goals. Thus, the most complete radical perspectives will address how race, class, gender and culture *intersect* to shape life chances and life choices (Lynch and Patterson, 1996a; Lynch, 1996; Lynch and Stretesky, 2000). Not all contemporary radical approaches to the causes of crime incorporate each of these factors. There is, however, a growing recognition that no single factor can explain why people commit crime.

Before beginning our discussion of the causes of crime, we introduce a few more general ideas relevant to this discussion. This includes a review of a) the radical preference for macro-level explanation; b) radicals' focus on economically, historically and culturally-relative explanations; and c) radicals' use of contextualized explanation.

## MACRO VERSUS MICRO EXPLANATION

Many orthodox explanations of crime emphasize *micro-level* analysis. Micro-level research attempts to identify causal explanations and variables that operate at or near the individual level, such as peer or family relationships, personality or an individual's ties to his or her community.

In contrast, radical approaches tend to search for causal explanations for crime at a more *macro level*. This has two consequences. First, radical theories of crime causation give particular attention to the ways that broad historical, cultural, social, political and economic contexts – or *macro-level* forces –shape the behavior of individuals. Second, the radical emphasis on macro-level explanations means that most radical theories of crime causation will focus on *overall patterns* of behavior. Thus, radical criminologists will be concerned with the grouping of criminal acts – such as the amount and type of crime in a city, county, state or nation – rather than with individual criminals. When radicals sometimes do focus on specific individuals, as in ethnographic studies of how people end up on the wrong side of the law, the experiences of these people's lives are treated as *examples of* wider social processes rather than as unique experiences (for examples, see Anderson, 1990; Bourgois, 1996; Maher, 1997; Maher and Daly, 1996; Miller, 1998). This micro/macro distinction means that while orthodox criminology tries to isolate factors that explain behavioral differences across individuals and to focus on why some people break the law when others do not, radical criminology seeks to explain *trends* in criminal behavior. For radicals, the goal is to understand why rates and types of offending change across time or differ from one place to another.

Given their focus on micro-level causes, orthodox criminologists frequently criticize radicals for ignoring policies directed at changing individual behavior through criminal justice strategies such as prevention, investigation, arrest, prosecution, punishment and/or rehabilitation. This criticism, however, is inaccurate on two levels. First, it assumes that the primary factors shaping human behavior arise at the individual level. Second, it overlooks the many radical criminologists who have developed macro-level policy proposals that could have dramatic consequences for improving individual lives and consequently reducing crime rates (see, for example, Currie, 1996, 1985; chapter 13).

## Macro- versus Micro-approaches and Empirical Analysis

Orthodox criminologists typically conclude that societal-level propositions about crime causation are less well suited to empirical testing than those focused on more micro levels. At issue here is whether macro- or micro-level models are more consistent with the empirical methods practiced by natural or hard scientists (e.g., chemists, physicists). We pursue this discussion by way of the following analogy.

Let us take as our example a chemist studying water. The chemist's experimental observations about water include the following facts. First, water has a chemical composition, $H_2O$, or is composed of two hydrogen molecules and one oxygen molecule. Second, the chemist discovers that water can be found in a liquid, gas or solid state at very specific temperature ranges under normal atmospheric conditions. These temperature ranges can be altered by changing the air pressure or by adding other chemicals to the water. Third, the chemist finds that he or she can measure how much water expands or contracts as it passes from one phase to another and that s/he can use this information to make predictions about how other bodies of water behave as they are exposed to different temperatures.

Following these experiments, the chemist can make *very accurate* predictions about the behavior of *bodies* of water or groups of water molecules. What the chemist cannot do, however, is predict how each *individual* molecule that makes up a body of water will behave. Chaos theory, which originated in the field of physics, has made it clear that such predictions are not possible in the material world (Gleick, 1987). Thus, in the present example, the chemist cannot predict the direction or speed of an individual water molecule as a body of water is heated; or how many other water molecules it will collide with; or which water molecules will escape first; or which water molecules will gain enough speed to become part of the water vapor; or where water molecules that escape into the gaseous form will come to rest as it cools, and so on.

Like the chemist, radical criminologists can make fairly accurate predictions concerning the behavior of social bodies made up of individuals. For instance, radical criminologists have predicted crime rates (Lynch, 1988a; Lynch et al., 1994; Carlson and Michalowski, 1997), rates of punishment (Greenberg,

1977a; Lynch, 1988a; Michalowski and Carlson, 1999), trends in law making (Barlow and Barlow, 1995; Barlow et al., 1996; Lynch et al., 1999), and changes in police strength (Nalla et al., 1997). Radical theories cannot predict how *specific* individuals within the social groups studied will behave. But a close analysis of orthodox theories of crime shows this to be true for them as well for a very good reason. Human beings are not inanimate objects, and each individual may not respond in the same way to a specific condition each time that condition is present. Rather, there is an average response evident in the mass of individuals, or in groups of individuals such as a society, that is easier to predict. In other words, it is possible to identify *general trends* in how people may respond to specific stimuli even though we can't predict how each individual will behave. For instance, we can say that American society is structured in a way that middle-class men will have more extensive opportunities to commit corporate crime than working-class men. We may even be able to predict the proportion of middle-class men with the opportunities available who will become corporate criminals. Because of human variation, however, what we cannot do is predict which of these middle class men will be criminal and which will remain law abiding.

Given this situation, why have criminologists traditionally selected micro- over macro-level explanations? There is no inherent advantage to micro-level analyses. There is, however, a strong and long-standing cultural bias in the U.S. toward seeing the decision making of *individuals* as the explanation for social outcomes (O'Connor, 1985), a characteristic of American culture first recognized over a century and a half ago by the French social analyst, Alexis de Tocqueville, in his classic study *Democracy in America*. Contemporary analyses of American culture (Bellah et al., 1987; Varenne, 1977) have similarly found a deep *belief* in the ability of individuals to control their own lives. Thus, when orthodox criminologists study the difference between individuals in order to understand criminality, they are not reflecting some neutral scientific principle, but a particular cultural construct – the idea of the individual. This taken-for-granted American pattern of thinking shapes public and scholarly ideas about crime and justice.

Take the following example. When asked what causes crime, or how they would explain crime, most people resort to individual-level explanations, and typically assert that criminals are people who "choose" to commit crime. At some abstract level, that may be true. But, this is not an explanation of crime because it does not explain *why* people chose to commit crime. Consider these questions and answers about choice and crime:

(1) *Is the choice the result of rational calculation?* Rational-choice theories of crime presume that criminals have chosen between two or more available options. If crime results from this type of rational calculation, however, it is never the result of some *fundamentally* free choice. At best, crime it is a decision to select among options that have already been determined by forces outside the individual's free will. Consider the choice to deal crack in a low-income housing project. How many individuals would choose to deal crack if the alternative were taking a decent job with excellent wages and benefits and being able to earn income and social status legitimately? Phillipe Bourgois's (1996) study of crack dealers in Spanish Harlem shows that those who dealt crack did so because it was the best option available to them. It may have been a "choice," but it was a choice among limited options. Rational calculation theories, if they are intellectually honest, must first of all recognize the theoretical importance of factors limiting the choices that can be made.

To the extent that external factors make the decision to commit crime a rational one, we have a dilemma. On one hand, we can accept crime as the natural outcome of social conditions that set choices, thus relocating the responsibility for the crime from the individual to the forces that created the conditions of choice-making. On the other, we can condemn criminals for their failure to make *irrational* choices, that is, for their failure to choose to remain law-abiding even when the rational thing to do would be to commit crime.

(2) *If the choice isn't influenced by specific factors or rational calculations, is the choice simply a random act?* If crime is a random act, the original premise that criminal behavior results from rational choice is unsupportable. For example, if an offender committed an assault by hitting someone, we would first ask, "Did he do it for a reason?" If the answer is that he had no reason, two issues arise. First, hitting someone for no reason is inconsistent with the idea of rational behavior. Second, if the assault was not guided by some rational selection of the victim, then it is a random act. If an act is random, however, it is often difficult to explain, and it certainly cannot be explained as a rational choice.

(3) *How would we know if an act was rational?* This question reveals the core weakness of rational-choice theories: they are tautological. Rationality is a condition of consciousness. Since we cannot enter other people's heads, however, we can only make assumptions about what pattern of thoughts or emotions led to their actions. Rational choice theorists assume people

behave for rational reasons, but since they cannot see the rationality, they impute rationality to a criminal act based on the fact that the person did it, or in their words, "chose" to do it – a perfect circle, beginning and ending with the assumption that people are rational.

Our point in using these examples is to illustrate how American cultural preferences for individualistic explanations translate into poor theories of crime. Crime can not be explained merely as a choice individuals make. To be sure, individuals are faced with making choices everyday, and the last event that leads up to the commission of a crime appears to be a choice. But, what if the offender tells us he/she felt compelled to act? Then, would we say that s/he had no choice? The larger issue is that crime is not simply a choice; it is not simply a result of choosing or not choosing to commit a crime. Choices are structured. Some people are faced with making choices that other people do not have to make. These choices may have nothing to do with any previous choice the person made in his or her lifetime. For example, as groups, men and women face different cultural, structural and institutional forces that limit or enhance the choices they can make. Research shows that young men are subject to less social control than women (Daly, 1994b; Schur, 1984; Hagan et al., 1985, 1987; Messerschmidt, 1986, 1997, 1993). Thus, men may be freer to make certain kinds of choices compared to women. In order to understand the nature of those choices, we have to come to grips with the impact of gender socialization and sex roles, and the structure of gender-linked opportunities and motivations. When we examine this situation further, we realize that not all men face the same structural conditions either. African-American men face racial biases that are different from the ethnic biases that face Hispanic men, which differ from the freer structural constraints placed on white men. In addition, we must consider that class affects the structural milieu of individuals, constraining or enhancing the ability to make free choices.

What we can say about choices, then, is that they are made with reference to the structural locations people occupy. To be sure, not everyone in the same structural location makes the same choices, nor are they confronted with the same choices to make in the first place. The macro-level approach taken by radicals makes it possible to explain why groups of similarly situated persons generally confront the same kinds of choices. It also makes it possible to understand why patterns of crime differ across groups that face different structured choice conditions. These broader patterns are useful to understand, because if they explain patterns of crime, they can also be employed to engineer socially responsive programs for controlling crime.

The radical position on structured choice can help explain crime patterns, but as we noted earlier, it cannot predict which specific individuals within given structural locations will make the choice to conform or the choice to deviate. But, actually, neither can micro-level theories of rational choice, even though when it comes to policy, orthodox criminologists opt for strategies targeted at individuals. We suggest that programs that can reduce the *rate* of crime choices within populations known to have higher propensities for those choices – such as street crime among young and poor men of color or corporate crime among affluent, middle-aged white men – make more sense than programs premised on the ability to manipulate specific individuals. (For those interested in exploring this position further, see the research on econophysics by Dragulescu and Yakovenko, 2000, 2001a, 2001b, 2003; Silva and Yakovenko, 2005.)

## Contextualized Explanation

As noted above, early radical approaches to crime causation favored macro-level explanations that began with economic relationships. The goal was not simply to understand economic and class relations nor to remain at this level of analysis. Rather, the goal was to create explanations that connect class and economic relations to social and political factors and to demonstrate how culture and history affect these connections (Mills, 1977). We call this kind of explanation *contextualized*. Contextualized radical explanations begin at the broadest levels of analysis and show the connections and interpenetrations among different levels of analysis. Thus, when individuals are the focus of analysis, they must be placed within their social *context*.

Locating individuals in their social context means recognizing that their behavior will be shaped by the intersection of culturally-ascribed identities. The broad meaning of identities such as gender, race, ethnicity, and social class are shaped by specific economic and political arrangements (e.g., patriarchy, capitalism, socialism, feudalism) at a specific period in time (i.e., history). Identities become part of the lived human experience, however, through face-to-face interaction within small groups such as families and neighborhoods and other important social institutions such as schools, workplaces, churches, and civic organizations. A radical approach to crime causation continually seeks to locate human behavior within the economic, cultural, historical and political forces that give meaning to identity, and the established social practices that apply those identities to specific individuals.

The radical commitment to contextualizing crime leads to questions such as: "How is the proportion of intact, two-parent families in a given neighborhood affected by the access that parents in that neighborhood have to work and wages?"; "Whose cultural preferences are embedded in the idea that the only social units that can effectively rear children consist of two parents, a heterosexual male and a heterosexual female?"; "How does the dominant racial and/or ethnic character of a neighborhood shape the likelihood that businesses will offer well-paying jobs that can improve the work options of parents in those communities?"; "How does the class position and cultural background of parents affect the kinds of behaviors they will expect of their children and the kinds of disciplinary practices they will employ when children fail to meet these expectations?"; or, "How do class composition, racial characteristics, status and preferred pleasures within a neighborhood increase or decrease the likelihood that police will focus on the residents of that area?" We will analyze this contextualized approach in depth later in the chapter. For now, we turn to the issue of generalization in criminology.

## General Theories versus Relative Explanation and Understanding

In recent years, orthodox criminologists have given considerable attention to general theories of crime (Hirschi and Gottfredson, 1983, 1988, 1989; Gottfredson and Hirschi, 1990; Tittle, 1995). The aim of a general theory of crime is to provide a conceptual framework that can be used to explain the causes of criminal behavior across time within a society or even to explain criminal behavior in different kinds of societies. In doing so, general theories tend to minimize the importance of historical, economic, cultural, political or economic differences in shaping both the definition of crime and the production of criminal behavior. In effect, general theories reduce human behavior to differences across individuals (for general criticism, see Mannheim, 1940; for criticisms specific to criminology, see Allan and Steffensmeier, 1989; Miller and Burack, 1993; Lynch and Groves, 1995).

In contrast, radical explanations of crime are economically, historically, culturally and politically *relative* – that is, they apply only to situations with specific characteristics. Radical theories are based on explaining how the contextual factors of a particular society during an identifiable historical context generate crime. As such, these theories should not be generalized beyond that context. For instance, analyses of crime in capitalist societies suggest that there is often a link between economic inequality and racial inequality, and this link increases the likelihood that the behavior of subordinate racial groups will be criminalized. We cannot assume, however, that this link will exist in other types of societies, without specific analyses of those societies. In short, radical explanations do not apply to all kinds of societies to all historical time periods, nor even to all kinds of crime.

Having summarized some key issues that orient radical theorizing, we are now ready to continue our discussion of radical theories of crime.

## SOCIAL CLASS, RACE, GENDER, STRATIFICATION AND ECONOMIC INEQUALITY

As noted in chapter 1, Marx defined social classes in terms of their relationship to the means of production. Since then, social theorists like Max Weber and Robert Merton have expanded Marx's conception to include unequal distributions of socially valued items such as power, prestige, wealth or income. By focusing on how class position affects life chances, political power and socialization patterns, radical theories affirm that economic factors exert a powerful influence on social life.

The most dramatic and decisive characteristic of social stratification is the distribution of wealth. In the U.S., wealth "is extraordinarily concentrated" (Gilbert and Kahl, 1982:105). For example, in Japan the richest 20 percent have four times as much wealth as the poorest 20 percent; in Germany, the top 20 percent is five times wealthier than the bottom 20 percent. In the U.S., the richest 20 percent of the population has *nine times* more wealth than the poorest group (United Nations Development Program, 1993). According to a 1995 report by the Organization for Economic Cooperation and Development (OECD), the U.S. has the most extensive level of inequality of any of the 15 highly industrialized nations that comprise its membership. Not coincidentally, at the time that report was written, the U.S. also had the highest rates of predatory crime and the least safe streets among the OECD nations.

In contrast to popular belief and ideology, in recent years wealth has become *more* – not *less* – concentrated in the U.S. For example, Edward Wolff (1995a:58) notes that "data from federal surveys shows that between 1983 and 1989 the top 20 percent of wealth holders received 99 percent of the total gain in marketable wealth, while the bottom 80 percent of the population got only 1 percent." Even among those who receive the most wealth, an extraordinary amount was concentrated in relatively few hands. From 1983 to 1989, the top 1 percent of *income recipients* took home one-third of all new wealth, while the *wealthiest* 1 percent – the "super rich" – received 62 percent of all *new* wealth (Wolff, 1995a). The trend in wealth concentration was even more exaggerated from 1989 to 1992 (Wolff, 1995a:58-59). By 2001, the wealthiest 10 percent of the American population owned 72 percent of everything of value in the U.S., while the bottom 80 percent shared in only 15.3 percent of America's wealth (see Table 5.1). This increased concentration is revealed in the following trend: At the same time that the number of millionaires and billionaires in the U.S. increased, homeownership and retirement savings declined for middle-income families (Wolff, 1995a, 1995b, 2004). These data show an increasing polarization of wealth in the U.S. over the past 30 years (see also Perlow, 1988).

### Table 5.1: Distribution of Wealth by Population Percentiles, U.S., 2001*

| Population Percentile | | Percent of Wealth Owned |
|---|---|---|
| Top | 1% | 34 |
| Next | 4% | 26 |
| Next | 5% | 12 |
| Top | 10% | 72 (total of top 1, 4 & 5) |
| Next | 10% | 13 |
| Next | 20% | 11 |
| Next | 20% | 4 |
| Next | 22% | 0.3 |
| Bottom | 18% | 0 |

\* Adapted from Edward N. Wolff, *Changes in Household Wealth in the 1980s and 1990s in the U.S.*, Jerome Levy Economics Institute, May, 2004.

### Table 5.2: Percent of Wealth Owned by the Super Rich (Top 1%) in Five Advanced Nations, 1989*

| Country | % Wealth | % Difference from U.S. |
|---|---|---|
| France | 26% | - 13% |
| Canada | 25% | -14% |
| Great Britain | 18% | -21% |
| Sweden | 16% | -23% |
| U.S. | **39%** | ----- |

\* Adapted from Wolff, 1995b.

While capitalism tends to produce disparities in both wealth and income, not all capitalist countries are the same. In many developed capitalist countries, strong labor movements have been able to offset, at least somewhat, the tendency to concentrate wealth at the top. In the U.S., however, there has been no such countervailing force since the late 1960s. As a result, the U.S. now has one of the most lopsided class systems among modernized capitalist nations (see Table 5.2).

Wealth concentrations are also skewed by race and ethnicity. For example, according U.S. Census Bureau data (*Current Population Survey, 2000*), the average white (non-Hispanic) household net worth was $198,184. Compare this to the average net worth for African-American households ($35,284) and Hispanic households ($51,908), and one can clearly see the relationship between economic security and advancement, and race and ethnicity in the Unit ed States. Also, it is important to keep in mind that averages conceal great disparities. For instance the nearly $200,000 average for white households does not mean that most white households in America are worth that much. The figure is grossly inflated by the fact that a few households enjoy multi-millions of dollars in net worth, while many have none.

In part, the increased concentration of wealth is a result of changes in the tax structure. President G.W. Bush's tax cuts, for example, were overwhelmingly lopsided. As noted by the organization, *Citizens for Tax Relief,* one-half of Bush's tax cuts benefit the top five percent of income earners, those earning more than $125,000 a year. Coupled with declining government relief for the poor, the eroding purchasing power of the minimum wage due to inflation, and increased government subsidies and lower tax rates for corporations (which have increased stock values, also a benefit to those who already hold wealth in the form of stock), the wealth and income disparity continues to grow.

Contributing to this lopsided class structure is the distribution of income (as distinguished from wealth). In 1996, the U.S. Census Bureau reported that in 1994 nearly half of all income was received by the top 20 percent of families and individuals, while the bottom 20 percent received only 3.6%. According to these figures, the top 5 percent of income earners take home a little more than 21 percent of all earned income in the U.S. As disturbing as these figures are, what is more disturbing is that the U.S. income picture has changed for the worse over the past 50 years, especially for the lowest classes (Currie and Skolnick, 1984; see also Wolff, 1987). Indeed, the lowest 20 percent of income earners saw their share of all income decline from 4 percent in 1967 to 3.6 percent by 1994 (U.S. Census Bureau, 1996a). At the same time, incomes for the top 1 percent more than doubled between 1979 to 1989 – a period where median income was relatively stable and the cost of living doubled (Frank and Cook, 1995). Contrary to capitalist ideology, these facts indicate that there is little chance for the vast majority of people within the lower class – and increasingly, the middle class – to improve their economic conditions. In 2004, someone whose parents were in the bottom 20 percent of income-earners in the U.S. has a 1 in 13 chance of reaching the top 20 percent of earners in their lifetime, while someone whose parents were in the top 20 percent of earners had a 1 in 2 chance of staying in the top 20 percent of income-earners. In addition, the child of affluent parents is six-and-a-half times more likely to be wealthy themselves than children of poor parents. In other words, class position for most people is not earned: It is inherited in the form of both money and the kinds of social capital that allows people to do well in society. Regarding this last point, consider that 72 percent of the students at America's top 146 universities come from the richest 25 percent of the population, while students from the bottom half of the U.S. earnings pyramid constitute barely 10 percent of the students at those schools (see Figure 5.1).

Conservative defenders of the inequalities produced by capitalist economic systems typically point to the person who has risen "by her bootstraps" from poverty to success through hard work or ingenuity as proof of the kinds of opportunities capitalism makes available to all. These explanations of income inequality illustrate the fundamental difference between an individualistic, conservative perspective and a radical, contextualized view. Conservatives point to what happens to *some* of the people *some* of the time. Radicals are concerned with what happens to *most* of the people *most* of the time.

The tendency toward increased concentration of wealth and income in the U.S. calls into question the idea that hard work gets you ahead because, clearly, many Americans work very hard *but have very little*. Indeed, recent studies show that many people are working harder and earning less, which is part of the reason why income and wealth inequality are increasing (Bluestone, 1995; Frank and Cook, 1995). As Juliet Schor (1993) noted in *The Overworked Americans: The Unexpected Decline of Leisure*, the returns that Americans received for their labor has decreased: "In the last twenty years the amount of time Americans have spent at their jobs has risen steadily. Each year the change is small, amounting to about nine hours, or slightly more than one additional day of work. In any given year, such a small increment has probably been imperceptible. But the accumulated increase over two decades is substantial… Working hours are… longer than they were forty years ago" (p. 1).

The increase in working hours offers an excellent example of the difference between orthodox and radical approaches to the problem of crime causation. One school of orthodox criminology focuses on the increasing failure of poor families to pass on appropriate "values" to children (Bennett et al., 1996), which is one reason the children of the poor fail to get a head. According to this thought, the root of this "failure" are the personal choices people make about raising their children. Yet, if families are "failing" to adequately socialize children (and it is not clear that they are, especially to the degree conservatives claim), one of the problems might be the increasing lack of time parents have to spend with their children, especially because of the increased need for families to have two paychecks instead of one. What might families be like if either a mother or a father, or a lesbian or gay partner in a household with children, could earn enough from a single job that requires no more than 40 hours a week to provide a dignified economic base for the family, thus freeing larger portions of collective household energy to be focused on the needs of children? Or how might childhood socialization improve if we defined child rearing as the responsibility of whole communities, not just isolated family units? Such linkages between structural conditions and everyday life are typically lacking within orthodox criminology, particularly its more conservative versions.

### Figure 5.1: Who Gets a Prestigious College Degree?

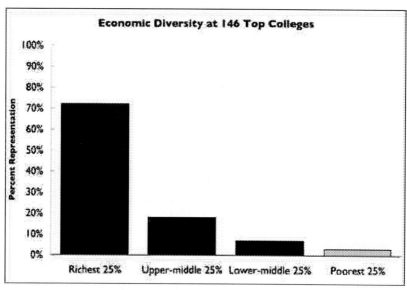

**Source:** Anthony B. Carnevale and Stephen J. Rose, "Race/ethnicity and Selective College Admissions," in Richard D. Kahlenberg, ed., *America's Untapped Resource: Low-Income Students in Higher Education* (Century Foundation, 2004).

Not only have working hours for the employed increased, so too has the productivity of American workers, which *doubled* between 1940 and 1990 (U.S. Office of the President, 1991). Thus, Americans are not only working longer but are more productive when they are working. Despite working harder and longer, workers are economically further behind today than they were 30 years ago (for discussion, see especially Frank and Cook, *The Winner-Take-All Society: Why the Few at the Top Get so Much More than the Rest of Us*). With its increasing ability to threaten whole communities with capital flight unless workers produce more for less, capitalists have found a way to expand profits without having to share their gains with workers (Greider, 1997). In short, the rich are getting richer – much richer – while most of the rest of us are working harder just to keep from losing ground.

In sum, in recent decades, the degree of social inequality has accelerated in America. The income and wealth data reviewed above indicate that the "trickle down" economics of the Reagan, Bush I and now Bush II years have done nothing to redistribute wealth. Indeed, as critics have observed, "mink coats do not trickle down." In fact, policies such as decreases in capital gains and income taxes ensured that the wealthy kept a larger share of their incomes (Barlett and Steele, 1992; Frank and Cook, 1995).

Data on occupational stratification also point to a similar decline in the quality and quantity of rewards associated with white collar work, a drop in blue-collar employment, an increase in menial labor and service-sector labor, permanent high levels of unemployment and decreases in leisure time (Schor, 1993; Frank and Cook, 1995). These trends suggest "an increased hardening of class lines" (Gilbert and Kahl, 1982:83).

Economic inequality also has important gender characteristics. Historically, women have had less access to economic and political power than men, and this remains true despite claims that affirmative action programs have eliminated discrimination against women (for a review, see Lynch, 1996). It is indeed true that relative to men, women's incomes have increased. For instance, while, women earned 72 percent of what men took home in wages in 1994, by 2004 this gap had narrowed by 7 percent, with women, on average, now earning about 79 percent of what men take home. This increase, however, was due to a *decline* in men's average wages rather than an increase in women's wages (Amott, 1995; U.S. Bureau of Labor Statistics, 2004). Over all, women continue to be employed primarily in the service sector (e.g., clerical positions, sales help) where low wages dominate (Figart and Lapidus, 1998, 1996).

Current evidence indicates that making better jobs available to women will not end the gender gap in wages. Even women in high-status positions, such as physicians, lawyers and accountants, earn less than men with the same jobs (Ruth, 1995; Figart and Lapidus, 1998). Gender inequality in both wages and occupational access has led to a *feminization of poverty,* a term used to identify the increasingly large numbers of those living below the poverty level – women (and children) in female-headed households (Sklar, 1995; Kozol, 1995; Rotella, 1995; see also Messerschmidt, 1986).

Many orthodox theorists link these female-headed households to a variety of social pathologies, including crime (Wilson, 1996). Having proposed this link, conservative solutions to crime tend to focus on decreasing the number of children living in female-headed households by denying welfare benefits for children born out of wedlock (even though families on welfare have, on average, fewer children than families not on welfare) or tracking down "deadbeat dads" who fail to pay child support. Omitted from consideration are alternative, better-informed policies that ensure that employed women who head households can earn a dignified wage that would enable them to adequately provide for their children. For example, if working women were paid the same as men, it would result in an average of $4,000 increase in household income. This alone would cut the U.S. poverty rate in half! Conservatives, however, would rather punish poor women for being sexually active rather than reduce the poverty of their children or the crime that such poverty generates.

In the U.S., economic inequality also has important racial dimensions. African Americans and Hispanics, in particular, are economically disadvantaged (see Carnoy, 1994). In 2004, for instance, the average employed African-American male earned only 77 percent of the income of a white worker, and Hispanic/Latino men fared even worse, with median weekly earnings that were only 62 percent of their white counterparts (U.S. Census Bureau istics, 2005). In 2003, the median *family* income for whites was $47,876, while black and Hispanic median family incomes were $29,668, and $33,429, respectively (U.S. Census Bureau, 2004). In other words, white families enjoyed household incomes that were 38 percent higher than black families and 30 percent higher than Hispanic/Latino families. Unemployment figures show a similar pattern of racial/ethnic disadvantage. In early 2005, African Americans were twice as likely to be unemployed as white workers, while the chance of a Hispanic worker being unemployed was about one-third greater than that of a white worker (U.S. Census Bureau, 2005). These figures represent the continuation of a process that began in the late 1970s, as African-Americans steadily lost economic ground to whites due to the elimination of well-paying jobs in the industrial sector (Carnoy, 1994; Wilson, 1985)

The case of African Americans who are the heads of households provides an excellent example of how class, gender and race intersect. Under U.S. capitalism, some types of work will be paid *substantially* less than others. America's history of racism has meant that African Americans, as a group, have typically been restricted to occupying lower-paying job categories. Segregation has ensured that African Americans remain detached from economic structures such as ownership of large financial, manufacturing and other institutions that would promote their financial independence (see Massey and Denton, 1993, 1989, 1988; Massey and Gross, 1991; Massey and Hajnal, 1995). Finally, because of the long-standing tradition that places greater value on men, the types of work performed by women (e.g., service work) are low paying even if these jobs are similar to those men perform (e.g., require similar levels of education, are/or equally difficult). Thus, the kind of work available to a working-class African American woman will often pay less and provide fewer benefits than work available to white men, white women and, in many cases, even black men. In other words, the concentration of impoverished female-headed households in African-American neighborhoods has far less to do with the choices these women have made than it does with the way class, gender and race have combined in their biographies to assign them the least-rewarded places in society.

The story from recent years is no better. According to U.S. Census Bureau (2005) data, since George W. Bush took office and instituted new economic policies, the following shifts have occurred:

(1)     the number of Americans without health insurance has grown from 39.8 million to 45 million by 2003 (+13 percent);

(2)     the number of African-American living in poverty increased from 7.9 to 9.1 million – a 15 percent increase – after declining during the Clinton administration by nearly 27 percent;

(3)     the portion of the population living below poverty increased from 11.7 to 12.5 percent from 2000 to 2003; and,

(4)     between 2002 and 2003, 1.3 million more children were added to those living below poverty.

These indicators of the economic situation point toward the generation of conditions that will force the rate of crime to rise in the near future.

To round out our discussion of inequality, we present a few "quality-of-life" indicators for persons in disadvantaged socioeconomic positions. Many indicators show that the number of negative quality of life indicators (e.g., the likelihood of illness, mental health difficulties, inadequate housing, limited access to health care, problems of self-esteem or living in proximity to pollution and hazardous waste) increase as we descend the economic ladder (e.g., see Stretesky and Lynch, 1999a, 1999b). We will limit discussion here, however, to those quality-of-life indicators that help us understand how stratification and inequality affect criminal behavior patterns. It is important to remember that these indicators are not qualities of poor people, but, rather, are qualities of living within a particular social class context that carries with it certain opportunities and liabilities.

Compared with the middle and upper classes, the poor have far less access to quality education and thus are more likely to have lower levels of educational attainment (DiMaggio, 1982; DiMaggio and Mohr, 1985). Recent studies demonstrate that lower-income groups have limited access to things that the more affluent take for granted, such as telephones, computers and the Internet (e.g., Associated Press, 1998). Individuals in these categories are also more likely to be unemployed or to be employed in secondary labor markets that offer undesirable work and inferior wages. Their families are more likely to be large, and they are less likely to remain cohesive. They are more likely to have hazardous waste sites in their neighborhoods, to live near polluting industries and to suffer from elevated levels of environmentally induced cancers (Gilman, 1995; Knox, 1996, 1994, 1992a, 1992b; Knox and Gilman, 1997; Stretesky and Lynch, 1999a, 1999b). And, last but not least, poor persons are more likely to be victims of violent crime.

Turning from the bottom to the top of the class structure, it comes as no surprise that those holding positions of relative advantage gain additional leverage by translating economic strength into political power. As Mills (1956) demonstrated in *The Power Elite*, wealthy people lobby for their interests, purchase political clout with campaign contributions, secure important positions in both the public and private sectors, involve themselves in corporate and government decisions at the highest levels, and generally use their political and economic power to shape national policy in their own interests (see Simon, 1999).

From a radical perspective, stratification and inequality are due to political, economic and cultural factors that shape the antagonism between capital and labor. If productive relationships influence social relationships, as Marx suggested, and if different social classes experience the system of production in different ways, then class location will have a significant impact on other types of social relationships such as those involving family, education and community. Because social relationships influence the likelihood of criminal behavior, the extent to which the social system increases or decreases the criminogenic content of these relationships is the extent to which it is one of the causes of crime.

The extensive review of economic conditions provided above provides the background for radical explanations of the relationship between inequality and crime. These materials also impact the development of theories discussed in the chapters that follow.

## INEQUALITY AND CRIME

Let us begin with a question: What do social class, menstruation, broken homes, race, unemployment and lunar cycles have in common? The answer is that each has been specified as a cause of crime, which tells us two things: first, that criminologists have traveled far and wide (even to the moon!) in their quest to discover the causes of crime; and, second, that causation is no simple matter. But where does this leave us in the search for the causes of crime? What allows one to choose among causes as dissimilar as I.Q. and capitalism?

To answer these questions let us review an issue raised in chapter 2. That chapter introduced the dialectic and argued that dialectical thinking, by including the effects of political and economic institutions on the problem of crime, broadened causal inquiry by directing radical analysts to explore how micro-level variables such as broken homes or defective educational institutions are "shaped by larger social structures" (Greenberg, 1981:86). With this strategy in mind, three British criminologists – Taylor, Walton and Young (1973) – wrote the now-classic, *The New Criminology*. In this book they argued that models of crime causation must include a macro-level analysis that incorporates a *political economy of crime*. Central to their argument is the need to address how crime is affected by "the overall social context of inequalities of power, wealth and authority in the developed industrial society" (Taylor et al., 1973:270).

In addition to their emphasis on political economy, which they see as constituting the "wider origins" of the deviant act, Taylor et al. also argue that radical criminology must explain the "immediate origins" of criminal behavior (Taylor et al., 1973:271). Reduced to its simplest terms, they suggest that the wider arena of political economy will condition more immediate social milieus, and that these two levels together cause crime (see also, Mills, 1977; Katz, 1989). To more fully understand what Taylor et al. meant, below we review research that examines how political economy and inequality bear on both the wider and immediate origins of criminal behavior.

In an attempt to specify how economic and social structures of inequality cause crime, Blau and Blau (1982) undertook an empirical study that relied explicitly on Marxist predictions. Comparing the crime rates of the 100 largest U.S. cities, Blau and Blau demonstrated that socioeconomic inequalities increased rates of violent crime, and concluded that inequality is the root cause of both social disorganization and crime. In their view, inequality increases alienation and undermines social cohesion "by creating multiple parallel social differences which widen the separations between ethnic groups and between social classes, and it creates a situation characterized by much social disorganization and prevalent latent animosities" (Blau and Blau, 1982:119). Michalowski (1985:410) makes this same point in simpler terms when he notes that "inequality tends to increase crime by weakening the social bond" (see also Sampson and Groves, 1989). Both the Blaus and Michalowski argue that it is inequality rather than simple poverty that produces crime (see Michalowski, 1985:406-409 for further discussion).

The radical proposition that class is related to criminal behavior has been subject to a great deal of criticism because there is a considerable body of research that demonstrates that social class has a weak or nonexistent effect on crime (Tittle and Villemez, 1978; Messner, 1982; Elliot and Huizinga, 1983). There are a number of reasons for such findings. First, radicals define social class as a relationship between owners and producers, while orthodox criminologists measure class by income or social status, both of which are incompatible with the radical concept of class (i.e., class as a relationship). Second, class variations are unlikely to surface in the self-report methods criminologists use to determine levels of delinquency among juveniles. There are two reasons for this. First, the majority of these surveys have been administered to public school students. Since school dropout rates are higher for working and underclass youths than for the middle and upper classes, these surveys underestimate social-class differences in juvenile wrongdoing. Second, many self-report surveys are heavily weighted toward questions concerning petty deviance (e.g., underage drinking, smoking, and sexual exploration), or behaviors that are widespread among youths of all social classes, thus obscuring social class differences associated with more serious offenses. Third, the radical argument about class is not limited to the kinds of street crimes most criminologists examine, but also includes corporate and white collar crimes along with the unique opportunities that owners and managers of capital have to commit those offenses – offenses that cannot be assessed using data about delinquency.

In short, despite micro-level empirical findings indicating that class appears to be unrelated to crime, logic and practical knowledge – the first criteria for scientific thinking – support radical contentions concerning the relationship between class and crime. As Braithwaite (1989) has noted, even criminologists who claim there is no link between class and crime avoid walking alone through urban ghettos at night. Class is related to crime and particularly to the kinds of crimes people have the opportunity to commit, as well as to the kinds of laws that are enforced against people from different classes.

A radical approach to the link between class and crime requires a careful analysis of how class inequality translates into increased rates of crime. For instance, Blau and Blau (1982) suggest that the effects of inequality are transmitted into peoples' lives through such things as family disorganization (e.g., percent divorced, percent female-headed families) that are felt hardest by African Americans living in inner cities (Sampson and Wilson, 1994). Similarly, Lee Rainwater (1970) posits a causal framework that links macro- and micro-level effects by exploring how inequality and racial oppression intersect to increase family disorganization and crime. Rainwater argues that the economic marginality of black men leads to tense and conflicting role relationships, increases marital instability and ultimately results in a pattern of female-based households and "matrifocal" family structure. Like Blau and Blau, Rainwater concludes that inequality, low economic status and race interact to produce crime by increasing social disorganization. Simply put, both studies suggest that those who are economically disadvantaged are more likely to experience "segregated" family structures and that strains experienced in these types of families provide a fertile precondition for increased rates of crime and delinquency. For radicals, then, the focus isn't on how family disruption affects crime, but on how families get disrupted in the first place and the consequences of that disruption.

## INEQUALITY, FAMILY DISORGANIZATION AND CRIME

Family measures such as the percentages of divorced and female-headed families have long been correlated with criminality, and many researchers have suggested that family disorganization is an important cause of crime (Nye, 1958; Hirschi, 1983). Consistent with their preference for contextual explanations, radical criminologists view family structure as an intervening variable in crime causation. The work of Colvin and Pauly (1983) provides a good example of how the macro-social organization of capitalism can affect the micro-social organization of the family.

Drawing on the works of Kohn (1976, 1977), Kohn and Schoolert (1969), Edwards (1979) and Etzioni (1970), Colvin and Pauly (1983) argue that coercive socialization experiences in the workplace spill over into socialization experiences in the home and that negative experiences in either setting increase the likelihood that children will "engage in serious, patterned delinquency" (p. 515). Colvin and Pauly conclude that stable socialization experiences in white-collar professions promote an internalized moral commitment to the workplace. Parents in these occupations encourage family socialization experiences that rely on internalized compliance structures, a type of control that

promotes sibling attachment to the socialization sequence. As a result, socialization experiences are "positive" in that children have "initial bonds of high
intensity" to the family unit.

In contrast, blue-collar employees work under a utilitarian control structure, which means that their bond to the organization depends on a calculation
of extrinsic material rewards (e.g., pay increases, seniority, job security). Workers socialized in this way tend to reproduce similar structures in the family,
producing "calculative bonds of intermediate intensity in their children"
(Colvin and Pauly, 1983:536).

Finally, parents holding low-skilled, low-paying, dead-end jobs are exposed to inconsistent coercive controls that are externally enforced. Such parents are likely to impose inconsistent controls on their children, oscillating between punitiveness and permissiveness. In this section of the working class we
can expect "more alienated initial bonds to be produced in children who experience...arbitrary, inconsistent, and coercive family control structures"
(Colvin and Pauly, 1983:536).

In sum, Colvin and Pauly (1983) suggest that persons socialized under coercive control structures at work will employ similar socialization methods in
the home, or, more generally, that different parental attitudes toward child
rearing will be produced in different work-related contexts. By combining a
sociological approach with established empirical findings in criminology regarding socialization and delinquency, Colvin and Pauly broaden the inquiry
and subsequently conclude that: (1) socialization patterns in both workplace
and family settings are distributed along class lines; (2) these patterns are defined by the relations of production underlying capitalism; and (3) these differential socialization sequences determine "the patterned processes of development of both delinquent and non-delinquent behavior" (Colvin and Pauly,
1983:525). Colvin and Pauly reframe the role of family structure as a cause of
crime from an "independent" force – as is often favored by orthodox criminologists – to an intermediary social context that is shaped by the wider political-economic system and, that in turn shapes the micro-level experience of
children being socialized within families. This is the essence of radical approaches to understanding crime causation: to identify the networks of sociological forces that continually move between the most macro and most micro-
levels of society.

Colvin and Pauly's (1983) model raises but does not answer several questions. One is how familial social control is established in economically marginalized families; that is, families with little or no connection to the workplace. In
these families, parents tend to lack strong ties to the economic system (e.g.,
parents are employed sporadically or are unemployed). Parents in marginal

families, therefore, are not exposed to socialization patterns that can be replicated within the family. Thus, the type of controls employed within marginal families are likely to be very unstable, differing from one family to the next and within the same family over time. Extending Colvin and Pauly's argument would suggest that economically marginal families are the least likely to employ social control processes that minimize criminal behavior among children. Consequently, children from these homes should manifest the highest rates of criminal activity.

Two other questions raised by Colvin and Pauly's (1983) work are: what is the role of school socialization on these patterns?, and how do work-derived family socialization patterns affect the production of corporate crime? Prior to their work experience, Americans undergo institutionally-based socialization in schools. Schools have clear social-class characteristics: elite private schools prepare children from upper class homes to rule; good schools in affluent, middle class neighborhoods prepare students to become managers; schools in stable, working-class environments prepare children to labor; and rundown, aging schools in decaying urban neighborhoods attempt to teach the bare-bones basics while maintaining control (Anyon, 1997; Carlson and Appel, 1998). How do these experiences intersect with home and street socialization to increase or decrease the likelihood of crime? Similarly, most corporate crime is committed by upper-middle-class managers. How do the socialization patterns learned by those working in upper-management jobs influence whether their children will or will not become white collar or corporate criminals?

## In Sum

Radical criminology approaches crime causation as a macro-social problem. This does not mean focusing only on large-scale social forces in the search for an understanding of why crime happens. But it does mean giving close attention to how large-scale social forces such as the systems of production and distribution, historically established gender and race relations, and powerful cultural beliefs such as "individualism," interact in ways that increase the likelihood of crime for some and decrease this likelihood for others.

The following chapter expands on these ideas by examining the ways in which the political economy, structure and identity have all been utilized in radical criminology's search for an understanding of crime that moves beyond the individual level of explanation.

# SIX.
# RADICAL THEORIES OF CRIME CAUSATION — PART II: ECONOMIC STRUCTURE, IDENTITY AND CRIME

Radical theorists are concerned with contextual explanation. These explanations examine a variety of factors including the powerful capacity of economic systems and social identities to shape social conditions, social meanings, and the likelihood that people will engage in, or be seen as engaging in, criminal behavior. We begin our review with the relationship between economic structures and criminality.

## ECONOMY AND CRIME

Many radical criminologists have explored the connection between economic conditions and criminal behavior. This focus began with the publication of Willem Bonger's (1969), *Criminality and Economic Conditions,* which systematized a Marxist theory of criminality. The link between criminal behavior and the economic context of society is logically appealing given what we know about crime. For example, of the more than 13.6 million arrests made in 2001, 85 percent were for property and victimless crimes where the motive was money (e.g., theft, burglary, prostitution, drug dealing), or for non-violent Part II Index Offenses against social order such as public drunkenness for which the poor are most often arrested (*Sourcebook...*, 2002, Table 4.1). And surely, the primary motivation behind white collar and corporate crime is economic. By contrast, serious violent crimes (Part I) that are not connected with money (e.g., homicides, rapes, assaults) constitute less than 4 percent of all arrests in the U.S. Thus, both the crimes of the powerful and the crimes of the powerless are overwhelmingly linked to economic motives.

There are a number of ways of connecting the economic system to criminal behavior. For example, radicals have examined how perceived and real economic inequality causes crime (e.g., Blau and Blau, 1982). Others have suggested that the class structure consistent with a capitalist economic system limits individuals' choices (Groves, 1981; Groves and Frank, 1987; Lynch, 1996). In this view, individuals from the lower class have limited choices, while the middle and upper classes have substantially more available avenues to achieve success. From a Marxist perspective, in the most extreme cases, the lowest social class faces the "choice" between starvation and crime. Engels (1973:154) suggested that "[w]ant leaves the working-man the choice between starving slowly, killing himself speedily, or...stealing. And there is no cause for surprise that most of them prefer stealing to starvation and suicide...." In the U.S., even the poorest of the poor rarely have to choose between crime and death by starvation. Soup kitchens, welfare checks, "will work for food" signs, and even the dumpsters of a wasteful, wealthy society offer alternatives to the steal-or-starve problem. But a life based on soup kitchens, welfare checks, begging or dumpster-diving offers little incentive to abide by the rules of the game. Thus, radical criminology seeks to understand how the economic conditions of the least well-off segments of society shape their disproportional participation in street crimes. This does not mean that radical criminology is concerned *only* with street crimes among poorer and less-powerful groups. Rather, it underscores the aim of radical criminology to understand how *class-specific* opportunities and motivations affect the comparative likelihood and rate of crime across classes.

In terms of street crime, radical theorists' concern with social class gives rise to the observation that those individuals most likely to become involved in street crime or to be labeled as criminals occupy marginal economic positions (Spitzer, 1975; Quinney, 1980; Platt, 1978). One way of assessing the relationship between economic marginality and criminal behavior is by examining the connection between unemployment and crime.

## Unemployment and Criminal Behavior

A number of radicals have found a relationship between crime and unemployment (Chiricos and DeLone, 1992; Allan and Steffensmeier, 1989; Quinney, 1980, 1979; Reiman, 1984; Box, 1987, 1984, 1981; Box and Hale, 1983a, 1983b; Greenberg, 1977a; Chiricos, 1987; Platt, 1978; Currie, 1985; Bohm, 1985; Gordon, 1973, 1971). While orthodox criminologists have also examined the impact of unemployment on crime, their approach generally does not address how the economic system functions to create unemployment in the first place. Radicals, however, are very concerned with this concept, and with the *structural causes of unemployment*. Specifically, radicals have investigated how increases or decreases in the rate of unemployment affect the rate of criminal activity and how the economy can be restructured to reduce unemployment (Currie, 1985, 1996). A brief overview of this explanation follows.

Unemployment is an unfortunate consequence of the normal operation of capitalist economies. In order to increase profit and produce more value (especially surplus value), the capitalist seeks out technological innovations (e.g., machinery, technology) that increase worker productivity. The more the capitalist employs machine labor in the production process, the more expendable human labor becomes, and each increase in machine labor frees workers from the production process. Thus, in its normal development, capitalism's increasing reliance on machine labor creates a surplus, or economically marginal population (Marx, 1967a). The surplus population exists in several forms including the unemployed, partially employed and underemployed (Marx, 1967a).

As a result of this process, at a certain stage of development, capitalist economies become incapable of maintaining full employment. In the U.S., full employment became a structural impossibility following the Great Depression in 1929. Since that time, policy makers have redefined "full employment" as 5 percent unemployed, which today means that a minimum of *five million* people out of a labor force of roughly 100 million will be without work. This is only part of the story, however. Unemployment figures are based on the number of people who are involuntarily out of work, are eligible for unemployment benefits and are actively looking for work. The so-called "discouraged workers" – those who have been unemployed for more than 26 weeks and who are no longer eligible for unemployment benefits, or who have given up hope of finding work and are no longer looking – are not included in official unemployment statistics. This latter population is usually about the same size as the officially unemployed population. In reality then, the term "full employment" means having more than *10 million* employable people without jobs. And none of this addresses the six million people who are working part-time, not because they wish to but because there is not enough work (U.S. Bureau of the Census, 1993). This inability of advanced societies to provide meaningful work for all their citizens on a regular basis is a prime example of what radicals mean by the contradictions of capitalism. Unemployment has thus become a fact of life associated with American capitalism.

In capitalist economies, unemployment can be controlled to a certain extent. But, historically, low levels of unemployment tend to generate inflation. Using the Phillips curve, economists have demonstrated that there is a tradeoff between inflation and unemployment. In the long run, low levels of unemployment create inflation; and inflation can be controlled by increased levels of unemployment (Dolan, 1977). At some point during "good economic times" (low unemployment), the government is pressured by business or the general public to do something about inflation. In recent decades the policy of choice has been to lower the inflation rate by contracting the money supply (the Federal Reserve raises interest rates) and thereby limiting the creation of new jobs and increasing unemployment. Thus, there has been a tradeoff between inflation and reductions in unemployment that appears difficult to solve within the confines of capitalism (Applebaum, 1979).

For much of the 1990s, a somewhat different pattern emerged as the U.S. enjoyed low levels of both unemployment and inflation. This apparent repeal of the Phillips curve, however, revealed some important elements of the link between unemployment and inflation. First, this link has always been based on the ability of workers to demand higher salaries when workers were in short supply. With the emergence of a global economy that includes global competition for jobs, what Marx called the "reserve army of the unemployed" is never depleted. Businesses can (and do) relocate to lower-wage nations to hold down labor costs, making it difficult if not impossible for workers to bid up wages; hence, there is no inflation (Greider, 1997). This practice, which is called "outsourcing," not only reduces the number of available jobs by moving them overseas; it also causes increased competition for available jobs, and in the process, helps suppress wages.

Second, the U.S. has a large surplus of economically marginalized workers who are not reflected in unemployment statistics. Thus, the U.S. *seemed* to enjoy low rates of unemployment during the 1990s in part because large segments of the inner-city youth populations were held out of the labor market and were not counted among the unemployed (Carlson and Michalowski, 1997).

Unemployment is an intractable feature of industrial and post-industrial capitalism whether one uses radical or orthodox economic approaches. This being the case, it makes sense to examine the connection between unemployment and crime, particularly since most crime is property crime. In this regard Greenberg (1977a:648) noted that: "Persons who are unemployed can be assumed to have a greater incentive to steal than those who are not. In addition, they may risk less when they engage in crime, for they cannot lose their jobs if caught. If this reasoning is correct, [the] crime rate will increase during periods of unemployment." In this view, crime becomes a rational response to the structural constraints (e.g., in this case unemployment) associated with capitalism (Quinney, 1980; Gordon, 1971, 1973), since unemployed individuals have fewer choices available to them (Groves and Frank, 1987; Box, 1987).

One mistake people often make when they think about crime and unemployment is assuming that it is the *officially unemployed* – those who have lost jobs – who commit crimes. During periods of high unemployment some people who lose jobs will be tempted to replace a portion of their lost income through crime. The majority, however, will not turn to crime because these are people who, until their recent job loss, were largely disciplined to uphold law-abiding ways of life through work and wages. Additionally, since those who lose jobs have work experience, they are often better able to compete for another job, although it will typically be one below the skill and wage level of the job they lost. This sets into motion a trickle-down effect; as the skilled unemployed enter the lower-wage labor market, less-skilled workers lose *their* jobs, and so on down the job ladder. At the lower end, new low-skill entrants into the labor force find little to encourage them. In the absence of effective government intervention to create economic opportunity and visions of a hopeful future, long periods of high unemployment tend to create a social climate that discourages law-abiding behavior among the least well off and increases temptations to seek criminal opportunities for money obtained through drug dealing or prostitution, or to engage in illegal or illicit pleasures such as drug consumption and casual sex. In addition, given the pressure to succeed – which in the U.S. is measured by material possessions – some individuals who are employed at jobs that leave them far from achieving any of their dreams will be tempted to make up the difference through crime. Crime is one avenue that some absolutely or relatively impoverished persons utilize to obtain the material trappings of a positive identity (Merton, 1979).

In his review of the literature on the unemployment-crime connection, Chiricos (1987) found that the majority of studies indicated a correlation between the rate of unemployment and levels of property crime. Not all studies reviewed, however, found a relationship between unemployment and property crime, and few found any association between unemployment and violent crime. Orthodox criminologists have employed these null findings on unemployment to criticize radical models that focus on the link between crime and economic conditions (Wilson and Herrnstein, 1985; Wilson and Cook, 1985; Fox, 1978; Freeman, 1983). Chiricos disputes this claim by pointing out that the greater weight of the evidence supports the idea that there is a causal link between unemployment and crime. Others have suggested the unemployment-crime question is the wrong one. Robert Bohm (1985), for instance, suggests that radical criminologists should not link crime to unemployment but should examine the broader social relationships that cause both crime and unemployment. Capitalism, for instance, fosters competition, self-interest and exploitation of the working class. In this view, crime is not simply the result of unemployment – it is the result of competition over scarce resources (including jobs) and the promotion of self-interest, which Bonger (1969) summarized when he noted that capitalism promoted egoism, which in turn created crime among all classes.

This approach is consistent with observable crime trends. The white collar or corporate criminal, for example, is employed and well paid, yet still commits crime. Why? The answer could be that he is pursuing culturally-induced aspirations that appear as self-interest (being economically egoistic); or that he is promoting corporate profits (in general, pursuing the goals of capitalism), and that these concerns induce him to violate the law. In Bohm's view, self-interest and competitive influences are part of everyday life in capitalist societies that establish conditions conducive to criminal behavior among all classes (for a similar argument, see also Engels, 1981).

While his approach downplays the significance of unemployment as a primary cause of crime, Bohm (1985) remains sensitive to the idea that unemployment creates additional strains that may lead unemployed individuals to commit crime. Unemployment is particularly high among young minority males, who constitute one of the large at-risk crime populations (Bohm, 1985). Bohm sensitizes us to the idea that unemployment is caused by the natural progression of capitalism and that it generates many forces in addition to unemployment that magnify the propensity toward crime among all social classes. For Bohm, the solution to the crime problem lies not in reducing unemployment but in transcending capitalism.

Other radical criminologists have argued that if there is a connection between unemployment and crime, creating more jobs will, in fact, reduce the property crime rate here and now (Currie, 1985, 1996; Quinney, 1980; Chiricos, 1987). Thus, there is some tension in the policy recommendations suggested by radical theorists about how to reduce crime. Short-term policies that can be instituted under the current system clash with the types of long-term policy Bohm (1985) prefers. In Bohm's view, creating jobs will not reduce crime since the overall experience of capitalism still alienates the majority of the population. The question of whether there is an alternative to capitalism seems further from resolution today after the collapse of state socialism worldwide. Yet the question remains. If much crime results from the cultural constructs typical of capitalist societies, and from the tendency of these societies to exclude significant portions of their populations from the world of work and wages, are there any possibilities for making significant inroads into the world's crime problem? We will explore this question further in our concluding chapter.

## Recession and Crime

Like others, Stephen Box (1987) has suggested that radical criminologists should downplay the significance of unemployment as a cause of crime and focus on broader economic conditions that affect all classes. For instance, Box argues that the unemployment explanation fails to account for the crimes of the powerful. For these reasons, Box argues that radicals should examine the connection between recession and crime.

In Box's (1987) view, recessions create conditions conducive to crime that affect all classes. The powerful are more likely to violate the law to increase profits during recessions, while the same unfavorable economic conditions drive the lower class further into poverty, block legitimate means to success and reduce commitment to the conventional social order, thereby making crime among the lower class more likely.

Recessions not only increase the types of economic inequality likely to lead to street crime but also affect the ways that the powerful view the powerless. During recessions, the unemployment rate increases, which translates into a growing surplus population. This surplus population is "viewed more suspiciously by the governing elite, not because it actually does become disruptive and rebellious, but because it might" (Box, 1987:62). Thus, the widening of economic inequality generated by recessions also increases the fear the powerful have of the powerless, and results in increased state coercion of the powerless in the form of rising arrest and incarceration rates (Box, 1987). Recessionary trends might also have an effect on the way police enforce the law, and Box claims that recessions can be linked to an increased number of police crimes, including fabrication of evidence, brutality and the killing of offenders who are perceived as threats to the social order (Box, 1987).

## Economic Trends and Crime

Another trend in radical theory examines the relationship between the rate of surplus value and crime (Lynch et al., 1994; Nalla et al., 1997; Lynch, 1988a, 1987). This research, which links the driving economic forces of capitalism to crime, is explained briefly below.

Surplus value is the value workers produce above what they are paid. Radicals identify this surplus as unpaid labor. For Marx, the rate of surplus value defined the core of capitalist economic systems. On the one hand, the rate of surplus value defined the capitalist's rate of profit, and, on the other, it also demarcated the degree to which labor was exploited. This dialectical relationship or opposition of interest also characterized the general class antagonism between the capitalist and working class. Capitalists derive their profits from the surplus value produced by the working class. Thus, it is in the best interest of capitalists to increase the rate of surplus value as much as possible; meanwhile, workers' interests lie in the opposite direction. One way to do this is to rely on machine labor, which in turn frees workers from the production process and expands the size of the marginal population. A rising rate of surplus value also means that employed laborers receive a smaller share of the surplus they produce. In short, a rising rate of surplus value affects both employed and unemployed laborers and benefits capitalists over workers (Perlow, 1988).

As the rate of surplus value rises, more and more people become economically marginal, which decreases commitment to the conventional order among the employed and unemployed and makes crime an attractive alternative. Lynch (1988a; see also Lynch et al., 1994) has shown that there is a statistically significant relationship between the rate of surplus value and property crime arrest rates in the U.S. This research demonstrates that Marx's key economic concept – the extraction of surplus value – is useful for explaining how capitalist economic systems generate conditions conducive to street crime – especially property crime, the most prevalent type of crime in our society.

## Economic Cycles and Crime

Radical economists have frequently noted that capitalist economies contain long-wave cycles (Gordon, 1978, 1980; Kondratieff, 1935; Mandel, 1979, 1980) that constitute *social structures of accumulation* or distinct ways of pursing profit making and economic stability (Gordon et al., 1982). Social structures of accumulation have three stages: *exploration, consolidation* and *decay. Exploration* consists of vigorous economic activity with high levels of capital investment, strong corporate profits, widespread job opportunities and improvements in average standards of living. At some point, when markets become saturated, and when production outstrips the ability to consume (Veblen, 1964), capitalists begin to *consolidate* holdings in order to retain high levels of profit. As this tactic fails, a *period of decay* occurs during which corporate profits fall, investors become increasingly hesitant, and the job market contracts, resulting in lower wages and a general erosion in living standards. This is the beginning of a downward economic spiral marked by inflation, declines in the rate of profit and intensification of capital disinvestment. Left unchecked, this spiral leads to recession, depression and even economic collapse. Attempts to find a way out of this spiral form the basis for new *periods of exploration* that offer the hopes of increased profitability, which entices capitalists to reenter economic markets (Bowles et al., 1990). This process of exploration, consolidation and decay is continual. These cycles, while interesting in themselves, have been used to provide a qualified and contextualized explanation of the relationship between unemployment and crime.

Until recently, both orthodox and radical criminologists viewed criminogenic forces such as unemployment as *time-invariant* social phenomenon; that is, as factors whose meaning and impact on social life do not change over time (for an exception, see Greenberg, 1977a). For instance, if unemployment has a tendency to increase rates of crime, then whenever unemployment increases by a certain amount, there should be a parallel increase in crime. Carlson and Michalowski (1997), however, have argued that unemployment is more than the simple condition of being without a job: it is a *social experience* whose meaning and impact will be sensitive to the social context within which it occurs. In other words, high levels of unemployment may or may not increase criminality depending upon whether they are associated with growing or contracting economic opportunities. Thus, a period characterized by low official unemployment but also a high proportion of low-wage, dead-end jobs (e.g., the 1990s) may produce nearly as much crime as one with a similar level of unemployment but also with "well-paying, benefit-eligible jobs for those who do work" (Carlson and Michalowski, 1997).

To test this proposition, Carlson and Michalowski (1997) analyzed the relationship between unemployment and crime in the U.S. between 1933 and 1992. They discovered that the impact of unemployment on crime was indeed *historically contingent,* meaning that the relationship changed from one economic stage to another. Specifically, they found that increases in unemployment were *not* linked to increases in homicide, assault, robbery and burglary during the period of consolidation from 1948 to 1966, but *were* strongly linked to those crimes during the period of economic decay that occurred from 1967 to 1979 (Carlson and Michalowski, 1997). These findings suggest that in order to understand the impact that economic conditions such as unemployment have on crime, we must develop a better understanding of how political and social factors intersect with economic ones to create the actual contexts within which criminal behavior will increase or decrease.

## Economic Cycles and Justice

Cyclic economic processes are related not only to the production of crime but also to the production of justice policies. A number of analysts have shown an association between economic long cycles and criminal justice practices (for examples, see Barlow and Barlow, 1995; Barlow et al., 1995a, 1995b, 1996; Greenberg, 1977a; Greenberg and West, 1997; Laffargue and Godefroy; 1989; Lynch et al., 1999; Jankovic, 1977; Michalowski and Carlson, 1999; Parker and Horwitz, 1986). In general these analyses indicate that periods of economic contraction generate harsher punishments and extensive criminalization of the deviant pleasures of the working class and the poor.

The primary focus of the justice system is to control those kinds of crimes most likely to be committed by the least well-off segments of the society. As German sociologist George Rusche noted over 50 years ago: "If penal sanctions are supposed to deter these strata from crime in an effective manner, they must appear even worse than that strata's present living conditions" (1978:3-4). In other words, as economic conditions decline, strict law enforcement and punishment increase as a means of exerting greater control over those who might be tempted to commit the kinds of street crimes that are the focus of the justice system. It is no mere coincidence that as economic conditions in older urban centers in the U.S. decay, and as the overall wages of workers decline, political leaders began to demand ever-increasing levels of punishment and ever more anti-crime legislation. The continually expanding "war on drugs," the criminalization of crack mothers, "three strikes and you're out" laws, registration of sex offenders, court decisions holding drunk driving to be a crime of violence, the declining age at which juveniles can be prosecuted as adult criminals, and America's imprisonment binge are all evidence of an increasingly frantic response to an underlying fear that if the society cannot provide meaningful places for everyone, it will have to face growing rates of crime among the excluded.

## The Limits of Capitalism as an Explanation for Criminality

Each of the political-economic models discussed above employs a contextual approach to crime and each expanded the radical understanding of crime causation. These explanations, however, are also limited by their focus on political-economic forces as the primary explanation for criminal behavior. A number of different kinds of societies experience crime or at least behaviors that are treated as reprehensible. The question is not whether capitalism causes crime but, rather, how the organization of life within specific capitalist societies leads to behaviors that are understood as criminal in those societies. The answer to this question involves more than the economic characteristics of a capitalist society. It involves understanding the dynamic processes through which economic characteristics intersect with other key elements of the human experience. In this sense, crime is not "caused" in any linear sense. Rather, acts defined as crime, like all behaviors, emerge as individuals attempt to negotiate social realities that they did not make, but which they attempt to influence in accordance with the opportunities, beliefs and desires available from the standpoint of the identities they inhabit. Beyond social class, social identities that have received the most attention from radical criminology have been those of gender, race and ethnicity.

# GENDER AND CRIMINALITY

*The Orthodox Approach*

From its beginnings in the nineteenth century until the middle of the twentieth century, "scientific" criminology overlooked the topic of female criminality. By the 1970s, however, the "women's movement" had begun to insert itself into criminology. The publication of two books in 1975 – *Sisters in Crime* by Freda Adler, and *Women and Crime* by Rita Simon – marked a turning point in the study of female criminality. Prior to that time, *if* female criminality was addressed at all, the discussion centered around the *essential* differences between men and women in order to explain the lower rates of female crime. These theories of female criminality tended to focus on what was assumed to be either the biological or psychological *essence* of women (see, for example, Lombroso and Ferrero, 1894; Warker, 1875; Adam, 1914; Bishop, 1931; Glueck and Glueck, 1935; Pollak, 1950). For example, Cesare Lombroso, the founder of "scientific" criminology, contended that female criminals were "born criminals" who exhibited masculine and atavistic (primitive) characteristics. Since far fewer women than men possessed masculine or atavistic characteristics, women were less likely than men to commit crimes. Others, like Pollak (1950), maintained that women committed as much crime as men. He argued that female crime had a "masked" character: meaning that females tended to commit crimes that were difficult to detect or were easily hidden (e.g., shoplifting, abortion, poisoning, domestic thefts). Pollak also believed that the masked character of female criminality was related to women's deceitful nature. This deceitfulness resulted from the interaction of social and biological factors essential to being female. A variety of other psychological, psychiatric, chromosomal and genetic explanations have been suggested as well (for a review, see Chesney-Lind and Shelden, 1992).

Simon (1975) and Adler (1975) rejected these explanations of female criminality, and instead focused on female social roles, thereby moving the study of women and crime from individual and biological explanations to sociological and contextual frameworks. Observing an apparent rise in female crime in that period, both Simon and Adler argued that increased liberation of women from traditional sex roles widened their opportunities for female crime. Both theorists applied the theory of "sex convergence" to explain male and female criminality. This approach suggests that as females were liberated from sex roles that defined housekeeping, childrearing and subservience to men as the proper place of women, and became more like their male counterparts – particularly in their participation in the economic, political and public life of the society – women's participation in crime would become more similar to that of men (the crime rates of the sexes would converge).

While Simon (1975) and Adler (1975) agreed that sex convergence would reduce differences in male and female criminality, they disagreed as to just how this would happen. Adler argued that the increase in female criminality was concentrated in violent crimes. In Adler's view, the women's movement led to the masculinization of female behavior, which increased aggressiveness among women and led them to commit more violent crimes. Simon, however, argued that the increase in female criminality was restricted to property crime, particularly occupationally-related theft such as white collar crime. Both supported their contentions by analyzing increases in the number of Uniform Crime Report arrests for women.

Adler (1975) and Simon (1975) made an important contribution by directing attention away from biological and psychological theories of female criminality and toward the social construction of gender roles as the explanation for female patterns of crime. Subsequent research, however, has called into question some of their underlying assumptions about the convergence of male and female patterns of crime. First, there has been no significant increase in female criminality relative to male criminality, especially in terms of violent crime (Messerschmidt, 1986). Where there have been increases in female crime, these have been in the areas of nonviolent and non-occupational crime (Messerschmidt, 1986; Steffensmeier, 1981). Second, research that specifically examined the link between "liberation" and crime among women using survey research methods found no support for the contention that women who held more liberated beliefs were more likely to commit crime than women with traditional beliefs (Figueria-McDonough, 1984; James and Thorton, 1980; see also Chesney-Lind and Shelden, 1992).

Fairly early in the development of radical criminology, a number of radical and feminist theorists contested Simon (1975) and Adler's (1975) claim that the liberation of women from so-called traditional sex roles is criminogenic (Klein, 1979; Klein and Kress, 1976; Box and Hale, 1983a, 1983b). Rather, they contended, the forces that influence female criminality are embedded in society's social and economic context.

## Radical Approaches to Understanding Female Criminality

The central concern in the study of female criminality is not explaining why women commit crime, but explaining why they commit significantly fewer crimes than men. Several radical theorists have taken up this challenge employing Marxist-feminist theory. Marxist-feminists contend that the sexual division of labor and social class position interact to determine a woman's position in society. In this view, the sexual division of labor and the construction of female bodies and female sexuality become important targets of capitalist social control as outlined by Engels (1968/1972) in *The Origins of the Family, Private Property and the State*. Thus, control over women and their productive powers is constructed and maintained through the economic system (see Messerschmidt 1986:10-11 for a review).

A number of radical criminologists have applied a Marxist-feminist perspective to the problem of female criminality (Klein, 1982, 1979; Klein and Kress 1976; Weiss, 1978; Box, 1984; Box and Hale 1983a, 1983b; Balkan et al., 1980; Danner, 1996, 1991; see also, Greenberg, 1995). Balkan et al. (1980), for instance, argued that women commit certain types of crimes because the sex-specific socialization of women limits their skills, self-image and access to criminal opportunities in ways that reduce female criminality. These factors not only exclude women from ready participation in street crime, they also minimize the likelihood of upper-world crime. Since opportunities to participate in business and industry at levels beyond the shop floor or the secretary's desk were historically rare for women, they have had few opportunities to commit white collar and corporate crime. Thus, the crimes women commit most often (e.g., shoplifting, forgery, fraud, abortion, "promiscuity") center on the opportunities and/or pressures associated with their roles as wives/mothers/homemakers (Balkan et al., 1980). The typical crimes of women reflect their lesser power in American society. Even the violence women engage in most often is an expression of their social roles. Most often female violence victimizes family members, particularly children, since children often represent the only people over whom a woman holds power. Additionally, female violence is much more likely to involve the use of household items such as knives rather than guns, which are more typically male weapons of choice (Messerschmidt, 1986).

In Schur's (1984) view, to be a woman in American society is to occupy a devalued status because she is *objectified* and *commodified*. First, women are seen as sexual objects. Women become the targets of the male gaze, continually being scrutinized for their outward physical appearance. Second, women are constructed as objects that can be *acquired*. When women internalize this objectified and commodified view of themselves, according to Schur, they will become submissive to men, and will therefore commit the types of crimes that fit their stereotype – nonviolent, powerless and sex-related crimes (e.g., prostitution, adultery, abortion, infanticide). From a Marxist-feminist perspective this devalued role of women is rooted in the organization of the productive system. This system first of all assigns the work of social reproduction (caring for children, tending homes, preparing food, etc.) to women, thereby limiting their impact on the public sphere (e.g., business, industry, education), and second of all assigns them primarily to subordinate positions when they are allowed into public spheres.

Hagan and his associates (see Hagan et al., 1979, 1985, 1987) have argued that the relationship between gender and delinquency can be linked to the forms of power and control exerted by the family, which in turn are related to the economic roles fulfilled by parents (see also Singer and Levine, 1988; Hill and Atkinson, 1988; for criticism, see Morash and Chesney-Lind, 1991). This theory is closely related to Colvin and Pauly's (1983) work. The resulting power-control theory implies that "dominance and control in the household organizes delinquent conduct by gender" (Singer and Levine, 1988:627). In this view, gender control is related to family patterns of control that vary according to the family's social class. Parents, in effect, reaffirm their own power relationships by the way they control their children (Hagan et al., 1987). Mothers locked into subservient roles attempt to raise daughters with similar values; they socialize their children to accept a sex-role structure in which women are subservient to the needs and interests of men (Hagan et al, 1987). This means keeping the daughter close to home, teaching her domestic chores and reaffirming domestic consumption patterns, all of which insures conformity among young women.

In patriarchal households, the father is the authority figure, while mothers remain relatively powerless except in relation to daughters and young sons. In these unbalanced households, the father is in a position of authority because of his economic status, while the mother is either "unemployed" in the traditional sense (for criticism of this view, see Warring, 1990) or employed in a low-status occupation. In these situations, the mother's control over all but the youngest male offspring is minimal, giving sons in male-dominated households greater freedom to deviate than daughters. In balanced households, mother and fathers are both in positions of authority in the workplace. Workplace equality translates into household equality between mothers' and fathers' authority. This should create egalitarian attitudes toward the control of male and female children, decreasing differences in criminality among male and female offspring.

Empirical analyses of this position support many of the contentions of power-control theory (Hagan et al., 1987, 1985; Singer and Levine, 1988; Hill and Atkinson, 1988). Singer and Levine discovered, however, that boys in balanced households were more likely than boys in unbalanced households to become involved in delinquency (though they confirmed a number of other hypotheses associated with power-control theory). In sum, this research demonstrates that the type of informal social control exercised over juveniles is related to economic positions occupied by parents *through its influence on gender roles in the family.* That is, social control techniques employed within the family "reflect gender divisions found in the workplace..." (Hill and Atkinson, 1988:144). Thus, the production of different patterns for male and female delinquency can be explained with reference to how the economic context and workplace position of parents creates gender-balanced or gender-imbalanced patterns of socialization within the family.

Marxist-feminist approaches assign a significant – and often primary – role to the economic organization of society in their efforts to understand the difference between male and female patterns of criminality. With the possible exception of Messerschmidt's (1986, 1993) work, what these theories do not explore is the ways in which gender (or other elements of identity such as race and ethnicity) influenced the production of crime in ways that were either independent from, or at least not subsidiary to, economic organization.

## From Marxist-Feminism to Socialist-Materialist Feminism

By the 1980s, a heated debate emerged between feminists and Marxists over the role of gender in both society and social analysis. Feminists increasingly argued that the Marxist emphasis on economic organization and social class as the "base" of society failed to adequately appreciate the central role that gender relations played in shaping social life. In a now-classic essay, "The Unhappy Marriage of Marxism and Feminism," Heidi Hartmann (1981:3) wrote: "The woman question has never been the 'feminist question.'" The feminist question is directed at the causes of sexual inequality between women and men, of male dominance over women. Most Marxist analyses of women's position take as their question the relationship of women to the economic system, rather than that of women to men, apparently assuming the latter will be explained by their discussion of the former."

According to the new wave of feminists, the problem was that in every society important elements of the experience of women *as women* could not be explained by the economic organization of society. This approach was animated by both the recognition that the dominance of men over women predated capitalism, and the realization that the development of "socialism" in many Eastern European countries, while it improved the access of women to paid work outside the home, did little to alter their subsidiary position within the household (Firestone, 1971). Indeed, some feminists argued that the position of women had deteriorated under socialism because they were now subject to the "double day": work in the factory, shop or office, and then all of the other responsibilities of wives and mothers at home (Heitlinger, 1979). This led to the development of what Young (1981) has termed a "dual systems" approach to social analysis. This approach posits two separate organizing systems: organized economic relations (e.g., feudalism, capitalism, socialism) that affect the relations of production, social class formation and class conflict; and gender relations, specifically patriarchy, which organized the dominance of men over women. These two systems interact and influence each other (for alternatives, see Hennessy and Ingraham, 1997).

The debates surrounding the respective roles of political economy and patriarchy in the organization of society significantly affect how radicals treat gender in the study of crime. This dual-systems approach is described below.

## A Dual-Systems Model of Gender and Crime

The work of James Messerschmidt (1986) provides a good example of a dual-systems approach to the question of gender and criminality. Following the Marxist anthropologist Marvin Harris (1986), Messerschmidt contends that economistic theories that divide society into an economic system and a social/cultural system suffer severe limitations. Messerschmidt posits that society really has three spheres: the economic, the social and the biological (i.e., the gendered reproduction of biological and social life). In this approach, social life is shaped and determined by both economic production and gendered reproduction. In other words, the individual's place in society is not merely a consequence of class but of the interaction between class and gender (i.e., how a society constructs sexual divisions). Thus, the role of women is not explicable in terms of class alone. In Messerschmidt's view, capitalism is not only a class society but a patriarchal (male-dominated) society as well.

In this view, capitalists control the labor of workers, while men control the economic and biological labor power of women. Thus, society contains both class and gender mechanisms of control. The subordination of women to both gender and class control may explain why women commit fewer and less serious crimes then men: "Individuals are enmeshed in class and gender structures that organize the way people think about their circumstances and devise solutions to act upon them. Gender and class shape one's possibilities... Criminality is related, then, to the interaction of patriarchy and capitalism and the structural possibilities this interaction creates" (Messerschmidt, 1986:41).

In patriarchial capitalist society, women commit fewer crimes than men because women are socially, economically and biologically less powerful. Women are isolated within the family and have fewer opportunities to commit crimes requiring power (e.g., white collar and corporate crime) than men (Daly,

1989). Furthermore, women are denied access to illegitimate means of success (i.e., street crime) since illegitimate opportunities are, like legitimate opportunity, controlled by men (Messerschmidt, 1986). In addition, women are less likely to receive social support for their violent actions (Braithwaite and Daly, 1994). Thus, Messerschmidt argues that "oppression and powerlessness in both the home and the labor market... generates specific forms of criminality on the part of women" (1986:72). Since women are less powerful than men, they tend to commit less serious, nonviolent crimes that reinforce gender stereotypes and gender hierarchies (West and Fenstermaker, 1995; West and Zimmerman, 1987; for a critique of Messerschmidt, see Schwendinger and Schwendinger, 1988; see also Messerschmidt's reply, 1988).

What distinguishes the socialist/feminist line of reasoning from more economy-based approaches is that many of the factors that keep women from committing crime are related to their position in the society *as women*, not just as workers. Thus, the socialization of women to be less aggressive than men, the greater control exerted over the out-of-home activities of girls than of boys, and the lack of social support for such things as fighting between girls as compared to fighting between boys, are seen as expressions of a systemic female subordination that exists, and has existed, independently of capitalism, even though it may express itself in particular ways in capitalist society.

## Masculinities and Crime

Feminists have long recognized that "maleness" is "normal" in patriarchal social systems, and all other categories and social behaviors are measured against the "normal male" (Rosaldo and Lamphere, 1974; Schur, 1984). This "male normalcy" is clearly evident in both the lack of attention devoted to female criminality and the *manner in which* it has been studied. In other words, if males are normal so are their high rates of offending, meaning that low rates of female offending require special explanations. Consider making the reverse assumption: that femaleness is normal. The question we might ask would be turned around: "Why are men so much more criminal than women?" In other words, the quiet operation of patriarchal concepts has for a long time shaped how criminologists – including many radical criminologists – have thought about the question of female criminality.

Feminist theories of crime have contributed considerably to explaining *differences* between male and female criminality (see, for example, Daly, 1989; Cain, 1990; Carlen, 1990; Daly and Chesney-Lind, 1988; Chesney-Lind, 1989; DeKeseredy and Hinch, 1991), and to establishing an understanding that gender mattered when criminologists thought about crime – at least when *some* criminologists thought about crime (Daly, 1994a). However, while gender construction became an important consideration relative to female offending (Simpson and Ellis, 1995), it continued to be neglected when criminologists examined patterns of male offending. Part of the reason for this is that when feminists turned their attention to crime, they were more likely to focus on the role of women in crime, either as offenders or victims. While male criminologists typically focused on male crime, the majority were relatively unschooled in feminist theory. Although many feminist criminologists considered how women became women, far fewer criminologists considered how men – the most criminal gender – became men. In other words, the construction of masculinity – or "maleness" – remained, for a time, an unexplored cause of crime.

According to Connell (1987, 1989, 1991, 1995), understanding social life requires attention to the ways that male identities (masculinities), as well as female identities, are constructed. In this view, there are numerous masculine identities, and the specific male identities we observe in a given society are the ongoing products of race, class and gender relations. With this recognition it becomes possible to examine the role played by historical, cultural, racial and class forces in the construction of masculinity. Using the concept of masculinities, Messerschmidt (1993) suggested that understanding patterns of crime requires attention to how men become men and how some men become the kinds of men who are more likely to commit crime.

Masculinities are identities, constructed as individuals internalize attitudes and behaviors they associate with other "normal males," and as they act out these identities in front of social and political audiences who respond either approvingly or disapprovingly. It is important to point out that the term "masculinity" is a generalization. In reality, masculinities are multidimensional, varying along cultural, class, race and ethnic dimensions, meaning that at any one time there are a variety of masculine identities being constructed within society. These identities, however, may share common dimensions associated with race, class or ethnic membership.

Masculine identity construction is an integrative process, involving micro (individual), middle-range (peers, communities) and macro (economic, racial, class and gender) structures and institutions. The construction of these identities demonstrates the impact of structures on the formation of individual psychology and behavior. Through masculine identity construction, individuals adapt their behavior and attitudes to reflect (and at times modify) class, race, cultural and ethnic structures that define maleness and the behavioral expectations associated with occupying a historically and culturally situated, race-class masculine identity.

This contextualized understanding of masculinity differs from the more usual biological and stereotypical notions of maleness (often regarded as *machismo*). From a biological perspective, males differ from females in terms of chromosomes, hormones and genitalia; male chromosomes and hormones, in particular, are believed to play an important role in male aggression and behavioral patterns. The problem with this view is that male aggressiveness varies both historically and cross-culturally, while biological differences among males across these dimensions are relatively constant. For example, in a recent White House lecture (C-Span, March 6, 1998), respected scientist Stephen Hawkins noted that there has been no change in human chromosomes over the past 10,000 years. Thus, a focus on the unchanging biology of maleness is a poor starting point for explaining historically variable male behavior. Unlike biology, the social construction of maleness – what it means to accept the identity of "male" – is a historically variable and highly contextual phenomenon that can better contribute to understanding what it is about men that make them so criminal. The following discussion of rape provides one example of how we can employ the idea of "masculinities" to the question of male criminality.

## Rape and Masculinity

### The Historical Context

Today, rape is commonly viewed by feminists as an expression of male power and dominance over females (Brownmiller, 1975). Indeed, this interpretation may be useful for understanding the prevalence of rape in modern societies such as the U.S. However, this view is less useful for explaining historical and cross-cultural variations in rape, or disparities in rape patterns (and the meaning of rape) across males from different social class or racial backgrounds. Historically, for instance, rape was a rare event in male-dominated hunting and gathering and horticultural societies (Messerschmidt, 1993; see also Sanday, 1981; Porter, 1986; Messerschmidt, 1986, 1988). In these societies, male domination was so well entrenched that rape would undermine the legitimacy of male rule (Messerschmidt, 1993), and therefore rape was not part of the construction of masculinity. There also appear to be tremendous differences in the prevalence of rape across cultures (Messerschmidt, 1993:48). If, for example, male rape behavior was either biologically programmed or the automatic result of male domination, these historical and cultural differences in rape would be much less dramatic. In contrast to the constant pressure to commit rape proposed by biologically based or male-dominance explanations for rape, the masculinity perspective posits wide variations in the historical and cultural construction of masculine identity (and within cultures, by race and class), making it useful for exploring variations in rape patterns.

## A Contemporary Example

Gary LaFree's (1989, 1985, 1980) examinations of how official reactions to rape vary according to the victim's and offender's race/ethnicity provides a good example of how masculine identities affect justice. LaFree found, for example, that white females were more likely to be protected by law than black females, especially when the supposed offender was black (on the behavior of law, see Black, 1976; see also Chambliss and Seidman, 1982). In turn, black offenders were more likely than white offenders to be prosecuted, convicted and sentenced to prison, especially when the accused was white. This pattern of treatment can be explained with reference to masculinity theory and perceptions of masculinity held by others. The process involves the role that stereotypes of black male sexuality play in their treatment by the criminal justice system (for discussions of black male masculinity as perceived by others, see Hernton, 1988; hooks, 1992; Staples, 1982). In short, black males do not necessarily have to behave any differently from white males in order for black male masculine identity to have an effect upon their treatment in the criminal justice system. Indeed, there are a variety of reasons to believe that assumptions about racially-specific masculine identities have an impact on how the sexually assaultive behavior of black and white males is treated.

To begin, views of white male masculinity are more favorable than assumptions concerning black male masculinity; this difference helps to protect white males from prosecution. An example is the case of sexual harassment. Many women admit to being sexually harassed in the workplace, yet their claims are often dismissed by workplace or other officials, and are often addressed informally rather than criminally even when the charges are serious (e.g., forced sex), especially when the purported offender is a white male with economic power. In effect, part of the construction of white male masculinity includes the idea that their sexual harassment is not really all that serious, as was alleged by Paula Jones in her accusations against former President Bill Clinton (see Gruber and Morgan, 2004; Painter, 1992; Burnham, 1992; Crenshaw, 1992; Williams, 1992; Lubiano, 1992; McKay, 1992; Bhabha, 1992; Stansell, 1992; Morrison, 1992b; and see generally, Morrison, 1992a). Thus, class and race play a role in the non-response to and construction of white male masculinity.

The connection between class and the construction of white male masculinity can be further exposed by examining differences between the kinds of sexual harassment corporate executives and shop-floor men practice (Gurber and Bjorn, 1987; Messerschmidt, 1993). The kinds of men who become corporate executives typically have learned a style of masculinity that is simultaneously less overtly aggressive and yet more able to call upon institutional power to help compel female employees (usually subordinates) into complying with the demands for sexual favors. Many working-class men, by contrast, have internalized images of masculinity that direct them to use more aggressive strategies such as groping or obscene, suggestive comments with their female co-workers. Nor can these men call upon powerful institutional resources to either compel women to comply with their desires or protect themselves against claims of harassment by victimized women. Thus, while the strategies of executives are no less harassing than those of shop-floor men, the behavior of the shop-floor man is more likely to be quickly labeled as sexual harassment.

The study of masculinities offers useful directions not only for reconceptualizing explanations of criminality, which is largely a male activity, but also for understanding both criminality and the response to crime. The concept of masculinities allows us to situate male crime in the same way that criminologists have situated female crime – at the place where gender, race, class and culture intersect.

## In Sum

This chapter reviewed both radical political-economic and identity-based theories of crime causation. The following chapter approaches the question of crime causation from another angle by examining parallels between radical and orthodox criminology. What we will see is that the etiological explanations used by many orthodox criminologists are actually unreferenced footnotes to Marx insofar as they emphasize the economic causes of crime.

# SEVEN.
# RADICALIZING ORTHODOX THEORIES OF CRIME:
# STRAIN, SOCIAL CONTROL AND LIFE COURSE

This chapter explores how orthodox criminological theories can be radicalized. Many orthodox explanations of crime have unexplored radical implications that emerge when they are linked to broader structural and contextual explanations of crime that incorporate race, class and gender relationships and power hierarchies. Below, we explore the radical potential of strain theory, control theory, life course analysis and the theory of cultural and social capital.

## Strain Theory

According to Robert Merton (1979:130), strain theory describes how "some social structures exert a definite pressure upon certain persons in society to engage in non-conformist rather than conformist conduct." The pressures Merton examined arise when there is a gap between socially induced desires (success goals) and access to legitimate means for satisfying those desires; when there is, in the words of strain theory, a disjunction between culturally-induced aspirations (goals) and the means available to achieve those goals. This disjunction creates a condition called *anomie*. These propositions are derived from several important observations about American society.

People typically pursue goals set forth by their culture. In the U.S., financial security and/or material success is an overriding life goal for many people (see Adorno, 1991; Messner and Rosenfeld, 1994; Michalowski, 1985; Varenne, 1977; for an analysis of the selling of culture, see Herbert, 1996; Zelnick, 1996, Kendall, 1996). This goal is more than a "natural" desire for material goods; it is the product of an elaborate system of cultural beliefs and values that support material success as a measure of personal worth. These beliefs are also supported by an enormous advertising industry designed to keep material desires at a feverishly high pitch (Henry,

1965; Varenne, 1977). Cultural institutions (e.g., schools, media, government, etc.) socialize people from all classes, races and genders to accept and expect the same level of material success (Henry, 1965). The means for achieving success, however, are limited and unevenly distributed, meaning that some portion of the population will be unable to meet success goals because its access to legitimate means for success are blocked. In short, the nature of the U.S. social structure inhibits many from achieving highly-valued cultural goals through legitimate means. In Merton's view, some of the people who experience significant gaps between their goals and their means resort to an alternative strategies for achieving success goals. For some, this involves using criminal means to achieve goals. Others turn to alcohol, drugs, depression, or suicide in response to the failure to achieve their success goals.

Radicals criminologists would agree with Merton's suggestion that structured inequalities prevalent in American society create pressures to commit crime. For radicals, however, there is a broader question that needs to be addressed: How can the origins of these cultural goals and the limitation of available means to achieve them be explained? Answering this question requires that we examine the relationship between the dominant cultural goals and the economic, class, gender and racial structures that influence what kinds of pathways to these goals people will enjoy.

## The Origins of Cultural Goals and Means

Strain theorists typically do not explore how American culture came to embrace materialist visions of success. For radicals, contemporary success goals can be explained, in part, by analyzing the underlying dynamics of capitalist economies. In order for capitalism to function effectively it must sell most of the commodities it produces. By the late nineteenth century, capitalism's ability to produce goods outstripped people's desire to consume them, generating the need for methods (i.e., advertising) to stimulate consumer demands (Greider, 1997; Ewen, 1988; Henry, 1965; Ohmann et al., 1996). Advertising is indeed an effective mechanism for stimulating the desire to consume. For example, today corporations spend about $250 billion a year in the United States in an effort to ensure that consumer demand will remain at profitable levels (Fish, 2003). To put this in perspective, consider that in 2005 these expenditures exceeded the total amount of money the U.S. government budgeted for agriculture, commerce, education, energy, health and human services, justice, labor and transportation (U.S. Office of Management and Budget, 2005). Some people have little chance of satisfying even a small portion of their heightened consumer aspirations. The lack of means to satisfy material desires is not randomly distributed through the society, but is shaped by the forces of class, race and gender, which, in turn, affect an individual's access to legitimate means for success.

In capitalist economies, the means of consumption are distributed unequally as a result of capitalist market dynamics. As a system for organizing production, capitalist labor markets have three characteristics. First, they are motivated by the desire of employers to pay the least they can to obtain the labor they need. Second, they ensure that some categories of workers will earn much more than others (e.g., skilled vs. unskilled labor). Third, they require a "reserve army" of unemployed labor to keep workers from using labor shortages to obtain increased wages. This creates one of the underlying contradictions of capitalist consumer societies: they require that everyone desires the products of capitalist industry, but they must also be organized in ways that ensure not everyone can enjoy these products. As a consequence, some people experience "strain," which Merton defined as the psychological cost of fueling aspirations to a feverish pitch.

## Adding Opportunity to the Strain Argument

Richard Cloward and Lloyd Ohlin (1960) expanded Merton's view by examining the role opportunity plays in conditioning peoples' abilities to respond to structurally-induced strain. Cloward and Ohlin (1960) recognized that *anomie* generated a variety of feelings including: discontent and frustration, indignation and problems of maladjustment, alienation and feelings of unjust deprivation that undermine the legitimacy of the social order (see also Merton, 1979). While many people might experience these feelings, they do not call forth the same reactions; for some, they might lead to theft, drug use or even an increased reliance on religion. Instead of positing an individualistic theory to explain these different reactions, Cloward and Ohlin suggested that responses were affected by the kinds of opportunities people from different classes enjoy. Consequently, they argued that crime would be most likely to occur among the lower classes, where the pressure of these strains are assumed to be the greatest and where individuals have a greater probability of encountering others who can provide them with the opportunity for street crime (see also Kornhauser, 1978). Cloward and Ohlin, however, also note that merely having the desire to commit crime is not sufficient. Many crimes of economic gain require access to criminal subgroups. Some individuals may be accepted into deviant youth groups or criminal gangs while others are not, and those who are will be far more likely to engage in criminal activity. While Cloward and Ohlin do not explicitly explore the gendered nature of admission into criminal subgroups, their proposition that criminality requires opportunity suggests that many pathways to crime may be more open for males than females.

## Strain, Class, Race and Gender

In their treatment of strain theory, Messner and Rosenfeld (1994:10) contend that:

> ...persistent economic inequality in the United States...[is] best characterized not as a departure from fundamental cultural values but rather as an expression of them. Despite the *universalistic component* of the American Dream, the basic logic of this cultural ethos presupposes high levels of inequality. A competitive allocation of monetary rewards requires both winners and losers; and "winning" and "losing" have meaning only when rewards are distributed unequally.

In short, "The American Dream . . . has a dark side that must be considered in any serious effort to uncover the social sources of crime" (Messner and Rosenfeld, 1994:10). The idea that the American dream has a "dark side" is consistent with radical discussions of crime. But what is this "dark side?" And how is it related to structural inequalities that have a differential impact on people situated in different race, class and gender positions? These issues are arguably *the most important* causes of strain in American society, and the most important for radical versions of strain theory.

In contrast to orthodox strain theories, a radical approach redirects attention toward the interaction among the political-economic characteristics of a given social system, the cultural construction and communication of desired goals within that system, and the origins of unequal distribution of opportunities to achieve those goals. This focus provides a rich and contextually grounded framework for exploring the ways in which structural strain conducive to criminality emerges within specific societies.

From a radical perspective, structural strain is a consequence of the particular class, race and gender divisions within a society because it is through these elements of hierarchy and identity that differential access to culturally-approved success is allocated. Social class location increases access to legitimate means for members of economically and socially advantaged classes, and reduces access for those in less advantaged classes. Indeed, *unequal access* to opportunity *is the essential character of social class divisions.* This means that legitimate opportunities for success will be most constrained at the lower end of the socioeconomic spectrum, and it is here that the strain between culturally-induced aspirations and culturally-approved means will be greatest. This does not mean, however, that the experience of structural strain is limited to the poor. As we discuss below, those from more advantaged social groupings also may also experience crime-inducing strain, but because they have different opportunities to commit crime than the poor, the criminality of the middle and upper classes differs from that of the poor.

Access to the means for fulfilling culturally-approved goals is shaped by the gender, racial and ethnic structuring of a society, as well as its class dynamics. The racial hierarchy that exists in the U.S., for instance, intensifies class inequalities by exposing African Americans and other ethnic minorities of color to additional barriers between themselves and the legitimate means for success. In the narrowest sense, these barriers include: restricted access to educational institutions, especially high-quality institutions (Gibbs, 1988); high-income occupations; and financial resources such as mortgages to buy homes and loans to start businesses. In a broader sense, these barriers reflect the institutional dynamics of racism and segregation (Massey and Denton, 1993, 1988; Massey and Hajnal, 1995). From a strain perspective, then, higher rates of offending among racial and ethnic minorities in the U.S. can be seen as a product of racially intensified gaps between desired goals and the means to attain them.

Strain theory has led to particularly curious attempts to apply its premises to women. As discussed in chapter 6, some theorists have argued that the feminist movement increased rates of offending among women because it elevated women's desires for economic success. This purportedly created increased strain for women since their economic opportunities, such as access to well-paying jobs and professional work, did not keep pace with increased aspirations. For radicals, this explanation is misleading on several accounts (Lynch, 1996). First, it misdirects attention to, devalues and blames the women's movement for crime (Chesney-Lind and Shelden, 1992). The feminist movement did not create the disjuncture between women's desires for success and the means to satisfy them. Rather, the problem is that the interaction of the *economic system* and the *gender structure* of American society created a labor market resistant to the full integration of women into the workplace. Thus, women frequently encounter situations where their legitimate economic aspirations are blocked by structural features of a gendered labor market that still divides jobs into "women's work" and "men's work," and typically assigns higher salaries to the work done by men, regardless of the skill or difficulty involved (Oakley, 1974; Warring, 1990).

Second, the claim that the feminist and women's movements form the basis for increased female criminality misrepresents the real effects of these movements. For instance, feminism has been far more influential in reordering life priorities among white, middle- and upper-class women than among working-class women and women of color (Brewer, 1989; 1993; Joseph, 1997), and there has been little increase in crimes by upper-class and middle-class white women (Simon, 1997). What appears to be more significant is that the feminization of poverty and the overall declining living standard associated with service jobs that typically employ working-class women. These conditions have placed many women in the kinds of fearful economic conditions that can generate either crimes of survival – such as petty theft, prostitution or bad check writing – or expressions of hopelessness such as alcoholism and drug addiction (Schur, 1984). Thus, even if the material desires of working-class women were wholly unaffected by the feminist movement, from the perspective of strain theory these women would still experience a growing gap between their desires and their access to the legitimate means to obtain them.

The third difficulty in applying strain theory to the gendered difference in crime is that it fails to account for the differential structure of crime opportunities available to men and women. One of the contributions made by Cloward and Ohlin (1960) was their observation that individuals need both the *opportunities* and the *skills* to commit crime before crime will occur. Cloward and Ohlin's analysis was focused primarily on male delinquency, but if we take a radical perspective we can extend their observation to female criminality as well. As discussed in chapter 6, the cultural structuring of gender in the U.S. leads to a variety of behavioral differences between women and men. To the extent that women are socialized to respond to the experience of frustration, disappointment or anger differently from men, they will develop distinct skills and have different opportunities for addressing the disjuncture they might experience between means and goals. These different responses, however, may not lead in the direction of increased criminality, but may lead to maladaptations such as depression or drug use, or to increased reliance on friends and family as mutual support networks, or to increased devotion to religion.

The application of strain theory to female criminality is a prime example of how orthodox criminologists employ theories developed by observing *male behavior* to explain *all behavior*. This approach ignores the fundamentally gendered nature of social behavior (Daly, 1994a). Radical interpretations of strain theory must remain alert to the gendered origins of theories of criminal behavior before assuming they can be readily applied to both men and women. In this case, for instance, this means paying attention to the ways in which the gendered patterning of behavior can alter the way social forces such as structured strain affect people's propensity to commit crime. The evidence suggests that males, more than females, are socialized to respond to structured strains by resorting to delinquency and/or crime to achieve frustrated material goals or to substitute goals such as "respect" within street culture (Anderson, 1990; Bourgois, 1996; Messerschmidt, 1997, 1993).

In sum, the underlying thrust of strain theory is consistent with the radical contention that crime is "a property of the social system in which... individuals are enmeshed" (Cloward and Ohlin, 1960:211). Strain theorists call attention to crime as a regular, institutionalized feature of a social system characterized by extensive stratification and inequality, and they oppose depicting the causes of crime as residing with the individual (Taylor et al., 1973; Bernard, 1987). Strain theorists, however, typically do not specify the structural sources of strain – differential opportunity or inequality – in the same way that radicals would (Colvin and Pauly, 1983). Additionally, strain theorists give little attention to the crimes of the middle and upper classes, the gendered nature of crime patterns or the ways in which race and ethnicity can affect the experience of structured strain. For instance, Messner and Rosenfeld (1994) say little about how class, race or gender dynamics shape access to legitimate opportunities for success or how they can influence the *kinds of crime* people might commit should they find themselves the subjects of strain. We now explore this last point further by considering how strain might be related to the crimes committed by those who would appear to enjoy the greatest access to the means to success.

## Strain and Crimes of the Powerful

The study of corporate crime has demonstrated that corporations commit crime or behave in socially injurious ways in order to reduce costs and increase their profit margins. This is achieved through acts such as: failing to comply with safety regulations (Aulette and Michalowski, 1996);

violating environmental regulations (Barnett, 1994; Block and Scarpitti, 1985; Kauzlarich, 1997, 1995; Kauzlarich and Kramer, 1998); engaging in predatory market practices such as price-fixing and violating anti-trust laws, such as Microsoft's efforts to keep Netscape out of the Web-browser market in the 1990s (Block and Bernard, 1988; Simon, 1999; Friedrichs, 1996b; Frank and Lynch, 1992; Jameison, 1994); false advertising and bribery of government officials (Michalowski, 1985); and inflation of stock value through false reporting of revenue (Tillman, 2005; Fox, 2003). These actions can be seen as resulting from intense competition over market share and profits. A particular corporation (e.g., Microsoft) may be performing very well, and may even be a leader within its industry. Yet its managers may still experience the strain generated by a competitive market environment where more growth is never enough. As Mankoff (1980:142) noted:

> The wealthy capitalist, if living beyond his or her means, may be tempted to engage in stock fraud, drink to excess, or even commit suicide. The poor can respond to a similar situation by engaging in the latter two activities, but have no opportunity to consider the first. Crime and deviance are a reflection of strains and opportunities, and one should expect them at all levels of society, albeit in different forms and quantities.

The same is true of corporations. Corporations that spend beyond their means in order to expand, create new products or defeat competitors may generate internal work climates where both upper- and middle-level managers are tempted to circumvent regulations designed to protect workers, consumers or the environment. Thus, while the types of opportunities and strain vary by class, they are nevertheless present across all social classes. Taylor et al. (1974:452) make this argument when they claim that "both working-class and upper class crime...are real features of a society involved in a struggle for property, wealth, and economic self-aggrandizement." These views are typical of radical political-economic analysts, who generally agree that the incentive structures of capitalist societies produce pressures to commit crimes across all social classes (see chapter 5). Thus, while most strain theorists have not explicitly analyzed crimes of the powerful, there is nothing within strain theory that negates its applicability to the study of crime by corporate and political elites (Clinard and Yeager, 1978; Passas, 1990).

It is also important to address how race and gender structures affect the relationship between strain and upper-world crime. For example, corporate and political criminals are not only from advantaged *classes*, they are also *typically male and white*. The construction of gender and race in America has systematically denied minorities and women access to the kinds of positions that would, first, expose them to the strains that could lead to upper-world criminality, and, second, provide them with the opportunities and skills necessary to commit corporate or political crimes. Thus, women and racial minorities are underrepresented among corporate and political criminals. This is not necessarily because, as people, they have any less potential than white male managers to commit such offenses (unless, of course, one wants to argue that white males are genetically predisposed to commit this kind of crime!). Instead, it's because the structure of gender roles and race relations in the U.S. substantially reduces the access of women and minorities to power.

In sum, by qualifying and elaborating strain theory, we can specify two areas of compatibility between strain theory and radical criminology. First, both view the cultural image of material goods as markers of success to be an important factor promoting criminal behavior in America. Radicals would deepen this argument by exploring how these aspirations are logical expressions of capitalist political-economic relationships. In doing so, they would also examine how the specific construction and character of these strains change with changes in labor force characteristics and in consumer culture. Second, both views recognize that unequal distribution of opportunities for success and incentives toward crime are related to social class. Radicals, however, extend the strain argument by relating the differential distribution of opportunity and incentive to class, race and gender structures found in American society. With these elaborations, strain theory provides a potentially fruitful framework for an inquiry into criminality at a social-system level. We next turn our attention to the radical potentials within control theory.

## CONTROL THEORY

Control theory became a popular explanation for criminality during the 1970s. This approach emphasizes the importance of families in producing law-abiding citizens by creating effective bonds between parents and children. The popularity of control theory has several sources. First, control theory makes intuitive sense to many people because it restates an underlying characteristic of social behavior – that we are generally less likely to harm people or things that we care about than those that either hold no importance for us or toward which we feel hostility. Second, control theory has been particularly appealing in a conservative political climate that embraces the idea that ineffective families are at the heart of most of America's social problems (Bennett et al., 1996). Finally, by focusing on family failure as the cause of street crimes among the poorer classes, control theory validates a hidden assumption of the middle class – that they are better parents than the poor. Given these characteristics, it would seem that control theory would have little radical potential. However, this is not the case.

## Control Theory: Assumptions

The central argument of control theory is that "delinquent acts result when the individual's bond to society is weak or broken" (Hirschi, 1969:16). For Hirschi, the question is not so much "why do people commit crime?" but "why don't people commit crime?"

What is a bond? How is it maintained? In theory, bonds form when adequate social controls exist. These bonds take two forms, one positive, one negative. The positive bond is called an *attachment*, symbolized by the closeness and ties people develop with family and friends. Attachments result when *ties are rewarding*. Where social ties are not sufficiently rewarding to induce conformity, *threats of punishment*, a kind of "negative" bonding or deterrent, are employed (Lynch et al., 1993). According to control theory, without these rewards humans have little reason to avoid pursuing their inherent desires to gratify their needs in whatever ways they can.

In order for people to establish social bonds that lead to conforming behavior, societies must provide individuals with minimal satisfaction of human and culturally-defined needs (Kornhauser, 1978). In accounting for the strength of social bonds as they relate to need gratification, Kornhauser (1978:39,47) noted that "the means by which wants are gratified are unequally distributed," meaning that the ability to meet needs is class-linked. Thus, some positions within the class structure are more conducive than others to establishing attachments through positive rewards. The not-so-subtle conclusion is that strategies of social control are class-linked. In particular, those within less advantaged social classes are likely to experience fewer positive rewards, and to be subjected to more negative attachment methods, than those who are better off. This applies to both the private and the public sphere. In the private sphere, parents who are less able to gratify the material and/or social desires of their children will tend to rely more heavily on punishment than on promises of reward to obtain conforming behavior (Colvin and Pauly, 1983). Without other compensating rewards, this pattern of control through punishment will lead to weaker attachment between children and parents and greater potentiality for youths to pursue attachment with other – possibly deviant – individuals outside the home.

At the public level, a similar pattern emerges. The unequal patterns of distribution in capitalist society can mean that promises of either material or social rewards for conforming behavior are less convincing for members of the less well-off classes because everyday observations in their communities suggest that rewards for conformity are limited.

As Rusche and Kirchheimer (1968) noted, the more a society is unable – or unwilling – to meet the needs and desires of the poorer classes, the more it will rely on harsh punishments to control them. Similar to the attachment process in private life, public reliance on punishment rather than reward to obtain social conformity fails to establish a strong attachment between citizens and the dominant social order, creating an increased likelihood that some individuals will prefer the pleasures of crime to the lack of reward for conformity. This view fits well with the radical expectation that inequality inhibits social cohesion, since individuals with weak attachments to others, groups and social institutions – alienated individuals – have little to gain by conforming. Kornhauser sums up this view in a passage that could have come from Marx: "The web of interdependency is weak where unequal exchanges prevail" (1978:46).

While control theory is usually applied to the process of bonding at the individual level, the relationship between attachment and social cohesion also operates at the level of institutions and communities. These processes are sometimes termed *inter-institutional bonding*. Durkheim (1983) argued that healthy societies exhibited a high degree of institutional integration, while low levels of institutional integration typified socially disorganized ones. Radicals argue that social disorganization is an inevitable feature of social systems organized around class, race and gender inequality. Such unequal structures impede institutional integration, and ensure that disadvantaged social groups believe that competition, rather than cooperation, will appear to be to their advantage.

In the U.S., for example, many communities do not have coherent social structures, and many are becoming increasingly isolated economically by the process of capital disinvestment (Bluestone, 1995; Gordon et al., 1982; Warren, 1978). *Community control theory* argues that ineffective institutional linkages will have negative consequences for the integration of institutions with each other, and between institutions and individuals. Unlike individual-level control theory models (Nye, 1958; Hirschi, 1969), "community control models assume that many controls are...affected by...

macro-social contexts" (Kornhauser, 1978:106). For example, because slums are "segmented" and resource-deficient, their institutions become unstable and ineffective as means of establishing attachments (Suttles, 1971).

In short, a society with a lopsided economic distribution is less well-situated to meet the human and cultural needs of all its citizens. As empirical studies of social disorganization demonstrate, the best single indicator of social disorganization and crime is poverty (Shaw and McKay, 1942; Sampson and Groves, 1989; for alternative evidence see Veysey and Messner, 1999). Thus, high rates of crime within American communities should be seen not simply as a failure to implement effective crime control strategies, but as a failure of communities – and, consequentially, society – to meet people's needs.

Community control theory and radical approaches to crime are clearly compatible. Taylor et al. (1974), for example, affirmed the underlying logic of community control theory when they argued that persons occupying different social-structural locations had different levels of commitment to the social order. Similarly, Spitzer (1975, 1981) acknowledged the theoretical significance of defective inter-institutional bonding when he referred to the relative weakness of primary socializing agencies. Colvin and Pauly's (1983) explanation, reviewed in chapter 5, also sits well with control theory expectations.

While community control theory and radical approaches share some common ground, community control theory has typically been limited to identifying and cataloging the correlations between community characteristics and crime. Community control theorists accept that poverty, inequality and crime are related. They do not explore the sources of poverty and inequality, taking their existence largely for granted. Community control theorists also speak about the relationship between race and crime but primarily as an empirical correlation. They give less consideration than radical theorists do to reasons *why* race is related to crime, how this relationship is affected by racially-linked hierarchies in American society, and how these hierarchies impede bonding and need-gratification within minority communities. When community control theorists do address the issue of race and crime, it is often through its connection to class – a view that basically dismisses the possibility that the construction of racial identities in the U.S. not only interacts with the economic system, but also exerts independent effects on social factors such as community control and crime (Massey and Denton, 1993).

In sum, control theory and radical theory are not wholly incompatible *if* we contextualize the processes they examine within the wider social system. Like strain theory, control theory can be consistent with the proposition that class, gender and race inequality play important roles in crime causation. By situating the control explanations within the broader contexts of political-economic organization and racial and gender regimes, it becomes possible to explore how the processes of individual and community bonding are either improved or undermined by the wider dynamics of social inequality. By embedding community disorganization within the political, economic, racial and gender structure of American society, criminologists can contribute to the development of a radical theory of social control. In the next section we review some additional ideas that can be employed to accomplish this task.

## PATHWAYS FROM CAPITAL TO CRIME: THE POLITICAL ECONOMY OF CITIES AND CRIME

In his book, *Crime and Disrepute,* John Hagan (1994) addresses several ideas that are consistent with those offered by radical criminologists. Our specific focus here is on *human capital, social* or *cultural capital* and *capital disinvestment.*

### Human Capital

Hagan describes *human capital* as "the skills and knowledge acquired by individuals through education and training" (1994:67). Marx referred to this same idea, breaking this concept into two related terms: labor value and reproductive costs. For Marx, the value of human labor and the types of skills a person brought to a job consisted of the amount of time needed to create and reproduce those skills. This included the knowledge people possessed through their educational or vocational training as well as the physical costs of reproduction (e.g., food, clothing, housing, health care, rest and recreational expenses, and family financial issues). Each of these reproductive costs has an economic and cultural dimension, and the requirements for food, clothing, recreation, and so on might vary from one society to the next (see Marx, 1967a).

## Social Capital

Human capital is a very concrete idea, and includes things that can be measured by prevailing economic indicators. *Social capital* is a more abstract concept, which Hagan (1994:67) defines as "the creation of capabilities through socially structured relationships." In the family, parents pass on specific norms, values and training to their children. For Hagan, family-based socialization provides children with the beliefs and values that enhance or diminish their life chances for success or failure, including the probability that children accept or reject values conducive to crime. In part, families act as the primary mechanism for socialization, and are responsible for creating conforming or non-conforming individuals. But social capital also has a structural dimension, and Hagan cites Cohen and Felson's (1979) findings – that modern work patterns have reduced home guardianship, enhancing the opportunities for certain forms of crime – as an example of how social capital affects social control.

From a radical perspective, Hagan's arguments can be expanded to include the roles that class, gender and racial structures in U.S. society play in altering work patterns and family organization in order to explain crime. As far as work is concerned, the long-term development of capitalism has concentrated capital in fewer and fewer hands (Frank and Cook, 1995). Capital concentration was initially manifest in the decline of home-based manufacturing and the demise of the family-owned workshop in nineteenth century America, which occurred as capitalists organized production around factories in an attempt to lower production costs. Factory organizational techniques diminished the ability of home-based producers to compete economically and provide for their family's needs (Hobson, 1906; Smith, 1982; Ricardo, 1978). The result was that people who previously owned their own means of producing their livelihood now became dependent upon others for employment and were increasingly required to work outside their homes and move from their communities in search of employment. Through this process, work and home became separated, fostering the spatial organization we now associate with modern cities – separate residential, manufacturing, business and commercial districts (Gordon, 1984; Ashton, 1984; Sawers, 1984a). By the 1830s to the 1840s, the wealthy began to move away from what they perceived as disorganized central cities and their constant transition (i.e., movement of people from different classes in and out of various communities in cities), using their wealth and time to commute via horse-drawn carriages and ferries (Ashton, 1984). By the 1850s, better-off members of the middle class soon followed, using newly built railroads and horse-drawn street cars. The electric trolley of the 1880s gave the middle class its "first real chance to escape the city" (Ashton, 1984:59), and the migration of the middle class from cities intensified. In short, cities became spatially segregated along class lines.

This process of wealth concentration and social class differentiation was not separated from the gender and racial regimes of the time. Upper-class and even many middle-class households were able to organize their lives in suburban contexts because they could utilize the cheap labor of working-class *women* as domestic servants. While upper- and middle-class women began to enjoy a new freedom from their daily labor, other men, women and children from ethnic minorities (most often Irish, French, Italian, German and Portuguese) worked long hours in textile sweatshops, factories, and mines, making the ready-to-wear clothes and labor-saving devices that were the hallmarks of the new consumer society (Coontz, 1994). Thus, the emerging social and spatial reorganization of American society in the nineteenth century relied on class, gender, race and ethnic inequality to fuel the new consumer system, using the labor and energy of many who would never enjoy the benefits of what they produced.

With the rise of the commercial city in the mid-1800s and the division of cities into distinct areas, industrial workers became increasingly segregated into their own districts or communities, and industrial northeastern cities came to be subdivided communities inhabited primarily by ethnic groups such as Irish, Italians, French, Chinese or African Americans. Working-class cohesiveness was intensified by this kind of living arrangement, and from 1880 through the early 1900s, worker resistance, machine breaking, strikes and riots increased across a number of American cities in which workers were spatially segregated (Gordon, 1984; Peterson, 1938; Ashton, 1984). In response, capitalists relocated manufacturing from central city areas to fringe and suburban locations, limiting working-class access to the machinery of industry (a process reintroduced in the 1970s). This relocation of industry required an extensive investment of capital, made available by the monopolization of capital in numerous industries, a practice that improved profit levels (Ashton, 1984; Dowd, 1977). Increasingly, the city's spatial character became class-linked with the upper class, middle class, working class and the underclass, each segregated into its own part of town. Later developments such as mass-transit systems, the automobile and highways contributed to this trend (Sawers, 1984b).

Similar processes of spatial racial segregation affected the development of cities beginning in the early 1900s. As Massey and Denton (1993) show, many U.S. urban areas were racially integrated prior to the early 1900s (see also Massey and Denton, 1988, 1989; Massey and Gross, 1991; Massey and Hajnal, 1995). Over the past century, however, institutionalized economic and political processes have helped to promote, often purposefully, the racial segregation of U.S. cities (Massey and Denton, 1993). Racially segregated areas, consisting almost solely of African Americans and Hispanics, are in turn removed from attempts to revitalize local economies (Massey and Denton, 1993). In part, the reason offered for this neglect – that African-American and Hispanic communities are isolated from the broader economy and, hence, investment in those communities will not have wide-ranging impacts – is part of an institutionalized self-fulfilling prophecy that helps keep minority communities generally, and African-American communities in particular, segregated (Massey and Denton, 1993). In short, it is difficult to discuss any forms of human or social capital, or the processes of capital investment and reinvestment, as these relate to crime without reference to the history and contemporary practice of racial segregation in the U.S. (Massey and Denton, 1993).

The observations above help to explain the distribution of human and social capital in American cities. The segregation of the poor, the working class, the middle class, and the wealthy into their own areas within cities created tremendous differentials in the kinds of resources each community possessed. The community's potential to transfer social capital to the next generation depended on its location within the hierarchy of spatially separated classes. In addition to class divisions, other processes were at work. The separation of home and work separated children from parents, and men as wage workers from women as domestic workers. The processes through which children learned about work, and through which parental values were passed on to subsequent generations, were radically altered once both work and education were relocated outside the home. Similarly, once men – particularly middle-class men – began earning a family's living outside the home, while their wives were increasingly relegated to the non-income-producing tasks of reproducing the daily life of the household, gender divisions increasingly incorporated a devaluation of women's labor and a growing inability of men and women to understand each other's labor (Ehrenreich, 1983). Finally, patterns of racism and segregation have created additional layers of disadvantage in minority communities. First, contemporary and historic patterns of racial prejudice have limited access to the kinds of capital that could foster local businesses and owner-occupied neighborhoods in minority communities. Second, the segregation of racial minorities – whether by law (historically) or by economics (contemporarily)

– reduces their ability to develop social capital through routine interaction with white America. In sum, it should be noted that racial segregation has important impacts on the distribution of capital in U.S. cities, and on the likelihood that minority communities will experience the infusion of capital necessary to revitalize their neighborhoods.

What do these historic processes have to do with understanding today's crime problem? First of all, if community cohesion, stable households, communication of values to children and the guardianship of private and public places are important for preventing crime, the conditions for today's crime problem were set into motion over 100 years ago, as the development of industrial capitalism reordered and disordered community life and familial relations within the context of the urban physical and social lives of American cities. Second, unless we can link contemporary patterns and problems of crime with the historical forces that generated them, we will fail to understand how contemporary forces can be altered to ameliorate the crime problem.

A central problem with much orthodox criminology is that it searches for the causes of crime – whether they be poor parenting, one-parent households, disorganized communities, or youths' drug use – in isolation from their origins in history. It is only by envisioning crime as a social phenomenon emerging from historical processes that we appreciate the complex ways in which factors such as the spatial and social reorganization of how Americans lived and worked help create today's crime problem.

Consider education. The ability of communities to fund schools through taxation and to assist them through voluntary services is class-linked. Affluent communities have both a stronger tax base with which to fund schools, and more parents with the free time and energy to contribute volunteer services. Consequently, children in affluent communities will typically obtain a better primary and secondary education, be more successful in gaining admission to higher-status colleges, and generally achieve higher levels of economic success in their lifetimes (Frank and Cook, 1995). Thus, accomplishment and its rewards, which are the basis of positive attachment to the social system, are not simply the result of life in the privacy of the family but are consequences of community conditions, which in turn are affected by broad economic transformations.

A 1998 study by the Urban League demonstrated how structural positions tend to reproduce themselves by exploring the impact that race has on wealth accumulation (see also Carnoy, 1994). In the U.S., African Americans own about *eight cents* for every dollar of wealth held by whites. Much of this disparity results from the way in which home ownership is affected by race and the wealth of one's parents. According to the Urban League's findings, young white families are better able to buy homes than African-American families because they are more likely to receive loans or cash gifts from parents with some accumulated wealth. When African Americans do buy homes, the value of these homes often rises more slowly than that of the homes bought by whites for two reasons. First, because they have less access to wealth, fewer African Americans can afford to buy homes in desirable neighborhoods where growth in home equity will be higher. Second, African Americans who are capable of buying homes in desirable neighborhoods that are predominantly white will find that the value of their homes will rise slowly or even decline. This results because white homeowners, fearing a decline in property values when blacks move in, bring about the decline they fear by moving out in large numbers, thereby depressing the neighborhood housing market. Taken together, these factors mean that African Americans will typically accumulate less wealth than whites because the increasing value of homes is the primary means through which middle- and working-class Americans acquire wealth. Finally, as the Urban League report indicates, because wealth accumulation is the most significant factor determining a family's ability to purchase a home in a neighborhood with good schools, African Americans have fewer opportunities to provide their children access to the educational opportunities that will help interrupt the cycle of economic disenfranchisement experienced by many black families (Shapiro and Oliver, 1998).

Family values, similarly, must be viewed in the context of intersecting structural forces that limit or enhance chances for success. The lower class, for example, has access to fewer opportunities for success. Moreover, the dynamics of contemporary capitalism have increased the social and economic differentiation among classes, particularly the income gap between those with a college versus a high-school-only education. During the last quarter of the twentieth century, the median family income for high school graduates declined by 13.1 percent, while family income for those with four years of college increased by 10 percent. By 2000, the median household income for college graduates was $32,000 higher than for high school graduates (Mortenson, 2002).

Consequently, it is inevitable that the social capital that families can provide children varies by class location. As Hagan (1994:69) writes: "Social capital is used to successfully endow children with forms of cultural capital that significantly enhances their later life chances." While we agree with Hagan's general conclusion, we suggest that understanding *why* this is the case and *how it came to be* requires a fuller exploration of the historical development of class, gender, racial and ethnic structures.

## Capital Disinvestment

Hagan (1994) links the transmission of social and cultural capital to the process of *capital disinvestment*. Capital disinvestment is the process of removing capital from specific areas of the economy, whether cities, nations, or geographic regions, and relocating it to places more favorable for profit making. Historically, the process of capital disinvestment has included: the transfer of capital and industry from cities to the suburbs (Gordon, 1984; Sawers, 1984b; Pred, 1966); capital transfers from manufacturing to, first, commercial ventures and, later, the service sector (Gordon, 1984; Offe, 1985); the relocation of white collar employment to the suburbs; the transference of capital overseas and the globalization of capital (Barnett and Cavanaugh, 1994; Barnett and Mueller, 1974; Evans, 1979; Greider, 1997; Karliner, 1997); and the movement of capital from the Rust Belt (northeastern and central states) to the Sun Belt (southern states).

Hagan's focus on disinvestment advances structural theories about crime because it links localized crime problems to the wider political-economic process. In order to extend this model, however, the connections between the disinvestment and the periodic process of capital reorganizing and accumulation need to be examined both *historically* (e.g., Marx, 1967a; Blake, 1939; Hobson, 1906; Braverman, 1974; Sweezy, 1942; Baran and Sweezy, 1966; Mandel, 1968a, 1968b) and *contemporarily* (Greider, 1997; Melman, 1985; Mandel, 1979; O'Connor, 1973; Rifkin, 1995). Here we confine our remarks to the contemporary period of disinvestment.

In an attempt to enhance profits and exert greater control over labor, capitalists began to reorganize the geographic distribution of capital rather extensively in the early 1970s. This process of disinvestment and reinvestment shifted capital from older industrial cities in the northeast to several locations, including the suburbs, the southern U.S. and overseas. In part, the capitalists fled older northeastern markets, with their strong histories of labor unionization and expanding environmental regulation, for the southeastern region and foreign lands with their weaker labor organization, fewer local environmental restrictions, and so-called "pro-business" governments. This was intended to reduce labor and production costs, thereby enhancing or protecting profit margins. As a result, unemployment in the older industrial cities such as New York, Chicago, Detroit, and Flint, MI skyrocketed. This loss of well-paying jobs was disproportionately felt in minority (particularly African-American and Latino) communities. First, since minorities were historically the last to be hired for well-paying, unionized industrial jobs, they were also the first to lose jobs as disinvestment took hold (Davis, 1986; Wilson and Cook, 1985). Second, whites who were displaced from manufacturing often sought employment in the service sector, thus displacing African Americans, Latinos and lower-skilled whites from that sector as well.

In short, the contemporary processes of capital disinvestment began by marginalizing older industrial cities, and particularly the minority communities within them. Disinvestment did not mean simply that some people were without work for a while. It meant the marginalization of entire neighborhoods and communities, creating in many places the underclass "'hoods," where good jobs were unheard of, where many young people increasingly resorted to gang life as an alternative source of social identity and economic support, and where community resources to address these problems were shrinking. As regions underwent disinvestment, an increase in both crime and criminal justice controls – including such things as mandatory sentencing, increased penalties for drug use, and hyper-policing of poorer neighborhoods – followed. This, in turn, fed a continuing expansion of incarceration rates (Irwin and Austin, 1994; Welch, 1996d; see chapter 10 below for further discussion of the relationship between marginalization and imprisonment). Both Carlson (1997) and Matthews (1997) provide empirical support for the argument that disinvestment was the underlying cause of both increasing crime and increasing social control in the older urban areas hardest hit by capital's search for new, more profitable locations.

These developments suggest several conclusions. One is that the contemporary disorganization of many communities is not the product of failure at the level of individual moral choices or family socialization habits. It is, rather, a failure of the social system to provide the basis for organized community life. Another conclusion is that we cannot hope to reduce crime in these areas simply by targeting the individuals who live there for deterrence, rehabilitation or punishment. We can only make substantial inroads into the crime problem in those places marginalized by disinvestment by reestablishing a basis for economically and socially viable community life.

Not only have African Americans and many Latinos suffered from heightened levels of poverty due to disinvestment, they have also been excluded by housing-market discrimination from full participation in economic and cultural development. When banks and insurance companies identify neighborhoods with a high proportion of minority residents as "unsuitable" for loans or insurance, property values in those communities decline, absentee ownership increases, and residents with stable incomes begin to move elsewhere (see Massey and Denton, 1993, for a general discussion of this process). Hagan (1994:71) asserts that "whites perceived a protection benefit to segregation because it isolated a high level of black poverty within black neighborhoods."

The isolation of African-American and Latino families resulted from more than racial prejudice on the part of European Americans, however. It was fueled by class-linked economic benefits derived from enhancing racial segregation and shifting capital from urban to suburban areas, with the consequence of benefiting European-American communities over African-American and Latino communities. As noted earlier, disinvestment occurs during periods of general economic decay and restructuring as capitalists reorganize to facilitate the growth of profits (Bowles et al., 1990; O'Connor, 1985). The physical segregation of classes along racial and ethnic lines intensified labor force competition, which increased the overall earnings gap between European-American and minority workers even while it caused a more general decline in working-class wages (Frank and Cook, 1995; Carnoy, 1994). Although both European-American and minority communities experienced the negative effects of economic restructuring, the effects were qualitatively different. European Americans experienced an increase in work hours, a decline in leisure and a decline in income relative to work time. In most places, however, they did not experience a wholesale displacement from the labor force (Schor, 1993). Specifically, while disinvestment reduced the overall social capital of both European-American and minority communities, the level of job loss in many minority neighborhoods, particularly in the older industrial cities of the Northeast and Midwest, was devastating. This unequal decline in the human, social and cultural capital in white, African-American and Latino working-class communities helps explain the long-term increase in crime in white and minority communities, *and* the greater increase in rates and seriousness of crime in many African-American and Latino urban neighborhoods compared to white communities.

## CRIME AND THE LIFE COURSE: CLASS, RACE AND GENDER EFFECTS

Earlier, we discussed how class, gender and race constitute intersecting structures that affect life chances, opportunities for success and the quality and quantity of choices people can make. Both theory and empirical evidence indicate that males have more opportunities and choices than females; that minorities have fewer choices and opportunities than whites; and that persons from higher social classes have a greater number of choices, opportunities and life chances than those in lower social classes. We also noted that race, class and gender identities are interconnected. No one is simply white or black, male or female, working class or middle class. Instead, individual identities combine these (and other) elements in interactive ways. Thus, for instance, those who are middle class, white and male will encounter different choices, life chances and opportunities as compared to those who are working class, Hispanic, and female. These ideas can be used to explore the radical potential of a theoretical approach that has received considerable attention from orthodox criminologists in recent years: the life course model (Lynch, 1996).

Over the past few years, criminologists have begun to investigate the ways in which an individual's life course affects his participation in crime (Sampson and Laub, 1993, 1990; Hagan, 1993). These researchers have identified specific events called *turning points* that act as *pathways* to crime or conformity. The idea of a course of life events that shapes pathways to crime and conformity has radical potential (Lynch, 1996). In the radical perspective, however, the ideas of a life course and turning points take on a very different meaning. The radical perspective treats life courses as *social* trajectories shaped by the broader structures of race, class and gender relationships, rather than a matter of individual biographies. In the orthodox view of life courses, emphasis is given to such things as the age at which a person marries and the age at which he takes a job, changes jobs, or loses a job. From a radical perspective, life course pathways are structural. This means that, to a large degree, people occupying similar class, gender and race locations in society will have similar life courses, including roughly similar chances of following or avoiding criminal pathways. In short, from a radical perspective, race, class and gender relationships can be used to explain the life course trajectories of *groups* of people in similar structural locations.

A radical reinterpretation of life course theory does not suggest that all people sharing the same composition of class, gender and race identities will behave identically. Rather, it proposes that the life course probability of certain outcomes, such as involvement in street crime, will be greater for some groups (e.g., young, poor, urban, Hispanic males) than others (e.g., young, white, affluent males living in the suburban world of gated subdivisions). This structural reinterpretation of life course theory and research offers ways of utilizing the intersection of class, gender and race to predict the distribution of criminal motivations, criminal and conforming opportunity structures and patterns of bonding and law enforcement (see Lynch, 1996). The following example provides a cursory overview of how this model can be applied.

We begin with our previous observation that economic success in the U.S. is structured along the lines of class, gender, racial and ethnic structures, and that despite various struggles for equality these factors still matter where economic success is concerned. To be sure, exceptional individuals may succeed despite the existence of structural barriers to success. In the big picture, however, what is important is not what happens to some of the people some of the time, but what happens to most of the people most of the time. Despite popular stories of people who triumphed over great social and economic odds, the real story is that most people attain positions in life that correspond to the opportunities for success typical of whatever particular intersection of class, gender and race they occupy. These stories begin at birth.

Each of us: (1) is born into a specific social class with its opportunities and disadvantages; (2) is socialized into a particular set of life-defining gender roles; and (3) lives with the positive and negative implications of belonging to some racial or ethnic group. Each of these characteristics connects us to social structures that shape access to life-defining institutions such as education, medical care, healthy eating habits and nutritious foods, access to social services, and pathways to crime or conformity. Children have little control over the kinds of access they have to socially valuable, stable institutions that promote their integration into society. They cannot affect their social class, where they live, whether their parents are employed, and if so, what kind of employment they have, or the content of the popular cultural to which they are exposed. Nor can they exert control over the broad cultural meanings assigned to their gender, race and/or ethnicity. In short, children grow up in circumstances created by previous generations, and are embedded in – and to a greater or lesser degree are socialized to accept – prevailing cultural norms, values and institutions. This process begins at home, but is soon transferred to day-care centers, schools, peers and the street.

Life courses are affected by early experiences through a process we will call *growing up as* (Lynch, 1996). By this we mean that people grow up *as* "white" or "black," *as* "male" or "female," *as* "Anglo" or "Asian American," and so forth. Each of these elements of identity brings with it a body of culturally-established definitions and expectations as well as structurally-determined opportunities and experiences. Thus, for example, growing up *as* white is different than growing up *as* Hispanic or *as* African American. We are not suggesting that these "growing up as" experiences are uniform; there are many different ways to grow up *as* white, *as* male, or *as* Native American. Nevertheless, individuals within specific identity groups will share with one another a number of experiences and opportunities (or lack of opportunities) that they do not share with people who represent a different intersections of class, gender and race/ethnicity.

Race and ethnicity, for instance, affect such things as access to health care and even the Internet (Associated Press, 1998). These characteristics affect how one is treated by others and whether one sees issues of racial and ethnic equality as important. Racial and ethnic equality is a much more important issue for minorities since they are likely to be treated differently because of how they look, to witness others being treated this way or to hear conversations about race and racism. Similarly, growing up as male is different from growing up as female. Despite the long history of struggle to create gender equality, the majority of boys and girls are still socialized differently in the home and treated differently in school where boys receive special attention from teachers and are channeled into sciences and math more frequently than girls (Fennema and Leder, 1990; Mickelson and Smith, 1995; Schur, 1984). As they prepare for the work world, male and female adolescents come to recognize that they face very different options in a labor market that is still largely characterized by sex-segregated work. They might hear about or see some female police officers, but they also know that most cops are men. There may be a few male secretaries or nurses around, but most such jobs remain "women's work." And certainly the "glass ceiling" ensures that the leaders of most business, educational and political institutions will be men. These factors will shape both the real opportunities available to males and females as well as their understanding of what it means to be male or female.

In a similar vein, growing up *as* lower class is different from growing up *as* upper class. Unlike upper-class children, lower-class children have few opportunities to attend costly, prestigious, well-equipped private schools staffed by highly skilled educators. Nor are they even likely to attend well-equipped public schools: instead, they will likely find themselves in overcrowded classrooms, in deteriorating buildings, being taught by overworked and exhausted educators. As a group, their educational development will be poorer than that of middle- and upper-class children, not because they are inherently any less intelligent, but because of the kind of education provided to people in their structural location. Additionally, the education of working-class youths will be designed to channel them toward working-class jobs, rather than giving them the intellectual tools and the *expectations* that will direct them to pursue professional, middle-class careers.

Now consider what it means when these various elements of identity intersect. Affluent, young white males and females have a higher probability of enjoying high-quality primary and secondary education, and of obtaining an undergraduate or advanced degree. The male, however, is more likely to be socialized and mentored into science, industry or medicine, while the female will be more likely to be steered toward "people-oriented" areas such as education, social service or law. There will, of course, be those who violate this pattern – men who become teachers and women who become physicists. But these *will not be the norm*. At the other end of the spectrum, poor, young, Hispanic males and females are likely to attend underfunded primary and secondary schools, and to move into working-class jobs. The young male (if he is lucky) will go to the factory, while the young woman goes to the day-care center or maybe the hospital as a nurse's aide. These, of course, are broad caricatures, and many people's actual lives diverge from the stereotypical. Nevertheless, the intersection of social class, gender and race plays an important role in outlining the likely pathways during the years of "growing up as."

Another aspect of life course development is social class location. Using a life course model, Hagan (1993) examined the connection between crime and periods of unemployment in the lives of juveniles. Hagan's argument reverses the more typical understanding of the relationship between unemployment and crime, i.e., that unemployment comes before crime (see: Chiricos, 1987; Chiricos and DeLone, 1992, and chapter 5). Instead, Hagan suggests that unemployment *follows* crime in the lives of juveniles: i.e., unemployment is a consequence of crime. Beginning with juveniles' life courses as the unit of analysis, this conclusion seems logically correct, and Hagan's results offer some limited support for this interpretation. A broader, structurally situated approach to life course analysis, however, reveals several shortcomings with this view. First, due to age restrictions on employment, juveniles have the opportunity to engage in crime well before they can engage in employment, meaning that the relationship Hagan observed may be unrelated to his explanation. Second, a broader structural life course context would direct us to inquire about the relationship of juveniles' criminality to the unemployment of parents and the opportunities for work within the community. During their life course, some juveniles encounter the effects of unemployment through the life course of their parents and other adults in their neighborhoods. As Wilson (1987, 1996) argues, children who grow up in neighborhoods where work pays poorly, is sporadic or nearly non-existent have a greater tendency to be drawn toward deviant activities at early ages because they see little evidence within adult life to support the idea that conformity and work have their rewards. This is an *intergenerational* view of the life course, which allows connections *among* generations to be assessed. A life course, as we argued above, is structured by the situation into which a person is born, and this includes not only prevailing race, class and gender relations, but relationships to caregivers and caregivers' structurally situated circumstances.

If we extend the above discussions, we can also see that by occupying certain structural locations, some people are more likely than others to be placed in circumstances that are conducive to crime (i.e., they have a higher probability of having access to crime pathways). Poor educational experiences, growing up in economically-deprived areas with detached and ineffective institutional support mechanisms and few community resources, living in economic contexts that make working difficult for parents – each of these conditions produces strains and minimizes individual bonding with social institutions. These circumstances of early childhood are not choices children make for themselves or that a parent would select given some other option. Rather, they result from the political economy of class, race and gender relations that affect the distribution of human and social capital that communities can access, as well as the kinds of economic capital invested in communities.

The life course is a complicated process, and there are numerous issues we could investigate at length. Our purpose, however, was to introduce this mode of analysis in order to demonstrate how life course theory can be extended and radicalized.

## In Sum

This chapter has reviewed methods of extending and radicalizing the findings and theories offered by orthodox criminology. Further development of this view represents an important challenge for radical criminology in the coming years if the radical impulse is to move beyond academic debates about crime and crime control and into the arena of policy development and policy change.

We could expand the perspective taken in this chapter to any number of other theories of criminal behavior. For example, consider routine activities theory, which explains crime as an outcome of the intersection of motivated offenders and suitable targets in time and space. While useful, this view has not been fully developed in a theoretical sense, and fails, for example, to explain what motivates offenders (since this is not the task of this view). But, more importantly, it does not explain the factors that make a target suitable in a broad sense, nor does it explain opportunity structures adequately, if at all. How, for example, are the criminal opportunities a person encounters shaped by that person's connection to class, race or gender structures? In what way does a person's structured life course intersection with opportunities for success and failure, conformity and crime? These questions, which have not been addressed by orthodox criminology, possess the potential to be developed by connecting the routine activities model to a radical criminological perspective.

Likewise, we could reconsider social learning theories, which explain crime relative to learning processes. Learning theory, especially in the view of its leading proponent, Ron Akers, is a general theory of crime. Because learning theories have been conceptualized as general theories, the specific ways in which learning encounters may be shaped by structural factors such as race, class or gender membership and structures, has not received much attention (except as empirical controls). Again, it would be possible to add a level of explanation to social learning theories by connecting them to radical criminological ideas.

Our point is that many of the ideas contained in orthodox criminology may be useful for explaining criminal behaviors. But, before they can make greater sense as explanations of crime these theories would need to be revised to explain the role of class, race, gender and culture in the causal mechanisms these theories explore in order to make them more relevant to the influences found in the real world.

# Eight.
# The Environment, Crime and Justice

Our physical environment connects to crime and justice issues in various ways. This chapter explores four critical areas where crime and justice intersect with concerns for protecting the environment and subject matter to which criminologist should pay greater attention. First, we review research relating to the impacts of environmental conditions on human behavior, particularly how industrial pollution contributes to levels of violent behavior in society. Second, we examine research generated by the environmental justice movement. This research demonstrates how race and class inequality ensures that the health hazards caused by toxic waste and industrial pollution will be imposed far more often on the poor, particularly poor people of color, than on any other sectors of society. The distribution of environmental hazards along class and race lines has important social justice implications. Moreover, this distribution also points to the possibility that environmental forces are implicated in the etiology of crime, especially when it comes to explaining the geography of violence and elevated rates of violence in lower income and minority neighborhoods. Third, we will consider the impact of global warming and the impending oil crisis on the criminal justice system, and on the world's environment and inhabitants. And finally, we will examine the potential of an emerging radical perspective, "green criminology," to unite the various types of environmental studies radicals have undertaken.

## Orthodox Criminology's View of the "Environment"

The view of crime and the environment developed in this chapter highlights several differences between radical and orthodox criminology. For the orthodox criminologist, the crime-environment connection has been limited to examining the association between crime and sociological environments such as neighborhoods and communities, or more proximate environments such as families or friends. A good example of this tendency is illustrated by the orthodox school of thought known as "environmental criminology," developed during the 1970s. In orthodox environmental criminology, "environment" meant the material environment constructed by humans, such as buildings, streets, walkways, stores and so one. The concern was with how these "built-environments" could be engineered to reduce crime by doing such things as providing enhanced lighting or designing buildings differently, or by creating "defensible space": that is, inducing people to be concerned with what was going on in the immediate environs beyond their front doors (Newman, 1973, 1996; Crowe, 2000). While these analyses recognized that human behavior takes place in and is shaped by a physical environment, the exclusive focus on the built environment failed to consider whether human degradation of the natural environment through air, water or soil pollution might also be part of the environment-crime equation. Interestingly, "environmental" criminology was invented at the very same time that a social movement to protect the natural environment was emerging in the United States and around the world. Yet, environmental criminology took no notice of the relationship between humans and their natural world. This, we suggest, is another example of the orthodox criminological tendency to overlook the importance of contextualizing problems within wider frameworks, in this case the broad framework of "mother earth" that supports all life.

## Taking a Radical Approach to the Environment/Crime Connection

James O'Connor argued that the history of nature, labor and class struggle cannot be separated (1998:25-28, 48-66), and that understanding how these entities intersect is important to developing a radical ecology. From this perspective, humans live within a natural environment or natural ecology that they constantly modify through their labor. This is not, however, a one-way street. At the same time that humans modify the natural environment, that environment modifies them by shaping and limiting the opportunities for human production and the social environments that depend upon how and what humans produce.

In some instances humans use their combined labor to modify and manage the natural or human environment in ways that have particularly negative consequences for the health and survival of both. Radical ecology focuses on the ways in which specific economic systems shape and modify the uses of human labor to transform natural and human environments. Thus, for instance, economic systems that are based on continually expanding the production and consumption of material goods, as is the case with contemporary capitalism, will have far more damaging consequences for the natural world than systems that are not driven by resource extraction and industrial production. Since its birth, capitalism has imposed great and growing costs on the natural environment because the primary engine of capitalist growth is organizing and exploiting labor to extract raw materials from nature, shaping them into industrial products that can be sold for profit, while feeding workers and consumers foods produced through toxic but ever more profitable systems of factory farming (Gorz, 1979).

Because capitalism necessitates the exploitation of natural resources and labor to produce commodities at profitable rates, capitalism and the natural environment are at odds in meaningful ways. First, capitalism promotes only a short-term environmental vision that focuses on immediate consequences. The long-term consequences of environmental degradation are of little importance to investors and managers, whose primary goal is to maximize short-term profit. Second, the pace of nature is slow and long term. In contrast, the pace of capitalism is rapid and short term. Under normal conditions, capitalist investors and managers neither see nor worry about the impact of their actions on the long-term balance of nature. Because capitalists can promise immediate material benefits, they tend to enjoy a political advantage over environmentalists, who are concerned with long-term, less obvious consequences. Third, capitalism requires continual growth in profits. This means that production and consumption must continually expand, resulting in a permanent upward trend in levels of resource extraction, pollution and other forms of environmental degradation. There is a tendency within capitalist consciousness to treat raw materials as if they are endless, and to view the world's ecosystem as vast, robust and largely unaffected by the demands for raw materials or the pollution that capitalism has imposed upon it.

To the extent that the capitalist mentality is aware of environmental threats, this awareness takes two forms. First, informed by market ideology, capitalists assume that if a raw material supply becomes limited, the invisible hand of the market will intercede and cause the price of raw materials to rise, thereby reducing demand and avoiding any potential ecological disaster. Second, when corporate planners become aware that some necessary resource is being depleted, they typically begin searching for replacement resources that can be exploited in an equally profitable manner. In the early years of the twenty-first century, for instance, as readily available supplies of petroleum began to dwindle and become more costly, the U.S. energy industry began to focus on the potential of a process known as coal gassification to fuel power plants (U.S. Department of Energy, 2003). Because energy industry profits depend upon selling large amounts of energy, the declining petroleum supply did not lead to a discussion of ways to reduce energy consumption; rather, the issue that emerged involved devising plans of how to obtain alternative material resources needed to keep energy consumption high (and profitable).

The problem with these supply-side responses to environmental threats is that they are based on tunnel-vision, and, to borrow an economic term, inelastic marketplace thinking and assumptions. On the one hand, leaders of industries wedded to capitalist market assumptions do not question the logic of continually expanding consumption and production because both are defined as healthy marketplace parameters. On the other hand, market mechanisms cannot protect the environment because they are based on the pursuit of short-term private profit, and omit long-term economic and environmental scenarios. The short-term market plans common to capitalist systems of production do little to protect the environment because they focus only on the particular resources of concern to an industry, with little recognition that these resources exist within ecosystems, and that continued extraction of resources from these systems and introduction of pollutants into them will have consequences far beyond the resource itself. Short-sighted and profit-driven industrial production has meant that more species have become extinct in the last 100 years than during any other time in the entire history of human habitation of the planet. We are currently witnessing the exhaustion of natural resources across the face of the globe. Water fit for humans, plants, and animals, as well as petroleum, rain forests, old-growth timber, fish, and numerous other components of planetary life are rapidly dwindling. Levels of environmental pollution continue to grow, harming the health of humans, animals, and plants, and increasing the threat of global warming. These are big, long-term issues that reach far beyond quarterly profit reports.

In order to expose the connection between capitalism and environmental degradation, it is necessary to be able to step outside of market assumptions promoted by a capitalist worldview. Because it contains a critique of capitalism, radical criminology provides one alternative theoretical lens that can be employed for this task. This critique can be broadened and strengthened by incorporating the lessons of radical ecology.

Radical ecology directs us to connect environmental issues to political-economic processes in order to create contextualized explanations of environmental harms. In the age of capitalist globalization this means examining how environmental threats to ecosystems and human populations are shaped by capitalist practices, and how justice systems might be used to address these problems.

## Focusing on the Environment

Concern with environmental issues has followed three lines of reasoning in radical criminology. One theme grows out of the definitional paradigm and is concerned with issues such as determining when environmental harms are or should be criminalized and controlled by the state, identifying the role played by economic and political power in shaping environmental legislation and enforcement, and determining the effect of the regulatory strategies used to control environmental harms. Another theme centers around issues of environmental justice. This approach is concerned primarily with identifying how race, class, and ethnicity shape the distribution of environmental hazards, with the greatest burdens being placed on minority communities within the United States, and on poorer countries around the world. The third and more recent approach derives from the behavioral paradigm, and is concerned with explaining how environmental pollution shapes human environments and human behavior.

Historically, the word environment has been used to refer to the natural world comprising air, land, water and the plants and animals that inhabit them. Until recently, human environments were considered to be fundamentally different from natural environments. In recent decades, however, both environmentalists and social analysts have become increasingly aware that there is no clear line separating human social environments and natural physical environments. The natural environment is part of the human environment. Human labor is constantly applied to natural environments to produce human survival and satisfaction, which can change the natural environment in ways that significantly impact human experience. Indeed, sometimes humans change the natural environment in ways that produce tragic consequences, such as when commodity production pollutes the air, water, or soil or destroys the natural balance of the ecosystem (Davis, 2002). This intimate link between human social processes and natural environments means that acts of environmental pollution have detrimental consequences for both human and natural environments. For instance, creating toxic waste sites can cause species extinction and habitat loss, and can contaminate waterways in ways that affect both humans and animals. At the same time, routine exposure to chemical hazards and pollutants can not only cause cancer or other illness, but can also modify human behavior (Colborn, Dumanoski and Myers, 1997). Pollutants that can modify behavior are found more often, and in greater concentrations, in lower-class and minority-populated urban neighborhoods, raising the possibility that the distribution of crime – which has for so long been taken as an expression of the kinds of people who live in these neighborhoods – may be the result, in part, of corporate environmental pollution. This is just one example of how exploring the close connections between human social processes and natural environmental processes may reveal patterns of crime causation that are completely obscured when we treat these two environments as separate, unlinked processes.

These are big issues. Understanding how toxins degrade human and natural environments, and studying this issue requires knowledge of several disciplines, including toxicology, chemistry, biology, medicine, environmental sciences, geophysics, geography, law and sociology. Taking this kind of knowledge and making it relevant to the study of crime and justice has been accomplished using the race and class models that radical criminologists prefer.

## Environmental Pollution and Crime

The scientific literature contains numerous studies of the effects of various chemicals on human development and health. Much of this literature focuses on chemical toxicity and negative health outcomes (for a review relevant to criminology see Lynch and Stretesky, 2001), while other segments of this literature focus on issues such as human growth patterns, developmental delays, and human behavioral effects (Lynch, 2004). One goal of these studies is to pinpoint the level of chemical exposure that can harm humans (e.g., Pueschel, Linakis, and Anderson, 1996; Roderick, 1992; Wargo, 1998).

As noted, studies that examine the health consequences of exposure to toxins are usually conduced in disciplines such as medicine and toxicology. At first glance, this emphasis appears inconsistent with radical criminology's focus on economic, race, class and gender structures. Connecting the harms cause by toxins to toxin exposure patterns associated with class, race or gender, however, is not difficult.

The processes through which chemicals alter behavior is biological, and thus it could be assumed that discussing the connection between behavior-altering chemicals and crime involves a biological argument concerning the causes of crime. While it is true that the proximate mechanism of causation in this case is biological (a chemical alters a biological process that impacts behavior), there would be no behavioral modification without chemical exposure. The point is that exposure to toxins is not only a biological issue; it is an issue with sociological relevance.

By focusing on the distribution of chemical exposure and potential routes of exposure, rather than on the biological processes affected by exposure, radical geo-spatial models that detail how race and class affect chemical exposure and the distribution of crime can be created. Consider, for instance, three community characteristics that affect the likelihood of exposure to environmental toxins: (1) location (more likely in urban than in rural areas); (2) class (more likely in low-income and poor communities); and (3) race characteristics of a neighborhood or community (more likely in African-American and Hispanic communities; see Lui, 2001 for extensive discussion). Interestingly, these community correlates of chemical pollution exposure are also correlates of crime (Lynch, 2004). High-crime areas are more likely to be urban rather than rural; African American or Hispanic compared to white; and, low-income or poor rather than middle- or upper-income communities. This raises the following question: Is it possible that these overlapping correlations reveal a causal relationship between patterns of toxin exposure and patterns of crime – both of which are associated with the political economy of race and class?

Within criminology, empirical studies of behavior-altering chemical substances have not examined this issue, and have been limited to studying the effect of prohibited drugs on behavior. The broader scientific literature, however, indicates that environmental toxins may play an important role in altering behavior by disrupting the central nervous system, and the hormonal and endocrine systems, and by affecting fetal development. In one of the most important examinations of toxins in the environment, Colborn, Dumanoski and Myers (1997:186) state that::

> Long before concentrations of synthetic chemicals cause obvious illness or abnormalities, they can impair learning ability and cause dramatic, permanent changes in behavior, such as hyperactivity. Save for a few compounds such as PCBs, we know virtually nothing about the hazards posed to thinking and behavior by the thousands of synthetic chemicals in commerce.

In comparison to medical and epidemiological literature on the behavioral effects of toxins and pollutants, criminological literature is extremely limited (e.g., on medical research see: Colborn, Dumanoski, and Myers, 1997; Needleman et al, 1996; Needleman et al., 2002; Pihl and Ervin, 1990; Dietrich et al., 2001; on criminological research see: Lynch, 2004; Lynch and Stretesky, 2001, 2004; Denno, 1990). To illustrate how environmental toxins can alter behavior, let us consider what is known about the effects of PCB and lead (Pb).

**PCBs**. Chemically, there are 209 possible PCB (polychlorinated biphenyls) combinations that have been used in manufacturing of paints, dyes, inks, adhesives, carbon paper, and electrical equipment (wiring, switches, capacitors, transistors, voltage regulators). Although a near-worldwide ban on PCBs was instituted in the early 1980s, PCBs continue to pose a health and environmental threat because they are contained in many widely dispersed products such as electrical transformers, and are found in large quantities as environmental pollutants. When released into the environment, PCBs biodegrade slowly and persist in the environment and human body for long periods of time (the half-lives of PCBs can be as long as six years). For example, while PCBs have been banned, currently the average American ingests between 5 and 15 micrograms of PCBs on a daily basis. Based on estimates produced by the Agency for Toxic Substances and Disease Registry (www.astdr.cdc.gov), the average American diet meets or exceeds by a factor of three the establish daily minimum intake risk level for PCBs. And small amounts of PCBs can have significant health consequences.

While scientists do not understand the exact processes involved, they know that PCB exposure harms human health. For instance, PCBs are now recognized as a cancer-causing agent by the U.S. Environmental Protection Agency (EPA). But, PCBs have other health effects as well. One effect appears to operate through the thyroid, which secretes hormones that influence brain and nervous system development in the fetus. Studies of animals and humans exposed to PCBs provide evidence of neurological impairments related to learning disabilities, decreased IQ, hyperactivity, impaired motor skills, attention deficits, and enhanced sensitivity to stimuli that can generate aggression (Colborn, Dumanoski and Myers, 1997:186-94). This research has interesting implications for the study of criminal behavior.

Studies of criminals and delinquents, for example, have discovered a long list of bio-behavioral characteristics that are correlated with crime including (but not limited to): low birth weight, attention deficit disorder, aggression patterns, mental retardation, learning disabilities, hyperactivity, low frustration tolerance, impulsivity, self-control deficits, antisocial behavior, neurological dysfunction, IQ deficiencies and poor academic achievement, and developmental delays. Insofar as we also know that exposure to chemical pollutants such as PCBs can lead to these bio-behavioral consequences, it suggests there may very well be a link between the distribution of pollutants and the spatial distribution of criminal and delinquent behavior in society.

There is a problem, however, when it comes to connecting the distributions of pollutants and crime. There are thousands of chemical pollutants in the environment. Identifying which of these may be responsible for changes in human behavior is a daunting task (Davis, 2002). As discussed above, some headway has been made with regard to PCBs. Another group of chemical elements suspected of having negative impacts on human health and behavior are known as heavy metals – metals with high atomic weights such as mercury, chromium, cadmium, selenium, arsenic, cooper, zinc, nickel and lead. Heavy metal exposure routes may be direct (e.g., exposure to air pollution) or indirect (as a bioaccumulate in the food chain). And, while a "trace" exposure (extremely low level) to some heavy metals such as copper and zinc contributes to good health, elevated levels of exposure are toxic to living organisms. Currently, there is limited knowledge of the behavioral effects of heavy metal exposure. One exception to this rule involves lead (Pb). In fact, while the health effects of lead exposure have been known for centuries, its behavioral effects have become the subject of more recent studies.

**Lead.** Earlier, we provided a short list of some correlates of crime and delinquency (e.g., low birth weight, attention deficit disorder, etc.). Take a moment to look over this list again. What is interesting about this list is that each outcome noted there is associated with lead exposure (see, Bellinger, 1996). Much of our knowledge of the relationship between lead exposure and delinquency comes from studies performed by Herbert Needleman, who pioneered these studies in the late 1970s (Needleman et al., 1979, 1990, 1996; Needleman and Gatsonis, 1990). Needleman's studies point to a persistent relationship between childhood lead exposure and adverse outcomes such as delinquent behavior.

Because lead exposure has been a significant health concern for many years, the lead content of commodities (e.g., paint, gasoline) was legally regulated in the 1970s and 1980s. The usefulness of these regulations can be assessed employing data from the federal National Health and Nutrition Examination Survey (NHANES), which has tracked many health indicators, including blood-lead levels for children, since 1976 (e.g., see, Pirkle et al., 1994). Several interesting facts emerge from NHANES. For instance, lead levels among the U.S. population have declined, indicating that federally imposed laws rather than free market mechanisms are more responsive to improving human health and environmental quality. Under free-market conditions (pre-1980s), environmental lead contamination rose, while concerns with lead exposure and lead contamination in the environment were dismissed as exaggerated by the lead industry (Davis, 2002). Despite the decline in blood-lead levels among Americans, the urban poor, African-American, Hispanic and Mexican-American children continue to exhibit higher blood lead-levels than whites, suburban or rural children, largely due to the concentration of lead paint and lead-laden pipes in older buildings and higher levels of industrial production around poor urban neighborhoods (Pirkle et al., 1994). The level of lead exposure for a significant portion of minorities in the U.S. remains higher than exposure levels known to cause physiological, psychological and behavioral impacts. For criminological purposes, these facts may help explain the distribution of crime.

Existing research indicates that lead exposure is a function of class and race (Stretesky, 2003; Lynch, 2004). Facilities that use lead and produce lead pollution, and hazardous waste sites contaminated with lead, are more prevalent in urban areas inhabited by the poor, and by racial and ethnic minorities. This spatial relationship between class, race and lead exposure is a historical process related to class and race segregation found in U.S. urban areas (see chapter 6), which forced minorities and the lower class into physical locations more proximate to sources of industrial pollution. When coupled with adverse economic conditions that limit access to health care, class and race segregation enhances the likelihood of negative health and behavioral effects from lead exposure, perhaps causing a rise in crime. In support of this argument, Stretesky and Lynch demonstrated a geographic relationship between air lead pollution and homicide rates (2001) and violent and property crime rates (2004) across all U.S. counties (N = 3,111). For example, counties with elevated air lead concentrations have homicide rates four times those found in counties with the lowest levels of air lead. This relationship is evident even though the researchers controlled for the impact of six other known correlates of homicide and the potential effect of nine other air pollutants (Stretesky and Lynch, 2001). This geographic pattern reinforces evidence on the relationship between lead exposure and crime that medical researchers have discovered using individual level data (e.g., see, Dietrich et al., 2001; for a summary see, Lynch 2004).

In addition to PCBs and lead, scientists have discovered that exposure to a number of synthetic chemicals – especially pesticides, fertilizers and herbicides – has negative human health consequences that elevate disease levels and stimulate aggressive behavior (Colborn, Dumanoski and Myers, 1997). These studies have clear criminological implications; they imply the need for further research that examines community crime rates in relation to synthetic chemical exposure patterns, including proximity of communities to facilities that produce and store hazardous synthetic chemicals that affect human health and behavior (e.g., landfills, toxic waste sites).

Criminologists are only beginning to examine how toxic chemical exposure affects criminal behavior, and how this relationship is mediated by the political economy of class and race. The study of the spatial proximity between hazardous waste locations and lower-class and minority communities, however, has been a central concern of environmental justice researchers for the past two decades.

## Environmental Justice

In the 1980s, radical social analysts combined research focused on social justice with research examining the distribution of environmental hazards to create a new area of inquiry: environmental justice (EJ). EJ research examines whether the racial, ethnic and class composition of a community affects the probability of residents' exposure to toxins and hazardous waste. To determine exposure patterns, EJ researchers examine environmental hazards sites and assess whether these locations are closer to lower-class and minority communities than to other communities.

EJ studies have important implications for criminology and criminal justice (Barnett, 1994). First, they tell us about the structure of justice within a society, the level of (in)justice a society is willing to tolerate, and the extent of a society's commitment to equal treatment of its citizens. Second, they can tell us whether people who live in neighborhoods with certain kinds of characteristics are more or less likely to be exposed to hazardous chemicals, including those that can affect human behavior. Combining these ideas, we can posit that the level of (in)justice (measured by variation in exposure to chemical harms) a society is willing to tolerate varies with the race and class composition of affected communities.

EJ studies begin with the assumption that, stated positively, every community has an equal right to be free from harms associated with exposure to toxic wastes; or stated negatively, that every community should bear an equal risk from exposure to the toxic effluents of our consumer society. EJ researchers test this assumption by collecting and combining census data on the characteristics of residential areas with Environmental Protection Agency data on the location of hazardous waste sites. Once these data are collected, the distances between communities and waste sites are determined and analyzed. Proximity and exposure to toxic waste is defined as unjust if a pattern indicates that hazardous waste sites are located closer to poor and minority communities than they are to white and affluent communities.

Toxic waste exposure patterns are an issue because they pose health and quality-of-life concerns. Exposure or proximity to hazardous waste production, treatment, storage and disposal facilities (TSDFs) increases the prevalence and incidence of disease across communities. These diseases include cancers and breathing disorders (Liu, 2001), as well as bio-behavioral outcomes such as increased levels of violence and crime associated with lead exposure.

Geographers and sociologists have produced the majority of environmental justice research. Up to this point, no orthodox criminologists and relatively few radical criminologists have devoted much attention to questions of environmental justice. As data regarding the link between environmental injustice and problematic behaviors such as aggression, school failure and crime become more available, we can anticipate increased attention to environmental justice from radical criminologists insofar as radical criminology, much more than orthodox approaches, emphasizes understanding all of the contextual forces shaping criminal behavior (see, Burns and Lynch, 2004 for a discussion).

## Examples of Radical Environmental Justice Research

In a series of studies, Stretesky and Lynch examined the associations among a community's race, ethnic and class characteristics and its proximity to a variety of hazardous wastes, including: (1) accidental chemical releases; (2) "Superfund" sites, which are the worst toxic waste sites identified by the EPA; and, (3) EPA toxic hazard measures (i.e., the Toxic Release Inventory [TRI], the Biannual Reporting System data [BRS], and Comprehensive Environmental Response and Liability Information System data [CERLIS]). They also examined the racial and ethnic composition of public schools and proximity to environmental hazards.

Using geographic information system (GIS) analysis, Stretesky and Lynch produced evidence of several persistent findings:

1. Minorities, especially African Americans, are more likely to live in census tracts that are proximate to hazardous waste sites than whites (Lynch, Stretesky and McGurrin, 2001; Stretesky and Lynch, 2003, 1999a, 1999b).

2.    Low-income groups are more likely to live in census tracts closer to hazardous waste sites than high-income groups. This relationship is enhanced by the racial composition of neighborhoods (Stretesky and Lynch, 2003, 1999a, 1999b).

3.    Census tract racial composition is associated with proximity to several different types of hazardous waste sources (Lynch, Stretesky and McGurrin, 2001; Stretesky and Lynch, 2003, 1999a, 1999b; Stretesky and Hogan, 1998).

These findings held when other dimensions of area racial composition were employed. For instance, Stretesky and Lynch (2003) found that the racial composition of public schools was related to the distance to hazardous waste sites. Specifically, the higher the percentage of African-Americans students in a school, the closer that school was to a hazardous waste site. This finding is of particular concern not only because of its racial dimension, but also because young children are more susceptible than adults to the long-term negative health consequences of exposure to hazardous wastes.

Not only are minority and low-income communities closer than white neighborhoods to hazardous waste sites, they are also in closer proximity to chemical accidents (Stretesky and Lynch, 1999a). In short, there is a predictable pattern to chemical accidents that is, in part, explained by the racial and class composition of an area.

Finally, the relationship between ethnicity and exposure to chemical hazards is complex and not easily discernible. Ethnicity effects for Hispanic communities, for instance, are evident in some studies, but absent in other tests. The presence or absence of Hispanic community effects are confounded by the unique location of some Hispanic communities in rural/farming areas and the lack of measurement of rural toxic waste problems (e.g., on waste produced by hog farming operations see, Stretesky, Johnston and Arney, 2003).

Lynch, Stretesky and Burns (2004a, 2004b) extended EJ research to examine penalties handed out for violations of environmental laws. Specifically, they examined whether community race and class characteristics affected fines handed out by the Environmental Protection Agency to oil refineries that violated three major federal environmental laws: (1) the Clean Air Act, (2) the Clean Water Act, and (3) the Resource Conservation and Recovery Act. The researchers found that penalties meted out to oil refineries in predominantly Black census tracts averaged

$108,563. This was only one-third the average amount of $341,590 given to oil refineries when they violated these laws in white communities. In addition, the study found that penalties for violations in poorer census tracts were significantly lower ($259,784 versus $334,267) than those handed out for violations in high-income census tracts. These differences were found after holding constant other important variables, such as the seriousness of the violation (i.e., violation history, facility inspection history), production levels, and the EPA region in which the violating refinery was situated. Based on these findings, we can conclude that the EPA does not provide equal protection to racially and economically diverse communities when applying penalties to oil refineries that violate environmental regulations.

## GLOBAL WARMING AND THE END OF OIL

Two of the most pressing issues in the modern era have not been the subject of criminological discussions: global warming and the end of the oil era. Before examining these issues as criminological subjects, we will provide some background on each problem.

**Global Warming.** The majority of scientists with expertise in climate change agree that we are experiencing the initial phase of global warming. For example, more than 2,500 scientists, policy experts, and economists contributed to the United Nations' report, *Climate Change, 2001* (Houghton et al., 2001). This report reviews the effects of global warming, including: increased average annual temperatures, decreased snow cover, a rise in global sea levels, shrinking of the polar ice cap, thawing of the permafrost, earlier egg laying among bird species, earlier emergence of insects, lengthening of the growing season, and an increase in extreme weather, among other findings.

Scientists have discovered that the most import cause of global warming is the increase in heat-trapping gases (especially carbon dioxide) produced by humans, linked to burning fossil fuels and deforestation. Fossil fuels – oil, natural gas and coal – are composed of complex hydrocarbon chains. According to the U.S. Geological Service, for the year 2000 in the U.S., 46 percent of the nearly 114 trillion cubic feet of carbon dioxide produced by burning fossil fuels results from burning oil and gas. Combustion releases energy from fossil fuels, and the more complex the fuel, the more carbon it contains (e.g., methane gas has 1 carbon and 4 hydrogen atoms; propane has 3 carbon and 8 hydrogen atoms; octane has 8 carbon and 118 hydrogen atoms), which increases carbon dioxide outputs when these fuels are burnt. (On global warming and deforestation see: http://www.ucsusa.org/ global_environment/global_warming/index.cfm.)

Working with the United Nations, governments of the world attempted to address global warming by creating the Kyoto Protocol, a treaty that pledges reductions in the production of global warming gases by each of the signatory nations (see, http://unfccc.int/resource/kpstats.pdf, for list of signatory nations). Unfortunately, the two nations that produce the greatest levels of global warming gases, the U.S. and Australia, have not signed this agreement. U.S. President G. W. Bush refused to sign the Kyoto agreement, claiming the greatest burdens in reductions would fall upon the U.S. and that this would hurt the U.S. economy. Bush's rationale for not signing the Kyoto Protocol illustrates the persistent tendency of conservative capitalist consciousness to favor class interests over human and environmental health. As the Union of Concerned Scientists (UCS) noted, this criticism of the Kyoto Treaty is the same as the one U.S. conservatives lodged against the Clean Air Act (CAA) before it was passed (www.ucsusa.org). On the surface, conservative capitalist opposition to treaties such as the Clean Air Act and the Kyoto Treaty is puzzling insofar as laws mandating environmental protection typically create jobs in industries that emerge to provide clean and alternative technologies when legal limits are placed on environmental pollution outputs. Likewise, failing to reduce global warming will cause more economic harm than would responding to the problem. For example, a study by the Union of Concerned Scientists into the likely effect of global warming on California indicates the likelihood of water shortages, decreased mountain snow caps and decreased agricultural production (especially for wineries); an increase in deaths from disease and heat stroke; diminished meat and dairy production; and loss of coastline to rising sea levels, with negative effects on real estate values and the insurance industry (www.climatechoices.org).

So why would conservative capitalists, epitomized by the neo-conservatives who have dominated the administration of George W. Bush, oppose environmental legislation? This takes us back to our earlier discussion about the short-term vision of capitalist consciousness. It is true that environmental legislation can create jobs by creating new, environmentally-friendly industries. But these industries do not currently exist, and the ones that do have no interest in loosening their stranglehold on the market to upstart green businesses. Furthermore, while environmental changes such as global warming may exert important negative impacts on the environment, these happen slowly; too slowly to affect any company's bottom line this year. Consequently, conservative capitalists see little reason to endorse long-term environmental protection, while they have considerable short-term incentive to oppose it.

Despite Bush Administration opinions that the potential consequences of global are exaggerated, there is little doubt that global warming is affecting the environment. In the opinion of environmental groups and political leaders from other nations, the U.S., and the Bush Administration more specifically, are acting in an immoral and illegitimate manner. More than 5,000 scientists from around the world have accused the Bush Administration of manipulating scientific data to support its destructive environmental policies (Union of Concerned Scientists, 2004; also see, Kennedy, 2004). Rather than address the pressing issues of global warming, the Bush Administration has rolled back the environmental regulation standards to allow increased global warming gas emissions, and expand U.S. reliance on fossil fuels that contribute to global warming (Kennedy, 2004; Burns and Lynch, 2004; Goodstein, 2004).

From a radical criminological perspective, the struggle over which laws and international mechanisms should be used to combat global warming constitutes a case study in how the definitions of right and wrong, or of criminal versus lawful behavior, are most often expressions of power. Because of its powerful position in the world, the United States can excuse itself from any effort to make global law governing the protection of the earth's environment. Moreover, it can do so based on selfish claims that reducing global warming might harm the U.S. economy, even if these claims are suspect. Orthodox criminologists are inclined to study street criminals when they harm others to satisfy their selfish desires for small amounts of money. They are less inclined, however, to study the motivations and actions of powerful leaders when they are willing to place much of the world's population at risk in order to preserve their system of power and privilege.

## The End of Oil

Many scientists agree that global warming is a grave problem that, if left unaddressed, threatens to alter or end life on our planet. The United States is the world's leading consumer of oil and the world's leading producer of global warming gases. Although the U.S. contains only 4 percent of the world population, it consumes 25 percent of all oil produced in the world annually. Interestingly, while burning fossil fuel is the primary source of global warming, the world faces an equally serious crisis because of the world's dwindling supply of oil.

Data on the world's oil supply has led a growing group of scholars to state that over the next decade, patterns of energy consumption will become a primary determinant of both economic development and the shape of social institutions (Rifkin, 2002). Research performed by M. King Hubbert in the late 1950s predicted the U.S. oil peak and crisis of the 1970s. Known as "Hubbert's Peak" or "Hubbert's Curve," the oil peak is the point at which one-half of known oil reserves have been pumped and placed into production. Building on Hubbert's research, scientists have estimated that one-half of the *world's* oil reserves (half of all available oil) will be depleted as early as 2007, and, in more optimistic views, as late as 2020 (Campbell, 2003, 1998; Campbell and Laherrere, 1998; Deffeyes, 2001; Goodstein, 2004; Heinberg, 2003; Roberts, 2004).

If we still have half the world's oil yet to consume, why are scientists so concerned? They are concerned because the rate of oil consumption is not constant, it is growing. Although it took more than a century to consume the first half of the world's oil reserve, at current rates of use (and depending on estimates for world population and economic growth) the remaining oil reserve will be depleted within 25 to 40 years after the world oil peak occurs (http:// www.lifeaftertheoilcrash.net) – sometime between 2032 and 2060. The rate of oil depletion poses a particular problem for the U.S. because it is not only the world's largest consumer of oil, but also because it currently imports nearly 60 percent of its oil. Without this imported oil, the United States would deplete its domestic oil reserve in about 12 years. The recent addition of the Alaska Arctic National Wildlife Refuge (former known as the National Petroleum Reserve) proposed by the Bush Administration (passed by Congress, March, 2005) as part of its national energy policy, will not expand this prediction significantly (estimates suggest that this addition will add two years to the oil peak). A law passed in 1923 required that the oil under the Refuge be maintained as a reserve for use by the Navy in the event of a national crisis. Opening the reserve to drilling not only threatens national security, but fails to make long-term energy sense. For example, other simple and currently achievable measures, such as raising average vehicle fuel economy to 40 miles per gallon, would save more oil than is found in the Arctic Reserve.

In a world marked by increasing global demand for oil and its declining supply, the United States risks economic and social collapse by ignoring the need to transform the nation's energy infrastructure. Any criminologist concerned with crime and violence should be concerned with how such a potential collapse of the oil economy would threaten the possibilities for social order at home and peace internationally.

The declining supply of oil is not news to some. The world oil supply has long been tracked, and has been a central concern of international politics, often guiding U.S. interventions in Middle Eastern nations. A recent case in point is the invasion and occupation of Iraq that began in 2003. Even U.S. government commissions have shown there was no substance to the claims that Iraq possessed weapons of mass destruction (WMD) or had links to jihadist terrorism (Linzer and Gellman, 2005; see also chapter 9). Scientists who study oil depletion are so concerned that they have formed associations (e.g., the Association for the Study of Peak Oil and Gas) and conferences (e.g., the Peak Oil Conference) organized to share oil data and forecasts, and develop alternative energy strategies.

The looming oil crisis requires that societies rethink the production and use of energy. This is no small task since it involves discovering and implementing new energy sources that are likely to alter modern economic and social structures. Planning for the decline of oil is necessary in order to avert the effects of a world wide oil shortage, and perhaps, a world wide economic recession or depression.

In addition to devising alternative energy schemes, formulating plans for implementing alternative energy delivery systems, and coordinating a smooth transition to an alternative energy economy at the national level, individual states and institutions must develop their plans for the future. Policy planners from a variety of fields must begin to consider how the end of oil will affect various social functions, and what plans should be implemented to minimize the impact of the declining availability of oil. Criminal justice policy planners are not exempt from these challenges.

The U.S. has the world's largest criminal justice system, which includes the world's largest prison system, the world's largest court system, and the world's largest policing apparatus. These systems have been driven by policies based on deterrence and incapacitation, which have led to the creation of larger and larger systems of justice to reduce crime. Not only has this approach failed to reduce crime, it fails to address energy consumption, availability and expenses. One might say that the expansion of the U.S. system of justice was in part a product of assumptions that the energy supply fossil fuels presented were limitless. Consider, for example, the organization of U.S. policing, which is highly centralized, and relies heavily on the patrol car for law enforcement. Likewise, the U.S. prison system, the world's largest, is based on locating offenders in large, out-of-sight locations that require large fossil fuel energy inputs to operate.

Ironically, the coming energy crisis may help radicals achieve the kinds of criminal justice reforms they see as appropriate crime strategies (e.g., neighborhood policing strategies that flow from left realism; community-oriented problem-solving strategies based on peacemaking; see chapter 10). But, these strategies, as well as orthodox crime control policies, will increasingly have to take energy issues into account, perhaps privileging energy conservation over philosophies of doing justice (or altering policies derived from different theories of justice so that they are consistent with energy issues). Accomplishing this task will require criminologists and policy makers to think about crime and justice in new ways, leading to redesigned criminal justice procedures and a new criminal justice architecture. Thus, the decentralized neighborhood police station fuelled by solar, geothermal, and photovoltaic energy, with neighborhood foot, bicycle and electric car patrols are likely strategies of the future, not for philosophical reasons, but because limits on natural resources will require these policies. Energy conservation strategies have already been put into use by police in Vallejo and Anaheim, California . Likewise, the massive prison complex the U.S. has built since 1973 will need to be redesigned. Alternative energy prisons are already in operation in Michigan, Utah, Tennessee, England and Sweden. But, making policing and the prison system energy efficient will also require redesigning laws. One possibility is a system of ticketing minor offenders instead of the booking practices that require the arrest and transportation of offenders. Another might be the widespread use of camera-operated, automated traffic control and ticketing procedure that does not require police to cruise roadways in search of traffic violators.

Before closing this section, let us briefly state that there are numerous energy alternatives being proposed that may address short-term energy demands, such as coal gasification, shale-oil conversion, and other fossil fuel-related options. In the long run, these alternatives will not solve the energy problem for two reasons. First, some of these methods are not only expensive, but they are net energy losers, meaning more energy goes into the production of, for example, shale oil, than is extracted. The Canadian experiment with this process illustrates both the costs and net energy loss issues. Second, oil derived from coal and shale produces more pollution in the form of air-born sulfur, and elevated levels of carbon dioxide. Thus, while these methods may produce more energy, they add to the greenhouse effect and exacerbate the level of other air pollutants.

Given the threat posed by environmental pollution, global warming and the peak oil problem, the street crimes that most criminologists traditionally have studied will become less important. In his recent book, Robert Kennedy, Jr. (2004) labels behaviors that contribute to and avoid these important environmental issues as "crimes against nature," and he details how G.W. Bush's presidential administration has helped contribute to elevated levels of environmental pollution and global warming. Within radical criminology, these important but neglect environmental problems are the subject of green criminology.

# GREEN CRIMINOLOGY

In the early 1990s, as the green environmental movement took hold, Lynch (1990; Frank and Lynch, 1992:79-96) suggested developing a green criminology that combined radical criminology's emphasis on class, race and corporate crime, with the political activism and orientation of the green environmental movement. Since then, a number of others have joined the call to develop a green criminology (Benton, 1998; Groombridge, 1998; Lane, 1998; South, 1998; Lynch and Stretesky, 2003; Beirne and South, 2006). To understand what green criminology is, we begin by defining the term "green."

## What is "Green?"

In common usage, the term "green" identifies environmentally-friendly practices. From an environmental perspective, this term has broader implications, and denotes actions and practices that are consciously designed to protect and preserve both natural and human environments. This is a subtle but important distinction, especially in light of corporate advertising campaigns that use the term green to enhance sales, even when the product in question is environmentally harmful (Lynch and Stretesky, 2003). Nevertheless, we can begin by stating that green practices do not harm (or do minimal harm to) the environment, and those who "act" green consciously consider the environmental ramifications of their actions. In contrast, anti-green practices generate environmental harms, and those who engage in these practices either do not consider environment harms as serious outcomes, or view these outcomes as a cost of doing business.

The common definitions described briefly above, however, fail to capture the full importance of the term green. During the late 1980s and early 1990s, environmental groups adopted the term "green" to signify a commitment to environmental preservation actions that involved political activism informed by political-economic, race and gender-based theories of inequality. This was most evident among Green political parties in Europe, which "viewed environmental destruction as an outcome of the structure of modern, industrialized capitalist production and consumption patterns" (Lynch, 1990:3). Today, green environmental groups are split into three broad types: (1) ecofeminist, which focuses on the patriarchal nature of capitalism's growth orientation and the relationship between the exploitation of women and nature; (2) environmental racism and environmental justice movements, that focus on racial inequities in exposure to environmental hazards, and the use of community-based political activism as an anchoring point for solutions to this problem; and (3) red-green groups, that focus on the inter-relationship between economic exploitation and oppression and environmental degradation (Lynch and Stretesky, 2003). These groups can be differentiated because each has a different primary focus that is uses to explain the unequal distribution of environmental harms: gender (eco-feminists), race (environmental racism), or class (red-greens). These groups are united, however, because they share a commitment to political activism and democracy at the local level, identifying sources of environmental injustice in forms of human oppression evident in historically rooted conflicts and unequal race, class and gender relationships (Lynch and Stretesky, 2003).

## What is Green Criminology?

Now that we have identified key characteristics of the term "green," we can define green criminology as: a form of investigation that examines environmental harms, justice and laws in relation to class, race and gender inequality, and offers sustainable environmental alternatives that employ community-based political activism as a mechanism for remedying environmental harms and limiting the effects of environmental destruction.

Thus, rather than simply expressing concern with environmental hazards and pollution, and studying its effects or the laws that regulate environmentally harmful actions, green criminologists seek to: (1) understand how race, class and gender inequality generates these harms, structures the laws and regulatory processes designed to control environmental harms; and (2) explore ways in which this situation can be changed.

Given this theoretical focus, green criminology can be and has been used to examine a wide range of environmental harms including crimes against animals (Benton, 2003; Beirne, 2001, 1999, 1997), deforestation, pesticides use and pollution, environmental harms in developing nations (South, 1998; Frank and Lynch, 1992; Lynch and Stretesky, 2001), and increasingly, criminological questions related to ecofeminism (Lane, 1998) and environmental justice (Lynch, Stretesky and Burns, 2004a, 2004b; Stretesky and Lynch, 2003, 1999a, 1999b). Thus, green criminologists examine the environment as a direct victim (e.g., air, water quality; animal and plant species health), and humans as indirect victims of environmentally harmful activities such as hazardous waste treatment and disposal facility placement, or the dumping of toxic waste in streams, rivers or in landfills (Groombridge, 1998; Barnett, 1999). More importantly, they do so, or should do so, by framing these various environment harms in the perspectives of radically-derived theories, including radical ecology.

Examples of this research were reviewed earlier in this chapter, and it should be clear from our description that green criminology is a broad research area capable of including the various kinds of environmental studies radical criminologists have undertaken. In our view, green criminology provides a theoretical starting point for undertaking radically-oriented environmental research related to crime and justice, and uniting the various forms of environmental research that radicals perform.

## In Sum

Environmental crime and justice is becoming an increasingly important concern in societies across the face of the globe. Generally, criminologists have had little to say about these issues, and criminological literature on environmental crime and justice is inadequately represented in the criminological literature, especially in journals (Lynch, McGurrin and Fenwick, 2004). In contrast to orthodox criminology, radical criminology has paved the way for reorienting the study of crime and justice to give serious attention to crimes against the environment. This focus should not be interpreted as merely "trendy" or "fashionable." Rather, environmental crimes deserve the attention of criminologists because they cause more death, injury and illness than the street crime on which criminologists concentrate their efforts.

Developing methods for controlling industrial pollution, environmental hazards and global warming will occupy the time of researchers and policy makers in a variety of fields over the next decade. Criminology should not be an exception. Clearly, environmental issues are among the most pressing facing the world's population today, and any criminology that fails to address them fails in its responsibility to contribute to the knowledge needed to improve society. To our knowledge, the level of ordinary crime has, in the history of human societies, never caused the demise of a society. Environmental hazards produced by humans, however, may, and are already altering the physical world around us.

Studying environmental crime presents numerous challenges. Historically, criminologists interested in these crimes were hindered by a lack of data. This can no longer be said to be the case (see, Burns and Lynch, 2004). Radical criminologists have led the way in identifying and researching environmental issues in criminology, and have, by their actions, set up a challenge to orthodox criminologists to follow suit and contribute to the study of these serious crimes.

# NINE.
## STATE CRIME AND TERRORISM

*"A person stands a better chance of being tried and judged for killing one human being than for killing 100,000." José Ayala Lasso, former United Nations High Commissioner for Human Rights*

No one gets away with murder (or other crimes) as easily as presidents, dictators, and kings. Modern history is dense with violence, brutality, and oppression committed in the name of state power. It is not, however, equally dense with the punishment and prosecution of the politically powerful. The reason for this imbalance lies at the intersection of ideology, political economy, and state power, a subject we will explore in more detail further on. First, however, it is necessary to define two overlapping terms central to discussing crimes in the political arena – political crime and state crime.

### FROM POLITICAL CRIME TO STATE CRIME

Analyses of wrongdoing in the political arena have tended to take one of two approaches. Earlier works used the term *political crime* to designate acts committed against established authority, such as revolutions, assassinations, demonstrations and other forms of public dissent committed by those *outside of government* (Schafer, 1974; Turk, 1982). Other analysts reversed the analytic lens to focus on *state crimes,* such as political repression, expropriation, genocide, and wars of aggression committed by those *inside government.* This broad definitional distinction is a useful, if admittedly incomplete starting point for analyzing crimes in the political arena.

Crimes against government can also be divided into those that undermine the goals of the state and those that support these goals. Barak (1990:15) suggested that "political state crimes...are motivated by a desire to maintain the status quo or curtail change," while "non-political state crimes...are committed by individuals employed by the government who take advantage of their positions to engage in crime for personal and/or monetary gain." Ross (2003) divides these crimes into *oppositional* political crimes that violate state interests, and *pro-systemic* political crimes that are committed on behalf of state interests. Other criminologists have combined these approaches, characterizing political crimes as encompassing both crimes *by* and crimes *against* the state (Beirne and Messerschmidt, 1991; Hagan, 1997). In general, these types of bivariate distinctions, though useful, fail to capture the complex nature of state crime, and can risk misclassifying crime types (e.g., placing dissimilar crimes in the same category, and similar ones in different categories). For instance, government leaders who keep important information from the public by lying to the press or the public (e.g., the supposed existence of weapons of mass destruction in Iraq), or who promulgate genocide, may both be acting to advance state interests. Yet, the human consequences of these acts are unique enough to make them fundamentally different crimes.

To encompass a broader range of politically-motivated and/or politically enabled crimes, we offer a typology of political criminality that considers actors' social locations and goals. Political crime actors can be either *insiders* who have access to delegated state power or *outsiders* who lack such access, giving each type different opportunities to engage in these crimes. The three goals are private economic gain, private political gain, and systemic advantage. Table 9.1 illustrates the intersection of social locations and goal orientation, and provides examples of behaviors that fall within each division.

The top four cells of Table 9.1 include crimes in the political arena for private economic or private political gain committed either by *insiders* or by *outsiders*. Insiders, those who occupy positions of authority within state institutions, have legitimate access to some degree of state power. The insider can range from the town cop who shakes down a local bookie for a little "walking around money," to a U.S. Congressman who accepts elaborate trips and gifts from corporate lobbyists in return for favorable votes in support of the lobbyists' positions (Smith and Grimaldi, 2005). Outsiders lack formally-delegated government authority, but interact with the state in criminal or wrongful ways. A government consultant who submits fraudulent bills, or campaign advisors who use hidden "slush" funds to promote their candidates' campaigns, enjoy opportunities for crime that are not available to people with no connection to the arena of political power and authority.

The bottom two cells of Table 9.1 encompass crimes for *system advantage* committed by insiders or outsiders. These wrongdoings are more appropriately termed *state* crime rather than political crime, because they are explicitly undertaken to advance or thwart the goals of a political state or some state-like entity, rather than for a personal benefit(s). For this reason,

## Table 9.1:  Varieties of Political Criminality

| Goal | Insiders (actors with state power) | Outsiders (actors lacking state power) | Type of Crime |
|---|---|---|---|
| Private economic gain | employee theft of government property; influence peddling; using campaign finances for personal expenditures; accepting or soliciting bribes and kickbacks from government contractors | individual or organized theft of government property; bribing government official for special benefits or contracts; submitting doctored or fraudulent bill to government purchasers | Political Arena Crime |
| Private political gain | using government agencies to "investigate" political opponents; election fraud; dirty electoral "tricks" | campaign "dirty tricks;" stuffing ballot boxes; vote buying; manipulating voter roles | Political Arena Crime |
| Systemic advantage | expropriation of tribal or ethnic lands; slavery; genocide; wars of aggression; state terrorism; repression of domestic political dissent; repression of identity groups (e.g., ethnic minorities, religions, women, etc.) | assassination; revolution; coup d'etat; anti-state terrorism; boycott; civil disobedience | State Crime |

Note: The offenses described are for purposes of illustration, and do not represent the full range of political crimes.

when we use the term *state crime* in this chapter we mean *socially injurious acts designed to alter, expand, or reproduce key elements of the political order.*

Outsider crimes against the state may have far-ranging goals, such as revolutions aimed at fundamentally altering a country's social organization, or wars of aggression designed to transform a particular nation-state into an empire. Other outsider crimes such as *coups d'etat* or assassinations often have more limited goals, such as replacing one leader with another, that leave the overall social order unchanged. Similarly, insider state crimes may have broad state goals such as increasing national identity and "patriotism" by persecuting a racial or ethnic group labeled an enemy of the state, as is typically the case with crimes of genocide. Alternatively, insider state crimes may be narrowly focused, such as using political police to silence particularly annoying and/or influential critics of the state.

## State Crime as Organizational Deviance

State crimes, particularly those committed by insiders, differ from routine political crimes in another important way: State crimes are more often *organizational crimes* rather than individual or small-group deviance. This distinction parallels the one made between white collar (personal gain) and corporate crime (business or corporate gain; see, Kramer, 1984; Frank and Lynch, 1992; Friedrichs, 1996; Tillman, 2005). Just as it is useful to distinguish between white collar and corporate crime according to who benefits, it is also useful to distinguish crimes in the political arena that emerge from individualized motivations from those generated by the structure and organizational culture of governmental agencies. The structure and ideology of totalitarian governments, for instance, are prone to create institutions of social control and political policing in which terrorizing, physically abusing, or even killing perceived political enemies becomes a taken-for-granted part of everyday life (Arendt, 1977). The police, prosecutors, prison guards and other government agents who carry out these acts are not morally depraved. Rather, they are ordinary workers who come to accept the normalcy of an organizational culture in which these acts, even if regrettable, are understood as simply part of their jobs as well as necessary means to achieve positive goals (Hamilton and Kelman, 1990).

The Nazi Holocaust is the archetypical example of how states create institutional frameworks in which ordinary people perform heinous acts (Alvarez, 2001; Arendt, 1977). But, we do not need to reach as far back as World War II, or to some other country to find examples of state crimes committed by ordinary people as a routine part of their government jobs. In 2004, for instance, U.S. soldiers and military contractors engaged in abuse, torture and killing of suspected terrorists and "enemy combatants" at Camp X-Ray (the U.S. detention facility at Guantanamo Bay, Cuba), in Afghanistan, and at Abu Ghraib and other prisons in occupied Iraq (Ratner and Ray, 2004; Hersh, 2004; Greenberg and Dratel, 2005). Existing evidence suggests that these actors were not sadists; rather, their actions resulted from an *institutional culture* that enabled or even produced these actions as appropriate strategies for "softening up" or "breaking" people who were suspected to possess useful information in the war on terror (Taguba, 2004). In order to understand the worst state crimes – those committed systematically by large numbers of people in their role as formal or informal agents of the state – we must remain alert to the way states create the organizational framework and ideological understandings that make brutal behaviors appear moral or normal and acceptable.

## State-like Actors

Although it may sound contradictory, it is not only states that are guilty of state crimes. Those who attack or seek to grasp state power for the purpose of changing rather than expanding or protecting an existing social order can commit crimes that imitate state crimes. For instance, revolutionary and insurgent groups such as the Bolsheviks in pre-Soviet Russia, the Falange in Republican Spain, the Viet Cong in South Vietnam, Hamas in Palestine, Hezbollah in Lebanon, or the FARC in Columbia, typically begin to mimic the characteristics of governments as soon as they take control of any portion of the country in which they are struggling. They levy taxes, enforce laws, distribute benefits, and train and field fighters. Once they take on the role of an "official authority" or state, they can also be guilty of committing state-like crimes, including: the use of torture, brutal and summary punishments for ordinary crimes or suspected collaboration with the enemy; expropriating the property of people deemed to be enemy sympathizers without formal legal processes; using children as fighters; or employing terror and rape as weapons of war (Human Rights Watch, 2004; Arenas, 1985; Guevara, 1998). In short, a conceptual framework for the study of state crime should include both formally constituted states and state-like organizations that are struggling to obtain political power.

## The Greatest Crimes

State crimes constitute one of the greatest threats to human peace and security. According to estimates by Rudolph Rummel in his book *Death by Government* (1994), during the twentieth century alone, 170 million *civilians* were killed by war, genocide and terrorism. This figure does not include the more than 23 million *soldiers* who died in twentieth century wars, the hundreds of millions of soldiers seriously wounded in battle, or the 2 million *child soldiers* who were killed and another 6 million who were injured in fighting between 1994 and 2003 alone. Nor does state crime promise to be any less of a threat in the twenty-first century. In addition to the continuing threat of wars and brutalities by established nation-states, we also face the threat of global terrorism, increasing ethno-violence, and the violence associated with America's quest for a global empire (Johnson, 2004).

Stephen Schafer (1974:1) noted that: "It is virtually impossible to find a history book of any society which does not record...those craftsmen of dreams who possess a gigantic reservoir of creative energy as well as destructive force." For Schafer, these "craftsmen of dreams" are individual political leaders inside or outside governments who lead masses into wars, revolutions, expropriations and brutality. His observation, however, apply equally well to the history of political states: Since the rise of civilizations, states, the greatest reservoirs of power, have routinely used that power in ways that have brought death, disease and destruction to human populations. Indeed, van den Berghe (1990:1) contends that the state "has been the prime killer in human history. Killing is, in fact, in the very nature of the state. States are killing machines controlled by the few to steal from the many." Even if one does not subscribe to van den Berghe's anarchist view of nation-states, recent history makes it clear that humans have far more to fear from the political projects of states and state-like entities than from one another as individuals.

The harms associated with political crimes are not, however, limited to physical violence; they include influence peddling, accepting bribes and kickbacks, and illegal campaign financing. Private political crimes weaken public confidence in political processes, often opening the way for even greater crimes as citizens disengage from active efforts to create participatory political systems. They also distort the distribution of governmental benefits and protections, with the frequent effect of increasing existing inequalities and intensifying existing injustices. Crimes in pursuit of state interests are far greater threats, however, because states exert power along a number of dimensions (see Turk, 1982 for discussion).

The ability of the state to control and mobilize law, police and military powers, ideological weaponry and other political and economic forces, allows it to involve more people in pursuing state goals than any other institution of society – with the possible exception of private economic institutions in societies organized around private (i.e., capitalist) rather than collective (i.e., socialist) means of production and distribution. The historical record shows that state mobilization has often resulted in widespread death, disease, damage and destruction. In its early years, for instance, the United States used laws, institutions of justice and military force to preserve slavery and annihilate Native peoples and their cultures. By the last quarter of the nineteenth century, having stolen everything "from sea to shining sea," the United States turned its corporate, military and political power to the task of defeating, dominating, or undermining other countries in order to create a global economic and political empire under the guise of bringing "democracy" to the rest of the world (Johnson, 2001; Ferguson, 2001; Williams, 1988). Throughout the twentieth century, other nations such as the Britain, Germany, Japan, and the Soviet Union also sought to establish imperial dominance over weaker nations; these acts have resulted in wars and political repression that dwarf most other sources of human misery. Yet, state crime rarely figures into our everyday consciousness of crime.

## STATE CRIME AND POLITICAL CONSCIOUSNESS

As discussed in chapter 4, the powerful classes in each society play a central role in shaping the dominant culture and institutional frameworks that determine what will and will not be defined as criminal. As part of this process, dominant classes actively promote or tacitly endorse laws that confirm their worldview and serve their political-economic interests. High-profile representatives of elite interests, such as office-holders and other political leaders, high-ranking educators, religious leaders and other public moralists utilize broadly accepted elements of their cultures to justify policies and practices that promote the interests of dominant classes, while deemphasizing other cultural beliefs that contradict elite views and goals. In doing so, they help create and/or reproduce a dominant worldview in which ruling class ways of seeing the world come to be understood as *natural, normal,* and *universal.*

## Consciousness, Crime and Hegemony

Where political elites are successful in making their interests appear to be everybody's interests, they can be said to have achieved what Antonio Gramsci (1971) termed, *hegemony*. Hegemony is a cultural condition in which the values, ideologies, and forms of social, economic and political organization that favor elites are widely accepted by other social classes. Hegemonic consciousness involves a belief in "political myths that involve the glorification and romanticization of the nation-state," so that "whether in war or in peace, the state is correct, and the enemies of the state are wrong" (Hirsch, 1995:164). As a result, hegemony plays a contradictory role with respect to state crime. Where hegemonic consciousness exists, crimes *against* the state are minimal because the majority of the population views the state and its actions as legitimate (Ward and Green, 2000). At the same time, hegemony increases the potential for crimes *by* the state, and hegemonic states are more likely to rely on the use of force as a solution. The problem, as Max Weber (1978) noted, is that force is an unstable basis for authority. When hegemony exists, rulers can exert control over subordinated populations, not through coercion, but ideologically, by convincing them to accept their condition as right and moral, or through "repression by consensus" (Michalowski and Bohlander, 1975). For instance, American slave owners used Christianity as a strategy to convince slaves to accept their subordinate condition rather than rebel. Similarly, contemporary capitalist elites labor to convince working class populations that large tax breaks for the wealthy will stimulate the economy, and are the route to eventual working class well-being.

Hegemony is also a central mechanism ensuring that brutal actions taken by states on behalf of ruling elites will not appear as state crimes in political discourse and popular consciousness. Consider the following historical examples.

As part of the legal foundation for a new nation, the framers of the U.S. Constitution authorized the permanent enslavement of captured Africans and all their descendants, and agreed to count individuals of African heritage as only three-fifths of a person in counting the population so as to apportion political representation. In this way, the Constitution confirmed the view of slave owners and their supporters that the black laborer was a *sub-human* whose enslavement was not a crime. Native Americans fared even worse when they were formally excluded from census and apportionment counts, which rendered them legal *non-persons*. This created the legal framework under which their lands would be stolen, their lives taken, and their cultures destroyed with little compunction or legal objection. The Constitution also legalized the second-class citizenship of women when it imposed subaltern citizenship on women by denying them rights to vote, own property, or testify against their husbands (Sklar, 2000). The point is that the Constitution weakened the political power of opposing views by granting *legal validation* to the view that white males of English descent had a natural right to dominate women and people of color.

The repressive constitutional endorsement of slavery, genocide and the subjugation of women was not simply a codification of dominant beliefs. It was part of the process of determining America's dominant belief systems. Imagine what the dominant worldview in the United States might look like today if the founding fathers had declared slavery illegal, and that all people – white, black, Indian, male or female – were equally empowered citizens in the building of a new nation.

The early constitutional provisions legitimizing slavery and allowing genocide have been invalid now for more than a century. Today, most Americans would condemn slavery and genocide (although some political and economic elites still turn a blind eye to slavery or near-slavery in poorer parts of the world when it serves U.S. corporate interests; Bales, 2004). Similarly, a large majority in the United States believes that women should have equal opportunities in the workforce and the political arena. It is important to remember, however, that when the Constitution was written, slavery, genocide, and the subjugation of women *served key political-economic interests,* and the politically powerful white men who signed the U.S. Constitution did not challenge the morality of this view even though a significant part of public discourse did (Genovese, 1967). Over time, however, as power structures change, hegemony's content must be modified. For example, advanced technology, the need for an expanded pool of industrial laborers, and the threat that slavery presented to the political-economic interests of powerful northern elites produced conditions under which moral arguments against slavery were acknowledged (Huston, 2003). Likewise, women's struggles for equality gained the most ground when the wage-labor and public participation of women were most needed: e.g., the era of rapid industrial expansion at the beginning of the twentieth century; World War II, when the male labor force was depleted by military service; and the 1970s, when business leaders came to understand that reducing sex discrimination in the work world would increase the size of the labor force, thereby slowing or reversing wage growth at a time when corporate profits were shrinking in the face of global economic changes and the power of domestic labor unions (see,

Baron, 1991). The rights of Native Americans were only recognized after the majority of their holdings had been stolen, leaving them with few resources to challenge their long history of oppression.

We are not suggesting that revisions in hegemonic ideologies and repressive laws are the direct result of self-conscious duplicity on the part of political-economic elites. In some cases that may be true. More often, however, economic and political elites begin to incorporate the claims of groups struggling for some measure of equality or liberation when the dominant consciousness can no longer adequately address the problems and needs of these leaders. At that point hegemony begins to crack, and formerly excluded ideas are reconsidered to help maintain the state's legitimacy.

It is relatively easy to recognize the hegemonic beliefs that supported gross violations of human rights long ago, and to condemn these actions as crimes. The challenge for radical criminology, however, it to identify, analyze, and challenge actions in the contemporary world that are equally wrong, even though they may be part of the taken-for-granted (i.e. hegemonic) understanding of legitimate state actions.

## Invading Iraq: A Case Study in Crime and Consciousness

On September 11, 2001, Al Qaeda suicide pilots murdered 3,000 people in the U.S., most of them ordinary workers going about their daily lives. This was the greatest single act of violence ever committed on American soil by a foreign actor (domestically, losses from single battles in the U.S. Civil War had exceeded this total). Yet, the human consequences of the September 11th attacks against the United States were small in comparison to the consequences of the 2003 invasion of Iraq.

Although a violation of international law, in March 2003, U.S. President George W. Bush authorized the bombing and subsequent invasion of Iraq. These actions resulted in the murder of between 20,000 and 100,000 Iraqi civilians (Roberts et al., 2004). Of course, given the objectives of the U.S., we do not ordinarily call the deaths of these Iraqi civilians "murder." In fact, many of you reading this section surely recoiled when we used the word *murder* to describe what U.S. bombs did to Iraqi civilians. However, ask yourself why you did not have a similar reaction to our use of the word "murder" to characterize what happened to those killed in the United States on September 11, 2001.

Most Americans do not view the deaths of Iraqi civilians that resulted from the invasion of Iraq as murder because they accept the hegemonic ideology of *intent*. Our dominant consciousness revolves around utilitarian logic which holds that as long as U.S. actions are undertaken to achieve moral outcomes, the killing and destruction that happens along the way is morally acceptable "collateral damage." Because the United States government argues that it authorized the bombing of Iraq to eliminate Saddam Hussein, not to kill Iraqis, the fact that we did kill them appears acceptable to many people. As long as our intent was moral, we need not concern ourselves with the outcome.

Of course, regardless of U.S. motives, the *behavioral* consequence of killing innocent Iraqis with "smart" weapons, cruise missiles and "dumb" cluster bombs is the same as killing innocent workers in New York City by flying fuel-laden Boeing 737s into buildings. It means people bleed, suffer and die, loved ones are bereft, and gigantic holes are blown in the social fabric of society. Nevertheless, once the utilitarian logic that the "ends justify the means" is accepted, the only challenge facing leaders is to convince the public that their motives are pure. That is, they must convince people that the killing is being done in the "best interests" of the nation, or if a country is attempting to create a broad empire, in the best interests of "humanity," or "civilization" (Hardt and Negri, 2004). The use of these kinds of thought and language processes has been fundamental for justifying state crimes throughout modern history.

One way to understand how state-initiated brutalities come to be interpreted as regrettable necessities or praiseworthy moral actions is to investigate the construction of our own consciousness about the harms caused by states. What, for instance, are the language and thought processes that enable many Americans to see foreign civilians killed by U.S. weapons as acceptable *casualties of war,* while U.S. citizens killed by terrorists are *victims of crime?* We are not trying to minimize the criminality of killing innocents through terrorist attacks. What we are suggesting, however, is that the tendency to minimize the criminality of killing innocents when one's own government is doing the killing is a particularly vivid example of hegemony at work. Another example is the inability of orthodox criminology to incorporate wrongdoing by states as a core concern for criminological inquiry.

## THE ABSENCE OF STATE CRIME IN CRIMINOLOGY

Despite their gravity, criminologists have given scant attention to state crimes (Schafer, 1974; Barak, 1991; Ross, 2000). A good indicator of this neglect can be found in key publications within orthodox criminology.

From January 2000 through December 2005, *Criminology*, the official journal of the American Society of Criminology, *Justice Quarterly*, the official journal of the Academy of Criminal Justice Sciences, and the *British Journal of Criminology*, published a total of 575 articles. Of these articles, 533 focused on issues related to lower class crime and/or its control. Explaining the causes of street crime or assessing the efficacy of policies designed to control street crime were, by far, the dominant themes. Eighteen articles – just 3 percent of the total – addressed crimes of the powerful, and only 7 of these – a mere *1.3 percent* of the total – concerned either political crime or state crime. State crimes are barely a blip on criminology's radar. There are a number of reasons for this.

First, most criminologists view their discipline as the study of crime as officially or legally defined by state lawmakers (Sellin, 1938). Insofar as laws are influenced by social structure, the harms committed by those acting under state authority will rarely be defined as crimes.

Second, state crimes frequently involve many people, complex chains of events, and elaborate structures of authority that place substantial distance between inaugural acts and eventual injury. This structure makes it difficult to directly link state criminals to the crimes they have authorized.

Third, the complex nature of state crimes also deflects questions about intent or *mens rea* onto subordinates, and allows political leaders to escape detection, blame and responsibility. In addition, hegemonic discourse aids this "deception" by allowing leaders to note that their "intent" was liberation rather than murder. In effect, the complex structure of state crimes, a seeming lack of harmful intent, and hegemonic discourse all allow state crimes to be "neutralized." For example, consider that the "cold war" (see Highlight #1") led to extensive death and injury, and the impoverishment of millions of people worldwide. Yet, no U.S. political leader has ever been tried for these consequences, and most criminologists easily dismiss the need to study these behaviors as crimes.

Fourth, state crimes are almost never committed directly by the government officials who authorize them: a long, multifaceted chain-of-command hides the identities of the higher-ups responsible for these crimes behind the faces of the front line solider, or other low-level operatives.

Fifth, state crimes typically stand outside of hegemonic consciousness, and government-controlled or -influenced media have successfully convinced populations that wars of aggression, genocide, displacement of peoples from hereditary lands, and political repression were necessary to preserve the integrity of some sacred national space – whether it is called "der faterland" (Nazi Germany), "Mother Russia" (Russia under the Czars

## Highlight #1: The Cold War — State Crime Hiding behind Complexity and Ideology

Hiding behind the complexity of the structures, events, processes and actions that contribute to state crime are disingenuous intentions and subterfuge that disguise state crimes and undermine the principles of democracy upon which our government is built. As an example that we cannot elaborate fully, consider the "cold war," or the foreign policy built to contain Communism that emerged following World War II (Keenan, 1967).

To begin, we must understand that a dense network of government relationships stood behind the effort to enforce cold war policy. First, this policy was transformed into *strategic* goals by leaders in the State Department, the Central Intelligence Agency, the Department of Defense, and the National Security Council. Next, these strategic goals were passed down the chain of command to military units, CIA operatives and clandestine agents responsible for carrying out *tactical* missions (e.g., bombings, assassinations, training of foreign "police," the use of torture, low intensity warfare) to support the strategic goals (Herman, 1982; Klare and Kornbluh, 1989). These chains of command, also a common feature of corporate crimes, focus attention on low-level actors rather than "masterminds" or organizational higher-ups who remain hidden.

To defeat communism and maintain its own world domination, the U.S. employed economic sanctions and its military might to "protect freedom" by preventing smaller, less powerful nations from installing socialist or communist leaders, even when these leaders were supported by their national populace. To do so, the U.S. engaged in a dark cornucopia of state crimes, including assassinations of foreign political leaders, the overthrow or subversion of legitimate governments, illegal wars of aggression, and violations of the civil rights of U.S. citizens (Herman, 1982). Various tools and tricks of the trade were employed, including spies, training of foreign "police," military aid, and aid to "contras" and other terrorist, anti-communist government organizations.

Within the U.S., media reports depicted the international and even the national scope of the "communist threat." These media stories legitimized the continued repression of any nation, organization, or person assumed to have links to the "evil empire" of communists and socialists, and focused on on-going "purges" such as the one waged against motion picture actors. For example, in the late 1940s under the leadership of its president, Ronald Reagan (1947-52), the Screen Actors Guild (SAG) required actors to complete anti-communism pledges, and blackballed those who refused as "communists." Reagan also appeared as a "friendly" witness before the House Un-American Activities Committee, and turned over names of persons he considered "disloyal" to the U.S. while serving as a secret agent, T-10, for the FBI. The news media also promoted anti-communist fervor in its coverage of the McCarthy anti-communism hearings.

and the Soviet Union under Communist rule), or "homeland" (the United States under George W. Bush (see "Highlight #2).

---

## Highlight #2: Beyond Media Moguls: When the Government Controls the News

In the United States, we often think of situations where the government controls the media as undemocratic and consistent with totalitarian regimes based on communism, socialism or fascism. But, a similar situation exists in the United State today. In the modern era, state leaders enjoy easy access to the media, and use it to shape popular images of government actions through either direct censorship or indirect influence (O'Shaughnessy, 2005). For example, according to a report by the U.S. Inspector General issued in March 2005, between 2000 and 2004 the Bush Administration produced *several hundred* "news" segments that were distributed to, and frequently broadcast by, local television stations around the United States. Unlike commercials and political ads, however, these government propaganda pieces masqueraded as "objective" news, without any indication they had been made by the government (Barstow and Stein, 2005). Instead of examining the legitimacy of these kinds of government actions that control the news, criminologists maintain a focus on the kinds of one-on-one crimes of violence that the news media feature, which also helps promote hegemony (Hamilton, 2000; Lichter and Lichter, 1988).

---

Sixth, criminology and criminologists are controlled (disciplined) by the organizational exigencies of higher education, including the ability to obtain research grants and publish research findings. Grant money is rarely available to research cases of wrongdoing by government officials or their elite business or military allies (Tombs and Whyte, 2003). Typically, crime grants are designated to study the causes and control of lower-class crimes (e.g., U.S. National Institute of Justice, 2005). Government-funded research shapes the careers of scholars, especially in an era where public financing of universities has shrunk and in which the most prestigious and well-funded private and public universities are closely linked to governmental and business interests. Scholars who pose serious challenges to the hegemonic social system by studying behaviors such as state crimes make unattractive candidates for employment or promotion in these schools. In short, the "structure" of research financing significantly affects the topics that the majority of criminologists will investigate.

## State Crime in International Law

As noted, despite their gravity, state crimes are rarely scrutinized by criminologists. We suggest, however, that state crimes such as wars of aggression, terrorism, genocide, political repression, revolution, and suppressions of mass political dissent should become, much like environmental crime, a core concern for twenty-first century criminology. But how do we determine when acts by governmental officials or those seeking state power are state crimes, and when they are legitimate uses of power to fulfill a state's obligation to provide peace and security to its people or to resist the brutalities of a criminal state?

Legal definitions are the typical starting point for criminological studies. Legal definitions created and enforced by a nation-state, however, are a problematic anchoring point for the study of state crime because states rarely criminalize their own wrongful actions, and taking this view would leave little for criminologists to study. Chambliss (1995b:9) suggested that one way to solve this problem is to define state crime as "behavior that violates international agreements and principles established in the courts and treaties of international bodies." In other words, state crimes are acts that violate *public international law*, even when these acts do not violate the domestic law of the countries responsible for them (see also, Kauzlarich, Kramer and Smith, 1992; Kauzlarich and Kramer, 1998; Michalowski, 1985).

Public international law consists of customary state practices and treaties that govern relations among nation-states, which set forth principles and standards of human rights that should guide state practices. Since the end of World War II, public international law has evolved via UN-sanctioned debates among nations. For this reason, international law is a better standard for determining when states behave criminally than the laws of individual nations.

To be sure, there is disagreement over whether the legal frameworks created by the United Nations reflect "universal" standards. Post-colonial and feminist theorists argue that contemporary international human rights standards are primarily reflections of white, Western culture (Lambert, Pickering, and Alder, 2003; Otto, 1998), and that these standards constitute a kind of "human rights imperialism" (Roy, 2004). And, using public international law to define state crimes is not without other problems. International law does not emerge from a universal conception of human rights, but rather is the product of political negotiations, international power relations, and multilateral treaties. Nevertheless, following World

War II, public international law – especially the United Nations Charter, the Universal Declaration of Human Rights, and UN conventions on Civil and Political Rights, Economic, Social and Cultural Rights, and the Prevention and Punishment of Genocide – has emerged as an increasingly coherent framework for judging the behavior of individual states. Despite uneven implementation, these doctrines remain the best available global standard for distinguishing between legal and illegal state actions (Schultz, 2003; Steiner and Alston, 2000). In addition, public international law has been accepted *as law* by the nations of the world – including the United States – and for that reason violations of international law can appropriately be analyzed as crimes.

Based on the proposition that we can evaluate the criminality of state behavior according to public international law, we now briefly consider the greatest crimes of political intent: war, terrorism and genocide.

## War as State Crime

In its most basic form, war is the organized use of lethal force by one society against another. Since the creation of the modern nation-state in the seventeenth century, the identity of *citizen* and the corresponding feelings of *nationalism* have been the foundations of war (Scheff, 1994; Anderson, 1991). These feelings do not arise automatically; they are socially construct-ed, and modern wars are the products of "the conscious manipulation of shared symbols by a limited group within the society for social, political, or economic objectives" (Vayda, 1968). The dominant class and political leaders intentionally manipulate symbols (including myths of national origin, collective suffering and past triumph, ideas of as a physical homeland, images of flags, sacred places or past heroes, common religious beliefs) to ensure that a majority of citizens are willing to fight the presumed enemy, or to support the proposed war as workers, taxpayers and conduits of government propaganda. This well known approach has been used both in the past (e.g., in Nazi Germany by propaganda chief Herman Göring), and in the present (e.g., the Bush administration's justification of the war in Iraq).

In view of the death, injury and destruction that accompany war, there is a strong moral basis from which to argue that leading people to war may be one the gravest of all state crimes. Of course, the political and economic elites who promote war, and the citizens who follow their lead, view their wars as heroic deeds rather than criminal acts. Indeed, most modern nations would claim they are a "peace-loving" people who only fight when urgent self-defense requires them to do so. However, much as ordinary criminal law enables us to judge claims of "self-defense" in cases of one-on-one violence, contemporary international law enables us to also judge claims of defensive war.

**Aggressive War, Defensive War.** In 1648, the Peace of Westphalia established the principle of *national sovereignty* as a strategy to end the bloody religious wars between Catholics and Protestant that plagued Europe for nearly a century. The idea was simple. If nations respected each other's sovereignty by keeping their military forces inside their own borders, war would come to an end. The Peace of Westphalia, of course, did not end war in Europe. What it did do, however, was establish the modern principle for judging wars of aggression as crimes (Papp, 1994).

The contemporary legal framework for judging aggression emerged following World War II, and was tied to the creation of the United Nations, the UN Charter, and the adoption of the Nuremberg Charter. The Nuremberg trials declared that wars of aggression were not just individual crimes committed by those acting on behalf of the aggressor nation: they were also state crimes (Henkin, 1995:111). In doing so, the Nuremberg Charter created a new body of international rules, known as *international criminal law*, that "proscribe international crimes" and that required governments to "prosecute and punish....these crimes" (Cassese, 2003:15).

Central to international criminal law is the UN Charter's prohibition against the use of military force for any purpose other than self-defense or as part of a military action agreed upon by the members of the United Nations as necessary to restore "peace and international security." The specific prohibition against aggressive war is found in Article 2(4) of the Charter, which states that: "All members shall refrain in their international relations from the threat or use of force against the territorial integrity or political independence of any state." Article 2(4) was established as a peremptory (i.e. fundamental) norm that cannot be modified by treaty or by ordinary customary law or practice, and as a former judge of the International Court of Justice noted, it "completely outlaws unilateral resort to armed force" (Weeramantry, 2003:22).

While the UN Charter outlaws wars of aggression, it recognizes in Article 51 that states have a legitimate right to self-defense, which comes into play when a nation has suffered or is about to suffer an armed attack if:

> ...an armed attack has been launched, or is immediately threatened, an urgent necessity for defensive action against that attack exists, there is no alternative to the preservation of life and

property, and the defensive action is limited to what is necessary to stop or prevent the imminent attack. [Ratner, 2002:2]

All other uses of military force against the territory or interests of another nation are state crimes, unless otherwise authorized by collective agreement among members of the United Nations to preserve global peace and security.

The creation of international legal prohibitions against aggressive war did not end aggressive wars. From a criminological standpoint, however, they established a global standard by which to distinguish criminal acts of war from legitimate acts of defense.

## The Invasion of Iraq: A Case Study in State Crime

The decision by the United States to invade Iraq, to topple its former ally, Saddam Hussein, and to occupy the country until it established a government more hospitable to U.S. interests, is an example of the kinds of state crime that require further criminological examination.

On its face, the 2003 invasion of Iraq by a U.S.-led coalition of forces was a clear violation of Article 2(4) since there was no evidence of an armed attack against the United States by Iraq, or that the Iraqi government was preparing to attack the United States. Nevertheless, the Bush administration claimed it possessed a self-defense right to invade Iraq in accordance with Article 51 because: (1) it believed Iraq was involved in the September 11, 2001 attacks against the World Trade Center and the Pentagon, and (2) Iraq possessed weapons of mass destruction (WMD) that it could use against the United States.

Despite the available counter-evidence, key Bush Administration officials repeatedly argued that Iraq was involved in the 9-11 attacks (Clarke, 2004). Almost immediately following the attacks, every major statement on Iraq by an administration official included references to terrorism in general and Al Qaeda specifically (Prados, 2004; Waxman, 2004). It was a successful propaganda campaign. A survey of U.S. citizens released prior to the 2003 invasion of Iraq showed that 70 percent of Americans believed that Iraq was directly involved in planning the September 11th attacks, and that over half believed that most of the hijackers were Iraqis (Corn, 2003). These opinions contradicted what was actually known about the attacks (see: U.S. National Commission on Terrorist Attacks Upon the United States, 2005; Rampton and Stauber, 2003; Scheer, Scheer and Chaudhry, 2003) In the midst of the nationalist fervor that swept America after September 11, 2001, however, truth became a casualty of government-stimulated war fever.

What we now know is that following the 9-11 attacks, key Bush administration policy makers ignored relevant evidence in order to exploit the tragedy to gain support for implementing a plan to invade Iraq that they had proposed five years earlier. For example, Richard Clarke, the administration's National Coordinator for Security, Infrastructure Protection and Counterterrorism, personally informed the President that the attacks had been orchestrated by Al Qaeda and did not involve the Saddam Hussein government in Iraq. Nevertheless, long-standing proponents of invading Iraq – including Vice President Cheney, Secretary of Defense Donald Rumsfeld and Assistant Secretary of Defense Paul Wolfowitz – continued to insist that there was a direct link between Iraq and the September 11th attacks, using this supposed link as a way to redirect public anger toward supporting an invasion of Iraq (Clarke, 2004).

In late 2003, once the invasion was over, President Bush and Secretary Powell admitted that they could produce no evidence linking Saddam Hussein to Al Qaeda (Eggen, 2004). The invasion of Iraq was made possible because the highest officials in the U.S. had lied, misled the public and other government officials, and used the media to support their claims, promote feelings of nationalism, and justify an illegitimate crime of international aggression. There is a strong case that can be made that the U.S. public was the target of a deliberate propaganda campaign designed to demonize Saddam Hussein and gain mass public support for what the Nuremberg Commission called the "supreme international crime," that is, a war of aggression (Cirincione et. al, 2004; Dreyfuss and Vest, 2004; Eisendrath and Goodman, 2004; Pollack, 2004; Prados, 2004).

The Iraq-Al Qaeda connection, however, was not the only justification offered for invading Iraq. As previously mentioned, Article 51 allows for limited *preemptive* action to stop an immediate threat of attack (Slomanson, 2003). In December, 2002, President G. W. Bush unilaterally revised the principle of preemptive defense in a new National Security Strategy that claimed the United States had a legal right of self-defense that allowed it to attack any country it believed might pose a future threat (Mahajan, 2003). Testifying in front of Congress on September 19, 2002, Defense Secretary Rumsfeld contended that invading Iraq would not violate international law because the United States had a legal right to prevent a possible future use of that country's WMD against the United States. This argument, however, falls well outside any reasonable interpretation of the Article 51 justification for self-defense.

The Bush doctrine authorizes *anticipatory* self-defense rather than preemptive self-defense. Anticipatory self-defense involves using force against a nation that has neither attacked nor is about to attack, but that you *believe might attack at some time in the future.* Accepting anticipatory self-defense as a justification for violence in everyday life would allow homicides and assaults on little more than the claim that we *believed* our victims planned to harm us in the future. However, domestic criminal law treats murders based on perceived rather than actual threats as crimes rather than as justifiable homicides. International law is no different. Simply put, "There is no basis in international law for dramatically expanding the concept of self-defense, as advocated in the Bush administration's September 2002 National Security Strategy, to authorize...strikes against states based on potential threats arising from possession or development of chemical, biological, or nuclear weapons and links to terrorism" (Ratner, 2002). *On this basis, the invasion of Iraq was a violation of international law and therefore a state crime.*

Not only are anticipatory self-defense wars illegal, the basis for such an action by the Bush Administration were lacking. Long before the invasion there was considerable evidence from a variety of sources that Iraq no longer possessed prohibited weapons (Pitt, 2002; Rai, 2002; Ratner, Green and Olshansky, 2003; Solomon and Erlich, 2003). The United Nations Special Commission (UNSCOM) inspection process that operated in Iraq from 1991 to 1998 verified that nearly all of Iraq's biological and chemical weapons and been destroyed, and that its nuclear weapons program had been dismantled (Pitt, 2002; Ritter, 2003). An Iraqi defector, Hussein Kamel, Saddam Hussein's son-in-law and a manager of Iraqi weapons programs, reported that Iraq had destroyed its stockpiles of weapons and the missiles to deliver them (Scheer, Scheer, and Chaudhry, 2003; Rampton and Stauber, 2003; Prados, 2004). The UN Monitoring, Verification and Inspection Commission (UNMOVIC), headed by Hans Blix, and the International Atomic Energy Agency (IAEA), which operated in Iraq until it was forced to leave in the face of impending U.S. air strikes, reported that they could find no operable weapons of mass destruction, nor any viable facilities to produce them (Blix, 2004). Furthermore, during the war the Iraqi military did not use chemical or biological weapons, and after the war none were found. Post-war investigations made it clear that that Iraq had, in fact, disarmed, and was in compliance with UN Security Council resolutions (Allman, 2004; Blix, 2004; Corn, 2003; Eisendrath and Goodman, 2004; Everrest, 2004; Gellman, 2004; Hiro, 2004; Prados, 2004; Rai, 2003; Rampton and Stauber, 2003; Scheer, Scheer and Cahaudhry, 2003). The final blow to claims that Iraq had weapons of mass destruction came from the report of the CIA's Iraq Survey Group, headed by former weapons inspector David Kay, which said that no evidence of any stockpiles of Iraqi weapons had been found. "It turns out we were all wrong," Kay stated (Prados, 2004:344). This conclusion was later confirmed by the final report of the Iraq Survey Group under the direction of Charles Duelfer (Priest and Pincus, 2004; Jehl, 2004).

It has been widely suggested that the Bush doctrine of anticipatory self-defense was used against Iraq to further the geopolitical goals of the neoconservative bloc that came to dominate Bush administration foreign policy after September 11th (Dorrien, 2004), especially those with oil and energy interests (Everrest, 2004). Using military force to achieve strategic political and economic interests, however, is exactly the type of international crime that the UN Charter condemns. Because our consciousness is fundamentally shaped by hegemonic ideology, however, it is difficult for both citizens and criminologists in the United States to recognize that we live in a country governed by people who, except for the fact that they control the most powerful military force on the planet, would be condemned and judged as war criminals.

## State and Anti-State Terrorism

Any attempt to analyze terrorism immediately stumbles over the lack of an agreed-upon definition of terrorism. In general, there are two competing approaches to terrorism, each of which has generated a number of specific definitions.

One approach takes a broad view of terrorism as any use of violence to achieve political goals by creating fear among civilian populations. The United Nations, for example, offers the following definition of terrorism: "Acts intended or calculated to provoke a state of terror in the general public, a group of persons or particular persons for political purposes" (United Nations Development Program, 1999). Terrorism experts offer similar, though more detailed definitions. What these definitions have in common is that each views terrorism as a particular way of using violence, regardless of whether that violence is committed by state or non-state actors. From this standpoint, terrorism is defined in terms of its targets (civilian populations) and its purpose (creating fear), not by who is committing the act. This approach suggests that states are as capable of being terrorists as are non-state actors.

The other approach, largely associated with official definitions offered by state agencies, removes states from the list of possible terrorists. For instance, the U.S. Department of Defense defines terrorism as "The calculated use of violence or the threat of violence to inculcate fear…to coerce or to intimidate *governments or societies* in the pursuit of goals that are generally political, religious, or ideological." Similarly, the FBI identifies terrorism as "the unlawful use of force or violence against persons or property *to intimidate or coerce a government*, the civilian population, or any segment thereof, in furtherance of political or social objectives." Finally, according to the U.S. Code, terrorism is "premeditated, politically motivated violence perpetrated against noncombatant targets *by subnational groups* or clandestine agents, usually intended to influence an audience" (U.S. Code, Title 22, Section 2656f[d]) [emphases added]. In every case, terrorism is limited to anti-state violence, while the terror-generating tactics of states are left outside the definition.

Criminologists must be careful not to accept politically-motivated state definitions of terrorism as the basis of inquiry precisely because these definitions rule out the possibility that states can act illegally. For this reason we subdivide terrorism into three types: idiosyncratic terrorism, anti-state terrorism, and state terrorism.

**Idiosyncratic terrorism** involves acts of violence committed by one or several individuals as private acts of revenge or rebellion, without the involvement or support of an organized political group, such as the bombing of the Murrah Building in Oklahoma City by Timothy McVeigh (with the help of Terry Nichols).

**Anti-state terrorism** is violence directed against civilian and/or government targets in order to achieve the political goals of some organized, anti-system group. What often goes unrecognized is that anti-state terrorism is a form of war that people who are otherwise powerless wage against governments that have caused them some real or imagined grievance and that they cannot directly confront by conventional means.

**State terrorism** includes both military and economic violence used by governments against the citizens of other nations or against dissidents in their own nation (Herman, 1987; see also Frappier, 1985; Boyle, 1985; Piesterse, 1985; Shank, 1987a, 1987b; Petras, 1987; Huggins, 1987; Chomsky, 1987; Stohl and Lopez, 1984; on economic terrorism, see Pfost, 1987; Simon, 1999). For example, governments have often employed air strikes against civilian populations in order to create fear and crush their will, which made terrorism a basic war-fighting strategy of the modern state. From the 1937 bombing of Guernica by right-wing forces during the Spanish Civil War; to the targeting of German V2 rockets on London and the Allied carpet-bombings of Hamburg and Dresden during World War II;

to the slaughter of civilian populations in Hiroshima and Nagasaki by U.S. atomic bombs in 1945; to the U.S. "shock and awe" bombing of Baghdad in 2003; the purpose of air strikes is to create public terror in order to weaken an enemy state. The fact that states call this war and not terrorism is a political language-game designed to protect states from the same kind of condemnation we reserve for "terrorists." But it does not change the fact that for the victims of organized political violence, terror is terror, regardless of who does the bombing.

The problem with defining terrorism is precisely the political dimension of the definitional process. Even before September 11th, the U.S. government had been an outspoken critic of governments that it claimed supported terrorism (e.g., North Korea, Libya, Iran, Iraq, Cuba and Nicaragua; see Herman, 1987). At the same time, it chose not to condemn the violence committed against civilians by "friendly" governments in a long list of nations: South Africa, whose apartheid regime destroyed the lives and spirits of millions of black South Africans; Guatemala, where over 80,000 indigenous Indians were killed to prevent the redistribution of land from large owners (many of them U.S. corporations) to impoverished peasants; Argentina, whose military junta conducted a "dirty war" that "disappeared" over 10,000 people it believed were in opposition to the government; South Korea, where terror tactics were an essential strategy to keep workers from forming unions in the 1970s; Chile, whose military dictatorship conducted its own dirty war against supporters of the former Allende government; and Israel, which repeatedly used disproportional military force against Palestinian civilians in retaliation for attacks against Israel (Herman, 1987; Chomsky, 1987; Piesterse, 1985; Shank, 1987a, 1987b; Huggins, 1987; Scott, 1987; Petras, 1987; Pfost, 1987).

Nor was this a passive toleration of state-terrorism by U.S. allies. The U.S. government actively promoted state terrorism among its less savory allies by providing financing, military equipment, and the training of foreign police and soldiers in torture tactics. In the case of Nicaragua, for instance, "[the] U.S. government... organized a mercenary army to attack Nicaragua, and even provided it with a printed manual of recommended acts of sabotage and murder, which has been implemented at the cost of well over a thousand Nicaraguan civilian lives" (Herman, 1987:1). Indeed, 74 percent of the countries that employed systematic torture (a form of state terrorism) in the 1970s were U.S. client-states (Herman, 1987, 1982).

In addition to state terrorism, one of the more neglected forms of terrorism is what we call *corporate terrorism*. Corporations help sponsor terrorism in three ways. First, corporations produce the hardware or weapons of terrorism that states employ, and benefit economically from state terrorism. Corporations engaged in these activities actively lobby the government to support state terrorism. Second, corporations support terrorist states by establishing profitable economic conditions within those states that help legitimize terrorist states. In addition, once established in terrorist states, corporations help shape public opinion of states that sponsor terrorism. For instance, the list of U.S. corporations that operated under apartheid in South Africa, and reaped handsome profits from a legally controlled labor market that systematically deprived the majority black population of its basic human rights, reads like the *Who's Who* of American industry: Bausch & Lomb, Borden, Bristol-Myers, Colgate-Palmolive, Chevron, Ford Motor Company, Gillette, Goodyear, Johnson and Johnson, Mobil, Tenneco, Texaco, Union Carbide and Warner-Lambert. In all, some 168 companies, 18 of which are on the Fortune list of the 50 largest corporations in America, were willing to profit from and support the apartheid regime of South Africa (see generally Cooper, 1987).

Third, corporations sometimes support state terrorism as outsiders by backing coups. As an example, Shell, Texaco and other major oil companies played a central role in impoverishing the Ogoni people of Nigeria in several ways: (1) through massive pollution of the land and water on which the Ogoni depend for survival; (2) by supporting government efforts to obtain Ogoni oil rights; (3) by supporting government repression of Ogoni efforts to fight against the destruction of the livelihoods and culture; and, (4) by backing regime changes in the Nigerian government to gain enhanced oil exploration rights (Saro-Wiwa, 1992).

In sum, when states engage in terrorist activities, they often do so in order to facilitate corporate interests in obtaining low-cost access to resources, labor, markets and financial institutions. Thus, any radical analysis of terrorism must examine the intersection of state and corporate interests in the production of violence against human populations (Michalowski and Kramer, 2005). Adhering to the hegemonic definition of terrorism as limited to only acts of violence by non-state groups does little to help us understand the role of terror in the modern world. It only serves to protect the interests of political and economic elites from scrutiny.

## Genocide

Genocide is the deliberate and systematic attempt to destroy some identity group, through outright slaughter or other strategies designed to undermine its viability as a people. Genocide is typically fueled by a desire on the part of the dominant group to acquire the resources of the targeted ethnic population, or by claims that the targeted group poses some mortal threat to the safety of the dominant group unless it is eliminated (Ignatieff, 1993).

Officially or legally, genocide is defined by the 1948 Genocide Convention (United Nations, 2005) as including any of the following acts committed with intent to destroy, in whole or in part, a national, ethnic, racial or religious group: (a) killing members of the group based solely on group membership; (b) causing serious bodily or mental harm to members of the group; (c) deliberately inflicting on the group burdensome conditions of life calculated to bring about its physical destruction in whole or in part; (d) imposing measures intended to prevent births within the group; or, (e) forcibly transferring children of the group to another group.

Like aerial bombing of cities or terrorist destruction of public buildings, genocide is a form of organized violence that, unlike combat between armies, makes no distinctions among men, women, children, young or old. Anyone unlucky enough to be within reach of the killing can be a victim. Genocides differ from war and terrorism, however, in several important ways.

First, war and terrorism are designed to extract concessions from an opposing political power. While innocent civilians may be targets of war or terrorism, they are not the *main* targets. The main target is always some larger political authority or government. By contrast, in cases of genocide the people being killed, driven to starvation or deprived of their children *is the main target*, and the goal is elimination of the target group itself.

Second, genocides most often target a group that is *internal* to the society, rather than some enemy outside it. The major genocides of the twentieth century took place not between separate nation-states, but between peoples inhabiting a shared land. These include the following examples: (1) the murder of over 1 million Armenians in the Turkish Ottoman Empire during World War I; (2) Soviet genocide against the Kulaks (large peasant landholders) in the 1930s; (3) the destruction of the Jewish and Roma (Gypsy) communities of Germany and wider Europe during the Nazi Holocaust; (4) the slaughter of Ibo tribespeople in Nigeria; (5) the "killing fields" of Cambodia in the 1970s that targeted Chinese, ethnic minority, and urbanized groups; (6) Serbian attempts in the 1990s to "ethnically cleanse" Bosnia and Kosovo of Muslim populations; (7) and the murder of Tutsi by Hutus in Rwanda.

Third, genocides frequently involve personalized violence. War and most terrorism involve the act of killing strangers. Genocides, in contrast, are often conducted by ordinary people against others in their own communities, sometimes even against people they know and have been friendly with in the past. Some of the most disturbing stories that emerged from the late twentieth century genocides in places like Rwanda and Bosnia revealed the power of genocidal movements to convince people to kill and brutalize their former neighbors, teachers, students, co-workers or friends (Gourevitch, 1999; Sudetic, 1999). In cases like the genocidal ethnic cleansing in Bosnia, many Serbian fighters resorted to raping Muslim Bosnian women as a way of destroying their self-worth before killing them, and to humiliate Bosnian Muslim men by demonstrating that they were powerless to protect their loved ones (Lewis, 1993; Neier, 1993).

Genocides, however, are not spontaneous acts of mass hate: They are sponsored and organized by political leaders for the purpose of achieving state goals, meaning that they can be considered state crimes. As Alvarez (2001:57) observes: "Responsibility for genocide rests invariably with the government in power, since the crime of genocide is largely planned and perpetrated by both the formal and informal agents of the state...public officials are the prime movers of genocide in the twentieth century. Participants do not act individually, but carry out mass murder as part of a larger movement." Political leaders typically resort to one or more of three strategies in to facilitate genocidal social movements: historic grievances, promoting false threats, and scapegoating.

**Historic Grievances.** One of the most common, yet least accurate characterizations of genocides is that they arise from "ancient ethnic hatreds" (Kressel, 2002). The idea that the roots of genocide lie deep in the past is particularly insidious because it suggests little can be done to prevent such eruptions. It is true that genocidal rampages are often justified by rhetoric that urges redressing old grievances. Whatever litany of historic grievances one group may have toward another, however, the mobilization of these grievances for genocide is always a deliberate and contemporary political *choice*. What is important in the production of genocide "is not how the past dictates to the present but how the present manipulates the past" (Ignatieff, 1994:21). Political leaders mobilize old cultural memories of pain and loss in order to generate present-day hostility toward the target group, memories that would otherwise not lead to violence, brutality and mass murder. In Rwanda, for example, Hutu leaders used stories about past killings of Hutu by Tutsi in Burundi to stir up Hutu hatred of Tutsi, while

Serb leaders emphasized ancient defeats at the hands of Muslims to foment anti-Bosnian sentiment (Mamdani, 2002; Gagnon, 2004).

**Promoting False Threats.** Another key strategy used by political leaders to drive populations to mass murder is to convince them that they themselves are facing an imminent threat from some ethnic group in their midst, and if they do not take action quickly, they will be destroyed. As the former state of Yugoslavia was being reorganized into separate nations of Croatia, Bosnia, Slovenia, Macedonia and Serbia in the early 1990s, for instance, Serbian leaders fabricated stories to promote the idea that Serbs were facing genocidal threats from Croats and Bosnians. One Serb propagandist, General Milovan Milutinovic, widely and falsely reported that: "Necklaces have been made of human eyes and ears, skulls have been halved, brains have been split, bowels have been torn" to create a sense of imminent threat among his Serbian audiences in order to stir up hatred for Bosnians (Gutman, 1993:ix). Similarly, Hutu leaders broadcast repeated radio announcements that if Hutus did not immediately rise up and slaughter their Tutsi neighbors, they would be the victims of mass murder by Tutsi..

**Scapegoating.** A third technique for mobilizing genocide is *scapegoating* ethnic minorities. In some instances ethnic minorities are accused of being responsible for dreadful current conditions. In Ottoman Turkey, for instance, ethnic Armenians were accused of collaborating with Russian forces during World War I, resulting in several devastating defeats to the Turkish army. This served as justification for mass slaughter and ethnic cleansing of Armenians from Turkish soil (Balakian, 2003). Similarly, anti-Semitic leaders in Germany, including most infamously Adolph Hitler, blamed Jewish collaboration with France and Britain for Germany's loss of World War I and for the devastating collapse of the German economy in the post-war era (Goldhagen, 1997). And in one of the most devastating slaughters of the twentieth century, Pol Pot and the Khmer Rouge in Kampuchea (then called Cambodia) targeted Chinese and "intellectuals" (including anyone who wore glasses) as responsible for Cambodia's internal economic and political troubles (Kiernan, 2002). Scapegoating enables political leaders to redirect public dissatisfaction away from the failings of government or the dominant social system and toward some vulnerable minority population. Although it has not been put to overtly genocidal purposes, frequent claims by political leaders in the United States that "foreign immigrants" are the cause of job loss and income decline for "honest" Americans is yet another example of how political leaders use scapegoating techniques to mobilize public sentiment against some "Other" (Perry, 2001).

In view of the gravity of genocide, the criminological similarities between ordinary murder and organized mass murder, and the fact that genocide has been defined as a crime under international law since 1948, "it is remarkable that no specific criminological explanations have been applied to genocide" (Alvarez, 2001:1). This is even more troubling in view of the fact that genocide may be the fastest-growing state crime of the twenty-first century. In many parts of the world, including the United States, ethnic nationalism is emerging as a last refuge from economic decline and political instability. Depending upon time, place and condition, it can be a short step from ethnic nationalism to genocidal, or near-genocidal practices.

## EXPLAINING TERRORISM

The task of explaining terrorism, like crime, is difficult. Orthodox explanations of terrorism focus on the behavior of the outsider, and tend to use personality theories to explain the behavior of terrorists. These explanations, which we cannot review here (for lack of space), clearly fail to provide a sufficient explanation for terrorism because they omit consideration of the political, economic, historic, and ethnic dimensions of the situation that generates anti-state terrorism. For example, to explain the September 11th attacks, the history of the problems that led to the attack would need to be fully detailed. This would include, among other topics, a discussion of the long history of U.S. international involvement in and foreign policy toward oil-producing nations, the links between oil manufacturers and government policy planners, and the connection between the oil industry, the nature of the U.S. economy and its energy needs, and the influence of oil companies on U.S. foreign policy. A detailed explanation of anti-state terrorism would require its own book-length manuscript, and even at that, it would not be sufficient to explain either state-sponsored terrorism, or terrorism by insiders.

As we noted previously, orthodox criminologists have devoted little attention to state terrorism. At the same time, however, radical criminologists have been equally slow to develop explanations of anti-state terrorism. A general explanation of terrorism consistent with radical expectations can, however, be found in Ihekwoaba Onwudiwe's book, *The Globalization of Terrorism*.

In *The Globalization of Terrorism*, Onwudiwe argues that the basic structure of terrorism can be understood by framing terrorism against the assumptions of world systems theory (WST). WST employs the general class framework Marx created to analyze class dynamics within capitalist society, but applies it to worldwide relations among nations. To make sense of this argument, WST demonstrates that the spread of capitalism created a worldwide division of labor based on capitalism. As Immanuel Wallerstein and other world system theorists argue, the process of establishing a world system based on capitalism began in the fifteenth century, and was completed by the end of the nineteenth century. And, despite the individual orientation of a nation's political and economic system, all nations participate in the capitalist world system.

In WST, nations occupy class positions similar to those found in a Marxian class model of capitalism. There are three primary world system positions. At the top of the hierarchy are core nations that produce and consume the majority of the world's commodities. These nations control trade flows and the formation of treaties that facilitate their global economic domination. In addition, they have greater access to and control of the labor and raw materials found in other nations, and use their economic and political power to maintain unequal relationships with other nations. These nations can be viewed as the capitalists among nations.

At the bottom of the hierarchy are peripheral nations. These nations have little in the way of an economic infrastructure, and they contain an abundant, cheap supply of labor and raw materials needed by core nation manufacturers. Politically, these peripheral nations are weak, and they tend to be protectorates in treaties which also limit economic trading partnerships. In effect, peripheral nations lack economic and political power, and occupy a position similar to that of the working and marginal economic classes.

Wedged between the core and peripheral nations are semi-peripheral nations which are either experiencing a developing or declining form of international capitalism. These countries typically are able to exploit peripheral nations, while they are simultaneously often exploited by core nations.

For his part, Onwudiwe argues that WST's political and economic model of world relationships can be used to explain general patterns in terrorism. State terrorism, for instance, is most likely to be a tool used by core nations against peripheral and semi-peripheral nations in order to facilitate advantageous economic conditions. This explains why, for example, core nations have historically intervened in the political situations in oil-rich nations, or in other nations with desirable raw materials. Likewise, the structure of the world system also explains why the majority of state-terrorism flows downward, that is, from the core to the semi-periphery and periphery, or from the semi-periphery to the periphery. But, this view also helps explain why the core is sometimes the target of non-state terrorism sponsored by groups in peripheral and semi-peripheral nations. Like the class system of capitalism, the global capitalist world system establishes a system of exploitation. When the exploited both understand and become aware of their subjugation, they develop a desire to strike out practical or at symbolic targets representing those they believe to be responsible for their subjugation. Not surprisingly, these targets are frequently persons or property associated with core nations.

In addition, Onwudiwe argues that WST helps us understand why peripheral and semi-peripheral nations are the sites for elevated levels of anti-state terrorism. Government officials in peripheral states in particular will tend to cooperate with core nations in ways that enhance the exploitation of people in the periphery. In addition, because peripheral states are underdeveloped economically, they have fewer military and political tools to control dissent within their national boundaries, and are less capable than core nations of defending themselves from anti-state terrorism.

Employing data on terrorist incidents, Onwudiwe is able to produce evidence supporting his contention of an association between the distribution, level and types of terrorist incidents that occur across nations of the world, and a nation's location in the world system. While this model of terrorism provides a constructive mechanism for studying generalities in terrorism, it is not capable of including contextual historical, cultural or geo-political issues that contribute to terrorism in specific cases. Nevertheless, Onwudiwe's model provides the basis for developing a radical explanation of terrorism that explains both state and anti-state acts of terror, and which is often omitted from radical criminological discussions of terrorism.

## In Sum

As the United States struggles to consolidate its positions as the global ruler, other nations and social groups attempt to resist this consolidation. Unfortunately, neo-liberal economic globalization extracts a fearsome economic toll on many poorer nations, and destroys their cultural traditions and values in ways that generate resistance. As globalization increases and numerous cultures are challenged and blended, and efforts to expand the hegemony of Western culture expand, so too will forms of state terror and the level of resistance to these forms of terror. These trends will lead to increasing state and anti-state violence. In the coming decades, far more people will be victimized, and victimized in far more devastating and brutal ways by state crimes than by common street crimes. However, without a serious radicalization in criminological thought that brings state crimes to the center of inquiry, the field of criminology is likely to remain largely oblivious to these epic forms of criminal violence. Meanwhile its practitioners will continue to delve ever more deeply into questions about the petty offenses of drug dealers, thieves and thugs.

# TEN.
# A RADICAL PERSPECTIVE ON POLICING

This chapter explores the role of policing in contemporary society, and how policing has been shaped by political-economic and cultural characteristics of society.

## Creating a National Culture of Control

Modern U.S. policing is a multibillion-dollar industry that is and has been shaped largely by funding and policy decisions at the *state and national* level. This was not always the case. During the nineteenth and first half of the twentieth centuries policing was a community concern managed at the level of towns and cities, with some assistance from state-level agencies. This all changed in the 1960s with the invention of "law and order" as a national-level political issue.

Three forces came together in the 1960s that resulted in a fundamental transformation of policing and social control in the United States. The first was social unrest on America's college campuses and urban ghettoes, along with other challenges to dominant cultural practices. The second was the emergence of broadcast television as the predominant news source in the United States. The third, and most important, was a desire among conservatives to identify political issues they could use to break the political strength that liberals had amassed as a result of Democratic Party leadership since the Great Depression of the 1930s and through the turmoil of World War II. The convergence of these three forces ultimately resulted in the transformation of urban police forces into militarized strike forces organized and trained according to national policies and national standards (Platt et al., 1982).

The early 1960s ushered in an era of social conflict that began with civil rights marches and sit-ins. These were soon followed by student protests against America's war in Vietnam and uprisings against racial discrimination in black ghettoes in many American cities. On their own, these events might have created public fear and a sense that society was "coming apart"; however, the image of a society descending into chaos was intensified by nightly television coverage that focused primarily on dramatic scenes of disorder while ignoring the social forces that were leading many people into the streets to demand fundamental social change – particularly the extension of civil rights to African

Americans, a re-thinking of U.S. war policy, and demands for greater social justice for urban minorities.

Those who opposed these social changes and/or sought to acquire political capital effectively mobilized media-intensified fears of disorder by portraying *all* civil rights, anti-war and social justice activists as "dangerous" people who belonged to "fringe groups" committed to destroying the American way of life. This process was facilitated by news media reports and conservative political rhetoric that presented the *most* vocal and aggressive dissidents as *typical* examples of the members and ambitions of these movements. The Black Panther Party provides an excellent example of this process. By focusing on Black Panther rhetoric about armed self-defense of their neighborhoods, the media and politicians created an image of Black Panthers as violent revolutionaries who would soon sweep out of their ghettoes and annihilate White America. Meanwhile, the fact that the Black Panthers were largely a localized political organization that worked to create such things as school breakfast programs, community health clinics, and other mechanisms that would improve life in their impoverished ghetto communities received little coverage by news media, and certainly wasn't addressed by conservative politicians. Instead of serving as an example of the need to end racial inequality and expand social justice, the Black Panthers became a symbol of why "upstanding" citizens should fear poor African Americans. In doing so, the media coverage and political rhetoric surrounding the urban uprisings of the 1960s and 1970s combined to create the cultural groundwork for what would eventually become national "wars" on crime and drugs, wars whose primary targets were young, poor men of color (Chambliss, 1999).

When it came to the war in Vietnam, the news media and political hawks focused primarily on the relatively small proportion of students and professors who were taking to the streets or shutting down college campuses for "teach-ins" opposing America's military intervention in Southeast Asia. By focusing on the disorderly aspects of protest, pro-war politicians obscured the growing legitimate controversy over the war in a fog of images and rhetoric about cowardly, draft-dodging students and the pampered left-wing protesters who supported them.

Ghetto uprisings came in for similar treatment. There is no question that the burning buildings and lootings of ghetto stores occurring in places such as the Watts neighborhood of Los Angeles and the 14th St. District of Detroit were dramatic and frightening events, both to those who lived there and those who observed them from the outside. The news media and politicians, however, focused most of their attention on images of violence and looting by ghetto residents, with little comment on the fact that almost every major urban uprising in the United States in the 1960s and 1970s was sparked by an act of police brutality in communities that had been targets of such brutality for decades (Kerner Commission, 1969). Nor was any attention given to the fact that most of the violence and looting was not "senseless" and random, but was targeted at businesses that had long histories of cheating or mistreating their ghetto clientele (Wilkins, 1994). Instead of recognizing and addressing the legitimate frustrations that eventually boiled over into street violence, conservative politicians saw the urban uprisings of the 1960s and 1970s as a clear mandate for militarizing the policing of these communities.

If urban ghetto militants were seen as a violent threat, other groups were portrayed as a threat because of their promotion of peace, interpersonal pleasure, and collectivism as ways of life. The appearance of "flower children," communes and other groups promoting various new approaches to social life – such as the environmental, feminist, and health food movements – were part of a wider process of social change that sought to promote virtues of simplicity and equality as alternatives to the growing obsession with competition and consumption of the ever-expanding array of commodities being produced by American industry and advertised by American media (Shi, 2001). By portraying these movements as consisting of little more than dope and sex-obsessed hippies, "bra-burners," "health food nuts" and "eco-freaks," conservatives worked to delegitimize the deeper social message of these movements.

The social movements of the 1960s and 1970s, in a variety of ways, represented the demands of excluded social groups for greater participation and a voice in determining the distribution of income and power and the creation of culture in the United States. Expansion of democracy, however, would threaten established arrangements of wealth and power. The view of conservatives was summed up by right-wing historian and political strategist Samuel Huntington, when he said that America's problems stemmed from "an excess of democracy" and that what was needed was a "greater degree of moderation in democracy." That is, demands for greater equality and democratic participation should be met with repression. And the first step in that direction was to build police forces that could keep civil peace while minimizing civic participation.

## Militarizing America's Police

Public fear has been used by politicians on many occasions to dramatically alter our perceptions of crime and the level of police control we will tolerate (Baer and Chambliss, 1997). Crime became a national political issue for the first time during the 1964 presidential campaign, with candidates promising to address the growing fear of crime among American citizens. Curiously, however, there were no actual measures of public fear of crime at that time.

In response to media-magnified public fear and conservative challenges in the wake of civil unrest, in 1965 President Lyndon Johnson impaneled the Kerner Commission to report on the causes of urban disorder in the 1960s. The commission's findings were summarized in *The Challenge of Crime in a Free Society* (1967). Radical criminologists criticized this report on the grounds that commission members manipulated research results to serve their own agendas and to preserve the status quo (Platt, 1971; Platt and Cooper, 1974; Quinney, 1974b, 1979, 1980). Although the commission did suggest various social strategies for dealing with unrest in urban ghettoes – such as reducing economic and racial inequality and improving educational, housing and occupational opportunities – the *only* commission recommendations pursued with any vigor involved increasing the size and fire-power of urban police.

In addition to examining the causes of urban unrest the administration of President Lyndon Johnson created the federal Law Enforcement Assistance Administration (LEAA), the primary purpose of which was to upgrade police power by funding sophisticated police technology and strategies, especially military weaponry and technology (Quinney, 1971, 1974b, 1979, 1980; Balkan et al., 1980; Platt et al., 1982; Michalowski, 1985). The creation of LEAA was soon followed by the establishment of the National Commission on Criminal Justice Standards and Goals (1973). The commission was charged with setting national standards for education, training, and technology in the U.S. criminal justice system.

LEAA and the Criminal Justice Standards and Goals commission produced more than just words: They provided money to police departments that complied with federal criminal justice policies and control strategies. In doing so, they represented the first steps toward creating what has become, in fact if not in law, a nationalized police force whose focus is increasingly shaped less by local concerns and more by the goals and vision of national politicians. Radicals have argued that this process has led to a militarizing of America's urban police forces which, in turn, has created "a police-industrial complex" that needs crime and criminals in order to keep both public funding and private profits high (Platt et al., 1982; Chamlin, 1990; Nalla et al., 1997; Kraska, 2001; see also Christie, 1994 for an analysis of police growth prior to this time).

The first steps toward militarizing America's police came at the height of the civil rights movement in the United States. In that context, "fear of crime" was really code for "fear of blacks." Politicians could not, however, openly address the race-based fears of white America, so they addressed them obliquely by promising to control crime. The strongest evidence that the crime control policies of the 1960s and 1970s were about race is the simple fact that most of the wars on crime and drugs since then have been fought in the urban ghettoes that are home to poor people of color, not on college campuses where drug use is widespread or in corporate boardrooms where grave crimes are committed regularly.

## Criminological Research and Nationalized Policing

Prior to LEAA and the 1960s' presidential commissions on crime, there was little academic interest in policing. Orthodox criminologists, however, were quick to seize upon the opportunity provided by LEAA to obtain federal funding for research. In contrast, radical criminologists showed little interest in police studies, entering this area of inquiry over a decade later in response to orthodox analyses of policing. As Sidney Harring, a radical police researcher noted: "… historians of the police have made little use of the Marxist theory of capitalist development and class struggle in their analysis. Yet, Marx's argument that the police serve 'to accelerate the accumulation of capital by increasing the degree of exploitation of labor' is a compelling synthesis of the actual function of the police" (1976:58; see also Harring, 1983).

In general, the radical analysis of policing considers the rise and development of modern urban policing as a manifestation of class struggle (Harring, 1981; Spitzer, 1981b). Since the 1970s, analyses of the relationship between class and policing have been relatively well developed within radical criminology. Analyses of the race (Takagi, 1981, 1979) and gender dynamics of policing have begun to develop more recently, though class-specific interpretation still remains the most common approach. As in other areas of radical research, an analysis of how class, race and gender interact needs to be more fully integrated into investigations of policing.

## POLICE AND THE STATE

Though it is difficult for modern people to conceive of societies without police, radicals argue that "[p]olicing is unique to *state societies*. In …nonstate societies…rules and customs are enforced and order maintained by ordinary individuals in the process of conducting their daily lives, not by designated representatives of state power" (Michalowski, 1985:170). In contrast to the consensus view that policing arose to protect shared societal interests, radicals contend that policing developed with the historical emergence of the nation-state, in order to protect the interests of ascendant power groups. In other words, policing arises when one group develops an interest in controlling other groups. Modern forms of policing emerged alongside the development of capitalist systems of production, and the interests they were designed to protect were related to the preservation of capitalism (Spitzer, 1981b). While we normally imagine that police exist to protect all citizens from crime, an examination of the history of policing reveals that its primary purpose was to protect the material and social relations of capitalism in both direct and indirect ways.

## A Radical History of Policing

In 1829, Robert Peel helped create the first modern police force in London. The creation of Peel's "Bobbies" changed the nature of law enforcement in several ways by centralizing the police function. Centralization was consistent with wider socio-political and economic trends that streamlined production, increased efficiency and reduced costs. The emergence and centralization of policing increased the population's reliance on state-assisted social control, and corresponded with the declining ability of communities to "police" themselves using informal mechanisms as social networks and relationships became more fragmented with the progress of capitalism (Spitzer and Scull, 1977a). As capitalism destroyed informal systems of social control, it became increasingly necessary to provide for some degree of social peace by using formal control strategies. The failure to do so would have made the development of capitalist society untenable.

Orthodox studies of policing treat the centralization of policing as a logical response to public concern over rising crime rates. Radicals, however, contend that centralization was designed to enhance urban elites' "control and discipline" over police, and helped "divide the police from the working class" (Platt et al., 1982:23). As Spitzer (1981, 1979) notes, elites saw expanding police powers, rather than the elimination of economic inequality, as the way to deal with rising levels of crime and disorder. In addition to centralizing the social control system, the creation of urban police also had an important ideological consequence. Because their focus was the criminal person, the new police helped promote the view that bad *individuals*, rather than larger-scale economic and social conditions, were the cause of crime.

The centralization of policing also changed the way people understood the control function of police. Traditionally, the response to crime always occurred *after* the crime had been committed. By the mid-nineteenth century, however, centralized police departments were engaging in *preventative* policing. The idea was that public police presence could deter crime. Initially, the central tool of crime prevention was the police patrol, which inserted police into the normal course of daily life (Parks, 1976; Platt et al., 1982). Everyone became subject to the observing eye of the police officer. One unintended result of this emphasis on preventing crime was that police often were held responsible for the crime problem. As Michalowski (1985:17) explains:

> The creation of a preventive police force tended to shift the responsibility for crime away from...society and onto the newly created professional police. If cities were crime ridden, it was not because the social order generated a class of impoverished and brutalized citizens but because the police had failed to prevent crime. This transition of responsibility to a professional police force effectively masked the role of the emerging capitalist economy in creating the conditions for crime and urban disorder.

According to orthodox thinking, increased policing was an appropriate response to the types of social disintegration and disorganization that accompanied urbanization and industrialization. "Working from such assumptions, historians have generally seen the development of the police institution as a natural consequence of the violent crime and disorder of city life" (Harring, 1976:54). In contrast, the radical perspective challenges this decontextualized analysis of policing by situating industrialization and crime within a wider socioeconomic framework.

While radicals agree that industrialization stimulated urban growth, they see the evolution of capitalism as the source of industrialization. In addition, although industrialization concentrated populations in cities, urbanization is viewed by radicals as neither the ultimate source of crime nor the simple product of industrialization. As noted in the previous chapter, the history and development of urban areas is closely connected to the distribution of capital in the spatial ecology of the city as well as to the nature of class struggle. In this sense, urbanization patterns correspond with the organization of production in urban areas both spatially and in terms of class distribution of power and resources. In short, urbanization and industrialization are not causes of policing, but rather may be covariates of policing or possibly intervening processes between capitalism and policing.

From a radical perspective, policing serves two key functions: it helps contain class struggle, and it helps control surplus populations produced by the normal progress of capitalist accumulation. Simply put, the same capitalist processes that generate value and wealth on the one hand, and criminal and surplus populations on the other, also create a need for strategies that can control populations marginalized by processes that divide societies into social classes (Spitzer, 1981; Quinney, 1980; Harring, 1976, 1983; Lynch, 1988a).

## Early Policing and Public Disorder

The first modern, centralized police departments in the U.S. developed in urban centers in the Northeast during a period of extensive immigration in the mid-1800s. The first of these emerged in New York City in 1845. This pattern of policing was adopted by other cities during that era in an attempt to "maintain order": In quick succession centralized police departments were established in Albany, NY and Chicago (1851), New Orleans and Cincinnati (1853), Boston (1854), Philadelphia (1855), and Newark, NJ, and Baltimore, (1857) (Fosdick, 1969; Richardson, 1974; Platt et al., 1982; Harring, 1983; Lynch, 1984).

Orthodox theory suggests that policing developed as a response to the crime and urban disorder resulting from immigration and rapid urbanization. This perspective accepts policing as an appropriate response to the appearance of social disorder and chaos. Radical criminologists, in contrast, raise questions about the idea of "order," such as: "*what* type of order does policing maintain?" and "*whose* idea of order does policing protect?" The answer to these questions from a radical perspective is that policing reinforces and maintains unequal class structures by focusing on behaviors most likely to be engaged in by working-class and marginalized populations. This interpretation of policing has been supported by studies that document how police reinforce property rights and maintain the interests of the powerful over those of the powerless.

For example, early in their history police were regularly called upon to disband striking workers (Harring, 1981, 1983; Platt et al., 1982). As Harring (1976) demonstrated, many of the so-called "riots" that nineteenth century American police disbanded were actually gatherings of strikers. He goes on to note that suppression of "riots" was: " ...advantageous to those with specific economic and political privileges to protect. Such protection is not... a value-neutral social control problem. Without real economic and political exploitation there would have been no riots, nor any need to create a police department to control them" (p.56).

Strikebreaking was a naked attempt to "break working class resistance to corporate power...by defining workers' struggles for better working conditions as criminal acts" (Harring, 1981:293). In addition to forced dispersal of groups of workers, police also used arrest for public order offenses as a "major weapon of class oppression permitting the indiscriminate arrest, jailing and fining of workers for behaviors that went unpunished among the ruling class and their allies" (Platt et al., 1982:26). This use of police was made possible by "ruling class domination of the state and its law making and law enforcement apparatus"(Platt et al., 1982:24; see also Parks, 1976; Quinney, 1979; Harring, 1983, 1982, 1981, 1977).

Evidence for these claims was provided by Harring's (1983) analysis of police arrests in Buffalo (1865-1915). Harring discovered that nearly 80 percent of all arrests were for public order offenses (pp.16, 46), which led him to conclude that these arrests were major weapons in class control. In another study, Harring (1981:296-297) noted that the Chicago Police Department was "viciously anti-labor...On a day-to-day basis it hauled nearly a million workers off to jail between 1875 and 1900... for trivial public order offenses." As further evidence of this bias, Harring (1977) noted that public order acts, such as the "Tramps Acts," were used to arrest traveling labor union organizers as well as unemployed laborers. Police were able to use these ambiguous laws to suppress the formation of workers' unions during the early decades of this century. Taken together, these data suggest that "[t]he police institution must be conceptualized as having been fundamentally bourgeois and anti-working class from its inception" (Harring, 1981:297).

In addition, Harring (1977, 1981, 1983; Harring and McMullin, 1975), provides extensive evidence of an intimate connection between big business and police commissions, using a case study from Buffalo, NY. These studies indicate that police commissions were "solidly in the hands of local commercial and industrial elites," with police chiefs often coming "directly from the ranks of businessmen, by-passing men with police experience" (Harring, 1981:297). Other studies indicate that local manufacturers and businessmen were appointed to important police offices (Platt et al., 1982), which gave local elite the ability to use local police for strike-breaking activities (Dawley, 1975).

The history of southern policing also illuminates how police institutions emerged to serve economic interests. The earliest form of southern policing, the "slave patrol" in South Carolina, dating back to 1712 (Platt et al., 1982), was responsible for apprehending runaway slaves, preventing slave riots and providing discipline and summary justice to blacks caught violating any law. Once the slaves were freed, the major impetus for policing shifted to controlling free black laborers to provide employers with a low-cost workforce (Platt et al., 1982; Adamson, 1983; Sheldon, 1981).

Police use of public-order arrests to control the lower classes has not disappeared in the modern world, and today police make more public-order arrests than arrests for serious "Index" crimes. We examine this issue further in the section entitled "Police Behavior." For now, we wish to complete our review of class issues and policing by focusing on the origins of private, state and federal police.

## Social Class and Policing by Private, State and Federal Agencies

Private, state and federal police originated from the need to exert class control. The most obvious example is private policing, which is particularly well-suited to take advantage of the contradictions of crime in a capitalist society (Spitzer, 1981; Spitzer and Scull, 1977b). We use the term "contradictions" to suggest that, while we normally assume it has no positive benefits, crime actually creates many opportunities for capitalist enterprises to generate profits. Crime, in effect, creates a way of life not only for well-entrenched members of the "criminal class," but also for those who own private security firms, produce security products (e.g., home burglar alarms, "the Club," personal mace), or run private, for-profit prisons. Privately owned security and control enterprises also provide a living for the working-class employees of these firms.

As an industry, private policing nets tremendous profits. In the U.S. in the mid-1990s, there were *three times* as many private security guards as public police, and private security firms collected more than $60 billion in revenues. Like public police, private police are a class-based institution, hired/purchased by those with the financial resources to do so and focused primarily on controlling lower-class threats. The irony of this situation should not be lost on observers, since those most in need of additional protection from crimes (lower and working classes) are least able to afford it (Platt et al., 1982).

The class bias of private policing can be traced back to its origins in the mid-1800s. During this period, as public policing developed to maintain public order and contain the "dangerous classes," private police emerged as a pay-for-service system that protected private property and helped those with resources to pursue justice privately (Weiss, 1978). For example, the first private police agency, founded by Allan Pinkerton during the early 1850s in Chicago, provided police services primarily to those who had industrial interests to protect. Consequently, Pinkerton's agency soon evolved into an anti-labor organization hired to spy upon workers. Less than 20 years after it began, breaking strikes and busting unions had become an important part of the Pinkerton agency's services. By 1892, the Pinkertons had participated in breaking more than 77 strikes nationwide (Weiss, 1978).

Pinkerton's agency used a variety of strong-arm tactics to break strikes. This, however, eventually resulted in growing public opposition to the idea of businesses hiring private "agents" to commit violence against workers. Further, evidence suggests that in small cities and towns, police, who were generally members of the working class themselves, refused to suppress striking workers (Guttman, 1977; Monkkonen, 1992). In order to preserve the legitimacy of strike-breaking, there needed to be some limits to the violence directed against workers. In response, states began adopting the idea of state police. In 1866, for instance, Pennsylvania formed the Coal and Iron Police to deal with striking coal and iron workers (Weiss, 1978). The loyalty of these state institutions to corporate interests was obvious, and they were often no less brutal than privately hired police. There was an important difference, however: the violence of state police appeared more legitimate because it was authorized by the state to preserve the "peace." In 1905, Pennsylvania created a general state police agency, which could be used for strike-breaking. As Weiss (1978:41) notes: "…[w]ith their creation, capital gained an efficient tax supported military force invested with public authority." Using Pinkerton-style, strike-breaking methods, the state police quickly dashed any hope that they would be a more humane strike-breaking force, and labor leaders described them as "legalized strikebreakers" who used violent methods similar to those of the "*Cossacks*" in Russia (Weiss, 1978:41).

Like state and local governments, the federal government also created new police forces to further the class war on workers and strikers. For instance, the Bureau of Investigation (later known as the Federal Bureau of Investigation, or FBI) was used throughout the early 1900s to infiltrate labor unions and other groups suspected of "radical" (i.e., socialist) activities. The bureau's extensive investigations of labor unions led them to charge a number of labor officials with violations of the Espionage and Sedition Acts (Belknap, 1977). In a relatively short period, the bureau's anti-labor and anti-communist sympathies became synonymous. The bureau claimed that communist doctrines were used to support labor union activities, a position clearly aligned with the interests of capitalists. In turn, the bureau was able to use its success at smashing labor unions to win additional funding (Belknap, 1977). Ironically, this bureau, created under the Sherman Antitrust Act – a legislative attempt to control big business – quickly came to protect big business. The first time the Sherman Antitrust Act was enforced it was directed against a labor union, the International Workers of the World, for supposed restraint of trade (Michalowski, 1985).

While the FBI provides a measure of protection for ordinary citizens, it continues to shape the image of crime as behavior engaged in by the lower classes, concentrating on crimes committed *against businesses* and publishing the Uniform Crime Report (UCR), a national measure of crime that excludes corporate and white collar crime. Below, we take a further look at the UCR and what it tells us about crime and police behavior in contemporary America.

# POLICE BEHAVIOR

Ordinarily, when criminologists speak of "police behavior" they are referring to the behavior of individual police officers, and the policing literature is replete with studies of police in action. Another way of studying police behavior is by examining police behavior in the aggregate, as revealed by arrest data. These data provide a record of the kinds of crimes that police encounter and act upon.

Most police agencies in the U.S. report arrest statistics to the FBI, which in turn records these data in the UCR. The UCR is divided into two parts: Part I includes the eight "most serious" crimes, while Part II keeps track of lesser offenses. Table 10.1 contains arrest patterns for Part I and Part II for 2002 (see Table 4.1 in the *Sourcebook of Criminal Justice Statistics, 2002*). These arrest data represent the general pattern of police behavior across the U.S. What do these data tell us about police behavior?

All told, police made over 13.7 million arrests in 2002. *Only 4.5 percent* of these arrests were for *serious violence* (murder, rape, robbery and aggravated assault), while 11.8 percent were for serious property crimes. In all, *only 16.3 percent* of arrests in 2002 were for crimes the FBI defines as the most serious. These Part I offenses declined 2 percent in proportion to the total number of serious arrests since 1995. Contrary to popular perception and news reports, *most police behavior involved responding to lesser crimes*. About *84 percent* of all arrests were for less serious, Part II offenses.

Furthermore *more than half* (56%) of all arrests made in 2002 involved "marginal population control offenses": these are crimes for which economically marginal persons are the most likely to be arrested, such as victimless crimes (prostitution, drug abuse and gambling) or population-control crimes (disorderly conduct, vagrancy, etc.). Since 1995, the greatest increase in arrests has been for drug offenses. The people arrested for these crimes are rarely from the middle or upper classes. Indeed, the overwhelming majority of people arrested for victimless, public-order and drug crimes are working class or poorer, not because they engage in these behaviors more frequently, but because they do so in public places that expose them to arrest. The high-priced call girl offered as a corporate perk to visiting executives will not find herself rousted off the street by police. The physician with a cocaine habit will not be arrested for buying crack on a ghetto street corner. Finally, the lawyers and executives in many cities who enjoy illegal, high-stakes poker games every weekend (poker games well known to the police) will not be arrested. No, the primary purpose of arrest is to punish the poor and minorities for *their* pleasures.

## Table 10.1: Police Behavior as Indicated by Part I and Part II UCR Arrests, 2002

| Crime Type | Number of Arrests | Percent of All Arrests | |
|---|---|---|---|
| **All Crimes**ᵃ | **13,741,438** | **100.0** | |
| **Part I or "Serious" Crimes** | | | |
| Violent | 620,510 | 4.5 | |
| Property | 1,613,954 | 11.8 | |
| Total | **2,234,464** | **16.3** | |
| **Part II or "Lesser" Crimes** | | | (CLASSIFICATION) |
| Other Assaults | 1,288,682 | 9.4 | Minor violent |
| Sex Offenses | 95,066 | 0.7 | offenses |
| Family Offenses | 140,286 | 1.0 | |
| Forgery/ Counterfeiting | 115,735 | 0.8 | Minor property |
| Fraud | 337,404 | 2.5 | offenses |
| Embezzlement | 18,552 | 0.1 | |
| Stolen Property | 126,422 | 0.9 | |
| Vandalism | 276,697 | 2.0 | |
| Weapons, Carry/Possession | 164,446 | 1.2 | Potential danger to |
| Driving Under the Influence | 1,461,746 | 10.6 | others |
| Prostitution | 79,733 | 0.6 | Victimless crimes |
| Drug Abuse | 1,538,813 | 11.2 | |
| Gambling | 10,506 | 0.1 | |
| Liquor Laws | 653,819 | 4.8 | Marginal population-control offenses |
| Drunkenness | 572,735 | 4.2 | |
| Disorderly Conduct | 669,938 | 4.9 | |
| Vagrancy | 27,295 | 0.2 | |
| All Other (except Traffic) | 3,671,058 | 26.7 | |
| Curfew/ Loitering | 141,252 | 1.0 | |
| Runaways | 125,688 | 0.9 | |
| **Total, Part II**ᵃ | **11,506,974** | ᵇ**83.7** | |

a. The totals for "All Crimes" and "Total, Part II" include arrests for "suspicion" (N = 8,899) under the category "All Other," a crime type that is not listed separately in Table 4.1 of the *Sourcebook for Criminal Justice Statistics, 2002.*

b. Due to rounding error, the total percentage for Part II crimes adds to 83.8%.

The class bias of policing is also evident in data omitted from this table. The UCR *does not* include arrests for white collar and corporate offenses because the types of offenses committed by middle-class managers and corporate capitalists fall under the jurisdiction of "regulatory agencies," not local police departments (see, Burns and Lynch, 2004, 2002). Moreover, corporate offenses are structured in such a way that individual offenders themselves will rarely be punished for their wrongdoing. Instead, penalties will be leveled against the offending company, thereby insulating the middle and upper class criminal from both punishment and stigma.

In addition to class bias, police behavior exhibits race and gender biases (LaFree, 1989, 1985, 1980). In terms of race, many have argued that minorities are overrepresented in police and crime data for a variety of reasons related to racial bias (Mann, 1993; Reiman, 1998; Tonry, 1994; Zatz, 1990; Lynch, 1990; Lynch and Patterson, 1990; Patterson and Lynch, 1991). When it comes to gender, police appear to provide less protection for crimes when women are the primary victims (LaFree, 1989; Schur, 1984). Let us take the following example.

## Policing Gender: Preliminary Comments

In 2002, police made arrests in nearly 57 percent of all reported assault cases, and 64 percent of all reported murders. The arrest rate for rape, however, was relatively low compared to these other serious offenses, with only 44 percent of all reported rapes resulting in arrest. There are a number of commonly heard explanations for this lower figure, such as women's unwillingness to participate in the investigative process, lack of witnesses, minimal evidence and so forth. Yet, many of these same problems also apply to homicides and assault (e.g., the victim certainly cannot participate, there may be no witnesses and little evidence) and other crimes. The difference is that dead bodies or beaten bodies elicit a different reaction from raped bodies, and much of this difference has to do with gender relations and the relative powerlessness of women in society. We will explore this idea further below. For now, we would note that in terms of gender bias and police behavior, it is revealing that the FBI does not report a category called "domestic violence," a crime in which women (and children) are the primary victims, despite the fact that domestic violence is estimated to be the *most common* form of ordinary criminal violence in the U.S. (see DeKeseredy and Schwartz, 1996). Furthermore, a woman's lifetime chance of being the victim of domestic violence substantially exceeds her lifetime chance of being the victim of any other type of violent crime (Websdale, 1997). While some crimes of domestic violence are included within the FBI category of assault, the majority are included under "other assaults" or "offenses against family and children" within Part II of the UCR (or excluded through lack of official police reaction). This reflects the fact that in most jurisdictions violence against women and children within the home is defined as a private matter (Websdale, 1997). In many places in the U.S., a man can face serious criminal charges for assaulting a stranger on the street or in some public setting. But the same level of violence committed by that same man against his wife or children is treated as a less serious crime, or, perhaps, not as a crime at all. While this trend is changing in some police jurisdictions, the tendency to treat domestic violence against women and children as "private" violence remains widespread.

## BROADENING OUR VIEW OF POLICING

Typically, discussions of policing *focus only on agencies* charged with *enforcing criminal law* that controls *street crime*. Yet there are a variety of other policing functions designed to control corporate and business crimes that criminologists have failed to examine as part of policing (Newman and Nalla, 1990). The omission of these latter forms of policing from criminology and criminal justice textbooks reinforces stereotypical notions concerning the kinds of crimes that most threaten our health and safety (e.g., Reiman, 1998; Frank and Lynch, 1992, chapter 4). While we cannot explore the full range of police-like agencies charged with detecting and controlling corporate and white collar crime here, we briefly explore this idea below in order to provide another example of the relationship between social class and social control.

### Corporate Policing

As noted in chapter 4, most crimes committed in the U.S. are corporate and white collar crimes. We reached this conclusion by comparing the number of street crimes recorded in the UCR to crimes committed by corporate criminals recorded in other sources (see Reiman, 1998:61-90). The difference between the level of street crime and corporate crime noted in that discussion could actually be extended further by counting *all* of the crimes recorded by *all of the agencies* charged with enforcing corporate regulations.

Table 10.2 includes a partial list of federal agencies that police corporate and white collar crimes (for more extensive discussion, see Meier, 1985). In addition to these federal agencies, most states have comparable regulatory bodies. Each state, for example, has rules that affect the banking and securities industries, the emission of pollutants and the rights of workers. Given the number of agencies charged with regulating business, it should come as no surprise that there are more business-related crimes than ordinary street crimes! The surprise, rather, is that *criminologists rarely investigate the activities of organizations charged with upholding laws aimed at controlling business crimes.*

### Table 10.2. Federal Agencies that Police Upper-Class Crime

| Agency | Focus |
|---|---|
| Office of the Comptroller of Currency | National banks |
| Federal Reserve System | Federal reserve banks |
| Federal Deposit Insurance Corporation (FDIC) | FDIC member banks |
| Federal Home Loan Board | Savings associations |
| National Credit Union Administration | Credit unions |
| Securities and Exchange Commission (SEC) | Investment companies, stock market, money market, mutual funds |
| Food and Drug Administration (FDA) | Foods and drugs |
| Food Safety Inspection Service (FSIS) | Meat and poultry products |
| National Highway Safety Administration (NHTSA) | Automobiles |
| Consumer Product Safety Administration (CPSC) | Over 10,000 consumer products not regulated by other agencies |
| Federal Trade Commission (FTC) | Unfair, deceptive trade practices, antitrust violations |
| Agricultural Stabilization and Conservation Service (ASCS) | Price support regulation |
| Agriculture Marketing Service | Agriculture marketing |
| U.S. Department of Agriculture (USDA) | Agricultural research & education programs; Soil conservation, FHA loans, Forest Service |
| National Air Pollution Control Commission (NAPCC) | Air quality and emissions |
| Environmental Protection Agency (EPA) | All industries that create waste products, waste water, Superfund sites and Cleanup |

| Agency | Focus |
|--------|-------|
| Occupational Safety and Health Administration (OSHA) | Workplace safety and health |
| Nat'l Institute of Occupational Safety and Health (NIOSH) | Worker safety research |
| Antitrust Division of the Department of Justice | Antitrust laws |
| Equal Employment Opportunity Commission (EEOC) | Unfair hiring practices |
| Federal Communication Commissions (FCC) | TV, radio regulations |
| Civil Aeronautics Board (CAB) | Airlines |
| Interstate Commerce Commissions (ICC) | Interstate commerce |

A number of the agencies listed in Table 10.2 have the power to use criminal sanctions (e.g., the SEC, EPA, FTC, OSHA). Oftentimes, however, these agencies rely upon their civil powers instead. For upper-class criminals, this means the ability to avoid the stigma associated with criminal penalties and the ability to avoid constructing a negative, personal self-image as "a criminal." Street criminals are not so lucky.

Regulatory agencies exist to protect people from harm. In some sense, these agencies act as balancing mechanisms, especially in capitalist economies where the push for profit can easily place people in danger of harm resulting from practices such as the manufacture of faulty products, false advertising, price-fixing, pollution and so forth. In a related sense, we might say that regulatory agencies are an expression of society's conscience, a constant reminder of how we *expect* corporations and businesspeople to behave.

Historically, the earliest federal regulatory/policing agencies focused on banking and agriculture (e.g., the Department of Agriculture, created in 1862; the Currency Act of 1863; the National Bank Act of 1864). During the late 1800s and early 1900s, a number of regulatory agencies were added to protect the public from corporate greed and predatory practices. It was at this point in history, *at the height of free-market economics*, that the many negative consequences of uncontrolled capitalist enterprises became a focus of public concern. During this period, it was typical for large corporations to lower their prices to drive competitors out of business. Once the competition was eliminated, the surviving corporation raised its prices and gouged consumers. Vast fortunes that still support some of America's richest families (e.g., the Rockefellers, the Du-

Ponts, the Morgans, the Carnegies) were made using this tactic. In addition to these unscrupulous practices, the marketplace was flooded with unsafe foods, drugs and consumer products as corporations sought to maximize their profits (Kallet and Schlink, 1933; Frank and Lynch, 1992; Pearce, 1976). The existence of these various forms of predation made it clear that there was a need for regulation in the marketplace. Laws promoting consumer protection, however, were not passed quickly. It took a long struggle, supported by "muckrakers" in the popular press, before agencies such as the Food and Drug Administration, established in 1906, the Food Safety Inspection Service in 1907, and the Federal Trade Commission in 1914 were reluctantly created to appease popular demands for protection against unscrupulous business practices (Morris, 2002). By the 1960s, there were 28 regulatory agencies policing corporate crimes. Over the next two decades, the number of regulatory agencies expanded to 56 (Meier, 1985). It was during this period that a number of important agencies that police workplaces (OSHA), airlines (CAB), automobile makers (NHTSA), and environmental safety (EPA, NAPCC) were created. Each appeared to mark an important step in controlling corporate behavior and in protecting people from harm.

Many people have argued that all this regulation and policing of corporations has driven up the costs of production, decreased the profit-making capacity of corporations, and placed an undue burden on corporations. Well-known apologists for *laissez faire* capitalism, such as Milton Friedman (1962), claim that corporations are capable of policing themselves. The historical record of corporate behavior clearly suggests otherwise. Early industrial capitalism, operating in a regulation-free environment, produced a great number of harmful and deadly products, wantonly destroyed competitors, engaged in price-fixing and showed little concern for the health and safety of workers, or for the well-being of the physical environment (e.g., Josephson, 1934, Ross, 1907; Kallet and Schlink, 1933; Silverman and Lee, 1974; Silverman et al., 1982; for a more contemporary example, see Glantz et al., 1996). Corporations did little, if anything, to police their own behavior during the heyday of free-market, unregulated economics, and there is little reason to believe they would do so today if regulations were removed.

Today, examples abound of corporations' inability to police themselves, especially when it comes to behaviors that threaten the life and/or health of people. For example, every major safety innovation found in today's automobiles resulted from government regulation, not corporate innovation or corporate concern for the safety of consumers (Burns, 1997). Even worse, automakers have a history of spending large sums of money to *defeat* legislation that would require enhanced automotive safety (Burns, 1997; Nader, 1965). Compounding this situation, when the auto manufacturers are punished, the costs of the hundreds of millions of dollars in fines are passed along to consumers in higher vehicle sticker prices (Burns and Lynch, 2002). In an automobile dependent nation, vehicle safety is an important issue, and on an annual basis nearly two-and-one-half times as many people die in automobile accidents as in homicides. But, there are numerous examples of the ways in which corporate behavior harms people each and every day.

In another example, corporations regularly export dangerous products to foreign nations *after* they are banned as dangerous in the U.S., and even after their products have been discovered to cause serious injuries and death (Weir and Shapiro, 1982; Silverman and Lee, 1974; Silverman et al., 1982; Braithwaite, 1984; Ermann and Clements, 1984). Sometimes, when products threaten the reproductive health and even the lives of women, they will not only be marketed overseas, but the U.S. government will help in this endeavor (Dowie, 1979). In cases such as these, the medical advances offered by pharmaceutical manufacturers become yet another challenge to the health and safety of people in poorer nations. This example also reinforces our claim that corporations do a very poor job of policing their own behaviors. Indeed, when the harms associated with their products are pointed out, and drugs are banned in the U.S., corporations continue victimizing customers by seeking out unregulated foreign markets of the type beloved by conservative economists.

The threats posed by corporations are not only exported to people in poorer nations, they are also "exported" to lower class and minority communities within the United States. Corporations, for instance, have knowingly dumped toxic waste illegally in ways that disproportionately affect minority and poor communities (Stretesky, 1997a, 1996; Stretesky and Hogan, 1998; Stretesky and Lynch, 2003, 1999a, 1999b; Lynch, Stretesky and Burns, 2004a, 2004b; Gibbs, 1995). They have even knowingly sold landfill sites polluted with known carcinogens to school boards for use as elementary school sites (Brown, 1980). Many of these cases involve deliberate and callous threats to human health and life. For example, executives of the Johns-Manville Company knowingly kept information about the lethal effects of asbestosis from their workers, just as major cigarette companies hid information about the lethal effects of smoking from the public for years (Brodeur, 1974; Glantz et al., 1996).

Corporate illegalities are not restricted to the sale of harmful products. At times, upper-world crime can even resemble the kinds of murders we associate with one-on-one violence. For instance, in 1995 the Nigerian government arrested and executed internationally acclaimed Nigerian environmental activist and Nobel Prize nominee Ken Saro-Wiwa. Saro-Wiwa had been instrumental in preventing several major oil companies from exploiting Nigerian oil reserves within native homelands. The actions of the Nigerian government to silence Saro-Wiwa were clearly in the interest of these oil companies, companies that not only did not add their voices to the international community calling for his release, but which have supported the activities of the Nigerian government (Michalowski, 1998).

In short, the argument that corporations and businesses will police themselves has no basis in either historical or contemporary fact. Indeed, today many major corporations are entering into a new era of relatively unregulated business by relocating to countries with far fewer regulations than are found in developed nations. In those countries they frequently resort to strategies of the past, including running sweatshops, sponsoring violent attacks on union members and organizers, and operating under dangerously unsafe working conditions (Karliner, 1997). Indeed, as William Greider (1997:334) notes: "...global commerce with all of its supposed modernity and wondrous technology" has restored "the barbarisms that had long ago been forbidden by law." Nevertheless, the contention by many business leaders and conservative politicians that business is "overregulated" and should be trusted to police itself is seen as a serious contribution to the national discourse on the appropriate use of law. If people who had a long history of burglary or robbery were to suggest that they were "overregulated" by police, we would laugh. The decisions made by corporate leaders in the pursuit of private profit, even when they are harmful, are treated with far greater caution by the system that polices corporations. There is no clearer example of the class-based nature of policing in the U.S.

## RACE AND POLICING

Up to this point, we have concentrated on the relationship between class and policing. Historically, American policing has had much to do with policing class conflict, protecting capital and maintaining class inequality, and, as a result, any discussion of policing and its development must pay close attention to these connections. Over the past four decades, however, the police have become much more involved in maintaining racial inequality, and it is no longer possible to examine policing without addressing its connection to America's racial hierarchy (on racial inequality generally, see Massey and Denton, 1993). Radical criminologists have long recognized this fact, and it is here more than anywhere else, that the issue of race has been emphasized by radicals (e.g., Takagi, 1979, 1981; Platt et al., 1982; Harring et al., 1977).

– 234 –

With respect to policing, radicals would agree with Walker et al.'s (1996: 115) conclusion that:

> There is persuasive evidence that minorities are more likely than white Americans to be shot and killed, arrested and victimized by excessive physical force. Despite some progress in recent years, significant racial and ethnic disparities remain. In addition, there is evidence of misconduct directed at racial and ethnic minorities and that police departments fail to discipline officers who are guilty of misconduct. Finally, employment discrimination by police departments continues to exist.

Below, we review some of the evidence that supports this claim.

## Policing Minorities

Both historically and contemporarily, police departments have typically conducted more surveillance in low-income minority communities than in white communities, even low-income white communities. The greater police presence in minority communities, particularly African-American and Latino communities, means that the people in those communities are more likely to become targets of police activity. For example, African Americans and Latinos are more likely than European Americans to be stopped for "field interviews," frisked, verbally abused for "suspicion," or "hassled" in other ways (for review, see Walker et al., 1996; on general issues of police abuse and deviance, see Kappeler et al., 1994; see also Chambliss, 1994). In addition, African Americans and Latinos, particularly men, are more likely to be arrested, and even more likely to be killed by police (Mann, 1993; Walker et al., 1996; Takagi, 1979; Harring et al., 1977; Robin, 1963; Knoohuizen et al., 1972; Milton et al., 1977; Kobler, 1975a, 1975b).

Orthodox and radical analysts of policing agree that African Americans and Latinos are arrested at rates that are disproportionate to their representation in the general population (Daly and Tonry, 1997; Tonry, 1995). There is also agreement that police presence is greater in African-American and Latino communities (see Mann, 1993). Orthodox and radical analysts do not agree, however, about why police are overrepresented there. Some argue that the police focus on African-American and Latino communities reflects established racial biases and practices rooted in the broader picture of race relations in America. Others suggest that police are more highly concentrated in minority communities because that is where crime is the highest. Still others contend that minorities contribute to racial disparities in arrest because they are either deliberately more disrespectful to police than European Americans, or because their cultural patterns of speech and interaction are more likely to be interpreted as disrespectful by police. Both the crime participation and demeanor arguments, however, suffer from several limitations.

First, demeanor is a subjective criterion that can be race-linked (see examples in Mann and Zatz, 1998). Like other citizens, police have expectations concerning others' behaviors. These expectations may be race-specific. If police expect African Americans to behave differently and to be more confrontational than European Americans, they may also be more likely to interpret African-American behavior in a manner that is consistent with these expectations, increasing the probability of arrest for minorities. This type of response does not require conscious and overt racism. Like others in our society, police have absorbed many taken-for-granted racial stereotypes from the larger culture (see Lynch and Patterson, 1996b, 1991). Thus, police can sometimes behave in racially biased ways without consciously intending or desiring to do so. Because these stereotypes construct African Americans and Latinos as generally less trustworthy and more likely to be criminals than European Americans, they are likely to be arrested on lesser evidence than whites (Petersilia, 1983).

Second, the issue of racial disparity in arrest must also be examined relative to the kinds of laws police have the power to enforce. As noted earlier, urban police patrols typically focus on the visible pleasures and problems of the poor, such as public intoxication, disorderly conduct, gambling and similar offenses. The enactment and enforcement of laws governing such behaviors frequently include clear racial biases (Tonry, 1994; Chiricos, 1996; see also Chambliss, 1995b). Betting with a bookie is illegal, while wagering your money on the stock market is not. Selling and using the street drug of choice for many African-American and Latino drug users – crack cocaine – is targeted by police and punished by law much more extensively than selling and using powdered cocaine, which happens to be highly favored among white middle-class and upper-class drug users. Likewise, the crimes for which whites make up the majority of offenders – white collar, corporate, environmental, medical and governmental crimes – are not the targets of urban police, and are excluded from crime statistics, contributing to the appearance that minorities represent the crux of the crime problem.

A third way of addressing the issue of racial bias in policing is to examine citizen complaints about police behavior. For example, in the early 1990s, over 70 percent of complaints lodged against New York City police were filed by members of minority groups (Walker et al., 1996). Nationwide, internal police investigations sustain only about 10 percent of citizen complaints of abuse, more often finding cause to support complaints filed by whites than those filed by African Americans (Walker et al., 1996). One explanation for higher levels of African Americans' complaints against police is that they typically have more negative attitudes toward police. The research evidence, however, contradicts this claim and shows no significant difference in white and black attitudes toward police (Smith et al., 1991). This suggests that there are, in fact, more complaints against police by African Americans because police are more likely to behave in disrespectful or overly aggressive ways toward them.

Finally, racial bias in policing can be examined from the perspective of hiring practices (Mann, 1993). For example, Nalla and Corley's (1996) historical and cross-city review of hiring, assignment and promotion practices shows continued racial discrimination even in the face of lawsuits filed against police agencies for racial bias and court judgments ordering police departments to remedy these situations. Racial bias in these areas is systematic, meaning that it is widely observable across American cities and persists over time (Nalla and Corley, 1996). Systematic racial discrimination has its greatest impact on Hispanic and African-American women, who are underrepresented on police forces and at all ranks and assignments (Nalla and Corley, 1996, for a review of these issues see also Walker et al., 1996).

## GENDER AND POLICING

In what ways does gender affect policing? Traditionally, this question has been examined relative to female representation on police departments, and there is fairly consistent evidence that women are discriminated against in hiring, promotion and assignments by police agencies (for review, see Lynch et al., 1992). Historically, policing has been constructed as "a man's world," and police agencies work hard to keep it that way, failing, for example, to recruit women from the many criminal justice, criminology and social work programs that exist on college and university campuses across the United States. There are more than enough women willing to work as police officers, but there is also great resistance to women in policing. That resistance has traditionally been legitimized in biased police performance requirements that favor men over women or that make women *appear* less capable because they are *only required* to meet reduced physical standards. Generally, policing is not physically demanding work, and current physical agility test requirements do not represent the tasks police officers typically encounter. "Reduced standards for women" is a tactic used to mark women as "less worthy" officers. In reality, agility standards should be reduced to levels that reflect the actual nature of the tasks police perform for *all* police officers, not just women. Further, the skills most useful to police officers include communication, negotiation and nonviolent problem solving – skills that many women perform better than men. Indeed, many of the violent confrontations that occur between police and citizens may result from the images of masculinity that men, particularly working- and lower-middle class white men bring to the job (Messerschmidt, 1993; for alternative feminist visions of how to enact justice, see Klein 1997).

The effects of gender on policing extend beyond these simple but visible acts of discrimination against women. Gender effects are also evident in the way police respond to women as victims. For example, the belief that it is acceptable for males to hit their female partners is still widely held (Gelles and Strauss, 1988), and is evident among police who deal specifically with violence against women (LaFree, 1989). These negative attitudes toward women are supported throughout American and other societies, and are in part responsible for the frequency of crimes against women, such as date rape on college campuses (DeKeseredy and Kelly, 1993; Schwartz, 1991), sexual harassment in the workplace (Rhodes, 1989) and spousal abuse and rape (Schwendinger and Schwendinger, 1981). How does policing contribute to the system of gender inequality that is responsible for these crimes against women?

First, policing is designed to ignore many of the crimes committed against women. In most jurisdictions, abusive events such as rape by a date or spouse are not defined as "real" crimes. In addition, many police officers believe that women share the responsibility for precipitating these events (LaFree, 1989). Workplace crimes such as sexual harassment – even when they escalate to serious levels of victimization – are normally outside the jurisdiction of urban police. Instead, businesses rely on a variety of informal and internal mechanisms to deal with sexual harassment, mechanisms that protect offenders from the stigma of crime (Rhodes, 1989; French, 1992). Because the established practice of policing treats many of the most common crimes against women lightly, or ignores them altogether, it reinforces the message that *victimizing women is not "real" crime.*

Second, when policing is supposed to respond to crimes that affect women, the response is often shaped by the way gender intersects with race and class (Websdale, 2002). For instance, the way many police officers deal with women reporting rape is shaped by the dominant standards for female behavior. These standards are based on how white, middle-class women dress, look, talk and act. Women who behave differently are more likely to be viewed as "trash" or "sluts." As a result, women of color, and particularly low-income women of color, are less likely to be believed when filing rape charges than white women (LaFree, 1989; Mann, 1993). This tendency on the part of police *reinforces established norms of gender-appropriate behavior* that justify differential treatment of women when they are victims of sex crimes.

Third, by restricting its view of which acts constitute "real" crimes against women, and by directing its gaze elsewhere, policing contributes to the more general cultural tendency to devalue women (French, 1992). By avoiding women's accounts of their victimization, *policing reinforces existing power relations that favor men over women* (Klein, 1997).

Fourth, as victims of crime, women are compelled to rely upon male institutions such as policing for protection. This reliance has two consequences. First, women have been unable to develop alternative strategies and practices of justice (Klein, 1997). Second, because policing remains a male-dominated institution, the need for women to rely on police *helps reinforce patriarchal stereotypes of men as protectors and women as helpless.*

In sum, from hiring through assignment and promotion practices found within police agencies, to the neglect and avoidance of and the tendency to discredit women's accounts of their victimization by men, policing reinforces gendered power structures and relationships that privilege men over women. The cultural message is that women are inadequate as law enforcers and unworthy as crime victims. These forms of neglect and bias contribute to the cultural construction of a "female identity" that emphasizes women's powerlessness relative to men. These patterns within policing are not caused by police. They reflect the wider construction of gender relations in society, and are unlikely to change significantly unless there is a change in the overall pattern of how men and women construct their identities and relate to one another.

## In Sum

Orthodox criminology treats police as the logical and necessary response to crime. Historically, policing has failed to control crime, has focused the majority of its attention on relatively minor crimes by lower-class and working-class citizens, has favored repressive rather than reintegrative crime control policies, and has denied women the same protection extended to men. These issues, however, have been largely ignored by orthodox criminologists.

The radical perspective explores the ironies and contradictions of policing, and, in so doing, directs us to inspect the connection between policing and maintenance of class, gender and racial hierarchies. In addition, the radical perspective disputes the idea that police forces were first created to deal with rising problems of predatory crime and instead suggests that urban policing emerged to control the working-class during a period of economic transformation and intense class struggle, and was later transformed into a coordinated national enterprise in an effort to control the rising tensions emerging from the persistence of social inequality in America's poor, non-white communities.

Thus, policing emerged as part of an ongoing effort to maintain the dominance of capital over labor, rich over poor, whites over minorities and men over women. These patterns are repeated in the American court and correctional systems, the focus of the next two chapters.

# Eleven.
# A Radical Examination of Courts

Contemporary law appears in two forms: *substantive* law and *procedural* law. Substantive law describes behaviors prohibited by the state and how they will be punished. Procedural law specifies the rules for prosecution and punishment. According to Western legal ideology, procedural law is the basis of civil liberties because it ensures that all citizens receive fair and equal treatment when they encounter the power of the state in the form of police, courts or penal systems. Whether or not this approach to justice actually guarantees equal treatment under the law, however, has been the cause of considerable social conflict, and the basis for a substantial body of legal commentary since at least the eighteenth century.

For the most part, contemporary orthodox criminology rests on the presumption that today's procedural laws provide a reasonably fair and equitable justice system. That is, orthodox criminologists study "criminals" *as if* contemporary systems of lawmaking and law enforcement accurately distinguish criminals from non-criminals, and apply rules in a fair and equal manner. In contrast, radical approaches to criminology contend that the designation of some people as criminal and others as law abiding is influenced by "extralegal" identities such as class, gender and race as much as by the actual harms people commit. In particular, the radical approach contends that historically-grounded structural inequalities have led to different laws for different groups of social actors. Thus, the most punitive forms of criminal law are applied to wrongdoing among socially disadvantaged groups such as the poor and people of color. In contrast, less punitive administrative or regulatory laws, or no laws at all, are applied to the wrongdoings of advantaged groups such as corporations and political leaders. In keeping with this proposition, our discussion of how the American courts handle people charged with wrongdoing focuses on how that system maximizes the punishment of some and minimizes the prosecution of others.

## Justice as Inequality

In previous chapters we considered how the social construction of class, gender and race in America is based on unequal relations between advantaged and disadvantaged groups. From a criminological perspective we are interested in the ways that unequal relationships and structures affect the nature of crime and justice. In this chapter, we explore this issue in two ways: (1) by examining theoretical issues concerning the practice of justice in a society characterized by widespread social inequality, and (2) by reviewing studies that examine how class, gender and race affect court processes. In doing so, we will expand upon the following three propositions:

> **Proposition 1.** The ideological basis of contemporary court processes legitimizes structural inequality by claiming that all people are treated equally under the law.

> **Proposition 2:** Unequal class, gender and race relations shape criminal court processes in complex ways that are often poorly measured by studies that rely on simple measures of court outcomes.

> **Proposition 3:** Because unequal relations of class, gender and race have led to different legal procedures being applied to different categories of behavior (e.g., street crime vs. corporate crime), a clear picture of how social inequalities affect court processes can only be developed by comparing criminal sanctioning systems with civil and administrative ones.

## Legal Ideology

The rules that govern how a society decides who is and is not a wrongdoer are typically based on a broad system of beliefs concerning the appropriate means of doing justice. That is, they are the expression of a *legal ideology*. Western legal ideology rests on the theoretical proposition that justice occurs when people are treated equally under law. According to American legal ideology, two related conditions must be met to achieve equality before the law. First, the legal process must be blind to the social differences among people. Second, judicial processes must focus only on the specific facts about a legal case. Identity characteristics such as class, gender or race are defined as extralegal, that is, outside the appropriate realm of the judicial process.

In principle, most people in the U.S. would agree that such rules are necessary if we are to ensure justice. Whether or not the goal of equal treatment before the law is achieved, however, depends upon what we might mean when we say people should be treated "the same." This question raises three related issues. First, is it possible for courts to provide equal treatment to people whose lives are shaped by whether they are the beneficiaries or the victims of inequality? In other words, is it "fair" for the legal system to ignore the impact of unequal relations of class, gender and race when these inequalities shape people's opportunities and life courses in fundamental ways? Second, if courts ignore inequality in the pursuit of equality, do they help legitimize the advantages enjoyed by some and the disadvantages suffered by others? Third, do American courts actually treat people equally according to their own definition of equality?

## INEQUALITY AND JUSTICE

Can justice be achieved in inherently unequal societies? To some degree, the answer to this question depends on what we mean by the word "justice." From our perspective, a just society would require three conditions (see Lynch and Stretesky, 1998). First, in a just society all people would have access to the fundamental minimum material and social resources required to lead a *dignified* existence, not merely to survive. Second, relations between members of all social groups would be relations of equality rather than relations based on privilege, difference and domination. Thus, for instance, men would have no structural or cultural power over women; European Americans would not enjoy structural or cultural power over those whose ethnic heritage or skin color identify them as non-Europeans; and workers would have as much power to determine the conditions of their work as those who employed them. In other words, individual and group characteristics such as class, gender, race, sexual orientation, religion and so on, would have little impact on the allocation of interpersonal respect, political power, economic opportunity or other life chances. Third, no one would have the power to create structural barriers that would promote their interests by fostering unequal social relations that disadvantage others.

Certainly, it is not easy to imagine how equality as we have defined it could be achieved in a world such as ours where one of the most basic principles of social organization is the struggle for competitive advantage. Like all ideals, however, our model of a just society is useful because it provides a standard by which we can judge the degree of social equality in American society and identify where there are shortcomings.

In previous chapters, we argued that major components of social identity, such as social class, gender and race, shape the access people will have to life chances and social power. If identity did not play a role in shaping life outcomes, an African-American, lesbian truck driver would have as much chance of becoming a U.S. senator as a white, male lawyer. Although we are surrounded by an ideology that claims America is the land of equal opportunity, a person's chances of ending up financially comfortable and/or politically powerful are significantly enhanced by starting out as a white male, raised by affluent parents, connected to a social network of people who are well placed in the worlds of business and politics.

When social inequality is a basic part of the structure of a society, it compromises the search for justice. First, real justice is elusive when the individuals over whom courts exercise power have differential access to the economic and social resources that determine the effectiveness of the case they can present. Contrary to movies like *The Rainmaker,* the quality of legal representation in the real world is not the same for the poor, who must rely on public defenders or legal aid attorneys, as it is for people who can afford private attorneys. The recent trials of football star and T.V. personality O.J. Simpson for the murder of his ex-wife and a male friend, and of T.V. and movie star Robert Blake for the murder of his wife, provide particularly dramatic examples of this link among money, power and the judicial process. Had Simpson been an impoverished, underemployed African-American man, rather than a rich and famous football star and actor, in all likelihood he would be spending time today in prison rather than on golf courses. Had Blake not been able to spend over a million dollars on his defense, whether innocent or guilty, he would have to learn if his tough-guy act works with real criminals behind bars.

Second, real justice is not possible when the kinds of law violations that are most likely to be committed by the poor – even minor violations – are treated as criminal offenses, while the law violations of the powerful, though serious, are often handled through non-criminal legal procedures. America's contemporary justice system imprisons lower-income youths from inner-city neighborhoods for drug crimes that in most other countries would result in community service, treatment or no punishment at all (Schlosser, 1998). At the same time, the legal system permits drug company executives to stimulate demand for questionable products through expensive advertising campaigns and free samples to physicians. All the procedures may be appropriate, but the outcome is not justice.

Some people might argue that a comparison between drug criminals and drug executives is unfair because the drug crimes of inner-city youths are "harmful," while the drugs sold by drug companies are helpful. This view, however, is just a restatement of an ideology that excuses the harms of the rich and penalizes the harms of the poor. As we discussed in chapter 4, more people die each year from the misapplication of so-called "legal" drugs – drugs that are subject only to administrative laws that protect executives from criminal liability for illness or deaths – than from "illegal" drugs. The difference in defining which drug offenses are considered a crime is not a result of the harm caused, but of the identity of the person causing the harm. This comparison can be highlighted by a further example: mismanufactured drugs – drugs placed on the market employing questionable, "faked," or poorly collected data on safety and effectiveness – that cause the death of humans are treated as an accident rather than a homicide or even a crime. This illustrates how equivalent harms are treated differently according to the classes of the people involved.

From our perspective, legal processes that ignore fundamental inequalities among people are inherently unjust even when they meet formal procedural criteria. For example, consider a poor woman prosecuted for selling crack, and a rich doctor administratively sanctioned for illegally prescribing Viagra to men who have no medical problem. Even if both were prosecuted according to legal procedures that were absolutely flawless, the difference in the systems that would judge them, and the resources each could muster in their defense, guarantee that the outcomes will be far removed from any standard of equality before the law. However, in a male- and white-centered society such as America, the legal system finds little reason to concern itself with a product that is promoted by white, male drug company executives and distributed by affluent white, male doctors to a clientele consisting primarily of white men who want to increase their sexual pleasure. In contrast, when poor people, particularly poor people of color, sell or use "illegal" drugs as part of a street-level system of self-medication, political leaders react with outrage, the legal system responds with drug wars and the courts lock up thousands of poor drug dealers and users behind bars. In the American way of doing justice, the sexual pleasure of white men is far more important than the lives of poor people of color.

The example above points to a fundamental flaw in American legal ideology – the belief that justice can be achieved simply by properly applying existing legal procedures. According to this belief, as long as the courts follow the procedures set forth for them, justice will result. This *juridical* (i.e., procedural), model of justice underlies much of orthodox criminology's approach to the courts. For instance, if all of those judged by a particular court to be guilty of assault received the same sentence regardless of their social class or race, many orthodox criminologists, operating from a procedural model of justice, would conclude that the court was class- and race-blind. What does not figure into their assessment of justice is that the dominant economic, political and social arrangements will deliver more working-class than middle- and upper-class men to court as defendants in assault cases, and that a disproportionate share of these working-class men will be African American or Hispanic.

In general, the orthodox view fails to consider how class, race and gender influence the behaviors included under a specific crime heading. For example, consider the case of Vioxx, an anti-arthritis medication marketed by Merck, which was claimed to relieve arthritis symptoms without damaging the stomach or kidneys. Merck marketed Vioxx in the U.S. and 80 other nations (as Ceoxx). But, after proving that Vioxx was "safe and effective" (even though clinical trials showed greater risk of heart attacks; see, Topol, 2004), and receiving FDA approval to market Vioxx, Merck later "voluntarily" recalled Vioxx because continuing clinical trials demonstrated that it was unsafe, inducing between 3.7 to 1.5 times (depending on dosage) as many heart attacks and strokes as other similar drugs. In an article published in the medical journal, *Lancet*, an FDA researcher concluded that Vioxx use led to an estimated 88,000 to 140,000 cases of serious heart events in the U.S. alone between 1999 and 2004, and that 44 percent died as a result (Graham et al., 2005). After "voluntarily" withdrawing the drug from the market at the request of the FDA , Merck is unlikely to be prosecuted, nor will this behavior be seen as the equivalent of an assault of a homicide, even though people who took Vioxx were physically injured or died. Yet, it is clear Merck executives knew about the risk associated with Vioxx use when it sought FDA marketing approval. And, while Merck is currently facing 700 Vioxx related lawsuits, it is unlikely that the victims' compensation will have much impact on Merck's Vioxx profits (Merck's Vioxx sales came to $ 2.5 billion worldwide in 2003 alone), and certainly no one will face a long prison sentence for the deaths they caused.

Under contemporary sentencing guidelines, it is increasingly difficult to detect significant differences in the sentences given to the rich and the poor when they commit street crime because very few rich men will ever have a reason to commit a street crime. Yet, as we will discuss below, many orthodox criminologists continue to insist that as long as those who commit similar crimes receive similar punishments there is no injustice in the American court system.

## Courts and the Legitimation of Inequality

The effects of a procedural model do not stay within the courthouse: they contribute to the legitimization of broader social inequalities. Courts reinforce and rationalize existing inequalities by applying rules. These rules, which are unequal in their *origin,* appear equal, neutral and unbiased in their *application.* This has several consequences. First, by treating the underlying inequalities that shape who is likely to end up in court as unimportant, the procedural model of justice helps validate the American belief in "meritocracy" – the idea that everyone gets what they deserve and, for the most part, deserves what they get.

Second, the procedural model of justice helps to validate an important corollary of the idea that America is a meritocracy – the belief that people are well off because they work harder and are more moral than those who are less-well off. By constructing an image of street crime as the work of the poor and minorities, the courts reinforce the notion that the "undeserving poor" are the cause of America's crime problem (Reiman, 1998). In other words, the appearance of equality under law reinforces the belief that the "kinds of people" who typify defendants in criminal courts – poor people and people of color – are simply not as good, hard working or humane as the rest of society, and therefore deserve to be punished far more for their wrongdoing than the "better people" who commit white collar crimes.

Third, the procedural model of justice legitimizes structural inequality by focusing on individual wrongdoers. The procedural model of justice is concerned with whether each *individual* received a fair and proper trial. The impact of how life-shaping identity characteristics – such as being male, female, European American, Hispanic, African American, affluent, poor and so on – affects the likelihood of people becoming criminal defendants in the first place is considered to be irrelevant to questions of justice. By focusing on the *behavioral* characteristics of wrongdoers (e.g., education, work history, prior criminal record), the procedural model directs us to consider only how the justice system can keep these people from offending, not how the crime problem they represent is an expression of broader structural forces. . This perspective both fueled and was fueled by a return to the belief that courts could punish crime out of existence.

Beginning in the 1970s, courts were increasingly viewed as key actors in determining crime rates. Justice system theorists argued that the rise in crime that took place during the 1960s was a consequence of the judicial system's failure to deter criminals through swift, certain, and equal punishment for equal crimes (Fogel, 1979). Conservative politicians took up this banner, adding that not only should punishment be swift, certain, and even-handed; it should be severe (see discussion in Greenberg and Humphries, 1980). Based on this perspective, courts, rather than social forces, are viewed as the key determinant of the crime problem. If crime goes up, it is because courts are being too lenient with criminals, thus failing to create a sufficient deterrent effect. If crime rates decrease, so the rationale goes, it is because harsh sentences have deterred more potential criminals while putting more convicted criminals behind bars and keeping them there for longer periods of time. This approach, however, ignores the many factors other than judicial sentences that influence the rate of crime. Courts do not determine crime rates, but many other factors do.

As discussed in chapters 5, 6 and 7, the rate of criminal offending is affected by structural factors that operate beyond the level of individual decision making. The most important of these is whether a society is capable of integrating all or most of its members into meaningful social roles, or isolates a significant portion of the population outside the social and economic mainstream. The more individuals are disconnected from the dominant order, the more likely it is that they will be drawn to criminal adaptations, regardless of the level of threatened punishment.

Given these circumstances, it is unlikely that courts can significantly reduce crime through the application of long prison sentences. The idea of rational calculus on which criminal penalties are sometimes built invokes the idea that the cost of punishment should outweigh the benefits of the crime, but that the punishment cannot be so severe as to be perceived as illegitimate (Newman, 1985). From a structural perspective, the problem becomes calculating the benefits of the crime and the cost of punishments to the offender. In a society where the majority of street criminals are poor and marginalized, the benefit of a crime may far exceed the value of the objects that are stolen. Likewise, because of these structural conditions, there may be no punishment severe enough to deter criminal offenders, and even long prison sentences or death may be preferred over a life of economic, social and political marginalization. Rather than attempt to deter individual criminals by manipulating the amount and type of punishment, it would appear to make more sense to engage in the kinds of social engineering that would eliminate the need or desire to engage in crime.

Nevertheless, many conservative thinkers and many Americans continue to believe that crime is primarily a matter of individual decision making, and that if courts were only harsh enough, crime could be dramatically reduced. By the end of the twentieth century, however, America had a larger share of its population behind bars than in *any other country in the world*, yet our crime rate, particularly the rate of violent crime, remained substantially higher than that of other developed nations with far less punitive court systems (Irwin and Austin, 1994; Welch, 1996b). In other words, if harsh punishments handed out by strict courts actually reduced crime, the U.S. crime rate should be one of the lowest among the richer nations of the world.

## Racial Discrimination and Court Processes

There is a substantial body of conflicting evidence concerning the effect of racial bias on court processes (see, generally, Walker et al., 1996; Mann, 1993). Rather than attempt to review this literature in total, our goal here is to provide a framework for understanding contemporary controversies over racial bias in the judicial process.

More than a decade ago, Marjorie Zatz (1987b) observed that findings on racial discrimination varied according to when the studies were conducted, the methods of analysis they employed and the time period from which their data were drawn. Typically, studies based on older data were more likely to show discrimination than more current court data, which seemed to suggest that, over time, racial discrimination in American courts had decreased. Zatz argued, however, that such a conclusion would be wrong. What has actually happened is that, over time, the *form* of racial discrimination has changed.

Earlier studies of discrimination in sentencing tended to find that race exerted a *direct* effect on sentences, such that African Americans were more likely to be convicted, more likely to be imprisoned, and when imprisoned more likely to be given longer sentences than white offenders. In the case of studies drawing on more recent data, the effect of race on sentencing is less obvious because changes in the criminal justice process have tended to relocate, rather than eliminate, the impact of racial bias. That is, the effect of race on sentencing tends to be *indirect*. For instance, mandatory sentencing laws and sentencing guidelines have reduced disparities at the *point of sentencing*. The hidden consequence of these laws, however, has made racial disparities *at the point of charging* more important. For instance, under sentencing guidelines, two people charged with felony possession of a drug with intent to sell will often receive similar sentences even if one is white and the other is not. However, even when similar quantities of the drug are involved, some people will be charged with felony possession and others with simple possession. The factors that influence these charging decisions are often race-linked, including whether a person is employed, whether the prosecutor thinks s/he can mount a powerful defense, whether the defendant has previous "street contacts" with police, and whether he has "known associates" with criminal records (Mann, 1994).

One well-known example of racial and ethnic biases can be seen in legal responses to crack and powdered cocaine use. The great American "crack attack," led by both the U.S. Congress and many state legislatures, established stricter penalties for people caught possessing or dealing in crack cocaine than in powdered cocaine. The justifications offered were that crack was more addictive than powdered cocaine, that crack users were more violent, and that crack distribution networks were more violent than other drug markets. None of these justifications is valid. Crack, for instance, is simply a solidified form of powdered cocaine, and they are chemically identical. Likewise, crack cocaine is no more additive than powdered cocaine, and crack users are no more violent than powdered cocaine users. At the international level, the violence associated with distribution networks of these drugs is identical because they are importing the same drug – cocaine – which is only later processed into crack to be sold in small quantities in poor communities whose drug users cannot afford the high-priced quantities of powdered cocaine sold in middle- and upper-class communities (Hawkins, 1997). The real fear that drove legislators to penalize crack possession and sales far more than cocaine was not the drug itself but a fear of the social group associated with its use – young men of color. Yet, within the procedural model favored by orthodox criminology, as long as those prosecuted for crack-related crimes were treated more or less equally *to each other*, even though they may have represented only one segment of the cocaine users in the society, the judicial system would be considered unbiased.

Because racial discrimination in the American justice system has become more covert, it has become more difficult to detect. This has led to a search for new modes of analysis that can capture subtle forms of racial bias. The work of Margaret Farnworth et al. (1991) provides a good example of how alternative approaches to studying racial biases in American courts can uncover subtle forms of racial bias in sentencing. Farnworth et al. employed two different methods to assess the effect of race on sentences given for the possession of marijuana with intent to sell. First, they analyzed the data in the traditional manner, dividing their data base into blacks and non-blacks and comparing average sentence lengths across these groups. This portion of their analysis showed no racial bias (i.e., no statistically significant difference in sentences given to black and non-black offenders). Farnworth et al. proposed, however, that this finding of no discrimination resulted from a failure to account for discrimination against Hispanic offenders, who are typically placed in the category of "non-blacks." They reanalyzed the same data after dividing the sentenced population into black, white *and* Hispanic groups. Controlling for a variety of other factors, this analysis revealed a statistically significant difference in sentence lengths among the three groups, with whites receiving the least severe sentences, Hispanics receiving the most severe sentences and blacks falling in between. Farnworth et al. concluded that the practice of placing Hispanics in the non-black category tended to inflate the measure of the average sentence given to whites. In effect, the reason that black and non-black sentences appeared similar was that the longer sentences given to Hispanic offenders were masked by the established research practice of combining them with white offenders.

In a similar exploration of new methods in sentencing research, Patterson and Lynch (1991) examined how guidelines for granting and setting bail contributed to racial discrimination. Bail schedules, like sentencing guidelines, were implemented to reduce racial bias in criminal justice decision making. Bail schedules are set by statute, and tell the judge the amount of bail that defendants should post for specific crimes. The assumption is that these guidelines will limit the impact of racial biases in setting bail.

In most bail studies, bail outcomes are divided into two types: excessive bail (persons receiving bail in excess of the stated guideline amount), and appropriate bail (persons who receive bail within stated guideline amounts). Patterson and Lynch (1991) argued that this technique of classifying bail decisions omitted a third possibility that could mask racial bias – – defendants who were assigned a bail amount that was *below* that set by law. They tested this proposition in two ways. First, they employed the traditional approach that divided bail outcomes into above and within established guidelines. This analysis found no evidence that race affected how judges set bail. Next, they divided their data into three categories: above, within, and below guideline amounts. This analysis revealed an important race effect: whites were more likely than blacks to receive bails *below* the stated guideline. Thus, while blacks were being treated appropriately according to bail guidelines (i.e., they were no more likely than whites to be subjected to excessive bail amounts), they remained at a disadvantage relative to white defendants, who were more likely to receive bail amounts below guideline levels. Thus, once again, the use of alternative research methods revealed that racial biases had not disappeared from judicial processes, but had changed form as legal procedures were altered.

The claim that racial and ethnic biases continue in the justice system is supported by a number of other studies (see, generally, Walker et al., 1996; Hawkins, 1997; Lynch and Patterson, 1996, 1991; Mann, 1993; Randall, 1997; Keil and Vito, 1995, 1992; Vito et al., 1988; International Commission of Jurists, 1997; Kennedy, 1997; Radelet, 1989). More specifically, Albonetti et al. (1989), Chiricos et al. (1991) and Farnworth and Horan (1980), for instance, found evidence of racial bias against African Americans in setting bail, a form of discrimination that exerts a cumulative, negative effect since defendants who are disadvantaged at the bail stage are more likely to be convicted, and, when convicted, more likely to be sentenced to time behind bars. Racial differences placing blacks at a disadvantage have also been found in the ways that prosecutors charge offenders with crime (Spohn et al., 1987; LaFree, 1980, 1989; Radelet, 1989). And a number of studies have found that at the state level, African-American juveniles typically face discrimination in juvenile justice systems (Pope and Feyerherm, 1990; Patterson and Patterson, 1996; Bishop and Frazier, 1988).

Finally, and perhaps most importantly, the research evidence strongly supports the conclusion that African Americans are significantly more likely than whites to be charged with capital crimes and sentenced to death if convicted of these crimes (generally, see, Harries and Cheatwood, 1997; International Commission of Jurists, 1997; Jackson, 1996; Keil and Vito, 1995; Zimring, 1986; U.S. Congress, 1986). In addition to being more likely to be charged with capital crimes and given death sentences if convicted, African-American, Hispanic, and Native-American men are substantially more likely to be *wrongfully* convicted of these crimes due to inadequate representation by counsel and based on weak, fraudulent, or inconclusive evidence (Radelet et. al., 1994; Westervelt and Humphries, 2001; Cohen, 2003).

Support for the death penalty in the United States is not racially neutral. Survey research findings further indicate that "white support for capital punishment is associated with prejudice against blacks" (Barkan and Cohen, 1994). Studies using mock juries have also found that white jurors are more likely to convict minority defendants than white defendants charged with the same offenses (Kileen and Creech, 1982). Perhaps the strongest evidence of the way the justice system values whites over blacks, whether as offenders or victims, is the finding that of the 15,978 executions conducted in the U.S. between 1608 and 1986, only 30 cases (less then 2/10ths of 1%) involved the execution of a white for a crime against a black (Radelet, 1989).

In sum, courts are not race-blind legal sites for justice. Rather, courts replicate and reinforce the racial biases evident in the broader society. In this sense, courts both reflect and contribute to the maintenance of hierarchies of racial inequality that characterize other social and economic institutions in America.

## Class Bias and Courts

Earlier, we noted that there were two methods for addressing class bias in the courts. The first, used by many radical and orthodox criminologists, examines outcomes in one kind of court (e.g., criminal court, civil court, administrative law court) to determine whether social class affects justice. In this approach, class bias is evident when people from different class positions receive significantly different penalties or outcomes, even though they are accused of similar crimes and have comparable criminal histories. Studies of class biases based upon this procedure have generated a conflicting body of evidence on class bias in the courts. From our perspective, the critical issue is not the diverse findings these studies have produced but the fundamental methodological problems they present.

First, these studies have tended to utilize a variety of different measures, such as educational attainment, various measures of income and occupational prestige scores, to determine social class. Consequently, it is difficult to compare the findings of one study with another. Second, the most commonly used measures of social class in these studies treat class as a continuum: that is, individuals are imagined to be arranged on a ladder with some having more or less income, more or less education, and more or less prestigious occupations than others. This approach does not tap the core of the radical concept of social class, which examines location within the social relations of production (i.e., is someone an owner, a manager, a technocrat, a fully employed wage laborer, an underemployed wage laborer, or a member of the underclass with no access to the labor market?) and associated forms of power and control (Wright, 1979). This is the essence of the radical concept of class, and it cannot be captured by simple measures of income or education.

Third, orthodox approaches to social class and judicial processes tend to focus on one kind of court, usually criminal courts, resulting in a substantial underestimation of the impact of social class on legal outcomes. Most studies of class bias in courts employ data from criminal courts. As noted in earlier chapters, the criminal law is primarily applied to the poor and the working-classes, which means there is little variation in the class characteristics of criminal law defendants. When most offenders are from working-class backgrounds, it is pointless to try to assess whether courts treat working-class criminals worse than middle-class criminals who commit similar offenses. The lack of variation in the social class of criminal defendants is sufficient grounds to reject criminal court data as appropriate to the task of assessing class bias. Instead, we suggest that *the best way to examine class bias in the justice system is to compare how defendants are treated in different kinds of courts.*

## Class Bias Across Courts

Throughout this book, we have discussed the effect of class structure on a variety of social, economic and political institutions. At the level of political institutions such as courts, class conflict is important because institutions will tend to develop in ways that *manage* class conflict without altering the existing class structure. In the legal arena, one way in which class conflict is managed is by directing typically working-class harms to one legal system and typical ruling-class harms to a different system. The importance of this becomes evident when we compare the forms of law and social control applied to criminal offenses versus violations of regulatory and administrative law (i.e., corporate wrongdoing). For example, criminal courts employ legal criteria such as *mens rea* (state of mind or criminal intent) that focus on individual wrongdoers. Much of the process in criminal courts involves demonstrating the offender's intent to do harm. The criminal court's focus on the "criminal mind" implies "evil" motivations and the conscious choice to commit "socially disapproved," and, in this case, illegal, behaviors. Additionally, criminal courts typically assign punishments whose goals are to disrupt criminal behavior and to force criminals to alter their entire way of life through surveillance (e.g., probation), rehabilitation (e.g., treatment) or incapacitation (e.g., incarceration).

Court processes that control corporate behaviors are based on a very different set of principles. In place of the focus on individuals, organizations are often the defendants. This focus often shields individual in organizations who contributed to the harmful outcome from prosecution. This distinction in the kind of defendant also affects other elements of the processes. In place of *mens rea,* we find concepts such as negligence. Unlike criminal defendants, corporate defendants can enter pleas such as *nolo contendere,* a legal option that allows corporations to accept the penalty without accepting blame for any wrongdoing. The penalties given to corporate defendants (if they can be called penalties), are quite different from those applied to criminal defendants. For example, the U.S. Food and Drug Administration and National Highway Traffic Safety Administration typically employ recalls in response to corporate violations of law (see Burns, 1997, 1999; Burns and Lynch, 2002). If a case does move out of the regulatory agency and into a court, the typical penalty is a cease-and-desist order. This is equivalent to a court saying to a drug dealer who had made thousands of dollars selling cocaine, "O.K., you've been caught doing something bad, but you can continue as a citizen in good standing as long as you agree to stop selling cocaine." In effect, when corporations violate the law, the legal response is simply to allow them to "correct" their behavior. In such cases, there is no implication of guilt even when corporations are forced to comply with recall notifications or other orders against their will. Corporate penalties are, in other words, corrective rather than punitive.

When we compare defendants in criminal and administrative/regulatory courts, we see that they have very different characteristics. Corporate crime defendants may have millions or billions of dollars in assets, as was the case in such landmark cases of the late 1990s as the wrongful death and illness suits against cigarette and gun manufactures, and the prosecution of Microsoft Corporation for restraint of trade. Some corporations maintain legal staffs that have worked for decades to build defenses against anticipated claims of wrongdoing long before any claims were ever made. In the case of the tobacco industry, for instance, lawyers for several cigarette companies began to work on legal defenses against suits for deaths and injuries caused by cancer as early as the 1950s (Glantz et al., 1996). In contrast to well-financed corporate wrongdoers, typical defendants in criminal court tend to be from the working class or the underclass, to have little net worth and to depend on overworked public defenders with little knowledge of their case and little attachment to them as a client (see Barak, 1980, 1974).

In sum, courts apply *different kinds of law,* use *different legal procedures,* and assign *different penalties* to defendants from *different* social classes. This differential treatment by class is more easily seen when looking across kinds of courts than within courts, since each court has a specific legal orientation that reflects its place in controlling class conflict. As a result, different courts contain defendants from vastly different social classes. The empirical evidence gained from comparing different kinds of courts supports the radical contention that class bias is an inherent part of the American court system rather than an aberration caused by prejudiced judges or juries.

## GENDER AND THE COURTS

Gender, like race and class, plays an important role in court processes (Dusky, 1996). A recent analysis of the role of gender in the courtroom in 30 states found strong evidence of gender bias in the juridical process. Gender bias against women was most common in cases of domestic violence, sexual assault and divorce, while gender bias against men was most common in cases involving child custody matters and criminal sentencing (Hemmens et al., 1998). This pattern demonstrates the ways in which judicial processes reflect and reproduce unequal gender relations in the wider society (Daly, 1994b; Daly and Tonry, 1997).

The widespread acceptability of male dominance is reflected in the tendency of courts to be biased in favor of men when they are charged with crimes against women, such as sexual assault or domestic violence. In contrast, when courts render decisions biased toward women in cases of child custody or criminal sentencing, they reinforce beliefs that women should be the primary caretakers of children, and that they are a "weaker sex" that must be protected from harsh treatment such as prison. The leniency that courts tend to show toward women in these situations, however, is only afforded women who conform to traditional gender roles. Women who "do" their gender improperly by behaving aggressively, by being sexually involved with women instead of men, or by rejecting motherhood will not be afforded the leniency typically given to women. In this way, the court helps enforce dominant gender role stereotypes by punishing women who fail to conform to them (Wonders, 1996; Schur, 1984).

During the last two decades of the twentieth century, feminist theory exerted a substantial influence on radical thinking about the role of gender in the judicial process. The underlying assumption of much of this work is that

"...gender is a major characteristic of the state and a principal domain of its operation. Indeed, in terms of personnel, style and function, the state is a masculine dominated institution" (Messerschmidt, 1993:155). There are several themes that figure prominently in the feminist assessment of legal and judicial processes.

First, the state plays a crucial role in defining and controlling gender relations (Levit, 1998; MacKinnon, 1989). Many of the decisions made by state officials through mechanisms such as legislatures and courts exert a direct influence on gender roles by defining what constitutes "appropriate" (i.e., normal) gender behavior. Every time some state passed or enforced a law prohibiting sodomy, denied the extension of employee benefits to couples who are not married, upheld the exclusion of women (or men) from some activity, or established a constitutional amendment specifying that marriage can only take place between partners of the opposite sex, it announced and enforced a particular conception of appropriate roles and relationships for men and women.

Second, state personnel responsible for rendering decisions that shape gender relations are most often male (Messerschmidt, 1993). As male social actors, these agents derive much of their identity and their authority from an existing pattern of gender relationships. This means that often (although not always) men who exercise state authority will perform their functions in ways that reflect male understandings and that preserve taken-for-granted male privileges (Minow, 1990). For instance, in the area of policing and prison work, masculine values such as power, dominance, force and weapons are accepted as the primary tools of social control. Accepting these values is a fundamental part of being able to claim a police identity. When women enter male-dominated sectors of the justice system, they are expected to endorse masculine ways of dealing with the world if they want to be treated as "real" cops, probation officers or prison guards (Jurik, 1985; Martin and Jurik, 1996). Similarly, American criminal courts are based on masculine values such as dominance and punishment rather than on ideals of communication, correction and reintegration that are more often associated with female gender roles in American society (Minow, 1997). In a patriarchal society, that is, a society where the foundation of identity is domination and privilege, courts will inevitably reflect a male-centered approach to doing justice.

It would be misleading, however, to conclude that the state in general and courts in particular always rule on behalf of the interests of men. While courts have been a central institution in maintaining a heterosexual, male-centered culture in American, they have also been an arena in which many important struggles for gender equality have been waged and won. In some cases, court decisions in favor of gender equality have created the basis for further challenging established gender relations. For instance, contemporary gender relations would be different if courts had not ruled that historic patterns of making decisions about such things as employment, salary, promotions, training or access to education in ways that favored men over women constituted a violation of law. Nevertheless, when someone engages in deliberate, overt discrimination against women (or men), this activity is defined as a violation of administrative or regulatory law, not as a crime. But then, most of the violators are middle-class white men.

## Gender, the State and Courts

The state has a long history of involvement in gender conflicts. Often, the state's primary role is to determine or define "appropriate" or "acceptable" gender behavior. In some broad sense, the historic process of defining and redefining "appropriate" gender roles can be viewed as a dialectic process where two opposing forces, in this case gender groups, confront each other. The process of resolving any particular issue, whether it is done within the court system or by some administrative unit of the state, will change the nature of the conflict between these groups by increasing, reinforcing or limiting the power of one group over the other. Put another way, we might say that the nature of gender conflicts can be seen as the tension between the desire of some to reinforce existing gender relationships, and the desire of others to expand the social, political and economic space women can occupy in society, that is, increase the life chances available to women. Courts play a role in deciding which of these sides "wins." Often, courts become involved in these struggles when women use the legal system, either through civil suits or legislative pressure, to alter existing practices that limit their access to opportunities typically available to men. Examples include suits by women challenging unequal pay for equal work, hiring or promotion decisions that are biased against women, denial of access to so-called "men's work," such as construction or military combat assignments, or the provision of more scholarship money for male college athletics compared to women's college sports (see Rhodes, 1989).

Victories in such cases do not constitute absolute changes in gender roles. Courts provide mechanisms for managing rather than eliminating gender conflict, just as they manage class or racial conflict. In some sense, the legal process through which courts resolve cases involving gender relations reflects what Michel Foucault (1979) termed "rendering the body docile." Attempts to render the body docile come in a variety of forms, and may involve the sciences, mathematics or other procedures that rely upon classification and division to establish order and hierarchy (e.g., Foucault, 1973, 1972, 1970, 1965). The courts, for example, are involved in rendering bodies docile by subjecting them to rules and procedures, as well as penalties, that fit or force people to occupy a specific, culturally-defined time-and-space-position – a location in society.

With respect to gender, the courts have typically issued decisions that require women to comply with complex rules and policies that claim to define precisely when a woman has been the victim of "discrimination." Once gender discrimination is legally defined, and rules for redress are spelled out in great detail, people can engage in a wide range of behaviors that are hurtful to women as long as they do not cross the bright legal line between legal discrimination and bad behavior. For their part, women must conform to a formal set of behavioral expectations if they wish to be able to claim they were "real" victims of discrimination. In this way of "rendering the body docile," the courts manage gender discrimination by providing some legal redress to women (or men), while requiring that they accept the broad framework of existing social, economic and political relationships.

Every society is characterized by specific social, economic, political, cultural and gender systems. These structural features define how individuals and social groups relate to one another. These structures allocate and define the roles needed to facilitate the reproduction, that is, the continued existence of the social order. In many modern societies, women's roles (the structural, cultural and geographic space women occupy) are restricted such that the range of activities permitted men is wider than that permitted to women. Where men have a wider range of action (i.e., more freedom), the relations between men and women typically evolve into relations of dominance and submission, with men in the dominant positions at nearly all levels of society – a pattern found in the court process just as everywhere else in the society.

In recent decades, courts have played important roles in managing conflicts created by America's male-centered gender hierarchy. Increases in the political power of women during the last three decades have forced the courts to respond to a number of gender-related conflicts over how we define and treat crime (Mackinnon, 1989; Smart, 1987). Radical inquiries into the gendered treatment of sexual activities, such as prostitution and pornography (Chancer, 1998; Miller, 1998; Wonders and Michalowski, 1998), rape reform efforts (Caringella-MacDonald, 1988); domestic violence (Ferraro, 1989; Stanko, 1985; Websdale, 1997); and the construction of female crime and female delinquency (Chesney-Lind and Shelden, 1992), have all explored how criminal justice systems manage the conflicts and contradictions arising from male-centered hierarchies of power.

There is an abundant and growing literature focusing on gender and judicial equality (see, for examples, Daly, 1994b; Dusky, 1996; Heprele and Crites,

1987; Levit, 1998; Minow, 1990). Radical criminologists, however, have given relatively less attention to how the management of gender conflicts by *civil* courts (for example, in cases involving employment discrimination, equal educational opportunities and reproductive rights) creates the basic legal framework of gender that is utilized in criminal courts, and how this management of gender conflict at the civil level protects men in positions of authority from criminal charges when they engage in discrimination against women or other minorities. In order to highlight these issues we will explore one type of gender conflict handled by courts: job discrimination.

## Gender, Discrimination and Decision-making Criteria in Courts

In *Justice and Gender*, Deborah Rhodes (1989) addresses the decision-making criteria courts employ in deciding gender discrimination claims. Rhodes noted that the courts assess gender discrimination claims with reference to the *equal protection doctrine*, which defines equality "as similar treatment for those similarly situated." As Rhodes (p. 3) explains, the implication of this doctrine in gender discrimination cases is as follows: "Within this framework, sex-based discrimination remains justifiable *if the sexes are different…*" (emphasis added). In other words, when a case claiming sex discrimination is brought, the defendants can escape the penalty if they demonstrate that men and women are biologically different and that this difference has some bearing on the performance of the activity or enjoyment of the benefit at issues.

In many cases, the courts accept biological evidence of sex differences as supporting the idea that men and women are different and inherently unequal. Consequently, in many major court cases involving claims of equal treatment relevant to gender, the courts have ruled that women can be treated differently than men *because they are different from men* (Rhodes, 1989). That is, the court's position on gender is not a simple reflection of "scientific" evidence, but also reflects cultural images and stereotypes that define appropriate roles, behaviors and abilities of women (see also LaFree, 1989; Schur, 1984). Rhodes (1989) suggests that the courts have not been willing to recognize or address this influence.

For instance, in deciding gender equity cases, the courts invoked the equal protection doctrine to create a legal position for assessing gender discrimination claims known as the *gender difference test*. Rhodes demonstrated how this "test" is biased, and is disadvantageous to women relative to men. We illustrate this point using the following fictional example that reflects circumstances found in real-world sex discrimination cases.

## Sex Discrimination? A Fictional Exploratory Case Study

*Gender Difference Model*

This example involves an automobile parts assembly plant. The plant managers advertise a position for a line worker. The job requirements include a provision that the successful applicant must be able to lift 150-pound objects (engine parts) repeatedly during the course of a working day. In the past, all jobs of this nature have been occupied by men, even though women have applied for these well-paying positions. The women who have been denied these positions file a class-action suit against the company alleging sex discrimination. Their claim is that males have been given a preference in hiring even though gender is irrelevant to the job task. The women allege that the 40 women who applied for these positions over the past five years were denied equal treatment under law based on their gender.

During the trial, the employer presents medical evidence that few women possess the kind of strength needed to meet the stated minimum qualification for this position (i.e., the ability to lift 150 pounds repeatedly). Further, the employers also present evidence from interviews with female job applicants indicating that only 5 percent of the women who have applied for these line positions can meet this particular job qualification. After hearing the evidence, the court rules that there is *no gender discrimination* evident in this case. The court accepts the gender difference argument offered by the defendants, and notes that they offered scientific and applicant-specific data indicating that women are generally incapable of meeting the stated job requirements.

In short, when employing existing legal standards (gender differences), this case cannot be said to involve gender discrimination. Below we reanalyze this case employing a different legal criterion, one that Rhodes (1989) argued is more appropriate for determining the existence of gender bias. This view is called the *gender disadvantage approach*.

*Gender Disadvantage Approach*

The gender disadvantage approach would require courts to examine whether a stated job criterion is disadvantageous to women relative to men. The important point is whether a job *could be* performed *differently*, thereby allowing *both* men and women to perform the task and have an equal opportunity to compete for the job. Let us return to our example to examine how it would be addressed from a gender disadvantage perspective.

In the previous example, we noted that women were generally less capable than men of repeatedly lifting objects weighing 150 pounds. The result was that women were not being hired to fill these positions. The gender difference model accepts this difference in outcomes because it can be shown that women and men are, on average, different biologically. The gender disadvantage model, however, does not accept this difference as a legitimate basis for discrimination for several reasons to be discussed below. Further, the gender disadvantage model challenges two taken-for-granted elements of how courts often think about gender difference. One is isolated outcome analysis, and the other is the focus on biological gender differences. In the gender disadvantage model, the real question is: "Do job requirements and the organization of a job create a situation that puts one gender at a disadvantage relative to the other?" For instance, in our example, the employer could easily restructure the job in question by installing chain pulleys, relatively inexpensive pieces of equipment found in most mechanics shops. With the chain pulley, both men and women could, with one arm, lift and move a 150-pound object repeatedly. The installation of chain pulleys, in other words, changes the nature of the job and eliminates the strength requirement for this position, thereby equalizing the opportunity for women to obtain these positions. It also reveals the degree to which *the meaning* of possible biological differences between the sexes is socially constructed, that is, transformed into a gender (rather than a sex) characteristic.

The question, in short, isn't whether genders are different in any particular respect, but rather, whether gender-specific employment criteria create unequal access to particular categories of jobs. The gender disadvantage model seeks to equalize access, and does not view gender-linked ways of working as either inevitable or insurmountable. One might be tempted to think that the reluctance of courts to use the gender disadvantage model reflects economic rather than gender relations, because such a test would require employers to spend money so that differently abled people (in this case, men and women) could do the same job. But if we examine how courts and legislatures have dealt with the biological differences between men and women in comparison to how courts have dealt with the biological difference between the disabled and those without disabilities, we can see the depth of established gender bias in American culture. The Americans with Disabilities Act requires that employers make "reasonable accommodations" that allow handicapped people equal access to employment, including the installation of specific equipment that will compensate for the worker's disability. This is the same requirement that Rhodes (1989) argued should be used in workplace gender discrimination cases.

In both cases, accommodations ought to be made for workers who cannot perform a task *the way it is currently organized*. With respect to disabilities, the legal system, for instance, has determined that all public-access buildings must be made wheelchair-accessible, that students who cannot hear must be provided with interpreters, that otherwise qualified wheelchair-bound applicants for jobs involving driving should be provided with hand-controlled equipped vehicles, and so on. The difference here is that the category of disabled includes *men* as well as women. Consequently, it has seemed sensible to legislatures and courts to establish and enforce accommodation-oriented rules for a mixed-gender category, while denying similar accommodation-oriented strategies for women. We are not implying that women are disabled relative to men. What we are arguing is that in many cases the reason that some jobs may be more difficult for the average woman to perform as compared to the average man (and even this is questionable in many cases) is that the *way of doing the work* was created by men for men.

## In Sum

American courts occupy a contradictory position. They are obligated to enforce existing rules that reflect a long history of unequal social relations in American society. Whether we are talking about relations among classes, genders, races, ethnic groupings, religious groups or generations, throughout American history some sectors of society have been privileged over others. The judicial system born of such a society cannot avoid incorporating historical patterns of inequality when dealing with difference. Thus, we find continuing patterns of class, gender and racial discrimination in the American court system, both civil and criminal. At the same time, American courts, particularly appellate courts, must adjudicate conflicts arising from unequal relations among social groups. This means that American courts will, at times, also make rulings that favor disadvantaged rather than advantaged social groups, whether they are welfare recipients, women, African Americans, Hispanics, the disabled or the underaged. If American courts were incapable of ruling at times in favor of the disadvantaged, they would escalate rather than manage social conflict.

When courts do move to protect the interests of disadvantaged groups, they seldom stigmatize as criminals those who continue to harm disadvantaged groups. Thus, harmful behaviors, such as discrimination against women, people of color, homosexuals or other citizens deemed to be second-class, are kept within the realm of civil courts. The American judicial system has historically placed the burden of obtaining redress for civil wrongs such as discrimination on the victim. Thus, while courts have at times expanded the legal avenues open to disadvantaged groups to *sue for* equality in civil courts, the courts typically have not mandated that the state play a proactive role in searching out and prosecuting those who engage in prohibited forms of discrimination, as they do in the case of criminal behaviors. Since most prohibited forms of discrimination can only be committed by people in positions of power, this means that, once again, the harms most likely to be committed by affluent white men remain free of criminal stigma.

In the final analysis, any attempt to understand the judicial process in America should proceed from an appreciation of its contradictory nature, particularly its role in preserving the legitimacy of the economic and political system by providing a controlled forum in which social conflicts can be managed, while leaving the essential inequalities on which the social system is based intact.

# TWELVE.
## PUNISHMENT AND CORRECTIONS:
## A RADICAL INTERPRETATION

The orthodox view of formal, state-imposed punishment of criminals is informed by four key assumptions. First, it is assumed that formal punishment is the imposition of a "collective will" necessary to reinforce consensually created law (Fine, 1980:19). The second assumption is that formal punishment is administered in a just and impartial manner. Third is the view that societies punish wrongdoers out of necessity rather than desire (Newman, 1985). fourth and finally, it is assumed that without the "necessary evil" of formal punishment societies would collapse under the weight of unchecked disorder (Sellin, 1968:vi). According to this perspective, punishment preserves social order by repairing the imbalance created by criminal behavior, satisfying the desire of victims for vengeance, and deterring criminal behavior. Although orthodox analysts of punishment recognize that punishment is the willful imposition of harm on the offender, this state-imposed suffering is justified according to the utilitarian assumption that it produces the "greatest good for the greatest number."

In contrast, radical criminologists reject the assumption that formal punishment by the state is necessary to the existence of social order. A radical perspective further contends that, because orthodox theories "consider punishment to be something eternal and immutable," these theories "interfere with historical investigation" (Rusche and Kirchheimer, 1968:4). In support of this contention, radical theorists point to the many societies that have existed *without formal systems* of punishment imposed by leaders, substituting instead informal social controls implemented by ordinary people utilizing established custom or tradition (Diamond, 1971).

While orthodox theorists accept punishment as a given, radical criminologists seek to discover the conditions under which formal, state-based punishment became *a regular feature of social control*. In so doing, radicals find historical links among three sets of forces: the division of societies into social classes, the concomitant emergence of political inequality, and the creation of ideological justifications for control of less powerful classes by more powerful ones. When viewed in historical perspective, these forces emerge as the real foundation for formal systems of punishment, rather than the necessity and even-handedness of punishment hypothesized within orthodox criminology. In addition to examining the historical origins of state-sponsored punishment, radical criminologists are also concerned with how the administration of punishment is influenced by the kinds of class, racial and gender biases that, as previously discussed, shape the creation and enforcement of law.

Radical criminologists have repeatedly demonstrated how state-imposed punishments generate more negative than positive benefits for society (see for instance: Lynch et al., 1993; Clear, 1994; Welch, 1999, 1996a, 1996c, 1996d). For instance, contrary to the idea that punishment creates order, John Cochran et al. (1994) and William Bailey (1998) have shown that there is a tendency for criminal activity to *rise* following executions as the result of what they have termed a *brutalization effect.* In *The Rich Get Rich and the Poor Get Prison,* Jeffrey Reiman (2002) demonstrates how America's punishment apparatus is designed for failure rather than for achieving its claimed goals of creating social order through even-handed punishment of those who cause harm. James Austin and John Irwin (2002) have detailed America's "imprisonment binge" of the 1990s, fueled by the conservative proposition that punishment is the best way to reduce crime. Although this punishment-oriented approach has failed to achieve its claimed goals, it has managed to create the most punitive country in world in terms of the proportion of its population behind bars. On balance, radical analyses of imprisonment raise serious questions about the claimed benefits of punishment as a route to social order and social peace.

## A RADICAL PERSPECTIVE ON PUNISHMENT

As a rule of thumb, radical criminology attempts to understand how the institutions of law and justice intersect with the dominant framework of society. To understand punishment from this perspective, we begin by asking how punishment evolved historically, how it relates to the contemporary operation of capitalism and how it helps reproduce class, gender and racial structures and identities.

The radical perspective contends that the forms of punishment favored in a society will reflect key features of its social system. In other words, some types of punishment will be more appropriate to slave societies, others to feudalism, others to capitalism, and still others to the emerging empire of postmodern, capitalist globalization. We begin our inquiry into punishment with four propositions.

**Proposition 1:** *"The nature of the basic productive activities of a given society will shape the forms of punishment appropriate to that society"* (Michalowski, 1985:225). Or, as George Rusche and Otto Kirchheimer (1968:5) observed in *Punishment and Social Structure,* the first Marxist analysis of punishment: "Every system of production tends to discover punishments which correspond to its productive relationships. It is thus necessary to investigate the origin and fate of penal systems, the use or avoidance of specific punishments, and the intensity of penal practices as they are determined by social forces, above all by economic and then fiscal forces" (1968:5). Below, we provide a few examples to help clarify this claim.

Rusche and Kirchheimer's (1968) analysis of punishment began with Europe during the early Middle Ages (circa 1100 A.D.). At that time economic production involved agricultural share-cropping centered on feudal manors under the control of lords. Production was agriculturally based, the population was widely scattered throughout the countryside, and life revolved around the manor. Authority and power resided within the boundaries of the manor, which served as the primary legal jurisdiction. Lords relied on a system of fines and corporal punishments to redress grievances brought before them. Rusche and Kirchheimer argued that these punishments were dictated by the nature of the agrarian economy of the Middle Ages. Specifically: (1) in the absence of strong centralized governments, fines and corporal punishments were easily administered by local elites; (2) as a punishment, monetary or in-kind fines generated income for the lord and allowed him to reduce the financial burdens of holding court; (3) corporal punishments were particularly appropriate for the class of serfs because they had little surplus with which to pay fines; and (4) punishments such as death or imprisonment would cost manor lords long-term loss of the serf's labor. This system of punishment established a class-based standard of justice with fines for the rich, and corporal punishments for the serfs.

By the mid-1500s, the European economy was in the midst of a transition from feudalism to capitalism, first evident in a major expansion of mercantile trade for profit. The decline of agrarian feudalism and the rise of capitalism meant a decline in the need for widely dispersed populations of agricultural laborers. Likewise, the rise of capitalism in the cities increased the need for the labor force to be centralized in growing cities and towns, and increasingly disciplined in their daily life by the necessity of working for wages. These changes created conditions conducive to the emergence of imprisonment as the punishment of choice for two reasons. First, imprisonment provided a source of free labor by congregating easily exploitable labor in one place (Rusche and Kirchheimer, 1968). Second, the centralization of economic and political power was justified by an emerging *ideology* that human life could – and should – be organized into institutional arrangements that would allow relatively few people to observe, record, and control the behavior of many (Bentham, 1995). The primary institutions for this regimentation were the hospital, the prison and the factory (Foucault, 1975; Melossi, 1988). Thus, in England and the rest of Europe the idea and practice of imprisonment emerged from the intersection of changing economic and cultural forces.

During the earliest stages of capitalist development, a significant gap emerged between the kinds of work that were increasingly becoming available and the kinds of people available to work. As the feudal system decayed and crumbled, many serfs were forced or sought to leave a system of agricultural production that no longer needed their labor. Because their skills and life histories were tied to agrarian ways of life, however, many resisted moving into urban areas and instead became "vagrants" and "vagabonds" who lived off the land, or in some cases, through rural banditry (Hobsbawm, 1981, 1963). During the feudal era, begging had been encouraged as both a crude form of social welfare and as a means for the devout to earn God's favor by giving alms to the poor. With the development of mercantile capitalism, however, serfs who turned to begging and wandering were no longer seen a theological benefit to society. Instead, they were a detriment because they had not made themselves available to the new system of producing goods for market. By evading the mercantile system of production, beggars reduced the overall population of available wage workers, thereby increasing the cost of labor and eroding potential profits for those who organized mercantile production and distribution. As a result, new laws were created that transformed beggars and wanderers into criminals called "vagrants" who could be imprisoned.

Defining displaced people who were unwilling to enter into the new production system as criminals had a number of positive consequences for an emerging system of capitalism. First, it supported the idea that working the way capitalism required was normal and that surviving in other ways was deviant (Rusche and Kirchheimer, 1968; Melossi, 1976, 1982; Ignatieff, 1978). Second, the practice of controlling people through discipline and surveillance either in the factory, the workhouse, or the prison was further normalized (Foucault, 1979). Third, once incarcerated and concentrated, the wandering population could be concentrated and forced to labor. Finally, this forced labor was available to help expand the system of capitalist production (Rusche and Kirchheimer, 1968; Melossi, 1982; Hogg, 1982; Fine, 1980; Foucault, 1979).

The workhouse, the precursor to modern imprisonment, emerged from these conditions and was first established in 1555 in Bridewell, London, UK. Typically, workhouse confinement was imposed on debtors, beggars, vagrants, recalcitrant workers and serfs who had been displaced from the land during the decline of the feudal era. Although the workhouse was a British invention, it reached its full potential in Holland in the late 1500s (Rusche and Kirchheimer, 1968; Sellin, 1944). At that time, Holland was the most advanced capitalist nation in Europe, but it lacked the reserve labor force of countries such as England. As a result, the working class of Holland was able to demand very favorable working conditions (e.g., high wages, short work hours, and a four-day work week). In an effort to tilt the balance in capitalism's favor, the Dutch government used workhouses extensively in an effort to "resocialize" workers into accepting longer work hours and an extended workweek. The idea, according to Rusche and Kirchheimer (1968:42) was that: "By being forced to work within the institution, the prisoners would form industrious habits and would receive vocational training at the same time. When released, it was hoped, they would voluntarily swell the labor market." Thus the workhouse, the forerunner of the prison, emerged at a time when labor market conditions *favored the working class.* The primary consequence of the workhouse, regardless of the values and rhetoric used to justify its use, was the reorganization of the labor market in ways that shifted the advantage away from sellers of labor to those who bought it (Rusche and Kirchheimer, 1968).

Our second proposition is a logical extension of the first.

**Proposition 2:** *As the type of production carried out in society changes, so, too, will the form of punishment* (Rusche and Kirchheimer, 1968). Behind this proposition stand several assumptions related to the Marxist strategies discussed in chapter1. First, since the form of punishment is shaped by a society's economic activity, each change in the method of production (i.e., a change from feudalism to capitalism) will produce changes in punitive practices. However, changes in the form of economic production and punishment do not occur simultaneously. Rather, punishments evolve slowly over time, reflecting the interplay between historically established beliefs about punishment and the requirements of the emerging system of production. In some instances punishments outlive the economic circumstances that caused them, and eventually evolve into different punishment strategies altogether. An example of one such punishment is galley slavery.

As the name implies, galley slavery was related to production based on an economic system that used slave labor. Many nations that colonized foreign territories, such as France and England, made extensive use of slaves to row galley ships. When slavery was outlawed the state found it difficult to recruit "freemen" to work galley ships. To address this problem, the state began sentencing criminals to galley slavery rather than death (Rusche and Kirchheimer, 1968). In this way, the state provided for its own labor requirements when administering punishment. The practice of substituting galley slavery for death sentences continued until technological innovations in sailing made the labor of oarsmen unnecessary (Rusche and Kirchheimer, 1968).

The idea of sending criminals to sea did not disappear with advances in sailing. Instead, it evolved into the practice of *transportation,* shipping criminals to colonial territories as forced labor. The transportation of criminals occurred most frequently when the supply of workers in the home country was high (Rusche and Kirchheimer, 1968). Countries could dispose of unemployed, marginalized populations that their economies could not support, and simultaneously create the labor force required to *profitably* exploit the riches of the "new worlds" by transporting criminals to colonies where they could be forced to work at relatively little cost to their colonial masters (Hughes, 1987; Newman, 1985, 1988).

The transportation of criminals from England is a good example of how the practice of punishment can be shaped by competing capitalist interests, in this case, the conflict between domestic producers versus those exploiting new worlds such as Australia and America (Newman, 1988; Hughes, 1987). As England's labor supply shrank, capitalists in England began to oppose transportation since "it reduced the number of working hands and robbed the country of their contribution to the wealth of the nation" (Rusche and Kirchheimer, 1968:59). That is, England's new industrialists preferred a large labor pool that would keep wages low by forcing workers to compete for jobs rather than forcing employers to compete for workers. Transportation worked against this goal by reducing the total number of workers available to compete for jobs. In opposition to England's native industrialists, colonial capitalists desired the relatively cheap, forced labor of deported criminals and sought more rather than less transportation. Parliament eventually struck a compromise between the competing employment needs of England's domestic industries and its colonial capitalists by agreeing to deport only those criminals who were condemned to death. This was not a small number because at the time English law prescribed death for over 200 offenses. This compromise would lessen the effect of transportation at home while still providing a number of laborers for the colonies (Christianson, 1981).

These examples show how systems of punishment and production interact with one another. The next proposition expands this link to the specific practice of *imprisonment.*

**Proposition 3:** *Imprisonment is "not only caught up in the economic structure of early capitalism, but is unable to be understood apart from it"* (Miller 1980:100). Several historical analyses of imprisonment (Hogg, 1982; Fine 1980; Miller, 1980; Sellin 1944, 1976; Rusche and Kirchheimer 1968) support the conclusion that "imprisonment... is a relatively recent historical phenomenon. Its rise can generally be reckoned to have accompanied the emergence of modern capitalism and its economic, political and ideological forms" (Hogg 1982:4). This change in the form of punishment resulted less from humanitarian concerns over the cruel nature of corporal punishment as traditional accounts suggest (for discussion, see Beirne, 1993), than from "certain economic developments which revealed the potential value of mass human material…" (Rusche and Kirchheimer 1968:24).

Beginning with the workhouse – the first widely used form of incarceration – imprisonment fostered the economic and ideological goals of capitalist production. Economically, imprisonment made sense for early capitalist societies. The tight labor markets of early capitalist systems mitigated against imposing death or corporal punishment on criminals when their labor could be used to help produce private profit (Rusche, 1982). Imprisonment was one attempt to harness the labor power of unproductive and even destructive people to the needs of a new economic system.

As capitalism evolved, however, so did the role of prisons. As labor markets became glutted through the combined effects of rapid population growth and technological changes that required less labor for any particular task, the prison's role in providing labor became obsolete. Under these conditions the prison no longer functioned to socialize people to accept capitalism or to supply manufacturers with workers. With this in mind, Rusche (1982:14) argued that prisons became a "leftover from a previous and quite different [historical] epoch…." Given the saturated labor market of the post-1929 depression period, for example, the focus of imprisonment shifted from providing laborers for the production system, to disciplining the lower social classes and surplus populations (Rusche and Kirchheimer, 1968; Rusche, 1982; Barak, 1982), to controlling potential criminals by warehousing them in prisons (Lynch 1988a, 1988b). Imprisonment was transformed from a strategy to help build capitalism into a means of managing one of the most serious contradictions of developed capitalism – its tendency to generate large numbers of people without work (Lynch 1988a, 1988b).

Within the radical perspective there is some debate over the cause of imprisonment. Some reject the argument that prisons emerged in direct relationship to the birth of capitalism. Others offer alternative models that place more emphasis on the importance of economic *context* and/or ideological forces in the creation of imprisonment (Foucault, 1979; Greenberg, 1977a; Box and Hale, 1982; Melossi, 1990, 1989, 1985). Ignatieff (1978), for instance, "places the penitentiary squarely in the midst of the Industrial Revolution in England" (Miller, 1980:100). His analysis suggests that the effects of the industrial revolution rather than capitalism *per se* gave rise to an increased use of imprisonment.

Foucault (1979) makes a similar argument. He contends that as industrialization advanced, corporal punishment disappeared because the functions of the penal ceremony associated with public corporal punishments were gradually beginning to be misunderstood by the general public. He writes: "It was as if the punishment was thought to equal, if not exceed, in savagery the crime itself, to accustom the spectators to a ferocity from which one wished to divert them, to show them the frequency of crime, to make the executioner resemble a criminal, judges murderers,...to make the tortured criminal an object of pity or admiration" (Foucault, 1979:9).

In effect, the ability of corporal punishment to create a climate conducive to law-abiding behavior declined as the rationalism of industrialization made it increasingly difficult for people to see the moral difference between the injuries caused by crime and the injuries caused by the state's use of the whip, the rack, or the noose. In Foucault's (1979) model, the importance of the prison was that it helped align the ideology of production and punishment, or that it helped restore legitimacy to the idea of punishment. In the prison, the focus of punishment was relocated from the bodies of criminals to their minds and habits. This allows the prison to regiment the inmate in ways that resembled and reinforced the work ethics and organizational form of the emerging factory.

Some radical theorists focus on the rise of capitalism and others focus on the Industrial Revolution to explain the invention of imprisonment. These positions, however, are compatible. The development of the prison as the primary form of punishment was a long process that involved both economic and ideological changes. While this process found its complete expression during the Industrial Revolution, industrialization was itself an outgrowth of the earlier shift from feudalism to mercantile capitalism. From the perspective of punishment, the evolution of capitalism has been a 500-year process that began with workhouses that set landless serfs to producing for capitalist markets, and continues with the modern prison, whose primary role is to warehouse today's version of the displaced worker – the underclass man of color.

**Proposition 4:** *Prisons in modern capitalist society reinforce ideological notions about criminals that justify the repression of the lower classes, and thereby reaffirm the class structure of capitalism* (Reiman, 1998; Fine, 1980).

In an advanced capitalist society such as the U.S., punishment serves many purposes, including reinforcing beliefs about appropriate behavior. By imprisoning certain types of people (especially the poor, African Americans, Latinos and the young), prisons create the belief that there is a "criminal element" that should be feared, not because of its actual behavior but merely because of the *potential* for criminality it represents (Reiman, [1979]1998; Quinney, 1980). This notion is similar to the eighteenth and nineteenth century concept of the "dangerous classes," and refers to roughly the same population – the least-well-off segments of the working class. Over time, then, imprisonment shifted from pursuing economic goals that reproduce capitalism economically by providing labor to capitalists or the state, to ideological goals that reproduce capitalism psychologically by enforcing the belief that the crimes of the poor are the greatest threat to our well-being.

While Rusche and Kirchheimer (1968) provided a powerful analysis of the economic foundations of punishment, many radical criminologists have criticized their work as overemphasizing the relationship between production and punishment and for being overly structural and economistic (see Miller, 1980; Hogg, 1982; Foucault, 1979; Ignatieff, 1978; Melossi, 1976; Fine, 1980; Jankovic, 1982a). As an alternative, various theorists have explored the relationship between ideology and imprisonment in capitalist societies.

The central theme of these analyses has been that imprisonment serves as a method for disciplining the workforce, directly thorough physical control of its poorest segments and indirectly by providing a model of human behavior based on the ideology of discipline and surveillance (Rusche, [1933]1982; Melossi, 1976, 1982; Melossi and Pavarini, 1980; Foucault, 1979; Ignatieff, 1978; Schwendinger and Schwendinger, 1981). These authors argue that the belief that human behavior is best organized according to fixed regimens overseen by others (i.e., discipline) emerged as the dominant ideology of capitalism because it best produced the qualities needed in an industrial working class. This approach incorporates Rusche and Kirchheimer's (1968) and Sellin's (1944) arguments that the emergence of the workhouse was linked in time to the emergence of capitalism. However, the approach goes beyond an economic explanation, and seeks to recover the political and ideological components of Rusche and Kirchheimer's work that had been previously overlooked (Michalowski and Carlson, 1999).

Some scholars – such as Greenberg (1977), Box and Hale (1982); Box, (1987); Hale, (1989) and Melossi (1985a, 1985b, 1989a) – argue against strict economic interpretations, and instead favor theories that allow for culture and human agency: theories that can integrate macro and micro explanations of punishment. In this view, criminal justice personnel (agents) are seen as participants in creating "moral panics" over crime. As news of worsening economic troubles spread, ordinary citizens and criminal justice agents are more likely to interpret their surroundings as dangerous insofar as economic decline typically creates a sense that the world is starting to "fall apart." In this climate, marginalized groups are easily transformed into concrete symbols of this vague sense of disorder as they become more evident during hard times. When people who are poor, unemployed or otherwise disconnected from the dominant order come into contact with the criminal justice system, they are likely to be treated more severely during times of economic troubles than when people feel secure about their world (e.g., Barlow et al., 1995a, 1995b).

The model for understanding imprisonment that Foucault (1979) put forward in *Discipline and Punish* focuses even more expressly on the ideological functions of imprisonment. Foucault suggested that there are two distinct periods in the Western history of punishment. The first period involved public spectacles of harsh corporal punishment directed at the body. These punishments were used extensively prior to the 1800s (Foucault, 1979). However, for reasons mentioned earlier, the use of corporal punishments was greatly curtailed during the 1800s in favor of the second phase of punishment: imprisonment.

While corporal punishment focused on the body of the offender, imprisonment targeted the offender's mind or "soul" (Foucault, 1979:29). This "grip" on the offender's mind marked the second phase in the European history of punishment: It signaled the decline of the spectacle of public punishment, the "slackening of the hold on the body," and the use of new technologies of power aimed at disciplining the "soul" of the offender (Foucault, 1979:10, 23-24).

For Foucault (1979), imprisonment served several ideological purposes. Unlike corporal punishment, in which the offender's suffering was deliberately revealed, imprisonment obscured the offenders suffering behind a guise of "correctional" strategies that were presumably undertaken for the prisoner's long-term benefit. Imprisonment replaced the obvious physical terror of public spectacles of corporate punishment with the hidden mental and emotional terror of being locked up, degraded and rendered a social non-person behind penitentiary walls. This shift made punishment appear to be both more humane and unemotional. In Foucault's (1979:11) words: "...the punishment-body relation is not the same [under imprisonment] as it was in the torture during public executions. The body now serves as an instrument or intermediary: if one intervenes upon it to imprison it, or make it work, it is in order to deprive the individual of a liberty that is regarded both as right and as property." That is, imprisonment restrains the physical body of offenders only as a means to reach their mind and limit their freedom. According to the dominant ideology, the suffering that occurs is only an indirect, and certainly justified, cost of the process, not its purpose.

Foucault's (1979) analysis is not limited to the ideological realm, however. His analysis rests on a complex understanding of the interaction between ideology and the political-economy. Foucault utilizes the insights of Rusche and Kirchheimer's (1968), and draws parallels between the economy of production and the ideology of punishment. He suggests that whether or not the body is the direct target of punishment, regardless of its form, punishment is a "political economy of the body"(Foucault, 1979:25-26). Central to Foucault's work is the idea that imprisonment is an instrument for making a complex series of power relationships seem normal (Foucault, 1979). He suggests that discipline and routinization pervade the social fabric of modern society. Industrial production requires work that is detailed and exacting as well as continuous. Accomplishing this task requires workers to be disciplined and routinized to the point where they accept as *normal* the idea that others will monitor every detail of their movements, controlling the space where they work, when they will work and the speed at which they will work. With this form of industrial production serving as the basic framework for society, Foucault (1979:228) asks, "…is it surprising that prisons resemble factories, schools, barracks, hospitals, which all resemble prison?"

Another example of an ideological analysis of imprisonment is provided by Reiman (1998), who claims – contrary to most radical perspectives – that prisons serve the interests of the powerful by *failing* at their mission of crime control. Reiman examines the pervasive racial and economic biases that characterize the American criminal justice system and that shape public opinion concerning who constitutes the criminal element. As it is used today, Reiman argues, imprisonment draws our attention to the acts of the poor and minorities, and in the process diverts our attention from the more harmful acts of the powerful. This occurs to the extent that the criminal justice system *avoids* corporate crime, and fails to label or perceive the violent nature of many acts committed by corporations.

## Social Class and Punishment

The criminal justice system in the U.S. weighs most heavily on the poorest segments of the society. Any doubt about this proposition evaporates in the face of U.S. jail and prison statistics. As we previously discussed, the majority of arrests are for relatively minor crimes, and those convicted of these crimes are most often sentenced to local jails or await trail while incarcerated in local jails. An examination of jail populations demonstrates that jails exist to control the public disorder crimes of the poor (Irwin, 1985; Goldfarb, 1969). The U.S. Department of Justice has estimated that 36 percent of male inmates in local jails were unemployed at the time of their arrest, and that among the 64 percent who were employed, another 11 percent held only part-time jobs (Pogrebin, Dodge and Katsampes, 2001). In other words, barely half of all those in U.S. jails were full-time workers. Moreover, economic disadvantage is the *pri-*

*mary* factor determining who spends time in a local jail. According to Pogrebin et al. (2001), 87 to 94 percent of all those in jail are there because they cannot obtain pretrial release by posting bond, or meet no-bail release standards (i.e., that they own property or have stable jobs). Clearly, those incarcerated in America's jails come from the least well-off segments of our society.

The story is similar for those incarcerated in state prisons. In comparison to the general public, prison inmates are more likely to have never worked, or to have held a wide assortment of short-term, unstable jobs. Occupational statistics for prison inmates in the 1980s revealed that: "before their arrest, 40 percent of all prisoners were working outside of what they considered to be their customary occupations. For many this suggests an inability to find work in their chosen field, and it also suggests some degree of underemployment" (U.S. Department of Justice, 1983:38). The portion of blue-collar workers in prison (69%) far outweighs the percent of blue-collar workers in the general population (47%). Not surprisingly, the 15 percent of the prison population who are white-collar workers substantially underrepresents the 40 percent of the general population in that category (U.S. Department of Justice, 1983).

More recent data suggest that the kind of people who are imprisoned has changed very little. According to the most recent survey of state prison inmates, 65 percent had not completed high school, and nearly one in five had not completed the eighth grade. Prior to their arrest, 45 percent of inmates were either unemployed (33%) or employed only part-time (12%). The majority of inmates (51%) had incomes under $9,999 in the year prior to their arrest. With these figures in mind, it becomes clear why Goldfarb (1969) called our prisons the "nation's poorhouses." In a similar vein, Jeffrey Reiman (1998:135) observes: "Our prisoners are not a cross-section of America. They are considerably poorer and considerably less likely to be employed than the rest of Americans."

In the next section, we examine the connection between race and imprisonment. While we shall have much more to say about the economic forces that structure imprisonment, it is important that we not overlook race-related explanations of imprisonment and punishment.

## Race and Punishment

It is not only the poor who are overrepresented in America's prisons. African-American and Latino men constitute portions of the prison population substantially larger than their shares of the general population. According to the Department of Justice (2004), about 63 percent of prison and jail inmates are African Americans or Hispanics. African Americans constitute only 12 percent of the general population, yet they make up *44 percent* of prison and jail inmates, while Latinos, at 7 percent of the general population, comprise 19 percent of the prison and jail population (U.S. Department of Justice, 2004). Population-specific incarceration rates (per 100,000 in the free population) for each of these groups were as follows as of 2003: 4,834 Black inmates per 100,000 Blacks; 1,778 Hispanic inmates per 100,000 Hispanics; and 681 white inmates per 100,000 whites. In other words, the Black incarceration rate was more than 7 times higher than the white incarceration rates, while the Hispanic incarceration rate was more than 2.5 times the white rate. As further evidence of this bias, it has been widely reported, for example, that there are more African-American men in U.S. prisons and jails than in American colleges and universities. How can the segregation of African Americans in prisons and jails be explained?

In the orthodox view, the explanation is self-evident: there are more African Americans in prisons and jails because they commit more crimes than whites. We have already discussed and rejected this claim at several points earlier in this book. Briefly, this view does not take into account: (1) biases in law and law enforcement that focus on behaviors that African Americans and Hispanics commit in public places and that whites commit in private such as drinking, drug use, prostitution etc.; (2) lack of enforcement of criminal laws against corporate criminals who are primarily white; and (3) processing biases that put minorities at a disadvantage and that cause them to be arrested, charged, convicted and sentenced to prison more often than whites.

In addition to these issues, the orthodox explanation for racially disparities in prison populations rely on misguided comparisons of white and minority rates of offending per 100,000 derived from police data. The reason this comparison is undertaken is to test whether minorities are overrepresented in prison in comparison to their rate of offending. The assumption is that if the ratio of minority-to-white prison population is similar to the ratio of minority-to-white offending, then minorities are not overrepresented in prison. Unfortunately, this comparison is misleading because policing data incorporate various reporting and institutional police behavior biases (e.g., more extensive patrols in minority communities) that lead to the overrepresentation of minorities as criminals. But this comparison is also misleading because of the way in which standardized population bases are used in the analysis.

When standardized population rates are used to make comparisons across racial groups, the researcher is creating a comparison that assumes that the general population is composed of an equal number of people from each race. For example, if we were to compare the rate of offending per 100,000 African Americans to the rate of offending per 100,000 whites, we would have made the size of the white and African-American population exact equivalents: 100,000 whites and 100,000 African-Americans. When we make this comparison, we find that there are more than six times as many African-American offenders per 100,000 population as white offenders per 100,000. When we compare this finding to the racial population percentages for U.S. prisons cited earlier, the fact that there are more African Americans in prison seems to make sense. What this comparison fails to take into account, however, is that in the real world there are six times as many white people in the U.S. population relative to the African-American population. In other words, using race-based police arrest and imprisonment data, we would conclude that Blacks were not overrepresented in prisons relative to whites *if the Black and white population in the U.S. were the same size*. But, these populations are not the same size in the U.S.

Now, let us examine race representation in a different way. Here, assume that crime was evenly distributed across race groups, and that the justice system was race-blind. If these assumptions were true, then the white prison population should be *six times* larger than the Black prison population. But, this assumption is faulty because, as victimization and self-report studies indicate, the rate of lawbreaking may be two to three times greater among Blacks compared to an equivalent white population. Even if this were true, the white incarceration rate should still exceed the black rate of incarceration – if incarceration were proportionate to the offending and population level for each group. In reality, however, the current level of incarceration for Blacks is seven times greater than for whites, or more than four times higher than what we would expect using race-based offending differences based on self-report and victimization surveys.

To be sure, differences in offending across race groups account for *some but not all* of the racial disparity in imprisonment rates. Before we can offer a radical explanation of these difference, some additional facts concerning imprisonment trends in the U.S. over the past decade are needed.

## The Recent Expansion of the Prison System

Between 1985 and 1995, the U.S. prison population more than doubled, when it expanded by 120 percent (U.S. Bureau of Justice Statistics, 1996). While the rate of increase has slowed in recent years, there are now more than 2 million people in U.S. prisons and jails, making the U.S. system of incarceration the largest in the world. If incarceration deterred crime, the U.S. would be expected to have one of the lowest rates of criminal offending in the world, but it does not.

Nils Christie (1994:14) argues that the rate of imprisonment in the U.S. is so high that "it cannot be compared to [the level] found in any industrialized country in the West." The reason for Christie's statement becomes obvious if we compare the U.S. rate of imprisonment, 714 per 100,000, to the rates for other nations: England and Wales, 140; Canada, 116; France, 72; Spain, 139; Japan, 58 (Walmsley, 2003). Also consider that the rate of crime in the United States is only 12 percent lower than in England, while the incarceration rate is five times higher. Similarly, the rate of crime in the U.S. is 33 percent higher than in France, where the imprisonment rate is nearly 10 times lower. And in the most extreme case, the rate of crime in the U.S. is 342 percent higher than in Japan, while Japan's rate of incarceration is a mere one-twelfth of the rate in the United States. These data make it clear that high levels of punishment do not lead to low crime rates, and low levels of imprisonment do not lead to high crime rates.

Today, there are more inmates in nearly every offense category in prison than there were in 1985. Over this period of prison growth, the characteristics of the prison population changed in important ways. First, there was a large increase in the percentage of inmates incarcerated for drug offenses. Second, there was a significant increase in the percentage of inmates serving time for public order offenses. Although the total *numbers* of inmates incarcerated for violent and property crimes increased, the relative size of these groups actually decreased in proportion to other categories of offenders.

The dramatic increase in U.S. prison populations is race-linked. For whites, the incarceration rate increased from 246 per 100,000 population in 1985 to 465 per 100,000 by 2003 — about an 87 percent increase. For Blacks, the rate changed from 1,599 per 100,000 to 3,405 per 100,000, an increase of 116 percent. These facts require some explanation.

The expansion of the U.S. prison system has typically been explained as an attempt to control crime. Simply put, the idea is that if we increase the costs of committing crime (i.e., increase the odds of incarceration), then crime rates will decline. The rate of incarceration has risen steadily since 1972. While official crime rates have gone down somewhat, very little of this decline can be attributable to patterns of punishment (Austin and Irwin, 2002; Lynch, 1999). The decline in crime rates heralded by conservatives as evidence of the deterrent power of imprisonment reflects the impact of broad social forces, not the efficacy of punishment. First, between 1973 and 1990, the U.S. crime rate rose consistently, even while the imprisonment rate increased dramatically. Second, the prime years of America's crime drop coincided with a decline in the proportion of the U.S. population in its most crime-prone years. Third, between 1984 and 1994 many urban areas in the United States experienced a significant growth in drug-related violence with the introduction of a new and disorganized market for cocaine and crack. During that same time period, arrests of juveniles for murder and assault nearly doubled, reflecting their role in the new drug markets. In the mid-1990s, ghetto drug markets became increasingly organized and routinized, with a corresponding decline in juvenile arrests for drug-related violence. If we subtract declines in rates of violence associated with the rise and routinization of illegal markets for drugs, the decline has only returned the United States to the levels of violence experienced before the wave of drug-market violence in the 1980s (Blumstein et al., 2000; Butts, 2000). In short, building more prisons and locking up more people has had little to do with changes in crime rates (see Welch, 1999).

Rather than being driven by rising crime rates, Nils Christie (1994) contends that the expansion of prisons has been driven by economic forces. Specifically, he suggests that crime control has become an industry that supports a growing private sector, which supplies crime control commodities and services. Michael Welch (1999) emphasizes this point by examining the growth in profit and earnings by private correctional corporations. With high profits at stake, for-profit prison corporations have been successful in gaining support from legislators for harsh prison sentences.

Economic models do not, however, explain why the expansion of prisons had a greater impact on minorities compared to whites. Building a reasonable explanation of racial differences in incarceration requires employing a combination of racially, culturally and historically-situated perspectives.

## Our Black Prisons

As noted above, the racial imbalance in U.S. prisons has long been debated. Some argue that the imbalance is due to differential rates of criminal offending by race. Others suggest that Blacks commit more serious crimes than whites, thus increasing their probability of incarceration. Still other posit that racial bias is the key to explaining racial differences in incarceration.

Differential offending and seriousness explanations are, as we argued in our discussion of policing and the courts, misleading. First, we have no accurate method for gauging all known crimes; nor do we have a way of knowing the real level of criminal offending — either over all or by race. Second, there is solid evidence of enforcement biases against minorities. Third, images and depictions of crime also contain cultural biases that generate expectations of heightened criminality among minorities that may affect official reactions to behaviors demonstrated by people of different racial and ethnic groups. Finally, the fact that we do not count or process corporate or white-collar offenders as criminals has a tremendous impact on the lower probability that white offenders are found in prisons.

Rising rates of incarceration emerged at the same point in history (1970s-1990s) as widespread economic restructuring of the U.S. economy (see chapters 6 and 7). Economic restructuring displaced black and white workers from the manufacturing sector, encouraged a shift in white employment from manufacturing to the service sector, displaced Blacks from the service sector, disrupted localized Black economies and further marginalized Black Americans. In short, as economic conditions for Blacks deteriorated, criminal justice controls that disproportionately affected Blacks increased.

During the same period, greater emphasis was placed on controlling drug offenses and public order crimes associated with marginalized groups in general, and Blacks in particular. These offenses have a cultural dimension that promotes race-linked stereotypes that have a negative impact on Blacks and Hispanics (Tonry, 1995). These factors have combined to produce what Scott Christianson (1981) calls "our Black prisons." An alternative explanation for this trend can be fashioned from Douglas Massey and Nancy Denton's (1993) book, *American Apartheid: Segregation and the Making of the American Underclass.*

## American Apartheid

Massey and Denton (1993:1) argue that "most Americans vaguely realize that urban America is still a residentially segregated society, but few appreciate the depth of Black segregation or the degree to which it is maintained by ongoing institutional arrangements …" (1993:1). That Black segregation has been institutionalized can be seen in a number of factors, primarily in the long history of physical segregation experienced by Black communities across the U.S. This segregation ensures that unstable economic and community characteristics will remain part of the structure of Black communities and that Black communities will become increasingly segregated "geographically, socially and economically" (Massey and Denton, 1993:2). The effect of segregation, which is structural, "lies beyond the ability of any individual to change; it constrains Black life chances irrespective of personal traits, individual motivations, or private achievements. For the past twenty years, this fundamental fact has been swept under the rug by policymakers, scholars, and theorists of the urban underclass" (Massey and Denton, 1993:3). While much more can be gleaned from their work, this summary is sufficient for discussion.

Massey and Denton's (1993) view provides two alternatives for explaining the disparity between black and white rates of incarceration. The first, which resembles traditional explanations and which we think is inconsistent with

Massey and Denton's overall view, is as follows. Racial segregation has established conditions conducive to crime in minority communities, from deleterious neighborhood conditions, community organization and ineffective forms of informal social control, to economic deterioration and joblessness. Thus, we should not be surprised to find higher rates of crime in Black communities, and, as a result, higher rates of incarceration among Blacks. This view, however, overlooks the broader importance and effects of segregation, and legitimizes higher rates of incarceration with reference to the idea that Blacks are more likely than whites to commit the kinds of offenses that land people in prison.

The second alternative is that imprisonment has become part of the institutionalized network for segregating Blacks in American society. In other words, imprisonment is part of the social-structural apparatus that has helped achieve and that maintains Black segregation. Imprisonment operates to segregate Blacks regardless of the volume of criminal activity differences between white and black communities. Further, as we argued earlier, these differences in criminal offending would disappear *if* we counted corporate and white-collar crimes as crime, and *if* we treated these offenses as serious events. In short, imprisonment – like housing and loan redlining, poor schooling, uneven urban economic development plans, etc. (see Massey and Denton, 1993, for discussion) – is part of the process that creates black segregation, and is not simply a result of black segregation.

## Unemployment and Imprisonment

The fact that prison and jail inmates are disproportionately poor and non-white has led many radical criminologists to theorize that there is a relationship between imprisonment and another social problem that disproportionately affects poor people of color: unemployment. In particular, radical criminologists have proposed that poor labor market conditions will lead to increases in the uses of punishment that are more than a reflection of increased crime rates. Analyses based on this proposition are important to the radical analysis of punishment for several reasons.

First, the radicals subject political-economic theories about punishment to quantitative analysis, thereby rebutting the criticism that it is impossible to construct empirical evaluations of Marxist approaches to criminology. Second, by employing empirical methods, these analyses meet orthodox requirements of the "burden of proof" for theoretical statements. While the validity of radical theories in criminology is not dependent on complying with orthodox views about how we can know what is true about society, the fact that radical theories of punishment *can* meet these methodological tests suggests they are able to move beyond orthodox theories by passing through them, rather than around them.

There is nothing inherently radical about the proposition that unemployment is related to imprisonment, since it is widely accepted that incarcerated populations are drawn mainly from the lowest classes in society. There are several factors, however, that differentiate the radical approaches to the link between unemployment and imprisonment from more orthodox perspectives.

First, radical theory links unemployment to the normal operations of a capitalist economy. In doing so it connects methods of capitalist production, particularly its reliance on labor-displacing technological advancements, to patterns of punishment. As capitalism develops, technological advancements render certain forms of labor obsolete, displacing individuals from the workforce. If the new technologies do not create equally good jobs as fast as they destroy old ones, this process swells the size of the surplus population, and the number of people with no solid footing in the society increases. Under these circumstances, labor displacement will lead not only to increases in crime but also to increases in rates of imprisonment that *are not caused by* increases in crime rates.

Second, unemployment is not only a consequence of capitalist production, it is a necessary *condition* of capitalist production. The existence of an unemployed or surplus population helps ensure that the supply of workers will exceed the demand for labor. This excess supply of workers limits wages, creates competition for scarce jobs, and keeps worker productivity high, all of which help secure a higher rate of profit (surplus value). Whenever the supply of workers for various job categories begins to drop relative to the demand for these workers, business leaders pressure government to institute policies that increase the supply of workers. In the case of high-tech jobs, these shortages of trained workers sometimes lead corporations to lobby for more and better education in the areas of science, mathematics or computers. If the labor shortfall is in the area of low-end service work there will be demands, as occurred in the 1990s, to force people off welfare and into the labor market, even if they are mothers with young children.

By definition, unemployed persons have a marginal relation to the means of production (Spitzer, 1975). Some people in this situation resort to crime as either a rational or an emotional response to conditions of their life (Bourgeois, 1996; Gordon, 1973; Katz, 1988; Quinney, 1980; Gordon, 1973). As the number of people who are unable to secure remunerative work and/or positive identities increases, both crime and imprisonment rates tend to rise, but not necessarily at the same rate and not necessarily for the same reasons.

In an early study of the relationship between unemployment and incarceration rates, Greenberg (1977b) hypothesized that imprisonment rates should rise and fall with changes in the unemployment rate. To test this hypothesis, Greenberg used unemployment and prison admissions data from Canada for the years 1925 through 1960. Greenberg found that prison admissions followed changes in unemployment rates quite closely, after allowing in his statistical model for a time lag in court processing. His conclusion that both unemployment and the business cycle have significant effects on incarceration rates in capitalist systems lends general support to the propositions outlined above.

In a similar study, Jankovic (1982a:96) theorized that a rise in unemployment would lead to increased prison commitments and increased prison populations "even if crime were decreasing, provided that unemployment is rising." In other words, Jankovic argued that rising levels of unemployment exert a pressure to increase rates of imprisonment that is *independent* of rates of crime. This proposition is consistent with the views of Rusche and Kirchheimer (1968) who argued that economic circumstances will have a direct impact on punishment *regardless* of the crime rate (see also Lynch 1988a, 1988b). Jankovic found support for his hypothesis in an analysis of U.S. imprisonment and unemployment rates for the years 1926 to 1974, and a study of an unidentified California county for the years 1969 to 1976. He concluded that the "relationship between unemployment and imprisonment was positive and statistically significant, regardless of the volume of criminal activity" (1982a:101). Similar statistical studies of unemployment and imprisonment were conducted by Yeager (1979) and by Box and Hale (1982) with similar results.

Chiricos and DeLone (1992) examined the results from 28 longitudinal and 16 cross-sectional studies of labor market effects on punishment. In most of these studies, labor market effects were measured using some type of unemployment statistic, although the specific measure varied. Longitudinal studies examined changes in either prison admissions or prison populations across time. Cross-sectional studies focused on changes in prison admissions and the severity of punishment from one place to another. The majority of the studies analyzed more than one specific relationship, resulting in a total of 247 different tests from the 44 different studies. The results of this analysis are summarized in Table 12.1.

Over all, 86 percent of the individual tests reported a positive association between labor market conditions and punishment, and more than one-half (55%) found the relationship between unemployment and imprisonment to be positive and significant. It was also found that results from time-series studies were more likely than those from cross-sectional studies to be significant and positive. These findings indicate that the greater weight of the evidence supports Rusche and Kirchheimer's (1968) basic proposition that as labor market conditions deteriorate, rates of imprisonment will rise, independent of rates of crime.

## Surplus Value

Research into the relationship between the extraction of surplus value and imprisonment has added new empirical evidence supporting the radical position. For Marx (1967a), the single most important characteristic of capitalism was the production of surplus value (see also Engels, 1973). As you will recall from our earlier discussion, surplus value is the value added to raw materials by labor during the production process. Historically, this kind of value could only be created by labor working on raw materials. In some cases, raw material is now turned into items of value with very little human labor, as computer-assisted production and robotics take over many of the jobs that human laborers once performed. This development, however, does not sever the connection between human labor and value insofar as nothing appears in the world, including high-tech machinery, without the efforts of flesh-and-blood workers. However, today these workers may more often be computer programmers and systems designers than machine-tenders on the factory floor.

The ratio of the value produced by workers to the wages paid them is the *rate of surplus value*. The rate of surplus value is an *empirical measure* of *labor's exploitation and alienation* that tells us how much uncompensated value workers produce. For example, if the rate of surplus value is zero, workers would not be exploited and would be paid the full amount of the values they produced. Capitalism, however, is based upon extracting more value from workers than is given back to them in wages. Without this exploitation capitalism would cease to function since the rate of profit would drop to zero. In reality, there are few enterprises where the rate of surplus value extraction is near zero. On the contrary, it is typically quite high. The current rate of surplus value for U.S. manufacturing industries is over 500 percent. This means that, on average, American workers produce commodities that are five times more valuable than the wages they are paid.

## Table 12.1: Summary, Time Series and Cross-Sectional Studies of Labor Market and Imprisonment Effects*

| | TIME SERIES | | | | CROSS-SECTIONAL | | | | ALL STUDIES | |
| | Prison Admissions | | Prison Population | | Prison Admissions | | Sentence Severity | | Total | |
| | N | (%) | N | (%) | N | (%) | N | (%) | N | (%) |
|---|---|---|---|---|---|---|---|---|---|---|
| **Relationship** | | | | | | | | | | |
| Significant/Positive | 59 | (57) | 53 | (60) | 18 | (53) | 6 | (29) | 136 | (55) |
| Positive (NS)*** | 29 | (28) | 25 | (28) | 13 | (38) | 9 | (43) | 76 | (31) |
| Significant/Negative | 5 | (5) | 4 | (5) | 1 | (3) | 1 | (5) | 11 | (5) |
| Negative (NS) | 11 | (11) | 6 | (7) | 2 | (6) | 5 | (24) | 24 | (10) |
| | 104 | (101)** | 88 | (100) | 34 | (100) | 21 | (101)** | 247 | (101)** |

*Adapted from Chiricos and DeLone, (1992).

**Rounding Error

***NS=not significant

As noted earlier, it is in capitalists' interests to increase the rate of surplus value. This is done in one of several ways. In modern societies, the main mechanism is by increasing mechanization, which simultaneously increases productivity and decreases the need for labor. The result is a reduced reliance on human labor, which translates into fewer and fewer manufacturing jobs. In the long run, then, there is a rise in the size of the economically marginalized population of under- and unemployed workers.

Earlier, we noted that radicals suggest that imprisonment is part of the social mechanism for controlling the surplus population. If imprisonment is an attempt to control the surplus population, and radical economists are correct in their interpretation of the theory of surplus value, then there should be a statistical relationship between the rate of surplus value and prison admission and incarceration rates (Lynch, 1988a, 1988b). In short, we can say that as the rate of surplus value increases, more people are made economically marginal, increasing the need for social control. Empirical analyses of this relationship (Lynch, 1988a, 1988b) have shown a direct and significant relationship between the rate of surplus value and prison admissions and incarceration rates for the U.S. That is, as the rate of surplus value has increased in the U.S., so too, has the rate of imprisonment.

## Historical Contingency

Most longitudinal studies of the unemployment-imprisonment relationship assume that this relationship, if it exists, will be constant over time. That is, if a 1 percent increase in unemployment produced a 5 percent increase in imprisonment during the 1980s, the assumption would be that the 5 percent increase would hold during other decades as well. This way of thinking imagines the relationship between unemployment and punishment to be *time-invariant*. There is another way to think about these relationships, however; that is, they might be *historically contingent*. This means that the effect of social forces is not constant over time, but instead changes with historical conditions. Historical contingency is easy to understand if we think about it in terms of personal life. For example, the consequences of having a romantic relationship come to an end are usually never good. But getting "dumped" by your boyfriend or girlfriend when you are 14 years old has a very different social meaning than having your wife or husband leave you when you are age 35 with a mortgage, two children and aging parents to care for. The same is true for larger social processes. In the case of unemployment, what it *means* to be unemployed can change from one time period to the next. For instance, losing a job during a widespread depression – when everyone else seems to be losing theirs and everyone's standard of living is declining – is different from losing a job when unemployment is declining.

Bowles et al. (1990) proposed that the recent political-economic history of the U.S. can be divided into four distinct phases: (1) a period of economic exploration from 1933 to 1947; (2) a period of consolidation from 1948 to 1966; (3) a period of economic decay from 1967 to 1979; and (4) a new period of exploration from 1980 to 1990. Each of these periods was characterized by a distinct collection of economic and political strategies for determining how production would be organized, how the wealth produced would be distributed among the population and how the government would help or not help those displaced from the economic system. Michalowski and Carlson (1999) have suggested that unemployment will have a different social meaning in each of these periods, and consequently the impact of unemployment on imprisonment will also be different from one period to the next. Specifically, they demonstrated that unemployment had the strongest impact on imprisonment during the 1967 to 1979 period of decay. During this time, good jobs were disappearing faster than they were being created, generating a growing surplus population. As people, particularly inner-city young men, became increasingly detached from the world of work, the state began to rely more heavily on repressive strategies of control such as imprisonment, rather than on more integrative strategies like job programs and expanded social welfare. Michalowski and Carlson found that unemployment registered less of an effect on imprisonment during the 1948 to 1966 period of consolidation and expansion when the unemployed had reasonable expectations of finding equivalent work within a short period of time. In this climate the state was free to utilize less repressive strategies, such as probation and community corrections, more extensively. Over all, their analysis of the relationship between unemployment and imprisonment for each of the four time periods, and over the entire period from 1933 to 1992, showed that the relationship was indeed historically contingent. This suggests that while there is a clear link between unemployment and imprisonment, the nature and strength of this link will be influenced by the surrounding economic and political conditions.

**In Sum**

Radical inquiry into the relationship between economic conditions and punishment has had a number of important consequences. First, it has offered empirical support for radical propositions regarding the link between the political-economy and patterns of punishment. Second, it has demonstrated how imprisonment serves to contain and control marginal segments of the population. Third, it has found support for Marxist propositions regarding the nature of class struggle in capitalist society. Fourth, it has generated a much better understanding of how class struggle involves political and ideological forces as well as economic ones.

Radical theorists suggest that in order to understand the role of punishment in modern society, specific forms of punishment (e.g., corporal punishment, imprisonment, fines) must be examined in light of the historic conditions in which they emerged and the concrete economic, political, and ideological climates in which they operate. Working from this assumption, radical criminologists have demonstrated that different forms of punishment have provided ideological and economic support for various systems of production. It is important to recognize that these relationships are never one-sided – specific forms of punishment seldom give support to economic and/or ideological arrangements without a return effect. Instead, the relationship is reciprocal, as Foucault (1979) argued. The ideology of surveillance, for instance, contributed to the rise of the penitentiary and the factory, while at the same time the existence of the penitentiary and the factory helped normalize the idea of surveillance.

As we conclude our brief review of radical approaches to crime and justice we want to emphasize this final point. Nearly all relationships in social life are reciprocal, just like the relationship between the ideology of surveillance and the reality of imprisonment. To fully understand crime and the systems designed to control it, we must always be alert to the ways in which different social forces intersect with one another and work in mutually supportive or mutually destructive ways.

In the final chapter we will briefly explore our vision of a radical response to the crime problem.

# Thirteen.
# Crime and Justice in the Twenty-First Century

The problem of crime and the challenge of justice are casting long shadows into the twenty-first century. As we noted earlier, the U.S. enters the new millennium with more people in prison than any other nation in the world, and a high level of crime, especially violent crime. Moreover, the number of street crimes in the U.S. pales in comparison to the crimes that orthodox criminologists and policy makers have tended to neglect: corporate crime, environmental crime and state crime. These latter crimes have a greater financial and physical cost to the American public than street crimes.

We have argued that these high levels of crime and punishment can be explained by the kind and quality of inequality found in the U.S. and elsewhere. There is little on the horizon that suggests we will soon see any significant declines in inequality, poverty and the kinds of social disorder, including crime, that they cause. Indeed, the current process of globalization contains a very real potential to *increase* rather than decrease pressures for both street crime and corporate crime in the U.S. and around the world (Amin, 1992; Burbach et al., 1997; Mander and Goldsmith, 1996.)

Most current indicators suggest that crime worldwide will remain high and true justice elusive well into the twenty-first century. Even more disturbing is the potential for increased resurgence of inter-ethnic warfare, genocide and desperate living conditions in many places in the world. To top off this pessimistic picture of the future, consider a future energy crisis described in chapter8, how that would affect inequality, and the role that state agents (politicians) and corporations continue to play in edging us closer to an energy-strapped, environmentally-destructive course of action.

This unhappy scenario, however, need not come to pass. While there are large-scale forces that threaten to create an increasingly criminal and violent world, it is also possible for people to take charge of the future of their societies by changing these forces. Humans need not be the mere objects of structural conditions and constraints. Rather, it is both possible and necessary for humans to become active agents who exert their energies in ways that can transform the future. In the U.S., the question we face is how to confront the challenge of crime without becoming captives of the punitive logic that has dominated crime control throughout the country.

## The Punitive Impulse

In recent years, street crime has dropped noticeably in the U.S. By 2002, the crime index had fallen 30 percent from its high point in 1991 (though it rose in 2000 and 2001; *Sourcebook...*, 2004, Table 3.103). This decline led to considerable self-congratulation in many political arenas. Yet, this decline still leaves the U.S. among the most crime-ridden industrialized nations, and, for women, one of the most dangerous nations in the world (e.g., 84 percent of all women killed by firearms in the 25 most populated, high-income nations live in the U.S.; see, Henenway et al., 2002). Nevertheless, conservatives took much of the credit for the crime decline, and pointed to two primary factors: (1) the increased use of imprisonment and the return to the death penalty; and (2) the police practice of "zero tolerance" for petty misbehaviors such as vandalism, public drunkenness, loitering, graffiti, wearing gang colors and drug use. This policy, often attributed to James Q. Wilson's "broken windows" concept, suggests that the best way for police to stop crime is to eliminate the kinds of minor disorders that might imply a tolerant attitude toward deviant behavior within a community (see Bernstein, 1998). Police and researchers have suggested that these zero-tolerance policies have lowered the incidence of all forms of crime, from petty theft to homicide.

As Peter Manning (1998) argues, there are many reasons to be wary of this claim. First, these changes occurred at a time when the economy was getting better for many people, and when numerous other changes related to crime were taking place. Second, as Manning points out, it is surprising that crime would decrease at the same time that police were being more vigilant about uncovering crime. That is, police claim that the success of the program lies in their increased number of arrests, while police data indicate a decline in arrests for most crimes. Third, Manning points out that the policy of zero tolerance is aimed at controlling the *visible* signs of disorder. The result is an increase in police presence and intervention in areas that appear disorganized, i.e., "slums" and ghettos, or underclass urban neighborhoods inhabited by the poorest people in the U.S. These areas also happen to consist primarily of African-American and Hispanic communities. Zero tolerance, in this view, is a mechanism for legitimizing long-standing biases in policing that have targeted the poor and people of color. Zero-tolerance policies put in place in Chicago and Fayette County, GA provide two examples of the consequences of this form of policing.

In 1992, Chicago police implemented a zero-tolerance city ordinance that permits police officers to order entire groups to move on and to arrest anyone who remains if there is reasonable evidence that the loiterer is a member of a criminal gang. Under this law, to loiter is "to remain in any one place with no apparent purpose," and may include sitting on one's own doorstep. Between 1992 and 1995 (when this law was declared unconstitutional by the Illinois Supreme Court), over 45,000 people were arrested under this act. Most were members of poor communities, and most were minorities (Greenhouse, 1998).

In March 1999, the sheriff of Fayette County, GA, the state's wealthiest county, filed felony charges under Georgia's Street Gang and Terrorism Act against five teenagers who styled themselves as the "Rollin 5 Crackas." The youths faced up to 10 years in prison for spray-painting their tag on a bridge and touting their crew on a web site. The official police response was as follows: "What's going on here is the same thing we've seen on [sic] other places where there are gang problems. First you got graffiti. Then you've got fighting. And before you know it, you've got the real thing, with drugs and guns and all the rest" (*Arizona Daily Star*, 1999).

Yet, consider the reality of this behavior. Ferrell's (1992) extensive research into gang and graffiti artists indicates that graffiti crews operate as *alternatives to and not as precursors to* violent drug gangs. But, even *if* the imagined sequence was correct, allowing the justice system to treat people who committed minor offenses as threats to society resembles the kinds of policing policies used in dictatorial police states – very undemocratic nations Americans find offensive. In both situations, there is an underlying willingness to trade citizens' rights for some vague promise of peace through greater repression.

In effect, the punitive and zero tolerance polices of the last three decades are, on the one hand, offensive and politically dangerous. On the other hand, these policies have been much less effective than their supporters claim. Consider the following simple example mentioned in chapter 12: from 1972 through 1995, the imprisonment rate in the U.S. steadily increased each year. At the same time, crime *did not decrease each time* incarceration increased. Table 13.1 contains the bivariate correlations for two analyses of time-series data for 1972 through 1995. The first half of the table shows the correlations and statistical significance for the relationships among the rates of arrests, crimes known to the police and imprisonment for this time period. The second half of the table shows the same information for changes in the rates of these variables.

The table indicates the following. The raw rates indicate that imprisonment, arrest and crimes known to police *all increased* during this time period; that these increases were related (i.e., as one increased the others increased as well); and that the relationships among these patterns of increase was statistically significant. The annual change data present a slightly different picture. First, as imprisonment increased, crimes known to police declined, while arrests increased. The relationships among changes in these rates was not statistically significant, indicating that the observed relationship is not meaningful. In short, in neither case was there evidence favoring the argument that getting tough on criminals by increasing levels of incarceration decreased crime.

### Table 13.1: Bivariate Correlations, Rates of (and Changes in) Imprisonment, Arrest and Crimes Known to Police in the U.S., 1972-1995*

| | RATES PER 100,000 POPULATION | | |
|---|---|---|---|
| | Imprisonment | Crimes Known | Arrests |
| Imprisonment | 1.00 | . 453 (.013) | .677 (.000) |
| Crimes Known | | | .851 (.000) |
| | ANNUAL CHANGE IN RATES PER 100,000 POPULATION | | |
| | Imprisonment | Crimes Known | Arrests |
| Imprisonment | 1.00 | -.230 (.147) | .144 (.256) |
| Crimes Known | | | .610 (.001) |

*statistical significance; one-tailed test

In addition to unfavorable evidence, "get-tough" policies were implemented at a time when the demographics, economy and culture of the U.S. were changing in ways that may have reduced crime without any increase in punishment. For instance, the proportion of "America's most crime-prone population," those aged 14 to 24, declined over this period, and this trend alone would have produced some change in crime. Further, since the late 1980s, the U.S. has enjoyed one of its longest periods of economic growth in recent history. Among other things, this growth created the lowest unemployment rates since World War II, even though not all segments of society benefited from this growth in employment (see Schor, 1993; Frank and Cook, 1995; Barlett and Steele, 1992). Nevertheless, evidence suggests that the return of a better economy contributed to a decline in street crime outside of communities inhabited by those displaced by technology and globalization (Carlson and Michalowski, 1997). Finally, cultural changes, such as the decline in the appeal of drugs between the 1980s and 1990s, also may have contributed to the decrease in crime.

In any event, it is difficult to establish how much *if any* of the reduction in crime that occurred in the 1990s resulted from changes in criminal justice policy, and how much was a consequence of broader societal changes, since all these factors changed simultaneously. We do know this, however: get-tough policies have been tried in many places and at many points in U.S. history. They have never proven to be a very effective mechanism for reducing crime. As we have already noted, if these policies had worked, the U.S. would have some of the lowest crime rates in the world, not the highest, since it has a very punitive criminal justice system compared to those that operate in other nations.

Even if the claims made for increased imprisonment, death sentences and zero tolerance were accurate, however, we would have to seriously question their practical and moral consequences. From a practical standpoint, punitive policies have resulted in far too little in the way of crime reduction to justify their economic costs and social consequences. We have spent billions of dollars on the war against drugs and billions more on prisons, but crime and drugs seem to remain intractable features of life in America. In short, the "orgy" of punishment our nation has engaged in has not made America safe. The U.S. remains a place where women are afraid to walk alone at night; where people's bodies and wallets are victimized each and every day by powerful corporations; where people fear strangers; and where few feel safe enough to leave their homes or cars unlocked. In the end, we have gotten very little for all the money we have spent fighting crime the old-fashioned way, while the corporations that make up America's criminal justice-industrial complex have gotten rich in the process (Schlosser, 1998).

From a moral standpoint, the small gains we have made have been purchased at a high cost to our moral sensibilities (Clear, 1995). Today there are nearly 1.5 *million* men and women behind bars on any given day in the U.S., and with 5 percent of the world's population, U.S. prisons hold 25 percent of all the world's inmates. According to the U.S. Bureau of Justice Statistics (Harrison and Beck, 2003), 1 in every 143 Americans was locked up in a federal or state prison or local jail in 2002, and fewer than half were incarcerated for violent offenses (Harrison and Beck, 2003). On December 2, 2005, the U.S. passed a grim milestone when it executed its 1,000th prisoner since the resumption of the death penalty in 1977. In recent years, the rate of executions, particularly in the southern states, has risen so dramatically that 500 inmates have been executed since December of 1998. Carrying out executions; sweeping 45,000 people off the street in Chicago through zero-tolerance policies; considering the imprisonment of teenagers for 10 years because their acts of tagging might develop into a drug gang; sending more and more people to prison to reduce crime when there is no evidence this policy works – each of these methods of crime control is taking us in a dangerous direction, increasingly justifying a police state. The primary justification for police states has always been restoring order. But at what price? At the cost of ensuring that being imprisoned will become a normal feature of life in minority communities? According to figures from the U.S. Department of Justice, this is exactly where we are headed if current trends continue. At the present time, it is estimated that one in every twenty citizens born in the U.S. in 1999 will serve some time in prison. For African Americans, the ratio is one in four, or, taking gender into account, over half of all African-American males. These figures are alarming. They are our future if we continue to allow our government to pursue get-tough policies that got us where we are today.

Americans' heightened fear of crime is instrumental in their embrace of punitive crime control strategies. Aided by conservative political leaders, many Americans have become so frightened of crime that they are willing to accept almost any amount of damage to our moral sensibilities and civil liberties if it will help keep the nation safe from crime. This is not only a bad bargain, it is a losing proposition. If the 17 percent decline in crime registered during the late 1990s is a result of tripling the prison population, how much more would we have to increase the incarceration rate to reduce crime even further? Would it be 30 percent or 4 million people behind bars? One of every two African Americans? To us, these terms are unacceptable.

Are there any alternatives? Can we avoid a future dominated by high rates of crime and staggering prison populations? Below, we offer three policies that draw on radical criminological ideas as means of reducing crime: left-realism, feminist theories of masculinity, and policies for political-economic change.

## GETTING REAL: LEFT-REALISM AND COMMUNITY CRIME CONTROL

As an intellectual movement, radical criminology has been recognized for focusing attention on the crimes of the powerful and for its attention to class biases in traditional criminological theories of crime and justice (Vold et al., 1998). At the same time, radical criminology has been criticized for devoting too much attention to the crimes of the powerful and for siding with the "underdogs" (i.e. lower-class criminals) while neglecting the crimes committed by the poor against those in their own communities. These criticisms are overstated, since numerous radical criminologists have, in fact, addressed the problem of street crime (e.g., Greenberg, 1995, 1985; Schwendinger and Schwendinger, 1997, 1993, 1985, 1983; Currie, 1996, 1985; Messerschmidt, 1997, 1993; Morash and Chesney-Lind, 1991; Colvin and Pauly, 1983; Grose and Groves, 1988; Lynch et al., 1994). In our view, these criticisms are also overstated because the amount of harm caused by the crimes of the powerful far outweigh those associated with street crime. Nevertheless, the criminal victimization of working-class citizens and strategies to reduce crime in working-class communities have received less attention than might be expected from an intellectual movement that claims solidarity with the working-class.

In response to these criticisms, a number of British and Canadian criminologists developed an alternative approach to doing radical criminology (Kinsey et al., 1986; Lea, 1987; Young, 1987, 1990; Lowman and MacLean, 1992; MacLean, 1991). Taken collectively, their work is known as *left-realism*, a movement that eventually exerted some influence on radical criminology in the U.S. as well (for an excellent overview see DeKesseredy and Schwartz, 1996; see also DeKesseredy and Schwartz, 1991). Left-realism focuses on working class victimization and concerns about neighborhood crime as a way of exploring alternative crime control strategies that arise, not from politicians or academics, but from working-class communities and peoples.

A central strategy of left-realism is the use of localized crime surveys, as opposed to national crime surveys, as the best method of pinpointing working-class crime-related fears and attitudes, as well as beliefs about crime (e.g., Jones et al., 1986; Crawford et al., 1990). By using these surveys, left-realists hope to identify crime control policies that would benefit the working class. One of the features of the local crime survey that distinguishes it from the typical governmental survey about crime is that it frequently includes questions about victimization by white-collar criminals as well as street criminals.

Like other radical criminologists, left-realists readily recognize that members of the working class are widely victimized by crimes of the powerful as well as crimes committed by members of their own communities (DeKesseredy and Schwartz, 1996). As noted earlier, because the crimes of the powerful involve indirect victimization, they do not often elicit the same kinds of responses as street crimes. As a result, working-class people are often unaware of the ways in which they are victimized by the powerful, and, instead, focus their attention on what appear to be more immediate and present dangers: crimes committed against them by other working-class people. However, when working people are asked specifically about corporate victimization, for example, they are quick to identify the various forms of victimization they have experienced (Wonders and Michalowski, 1996). For left-realists, the community crime survey serves not only as an information-gathering tool but as a mechanism for helping working-class communities develop strategies to protect themselves from crimes of the powerful.

Nevertheless, another goal of left-realism is to draw attention to intra-class victimization. Detailed local surveys can reveal a good deal of information about crimes in lower, working-class and minority communities. Since the majority of street crime is intra-class and intra-racial, this kind of information can serve as a realistic basis for developing effective crime control strategies in these communities. In short, left-realists are to be commended for pointing out that these kinds of criminal events have important consequences for working-, lower-class and marginalized peoples, and for calling upon radicals to devise specific policies that deal with these forms of criminal victimization.

Left-realists have also promoted the development of specific, community-designed crime policies that provide proactive alternatives to conservative, repressive crime control strategies based on a law-and-order mentality. The conservative response to crime in working- and lower-class communities has centered on increased police presence as a deterrent to crime. These policies typically originate outside the boundaries of working/lower-class communities by political and economic elites whose way of life has little connection to communities affected by crime. In contrast, left-realists argue for the empowerment of local communities so that they play a greater role in determining the kinds of crime control strategies that will be enacted in their communities.

Based on research into local community needs and desires, left-realists have promoted establishing responsive, localized police initiatives characterized by decentralization and democratization of policing. Once police are organized in this way, left-realists argue, they will be better equipped to respond to variations in community desires and in crime patterns across communities.

Left-realists' concern with the development of decentralized policing has a strong resemblance to the community policing movement in the U.S. In theory, the goal of community policing is to transform police from "outside" agents who impose "law and order" on communities, to active participants who work with community members to discover solutions to the problem of crime in the community (Peak, 1999; Rosenbaum, 1994). In this sense, both community policing and left-realism focus on *preventing rather than controlling crime once it occurs*. The left-realist movement, however, is clearly the more radical of the two insofar as it includes strategies that help communities develop and rely upon their own economic resources in an effort to reduce crime. Enhancing local economies, establishing economic well-being and reducing marginalization are central strategies for left-realists struggling to reduce crime in working-class communities. In contrast, standard community policing initiatives are an extension of more traditional crime prevention programs that control crime through surveillance and visibility.

In theory, both left-realism and community policing movements offer promising alternatives to the current repressive crime control strategies. Each approach, however, also incorporates a potential danger. That danger is that the implementation of such policies will be dominated by already established cultural images that define crime and how it should be controlled. One of the key problems for left-realists is that members of working-class communities are likely to continue to endorse established, coercive forms of social control (e.g., see Colvin and Pauly, 1983) such as intensified policing and prison expansion as appropriate responses to crime. The challenge for left-realists is to facilitate community-based discussion of non-repressive alternatives to crime control and to help make community policing, in its broadest sense, a reality. This involves helping communities find alternatives to traditional crime control strategies (increased arrests, zero tolerance, increased police presence), helping police understand that they are part of the community they serve, and establishing the conditions for local economic well-being that will liberate communities from oppressive economic conditions that produce crime.

# CRIME, GENDER AND MASCULINITY

Existing statistics, both for street crimes and the crimes of the powerful, indicate that the vast majority of crimes are committed by men. What is it about being male that increases the likelihood of becoming criminal? Clearly, as feminists have argued, the construction of gender in American society is a key factor in determining the character of the nation's crime problem. As we discussed in chapter 6, men and women are socialized to act in gender-specific ways that increase the likelihood that men will be more violent and more criminal than women. Three aspects of Americans' gender culture that contribute to the crime problem are: socialization into violence, competition, and gender inequality. Any real effort in reducing crime will have to address these patterns of culture-specific socialization.

## Socialization into Violence

The dominant male culture in the U.S. is a culture of aggression and violence. Men are trained to understand violence against "enemies" as not only acceptable but heroic. Gibson (1994:7) observes that: "America has always had a war culture... This culture has two fundamental stories: one celebrating the individual gunman who acts on his own ...; the other portraying the good soldier who belongs to an official military or police unit and serves as a representative defender of national honor." From an early age, most American boys learn that force is something to be admired and emulated rather than something to be deplored and avoided. This learning takes both secondhand and firsthand forms. Secondhand forms include the accepted violence that accompanies stories about the military that are taught in schools and promoted by popular culture (e.g., movies, TV and comics featuring sheriffs, detectives, private eyes and crime fighters like Batman). American males are surrounded by secondhand images that tell them if they want to be "real men" they must be strong, tough, and, above all, individual masters of violence (Gibson, 1989).

American males also experience violence firsthand as the recipients of corporal punishment and/or physical abuse at the hands of parents, caregivers and teachers. Indeed, many American boys have the curious experience of being hit in order to teach them that hitting is wrong. Whatever the reason for the physical punishment, the underlying message is that when someone is troubling you, you can resort to violence as a solution. While these cultural legacies do not make all men violent, they present alternatives that are less acceptable for women, and more acceptable for men who find themselves enmeshed within specific structural locations in American society (e.g., lower- and working-class men). The current widespread acceptance of punitive justice is a direct reflection of the comfort American men feel with inflicting physical harm on others. Changing these patterns of violence requires socializing men *not to accept* violence as a desirable part of male identity.

## Socialization for Competition

American culture values rewards (Bowles, 1976; MacPherson, 1962), and the ideological essence of capitalism is that "the best" — those who survive competition — reap the greatest rewards. To a large extent, this ideological message is a myth. Most people who succeed and are rewarded had a head start. Socialization into competitive values varies by gender. In American culture, females were/are socialized to imagine their desires in terms of domestic success and to compete in the marriage market. In contrast, men were/are socialized to imagine their desires in terms of economic success and to compete for success in the labor market (Ehrenreich, 1983; Coontz, 1994). Today, females continue to experience socialization routines that emphasize care-giving in the domestic sphere, while males continue to be channeled toward competition (through sports). Part of this socialization includes learning aggression and passivity. Males are taught that to win they must be aggressive. For women, the socialization rules are reversed; for them to win they must be passive. The distribution of aggression and competitiveness by gender in capitalist societies helps explain why males dominate many forms of competition, and why they are more often the criminals whether we are talking about street or corporate crime. In short, solving the problem of crime requires that we restructure male socialization experiences and deemphasize competition, aggression and domination as important values.

## Gender Inequality

In the U.S., the only people who are victimized by criminals expressly because of their gender are women. True, sometimes gay men are victimized because of their gender identity; they are victimized largely because they are not behaving like "real men," and rather are acting like women. Unlike men, there are many crimes by which women are regularly victimized simply because they are women. Every years, tens of thousands of women are raped and murdered because they have female bodies; up to two million more are assaulted in their homes in acts of domestic violence; and several million more women are the victims of sexual harassment in the workplace.

Feminists have pointed out that this wide-scale acceptance of the normalcy of violence against women is part of the "rape culture" in the U.S. (Brownmiller, 1975). That the sexual and physical assault of women is so prevalent underscores the privileged position of men in American society (Schur, 1984), which involves evaluating and using female bodies as objects of pleasure and power (Stanko, 1985). This culture is reinforced on a daily basis by socialization routines that emphasize the cultural acceptability of male dominance and differences in male-female behavioral expectations (aggression versus passivity) as well as by objectification processes found in popular culture and mass media (Schur, 1984).

There is also a racial dimension to this problem, discussed earlier, that should be emphasized. Minority women are seen as "less valuable" in American culture, and, therefore, their victimization is more widely accepted. This is particularly true when minority women are victimized by white males. Sexual stereotypes tied to race also play an important role in ensuring that minority women receive less protection at the hands of the law than other women (Schur, 1984).

In short, the majority of crimes committed against women by men – from street crimes to crime committed by powerful people, including the sale of dangerous women's "health care" products from cosmetics, to tampons, to drugs and surgeries – are the product of socialization into markets of gender inequality. Again, these socialization patterns must be transformed to make the U.S. a safer place.

## Changing Gender

In sum, what the discussion presented above has emphasized are ways in which the performance of masculinity in the U.S. is a crucial factor underlying the crime problem. Over the past decade, James Messerschmidt (1986, 1993,

1997) has been instrumental in developing a radical understanding of how the construction and performance of masculinity underlies every major form of male criminal activity from street crime to suite crime. Changing crime thus requires that we change masculine culture. This is no easy task, but it is one form of social change that people can engage in through their daily lives. First, men must decommodify sex, meaning that sex must change from something you get or buy to something two consenting adults share. Further, it is only by breaking the link between sex and commodities that we can end the culture that transforms women into objects that men feel free to own, dominate, violate and abuse.

Second, the socialization of men must de-emphasize violence and competition, and increase the emphasis on caregiving as a valued male — not just female — trait. There are many ways to accomplish this task, and individuals may participate in creating these kinds of changes through their own childrearing practices. As young boys observe their fathers engaging in caregiving, they will learn to construct their male identities differently. We do not mean to imply, however, that the responsibility for the construction of masculinity rests wholly on families, since the educational system in particular is capable of socializing children in ways that remain consistent with the construction of traditional forms of masculinity. Further, it is easier for white, middle-class males, for instance, to engage in alternative forms of masculine identity construction for a variety of reasons. Among these are safety factors that relate to class, race and neighborhood living conditions in the U.S. Thus, the process of changing masculine identity is both an individual and a social problem.

Third, formal educational values and mass-media messages must be changed so that they no longer value male violence and aggression as acceptable solutions to problems or events encountered in life. Males cannot be expected to refrain from violence when the culture that surrounds them endorses domination and aggression as appropriate values. These are values that individuals can help shape by, for instance, refusing to attend violent movies; writing producers and movie companies about their concerns; and attending local school board meetings to discuss how violence is portrayed in the classroom, how those images might be changed and how adults in the community can volunteer and become involved to help make those transformations possible.

It may be noted, with some irony, that the policies reviewed above emphasize the relationship between child-rearing practices and crime, a policy long associated with conservative forms of criminology. Radicals like Colvin and Pauly (1983), and John Hagan and colleagues (1987), however, have recognized the need to understand the context in which crime is created, and, for them, this has included family socialization processes. Part of that context involves child-rearing practices. The practices we highlight, however, are quite different from those examined by traditional criminologists, who emphasize the impact of broken or single-parent homes (especially, it seems, in minority communities). Single-parent homes per se are not the problem; the larger problem is the socialization mechanism and message that most homes in the U.S. pass on to their children. These messages, which often speak of male dominance, affect the quantity and quality of crime among families of all social classes, and allow children who grow up with them to accept the kinds of crimes the messages rationalize. Current socialization practices rationalize crimes of domination, whether they are violent or related to acquisition of property; whether they are street or suite crimes; in whatever form they victimize women – through rape, sexual harassment, unequal pay or suppression in the classroom. When creating policies that reduce crime, these issues must be addressed *alongside of* (not in isolation from) broader economic and structural forces underlying crime in America.

## CRIME, POLITICAL ECONOMY AND JUSTICE POLICY

There are a number of political-economic changes that eclipse the scope of traditional crime-control policies that must be addressed in order to reduce crime (see Currie, 1996, 1985; Welch, 1996a, 1996d). One such issue involves remaking democracy and enhancing people's control over their own lives through the creation of public trusts (Korten, 1998). A public trust gives citizens a role in determining the direction that a corporation takes. As noted earlier, the primary interest of the corporation is profit, and this interest often comes into conflict with those of a specific community, or with most people's (non-stockholders') interests. The result is corporate misbehavior, from the production of faulty products to the dumping of hazardous waste, the flight of capital overseas and downsizing, to practices that injure, kill, or otherwise have a tremendous adverse impact on many people. Placing corporations in public trusts will temper the lust for profit by balancing that desire against the best interests of people in the community. This solution would also reduce the tendency for corporations to cast aside workers in favor of machinery, a process that produces marginalized populations whose identities can become bound up in the underworld of crime.

The idea of transforming corporations into public trusts may seem far-fetched, but there was a time in American history when the idea of granting citizenship to people of African descent or allowing women to vote or to become truck drivers, pilots and doctors also seemed absurd — especially to those in power. Change does not come easily, and it requires radically rethinking how we understand our own lives, how we decide what matters to us and what we are willing to do to create a better world. This requires that people organize themselves and invent political and cultural strategies that contribute to changing the American agenda. This takes work and commitment, but it is not impossible. It takes being involved, taking a stand, and, perhaps, taking a role organizing such groups. This has been done before, and it will be done again. And, unless we at least *talk about* a different way of doing things in America *as being possible*, it will never become probable.

There are many smaller public policy changes that can redirect the American way of life and justice that exist beyond the radical restructuring of corporations. One of the most important is to bring criminal penalties in line with the harms that offenders commit. For conservatives, this observation is translated into the simple idea of controlling violent criminals, and we have no objection to this idea. Most certainly, there are those in society who pose such a physical threat to the well-being of the rest of us that they should not be allowed to circulate freely in society. But we have already created a penal machine that is out of control and out of line with the scope of this problem (Welch, 1996d; Irwin and Austin, 1994). Approximately 400,000 violent street offenders (people who committed murder, rape, robbery and sex offenses) were behind bars in 1998, constituting about 29 percent of state and federal inmates (Schlosser, 1998). The increases in prison populations have not, however, simply resulted from incarcerating more violent inmates: an increasingly larger percentage of the prison population is made up of lesser offenders, including drug and public-order offenders. In fact, the majority of people in prison are not incarcerated for violent offenses. Because prisons impose severe emotional harm on people (Amnesty International, 1998), they should be reserved for those who commit the most serious crimes against society. Most certainly, some of these people are corporate criminals, who generally receive fines as a penalty. For other types of offenders, we must search for more productive and creative mechanisms for dealing with the problems they pose to social peace and order.

Substantial headway can be made in reducing America's prison population simply by decriminalizing drug use and using the savings to pay for drug rehabilitation (Drug Policy Foundation, 1999). We can also make our world safer by rethinking our dependence on the justice system. Public safety can be assisted but is not created by police, and active community involvement in the justice system, as advocated by left-realists, provides an alternative to the way we presently do justice. Extensive public involvement with community systems of justice would require the cooperation of businesses, which would have to be willing to allow people to shift a portion of their private-sector responsibilities to public-sector responsibilities without penalty (Rifkin, 1995). The public trusts mentioned earlier could be instrumental in establishing these policies.

An extensive array of corporate harms occur through environmental degradation, including natural resource exploitation, air and water pollution, and the dumping of chemicals to create hazardous waste sites. Many in the environmental movement argue that these kinds of events are associated with the tendency for corporations to globalize, which detaches corporate concerns from local interests in environmental health and preservation (Agyeman and Evans, 2003; Shutkin, 2000). In effect, the sustainable development literature suggests that community members need to organize themselves and use democratic processes to counter globalization (Agyeman and Angus, 2003; Agyeman and Evans, 1995). The idea here is that local community residents, who have clear interests in preserving the quality of local environments, must recognize their common interests and join together to protect the environment while providing for sustainable economic development. Creating sustainable, localized communities of this type is, to be sure, a difficult process. It involves creating an economic climate that favors localized, small business over regional, national or global corporations. Where this process has been implemented, however, local businesses develop a greater environmental ethic, and improvements in local environmental conditions and management have been observed (Agyeman and Evan, 2003). Likewise, because sustainable economic development is a local phenomenon, profits remain in the community and enhance job creation. Sustainable enviro-economic policies also have the potential to address race and class equity concerns, such as unequal exposure to toxic waste and other environmental hazards (Agyeman and Evans, 2003). In sum, sustainable enviro-economic approaches can address pollution and social justice issues of concern to radical criminologists.

Finally, and most importantly, we must pursue strategies that ensure that everyone has a *meaningful place* in society. This does not mean that everyone must have identical incomes or statuses, but that we learn to value equally everyone's input to the maintenance of the social and economic order. It means that everyone must have a dignified existence for themselves and their children. It also means that dignity cannot be tied to identity markers such as gender, age, race, ethnicity, religion or sexual preference in ways that automatically confer dignity on some and disgrace on others. Achieving these goals is a big challenge, and is certainly an idea contained in *many* theories of crime, from traditional ones such as anomie, control and social disorganization, to the radical theories discussed throughout this book. The problem is that our present social system is based on depriving some people of their dignity so that others can live lavishly, and allowing some to heap dignity upon themselves and others like them because they view themselves as superior. We must come up with creative means for altering these forms of inequality, along with other forms of inequality (class, race, gender), if we want to reduce crime.

The U.S. is a wealthy nation, and is viewed as a leader among the nations of the world. But wealth and wisdom don't always go hand in hand. How wise is a wealthy nation that: Accepts millions of people behind bars as the answer to crime, when other nations have lower levels of crime and have not relied on prison as the answer? Watches as more than one-third of its children grow up at or near the poverty level? Allows huge gaps in income, wealth and social status as an acceptable price for being the most powerful nation on earth? Accepts regular violence against women as an acceptable cost for establishing male superiority? And has institutionalized mechanisms of racial oppression?

We are a nation that prides itself on its commitment to democracy and human rights. We need to think long and hard about these questions and the mechanisms we have employed to ensure "freedom and justice *for all*" if we wish this phrase to be more than ideology. Crime is the result of the structure of various kinds of inequality in society. In the end, the only way we can make any real headway against crime – headway that can be counted in more than a trend here and there, marked by some small decline in crime — is to embrace significant changes that erode and replace the forms of inequality upon which our nation is built.

# REFERENCES*

Ackerman, F. (1982). *Reaganomics: Rhetoric vs Reality*. Boston, MA: South End Press.

Adam, H. (1914). *Women and Crime*. London, UK: Werner-Laurie.

Adamson, C. (1983). "Punishment After Slavery." *Social Problems* 30(5):555-569.

Adler, F. (1975). *Sisters in Crime*. New York: McGraw-Hill.

Adler, J. (1989). "A Historical Analysis of the Law of Vagrancy." *Criminology* 27(2):209-229.

Adoratsky, V. (1936). *The Selected Works of Karl Marx*, vol. 3. New York: International Publishers.

Adorno, T. (1991). *The Culture Industry*. London, UK: Routledge.

Agyeman, J., and B. Angus (2003). "The Role of Civic Environmentalism in in the Pursuit of Sustainble Communities." *Journal of Environmental Planning and Management* 46(3):345-63.

—— and B. Evans. (1995). "Sustainability and Democracy: Community Participation in Local Agenda 21." *Local Government Policy Making* 22(2):35-40.

—— and T. Evans. (2003). "Towards Just Sustainability in Urban Communities: Building Equity Rights with Sustainable Solutions." *Annals of the Academy of Political and Social Science* 590:35-53.

Akers, R.L. (1980). "Further Critical Thoughts on Marxist Criminology." In: J. Inciardi (ed.), *Radical Criminology: The Coming Crisis*. Beverly Hills, CA: Sage.

—— (1979). "Theory and Ideology in Marxist Criminology." *Criminology* 16:527-543.

Albonetti, C., R.M. Hauser, J. Hagan and I.H. Nagel (1989). "Criminal Justice Decision Making as a Stratification Process: The Role of Race and Stratification Resources in Pretrial Release." *Journal of Quantitative Criminology* 5:57-82.

Allan, E. and D. Steffensmeier (1989). "Youth, Underemployment and Property Crime." *American Sociological Review* 54:107-123.

Allman, T.D. (2004). *Rogue State: America At War With The World*. New York: Nation Books.

Altheide, D. (2002). *Creating Fear: News and the Construction of Crisis*. New York: Aldine.

Althusser, L. (1972). *Lenin and Philosophy and Other Essays*. New York: Monthly Review (B. Brewster, translation).

—— (1969/1996). *For Marx*. New York: Vintage.

---

*Where there are multiple editions of a work, citations omit the dates of the earlier edition(s): e.g., a citation of "Rusche, 1982" refers to the reference entry for Rusche, G. [1933]1982.

—— and E. Balibar (1977). *Reading Capital.* Paris, FR: Francois Maspero.

Alvarez, A. (2001). *Govermenents, Citizens, and Genocide.* Bloomington: IN: Indiana University Press.

Amar, A. R. (2000). *The Bill of Rights: Creation and Reconstruction.* New Haven: Yale University Press, 2000.

American Civil Liberties Union. "Free Speech." http://www.acluohio.org/issues/free_speech/free_speech.htm

Amin, S. (1992). *Empire of Chaos.* New York: Monthly Review Press.

—— (1990). *Maldevelopment: Anatomy of a Global Failure.* Tokyo, Japan: United Nations University Press.

Amnesty International (1998). *United States of America: Rights for All Betraying the Young.* New York: Amnesty International, USA.

Amott, T. (1995). "Shortchanged: Restructuring Women's Work." In: M.L. Anderson and P.H. Collins (eds.), *Race, Class and Gender.* Belmont, CA: Wadsworth.

Amsterdam, A. (1993). "Race and the Death Penalty." In: R. Monk (ed.), *Taking Sides.* Guilford, CT: Dushkin.

Anderson, B. (1991). *Imagined Communities: Reflections on the Origin and Spread of Nationalism.* London:Verso.

Anderson, E. (1990). *Streetwise : Race, Class, and Change in an Urban Community.* Chicago, IL: University of Chicago Press.

Anderson, P. (1974). *Lineages of the Absolutist State.* London, UK: NLB.

Anyon, J. (1997). *Ghetto Schooling: A Political Economy of Urban Educational Reform.* New York: Teachers College Press.

Applebaum, E. (1979). "The Labor Market." In: A.S. Eichner (ed.), *A Guide to Post-Keynesian Economics.* White Plains, NY: M.E. Sharpe.

Arenas, J. (1985). *Cese el fuego: Una historia política de las FARC.* Bogata: Editorial Oveja Negra.

Arendt, H. (1977). *Eichmann in Jerusalem: A Report on the Banality of Evil.* New York: Penguin Books.

*Arizona Daily Star* (1999). "Five Wannabe Teen-Age Thugs Face Gang-Law Counts for Web Site." March 22:A1.

Arrigo, B. (1996). "Postmodern Criminology on Race, Class and Gender." In: M. Schwartz and D. Milovanovic (eds.), *Gender, Race and Class in Criminology.* Hamden, CT: Garland.

—— (1995). "[De]constructing Classroom Instruction: Theoretical and Methodological Contributions of Postmodern Science for Crimino-Legal Education." *Social Pathology* 1(2):115-48.

—— (1993). "Deconstructing Jurisprudence: An Experiential Feminist Critique." *The Journal of Human Justice* 4(1):13-30.

Arrigo, B., D. Milovanovic and R. Schehr. (2005). *The French Connection in Criminology: Rediscovering Crime, Law, and Social Change.* Albany, NY: SUNY Press.

Ashton, P.J. (1984). "Urbanization and the Dynamics of Suburban Development Under Capitalism." In: W.K. Tabb and L. Sawers (eds.), *Marxism and the Metropolis: New Perspectives in Urban Political Economy.* New York: Oxford University Press.

Aulette, J. and R. Michalowski (1996). "Fire in Hamlet: A Case Study in State-Corporate Crime." In: K. Tunnel (ed.), *Political Crime.* New York: Garland.

Associated Press (1998). "Magazine Study Finds Racial Divide on Internet Use, Computer Ownership." *The Tampa Tribune,* April 17(1):3.

Austin, R. (1984). "The Court Sentencing of Black Offenders." In: D. Georges-Abeyie (ed.), *The Criminal Justice System and Blacks.* New York: Clark-Boardman.

Austin, J. and J. Irwin. (2002). *It's About Time: America's Imprisonment Binge.* Belmont, CA: Wadsworth.

Baer, J. (1983). *Equality Under the Constitution : Reclaiming the Fourteenth Amendment.* Ithaca, NY: Cornell University Press.

—— and W.J. Chambliss (1997). "Generating Fear: The Politics of Crime Reporting." □ *Crime, Law and Social Change* 27(2):87-107.

Bailey, W.C. (1998). "Deterrence, Brutalization, and the Death Penalty." *Criminology* 36(4):711-733.

Balakian, P. (2003). *The Burning Tigris: The Armenian Genocide and America's Response.* New York: HarperCollins.

Balbus, I. (1977). "Commodity Form and Legal Form: An Essay on the Relative Autonomy of the Law." *Law and Society Review* 11:571-588.

—— (1973). *The Dialectic of Legal Repression.* New York: Russell Sage Foundation.

—— (1971). "Ruling Elite Theory vs. Marxist Class Analysis." *Monthly Review* 23:37.

Bales, K.. (2004). *Disposable People: New Slavery in the Global Economy.* Berkeley, CA: University of California Press.

Balkan, S., R. Berger and J. Schmidt (1980). *Crime and Deviance in America: A Critical Approach.* Belmont, CA: Wadsworth.

Ball, R. (1979). "The Dialectic Method: Its Application to Social Theory." *Social Forces* 57(3):785-98.

—— (1966). "An Empirical Examination of Neutralization Theory." *Criminology* 4:22-32.

Barak, G. (1998). *Integrating Criminologies.* Boston, MA: Allyn and Bacon.

—— (1996). "Mass-Mediated Regimes of Truth: Race, Gender and Class in Crime News Thematics." In: M. Schwartz and D. Milovanovic (eds.), *Gender, Race and Class in Criminology*. Hamden, CT: Garland.

—— (ed.), (1994). *Media, Process and the Social Construction of Crime: Studies in Newsmaking Criminology*. New York: Garland.

—— (ed.), (1991). Crimes by the Capitalist State: An Introduction to State Criminality. Albany, NY: State University of New York Press.

—— (1990). "Crime, criminology and human rights: Towards an understanding of state criminality." *The Journal of Human Justice* 2:11-28.

—— (1988). "Newsmaking Criminology: Reflections on the Media, Intellectuals and Crime." *Justice Quarterly* 5:221-246.

—— (1987). "Comment on Traditional as Radical Criminology by Groves and Sampson." *Journal of Research in Crime and Delinquency* 24(4):332-335.

—— (1982). "Punishment and Corrections." *Crime and Social Justice* 18:108-117

—— (1980). *In Defense of Whom? A Critique of Criminal Justice Reform*. Cincinnati, OH: Anderson.

—— (1974). "In Defense of the Rich: The Emergence of the Public Defender." *Crime and Social Justice* 3:2-14.

Baran, P. and P. Sweezy (1966). *Monopoly Capitalism*. New York: Monthly Review Press.

Baritz, L. (1988). *The Good Life : The Meaning of Success for the American Middle Class*. New York: Knopf.

—— (1985). *Backfire : A History of How American Culture Led Us into Vietnam and Made Us Fight the Way We Did*. New York: Morrow.

Barkan, S.B. and S.F. Cohen (1994). "Racial Prejudice and Support for the Death Penalty by Whites." *Journal of Research in Crime and Delinquency* 31(2):202-209.

Barlett, D.L. and J.B. Steele (1992). *America: What Went Wrong?* Kansas City, MO: Andrews and McMeel.

Barlow, D.E. and M.H. Barlow (1995). "Federal Criminal Justice Legislation and the Post-World War II Social Structure of Accumulation in the United States." *Crime, Law and Social Change* 22:239-267.

—— M.H. Barlow and T. Chiricos (1995a). "Economic Conditions and Ideologies of Crime in the Media: A Content Analysis of Crime News." *Crime & Delinquency* 41(1):3-19.

—— M.H. Barlow and T. Chiricos (1995b). "Mobilizing Support for Social Control in a Declining Economy: Exploring Ideologies of Crime within Crime News." *Crime & Delinquency* 41(1):191-204.

—— M.H. Barlow and W. Johnson (1996). "The Political Economy of Criminal Justice Policy: A Time Series Analysis of Economic Conditions, Crime and Federal Criminal Justice Legislation, 1948-1987." *Justice Quarterly* 13(2):223-242.

Barnett, H. (1999). The land Ethic and Environmental Criminology. *Criminal Justice Policy Review* 10(2):161-192.

—— (1994). *Toxic Debts and the Superfund Dilemma.* Chapel Hill, NC: University of North Carolina Press.

—— (1981a). "Wealth, Crime and Capital Accumulation." In: D. Greenberg (ed.), *Crime and Capitalism.* Palo Alto, CA: Mayfield.

—— (1981b). "Corporate Capitalism, Corporate Crime." *Crime & Delinquency* 27:4-23.

Barnett, R.J. (1994). "Stateless Corporations." *The Nation* (December) 19:755.

—— and J. Cavanagh (1994). *Global Dreams: Imperial Corporations and the New World Order.* New York: Simon and Schuster.

—— and R.E. Mueller (1974). *Global Reach: The Power of Multinational Corporations.* New York: Simon and Schuster.

Baron, A. (ed.), (1991). *Work Engendered: Toward a New History of American Labor.* Ithaca, NY: Cornell University Press.

Beard, C. (1916). *An Economic Interpretation of the Constitution of the United States.* New York: MacMillan.

Becker, H. (1963). *The Outsiders.* New York: The Free Press.

Beirne, P. (2001). "Peter Singer's "Heavy Petting" and the Politics of Animal Abuse." *Critical Criminology* 10,1: 43-55.

—— (1999). "For a Nonspeciesist Criminology: Animal Abuse as an Object of Study." *Criminology* 37: 117-148.

—— (1997). " Rethinking Beastiality: Towards a Concept of Interspecies Sexual Assault." *Theoretical Criminology* 1,3: 317-340

—— (1993). *Inventing Criminology.* Albany, NY: State University of New York Press.

—— (1987a). "Adolphe Quetelet and the Origins of Positivist Criminology." *American Journal of Sociology* 92:1140-1169.

—— (1987b). "Between Classicism and Positivism: Crime and Penalty in the Writings of Gabriel Tarde." *Criminology* 25:785-819.

—— (1982). "Marxist Theories of Law: An Introduction." In: P. Beirne and R. Quinney (eds.), *Marxism and the Law.* New York: Wiley.

—— (1979). "Empiricism and the Critique of Marxism on Law and Crime." *Social Problems* 26:373-385.

—— and J.Messerschmidt (2005). *Criminology.* Los Angeles: Roxbury Publishing Co.

Belknap, M.R. (1977). "The Mechanics of Repression: J. Edgar Hoover, The Bureau of Investigation and the Radicals, 1917-1925." *Crime and Social Justice* 7:49-58.

Bell, D. (1973). "Racism in American Courts." *California Law Review* 61:165-204.

Bellah, R.N., R.A. Banes and P.J. Brewer (eds.), (1987). *Individualism and Commitment in American Life.* New York, NY : Perennial Library.

Bellinger, D. (1996). "Learning and Behavioral Sequele of Lead Poisoning." In: S. M. Pueschel, J.G. Linakis, and A.C. Anderson (eds.), *Lead Poisoning in Childhood*. Baltimore: Paul H. Brookes.

Bendix, R. (1973). "Inequality and Social Justice: A Comparison of Marx and Weber." *American Sociological Review* 39:149-161.

Benedetto, R. (2003). "Poll: Support for U.S. Handling of Iraq War Drops." *The Washington Post*, November 11, p. A1.

Benhabib, S. (1996). *Democracy and Difference*. Princeton, NJ: Princeton University Press.

Bennett, W.J., J. DiIulio and J. Walters (1996). *Body Count: Moral Poverty — And How to Win America's War Against Crime and Drugs*. New York: Simon & Schuster.

Bennice, J. A. and P. Ressick (2003). "Marital Rape." *Violence & Abuse*, 4(3):228-237.

Bentham, J. ([1838]1995). *The Panopticon Writings*. M. Bozovic (ed.) New York: Verso.

Benton, Ted (1998). "Rights and Justice on a Shared Planet: More Rights or New Relations." *Theoretical Criminology* 2(2):149-175.

Bernard, T. (1987). "Testing Structural Strain Theories." *Journal of Research in Crime and Delinquency* 24(4):262-280.

—— (1983). *The Consensus-Conflict Debate*. New York: Columbia University Press.

—— (1981). "The Distinction between Conflict and Radical Criminology." *Journal of Criminal Law and Criminology*. 72(1):362-379.

Bernstein, R. (1998). "James Q. Wilson: Fertile Thinker, Friend of Facts." *New York Times*, August 22.

Best, J. (1995). *Images of Issues: Typifying Contemporary Social Problems*. New York: Aldine.

Bhabha, H.K. (1992). "A Good Judge of Character: Men, Metaphors and the Common Culture." In: T. Morrison (ed.), *Race-ing Justice, En-Gendering Power*. New York: Pantheon.

Binford, S. (1976). "Apes and Original Sin." *Annual Editions: Readings in Anthropology*, 75/76. Guilford, CT: Duskin.

Bishop, C. (1931). *Women and Crime*. London, UK: Chatto and Windus.

Bishop, D. and C. Frazier (1988). "The Influence of Race in Juvenile Justice Processing." *Journal of Research in Crime and Delinquency* 25(3):242-263.

Black, D. (1976). *The Behavior of Law*. New York: Academic Press.

Blake, W.J. (1939). *Elements of Marxian Economic Theory and its Criticism*. New York: Cordon.

Blau, P. and J. Blau (1982). "The Cost of Inequality: Metropolitan Structure and Violent Crime." *American Sociological Review* 47:114-129.

Blix, H. (2004). *Disarming Iraq*. New York: Pantheon Books.

Block, A., and T. Bernard (1988). "Crime in the Waste Oil Industry." *Deviant Behavior* 9:113-129.

—— and F. Scarpitti (1985). *Poisoning for Profit.* New York: William Morrow.

Block, F.L. (1977). *The Origins of International Economic Disorder.* Berkeley, CA: University of California Press.

Bluestone, B. (1995). "The Inequality Express." *The American Prospect* 20:81-93.

—— and B. Harrison (1982). *The Deindustrialization of America: Plant Closings, Community Abandonment, and the Dismantling of Basic Industry.* New York: Basic Books.

Blum-West, S. and T.J. Carter (1983). "Bringing White Collar Crime Back In: An Examination of Crimes and Torts." *Social Problems* 30:545-554.

Blumer, H. (1969). *Symbolic Interactionism: Perspective and Method.* Englewood Cliffs, NJ: Prentice-Hall.

Blumstein, A., J. Wallman, and D.Farrington (2000). *The Crime Drop in America.* New York: Cambridge University Press.

Bohm, R. (1987). "Comment on Traditional as Radical Criminology by Groves and Sampson." *Journal of Research in Crime and Delinquency* 24(4):324-331.

—— (1985). "Beyond Unemployment: Toward a Radical Solution to the Crime Problem." *Crime and Social Justice* 21-22:213-222.

—— (1982a). "Capitalism, Socialism and Crime." In: H. Pepinsky (ed.), *Rethinking Criminology.* Beverly Hills, CA: Sage.

—— (1982b). "Radical Criminology: An Explication." *Criminology* 19(4):565-589.

Bonger, W. ([1916]1969). *Criminality and Economic Conditions.* Boston, MA: Little, Brown.

Bonsignore, J.J., E. Katsh, P.D. Errico, R.M. Pipkin, S. Arons and J. Rifkin (1984). *Before the Law.* Dallas, TX: Houghton-Mifflin.

Bottomore, T. et al.(eds.), (1983). *A Dictionary of Marxist Thought.* London, UK: Oxford.

Bourgois, P. (1996). *In Search of Respect: Selling Crack in El Barrio.* Cambridge, UK: Cambridge University Press.

Bowles, S. (1986). *Democracy and Capitalism: Property, Community, and the Contradictions of Modern Social Thought.* New York: Basic Books.

—— and H. Gintis (1976). *Schooling in Capitalist America.* New York: Basic Books.

—— D.M. Gordon and T.E. Weisskopf (1990). *After the Wasteland: A Democratic Economics for the Year 2000.* Armonk, NY: M.E. Sharpe, Inc.

Box, S. (1987). *Recession, Crime and Punishment.* Totowa, NJ: Barnes and Noble.

—— (1984). *Power, Crime and Mystification.* London, UK: Tavistock.

—— (1981). *Deviance, Reality and Society.* New York: Holt, Rinehart and Winston.

—— and C. Hale (1983a). "Liberation and Female Criminality in England and Wales Revisited." *British Journal of Criminology* 22:35-49.

—— and C. Hale (1983b). "Liberation or Economic Marginalization? The Relationship of Two Theoretical Arguments to Female Crime Patterns in England and Wales, 1951-1980." *Criminology* 22(4):473-497.

—— and C. Hale (1982). "Economic Crisis and the Rising Prisoner Population in England and Wales." *Crime and Social Justice* 17:20-35.

Boyle, F. (1985). "International Lawlessness in the Caribbean Basin." *Crime and Social Justice* 21-22:37-57.

Bradburn, N.M. and B. Calpovitz (1965). *Reports on Happiness*. Chicago, IL: Adline.

Brady, J.P. (1977). "Political Contradictions and Justice Policy in People's China." *Contemporary Crises* 1:127-162.

—— (1974). "Revolutionary Justice in Cuba and China." *Crime and Social Justice* 1:71-75.

Braithwaite, J. (1989). *Crime, Shame and Reintegration*. New York: Cambridge University Press.

—— (1984). *Corporate Crime in the Pharmaceutical Industry*. Boston, MA: Routledge and Keegan Paul.

—— and K. Daly (1994). "Masculinities, Violence and Communtiy Control." In: T. Newborn and E. Stanko (eds.), *Just Doing Business?* New York: Routledge.

Braverman, H. (1974). *Labor and Monopoly Capitalism: The Degradation of Work in the Twentieth Century*. New York: Modern Reader.

Brewer, R.M. (1993). "Theorizing Race, Class and Gender." In: S.E. James and A.P.A. Busia (eds.), *Theorizing Black Feminism*. New York: Routledge.

—— (1989). "Black Women and Feminist Sociology: The Emerging Perspective." *The American Sociologist* 20(1):57-70.

Broder, P. (1974). *Expendible Americans*. New York: Viking Adult.

Brown, M. (1980). *Laying Waste: The Poisoning of America by Toxic Chemicals*. New York: Pantheon.

Brownmiller, S. (1975). *Against Our Will: Men, Women and Rape*. New York: Bantam.

Brownstein, H. (1996). *The Rise and Fall of a Violent Crime Wave : Crack Cocaine and the Social Construction of a Crime Problem*. Monsey, NY: Criminal Justice Press.

—— (1990). "The Media and the Construction of Random Drug Violence." *Social Justice* 18:85-102.

Buffalo, M.A. and J. Rogers (1971). "Behavioral Norms, Moral Norms and Attachment: Problems of Deviance and Conformity." *Social Problems* 19:101-113.

Bullock, H.A. (1967). "The Significance of the Racial Factor in the Length of Sentencing." *Journal of Criminal Law and Criminology* 52:411-417.

Burbach, R., O. Núñez, and B. Kagarlitsky (1997). *Globalization and its Discontents: The Rise of Postmodern Socialism*. Chicago, IL: Pluto Press.

Burke, P. and A. Turk (1975). " Factors Affecting Post-Arrest Disposition." *Social Problems* 22:213-223.

Burnham, M.A. (1992). "The Supreme Court Appointment Process and the Politics of Race and Sex." In: T. Morrison (ed.), *Race-ing Justice, En-Gendering Power*. New York: Pantheon.

Burns, H. (1973). "Black People and the Tyranny of American Law." *Annals of the American Academy of Political and Social Science* 407:156-166.

Burns, R. (1999). "Realities of Automotive Safety." *Transportation Quarterly* 53(1):83-92.

—— (1997). "Denying Harm: The Social Construction of Harm in the Automobile Industry." Unpublished doctoral dissertation. Florida State University, Tallahassee, FL.

—— and M. J. Lynch (2004). *Environmental Crime: A Sourcebook*. New York: LFB Scholarly Publishers.

—— and M. J. Lynch (2003). "A Space for Safety: The Transformation of Automobile Safety Advertising in Response to NHTSA Crash Test Implementation, 1977 and 1981. *The Social Science Journal*. 40(4):635-641.

—— and M. J. Lynch (2002). "Another Fine Mess… A Preliminary Examination of the use of Fine by the National Highway Traffic Safety Administration." *Criminal Justice Review* 27(1):1-25.

Bursik, R. (1988). "Social Disorganization and Theories of Crime and Delinquency." *Criminology* 26:519-551.

—— (1984). "Urban Dynamics and Ecological Studies of Delinquency." *Social Forces* 63:393-413.

Butts, J. A. (2000). *Youth Crime Drop*. Washington, DC: Urban Institute, Justice Policy Center.

Cain, M. (1990). "Towards Transgression: New Directions in Feminist Criminology." *International Journal of the Sociology of Law* 18:1-18.

—— and A. Hunt (1979). *Marx and Engels on Law*. New York: Academic Press.

Calavita, K. (1993a). " Worker Safety, Law and Social Change: The Italian Case." In: W. Chambliss and M. Zata (eds.), *Making Law*. Bloomington, IN: Indiana University Press.

—— (1993b). "The Contradictions of Immigration Lawmaking: The Immigration Reform and Control Act of 1986." In: W. Chambliss and M. Zata (eds.), *Making Law*. Bloomington, IN: Indiana University Press.

—— H.N. Pontell, and R.H. Tillman (1999). *Big Money Crime: Fraud and Politics in the Savings and Loan Crisis*. Berkeley: University of California Press.

Campbell, C.J. (2003). *The Coming Oil Crisis*. Multi-Science Publishing Company & Petroconsultants S.A.

—— (1998). "Running out of Gas: This Time the Wolf is Coming." *The National Interest* 51:47-55.

—— and Jean Laherrere (1998). "The End of Cheap Oil?" *Scientific American*, March (http://dieoff.org/page140.htm).

Cardarelli, A.P. and S.C. Hicks (1993). "Radicalism in Law and Criminology: A Retrospective View of Critical Legal Studies and Radical Criminology." *Journal of Criminal Law and Criminology* 84(3):502-553.

Caringella-MacDonald, S. (1990). "State Crisis and the Crackdown on Crime Under Reagan." *Contemporary Crises* 4:91-118.

—— (1988). "Marxist and Feminist Interpretations of the Aftermath of Rape Reforms." *Contemporary Criminology* 30(2):261-291.

Carlen, P. (1990). "Women, Crime, Feminism and Realism." *Social Justice* 17:106-123.

—— and M. Collison (1980). *Radical Issues in Criminology.* London, UK: Oxford.

Carlson, D. and M. Appel (1998). *Power, Knowledge, Pedagogy: The Meaning of Democratic Education in Unsettling Times.* Boulder, CO: Westview Press.

Carlson, S. and R. Michalowski (1997). "Crime, Unemployment and Social Structures of Accumulation." *Justice Quarterly* 14:209-241.

Carmichael, S. and C.V. Hamilton (1967). *Black Power: The Politics of Liberation in America.* New York: Random House.

Carnoy, M.D. (1994). *Faded Dreams: The Politics and Economics of Race in America.* Cambridge, UK: Cambridge University Press.

Carroll, L. and M.E. Mondrick (1976). "Racial Bias in the Decision to Grant Parole." *Law and Society Review* 11(1):93-107.

Cassell, J. (1977). *A Group Called Women: Sisterhood and Symbolism in the Feminist Movement.* New York: David McKay.

Cassese, A. (2003). *International Criminal Law.* Oxford: Oxford University Press

Carter, T. and D. Clelland (1979). "A Neo-Marxist Critique, Formulation and Test of Juvenile Dispositions as a Function of Social Class." *Social Problems* 27:96-108.

Castles, S. and M. J. Miller (2003). *The Age of Migration, International Population Movements in the Modern World.* Guilford, NC: The Guilford Press.

Caufield, S. and N. Wonder (1994). "Gender and Justice: Feminist Contributions to Criminology." In: G. Barak (ed.), *Varieties of Criminology.* Westport, CT: Praeger.

Caute, D. (1978). *The Great Fear: The Anti-Communist Purge Under Truman and Eisenhower.* New York: Simon and Schuster.

Chamlin, M.B. (1990). "Determinants of Police Expenditures in Chicago, 1904-1958." *Sociological Quarterly* 31:485-494.

Chambliss, W.J. (1999). *Power, Politics and Crime.* Boulder, CO: Westview Press

—— (1995a). "Another Lost War: The Cost and Consequences of the War on Drugs." *Social Justice* 22(2):101-109.

—— (1995b). "Crime Control and Ethnic Minorities." In: D. Hawkins (ed.), *Ethnicity, Race and Crime*. Albany, NY: State University of New York Press.

—— (1994). "Policing the Ghetto Underclass: The Politics of Law and Law Enforcement." *Social Problems* 41:177-194.

—— (1993a). "Criminal Law and Crime Control in Britain and America." In: W. Chambliss and M. Zata (eds.), *Making Law*. Bloomington, IN: Indiana University Press.

—— (1993b). "The Political Economy of Opium and Heroin." In: W. Chambliss and M. Zata (eds.), *Making Law*. Bloomington, IN: Indiana University Press.

—— (1993c). "On Lawmaking." In: W. Chambliss and M. Zata (eds.), *Making Law*. Bloomington, IN: Indiana University Press.

—— (1984). "White-Collar Crime and Criminology." *Contemporary Sociology* 13:160-162.

—— (1976a). "Functional and Conflict Theories of Crime." In: W. Chambliss and M. Mankoff (eds.), *Whose Law? What Order?* New York: Wiley.

—— (1976b). "The State and Criminal Law." In: W. Chambliss and M. Mankoff (eds.), *Whose Law? What Order?* New York: Wiley.

—— (1975). "Toward a Political Economy of Crime." *Theory and Society* 2(2):149-170.

—— (1974). "The State, Law and the Definition of Behaviors as Criminal or Delinquent." In: D. Glaser (ed.), *Handbook of Criminology*. Chicago, IL: Rand McNally.

—— (1969). *Crime and the Legal Process*. New York: McGraw-Hill.

—— (1964). "A Sociological Analysis of the Law of Vagrancy." *Social Problems* 12:67-77.

—— and M. Mankoff (eds.), (1976). *Whose Law? What Order?* New York: Wiley.

—— and R. Seidman (1982). *Law, Order and Power*. Reading, MA: Addison-Wesley.

—— and M. Zata (eds.), (1993). *Making Law*. Bloomington, IN: Indiana University Press.

Changnon, N. (1977). *The Yanomano: The Fierce People*. New York: Holt, Rinehart and Winston.

Chancer, L. (1998). *Reconcilable Differences: Confronting Beauty, Pornography, and the Future of Feminism*. Berkley, CA: University of California Press.

Chasin, B.H. (1997). *Inequality and Violence in the United States: Casualties of Capitalism*. Atlantic Highlands, NJ: Humanities Press.

Chesney-Lind, M. (1996). "Sentencing Women to Prison: Equality without Justice." In: M. Schwartz and D. Milovanovic (eds.), *Gender, Race and Class in Criminology*. Hamden, CT: Garland.

—— (1989). "Girl's Crime and Woman's Place: Toward a Feminist Model of Female Delinquency." *Crime & Delinquency* 35(1):5-29.

—— and R. Shelden (1992). *Girls, Delinquency and Juvenile Justice*. Pacific Grove, CA: Brooks-Cole.

Chiricos, T.G. (1996). "Moral Panic as Ideology: Drugs, Violence, Race and Punishment in America." In: M.J. Lynch and E.B. Patterson (eds.), *Justice with Prejudice*. Albany, NY: Harrow and Heston.

—— (1987). "Rates of Crime and Unemployment: An Analysis of Aggregate Research Evidence." *Social Problems* 34(2):187-212.

—— and W.D. Bales (1991). "Unemployment and Punishment: An Empirical Assessment." *Criminology* 29(4):701-724.

—— and M.A. DeLone (1992). "Labor Surplus and Punishment: A Review and Assessment of Theory and Evidence." *Social Problems* 39:421-446.

Chodorow, N. (1978). *The Reproduction of Mothering: Psychoanalysis and the Sociology of Gender*. Berkeley, CA: University of California Press.

Chomsky, N. (1987). "International Terrorism: Image and Reality." *Crime and Social Justice* 27-28:172-200.

Christianson, S. (1984). "Our Black Prisons." In: D. Georges-Abeyie (ed.), *The Criminal Justice System and Blacks*. New York: Clark Boardman.

—— (1981). "The American Experience of Imprisonment, 1607-1776." Doctoral dissertation, School of Criminal Justice, State University of New York at Albany, Albany, NY.

Christie, N. (1994). *Crime Control as Industry*. London, UK: Routledge.

Christainson, J., J. Schmidt and J. Henderson (1982). "The Selling of the Police: Media, Ideology and Crime Control." *Contemporary Crises* 6(2):227-239.

Cirincione, J., J. T. Mathews, G. Perkovich, and A. Orton (2004). *WMD in Iraq: Evidence and Implications*. Washington, DC: Carnegie Endowment for International Peace.

Clarke, R.A. (2004). *Against all Enemies: Inside America's War on Terror*. New York: Free Press.

Clear, T. (1994). *Harm in American Penology*. Albany, NY: State University of New York Press.

Cleaver, E. (1968). *Soul on Ice*. New York: Delta.

Clinard, M.B. and R. Quinney (1973). *Criminal Behavior Systems*. New York: Holt, Rinehart and Winston.

—— and P.C Yeager (1978). "Corporate Crime: Issues in Research." *Criminology* 16:255-262.

Cloke, K. (1971). "The Economic Basis of Law and the State." In: R. Lefcourt (ed.), *Against the People*. New York: Vintage.

Cloward, R. and L. Ohlin (1960). *Delinquency and Opportunity*. New York: Free Press.

Cochran, J., M. Chamblin and M. Seth (1994). "Deterrence or Brutalization? An Impact Assessment of Oklahoma's Return to Capital Punishment." *Criminology* 32(1):107-134.

Cohen, A. (1955). *Delinquent Boys: The Culture of the Gang*. New York: Free Press.

Cohen, L. and M. Felson (1979). "Social Change and Crime Rate Trends: A Routine Activities Approach." *American Sociological Review* 44:588-608.

Cohen, S. (2003). *The Wrong Men: America's Epidemic of Wrongful Death Row Convictions*. London: Carroll & Graf Publishers.

—— (1979). "Guilt, Justice and Tolerance: Some Old Concepts for a New Criminology." In: D. Downes and P. Rock (eds.), *Deviance and Social Control*. London, UK: Martin Robertson.

—— (1972). *Folk Devils and Moral Panics: The Creation of the Mods and Rockers*. Oxford, UK: Blackwell.

—— and J. Young (eds.), (1973). *The Manufacture of News*. Beverly Hills, CA: Sage.

Colborn, T., D. Dumanoski, and J. P. Myers (1997). *Our Stolen Future: Are we Threatening our Fertility, Intelligence and Survival?* New York : Penguin Books.

Coleman, W.J. (1989). *The Criminal Elite*. New York: St. Martin's Press.

Collins, H. (1982). *Marxism and Law*. Oxford, UK: Clarendon.

Colman, R. A. and C. S. Widom (2004) "Childhood Abuse And Neglect And Adult Intimate Relationships." *Child* Abuse *& Neglect* 28-11: 1133-1142.

Colvin, M. and J. Pauly (1983). "A Critique of Criminology: Toward an Integrated Structural-Marxist Theory of Delinquency Production." *American Journal of Sociology* 90(3):513-551.

Commons, J. (1957). *Legal Foundations of Capitalism*. Madison, WI: University of Wisconsin Press.

Conklin, J. (1977). *Illegal but not Criminal: Business Crime in America*. Englewood Cliffs, NJ: Prentice Hall.

Connell, R.W. (1995). *Masculinities*. Berkeley, CA: University of California Press.

—— (1991). "Live Fast and Die Young: The Construction of Masculinity among Working Class Men on the Margin of the Labour Market." *Australian and New Zealand Journal of Sociology* 27(2):141-171.

—— (1989). "Cool Guys, Swats, and Wimps: The Interplay of Masculinity and Education." *Oxford Review of Education* 15(3):291-303.

—— (1987). *Gender and Power*. Stanford, CA: Stanford University Press.

Coontz, S. (1994/2000). *The Way We Never Were*. New York: Basic Books.

Cooper, A. (1987). *U.S. and Canadian Business in South Africa*. Washington, DC: Investor Responsibility Research Center.

Corn, D. (2003). *The Lies Of George W. Bush: Mastering the Politics of Deception.* New York: Crown Publishers.

Cornforth, M. (1977). *Historical Materialism.* New York: International.

Coser, L. (1956). *The Functions of Social Conflict.* Glencoe, IL: Free Press.

Cox, H. (1999). "The Free Market: America's New Religion." *Atlantic Monthly* March:82-83.

Crawford, A., T. Jones, T. Woodhouse and J. Young (1990). *Second Inslington Crime Survey.* London, UK: Middlesex Polytechnic Centre for Criminology.

Crenshaw, K. (1992). "Whose Story It Is Anyway? Feminist and Antiracist Appropriations of Anita Hill." In: T. Morrison (ed.), *Race-ing Justice, En-Gendering Power.* New York: Pantheon.

Crites, L.L. and W. Hepperle (1987). *Women, the Courts and Equality.* Beverly Hills, CA: Sage.

Crockett, G.W. (1971). "Racism in Courts." *Journal of Public Law* 20(2):385-402.

—— (1969). "Racism in Law." *Science and Society* 33(2):3-30.

Crowe, T. (2000). *Crime Prevention Through Environmental Design* (2nd ed.). London: Butterworth-Heinemann.

Cullen, F. and J. Woziak (1982). "Fighting the Appeal of Repression." *Crime and Social Justice* 18:23-33.

—— W. Maakestad and G. Cavander (1987). *Corporate Crime Under Attack.* Cincinnati, OH: Anderson.

—— W. Maakestad and G. Cavander (1984). "The Ford Pinto Case and Beyond." In: E. Hochstedler (ed.), *Corporations as Criminals.* Beverly Hills, CA: Sage.

Currie, E. (1996). "Missing Pieces: Notes on Crime, Poverty and Social Policy." *Critical Criminology* 7(1):37-52.

—— (1985). *Confronting Crime.* New York: Pantheon.

—— and J. Skolnick (1984). *America's Problems.* Boston, MA: Little, Brown.

Curtis, L. (1985). *Violence, Race and Culture.* Lexington, MA: DC Health.

Dahrendorf, R. (1968). *Essays in the Theory of Society.* Stanford, CA: Stanford University Press.

—— (1959). *Class and Class Conflict in Industrial Society.* Stanford, CA: Stanford University Press.

Daly, K. (1994a). "Class-Race-Gender: Sloganeering in Search of Meaning." *Social Justice* 22:56-71.

—— (1994b). *Gender, Crime and Punishment.* Princeton, NJ: Yale University Press.

—— (1989). "Gender and Varieties of White Collar Crime." *Criminology* 27:769-793.

—— and M. Chesney-Lind (1988). "Feminism and Criminology." *Justice Quarterly* 5(4):497-538.

—— and L. Maher (1998). *Criminology at the Crossroads: Feminist Readings in Crime and Justice.* New York: Oxford University Press.

—— and M. Tonry (1998). "Gender, Race and Sentencing." *Crime and Social Justice* 22(2):201-252.

—— and M. Tonry (1997). "Gender, Race and Sentencing." In M. Tonry (eds.), *Crime and Justice: A Review of Research*, vol. 27. Chicago, IL: University of Chicago Press.

Danner, M. (1996). "Gender Inequality and Criminalization: A Socialist Feminist Perspective on the Legal Control of Women." In: M. Schwartz and D. Milovanovic (eds.), *Gender, Race and Class in Criminology*. Hamden, CT: Garland.

—— (1991). "Socialist Feminism: A Brief Introduction." In: B. MacLean and D. Milovanovic (eds.), *New Directions in Critical Criminology*. Vancouver, CAN: Collective Press.

Davis, D. (2002). *When Smoke Ran Like Rain: Tales of Environmental Deception and the Battle Against Pollution.* New York: Basic Books.

Davis, M. (1990). *City of Quartz: Excavating the Future in Los Angeles.* London, UK: Verso.

—— (1986). *Prisoners of the American Dream: Politics and Economy in the History of the U.S. Working Class.* London, UK: Verso.

Dawley, A. (1975). *Crime and Community: The Industrial Revolution in Lynn, Massachusetts.* Cambridge, MA: Harvard University Press.

de Beauvoir, S. (1952). *The Second Sex.* New York: Knopf.

Deffeyes, Kenneth S. (2001). *Hubbert's Peak: The Impending World Oil Shortage.* Princeton, NJ: Princeton University Press.

DeGeorge, R. and F. DeGeorge (1972). *The Structuralist from Marx to Levi-Strauss.* New York: Anchor.

DeKeseredy, W. (1996a). "The Left Realist Perspective on Race, Class and Gender." In: M. Schwartz and D. Milovanovic (eds.), *Gender, Race and Class in Criminology*. Hamden, CT: Garland.

—— (1996b). "The Canadian National Survey on Women Abuse in University/College Dating Relationships: Biofeminist Panic Transmission or Critical Inquiry?" *Canadian Journal of Criminology* 38(1):81-104.

—— and C. Goff (1992). "Corporate Violence Against Canadian Women." *The Journal of Human Justice* 4:55-70.

—— and R. Hinch (1991). *Women Abuse: Sociological Perspectives.* Lewiston, NY: Thompson Educational Publications.

—— and K. Kelly (1993). "The Incidence and Prevalence of Women Abuse in Canadian and University College Dating Relationships." *The Canadian Journal of Sociology.* 18:137-159.

—— and M. Schwartz (1996). *Contemporary Criminology.* Belmont, CA: Wadsworth.

—— and M. Schwartz (1991). "British Left Realism on the Abuse of Women." In: H. Pepinsky and R. Quinney (eds.), *Criminology as Peacemaking*. Bloomington, IN: Indiana University Press.

Denison, R.S. and D. McQuaire (1975). "Crime Control in Capitalist Society: A Reply to Quinney." *Issues in Criminology* 10:109-119.

Denno, D. (1990). *Biology and Violence from Birth to Adulthood*. NY: Cambridge University Press.

Dentan, R.K. (1968). *The Semai: A Nonviolent People of Malaya*. New York: Holt, Rinehart, and Winston.

D'Ericco, P. (1984a). "Law is Terror Put into Words." In: J. Bonsignore, E. Katsh, P. D'Ericco, R.M. Pipkin, S. Arons and J. Rifkin (eds.), *Before the Law*. Dallas, TX: Houghlin-Mifflin.

—— (1984b). "The Mask of Law." In: J. Bonsignore, E. Katsh, P. D'Ericco, R.M. Pipkin, S. Arons and J. Rifkin (eds.) *Before the Law*. Dallas, TX: Houghlin-Mifflin.

Derber, C. (1998). *Corporation Nation*. New York: St. Martins.

Dietrich, K.N., P.A. Succop, O.G. Berger and R.L.Bornschein (2001)."Early Exposure to Lead and Delinquency." *Neurotoxicology Teratology*. 6:511-18.

DiMaggio, P. (1982). "Cultural Capital and School Success." *American Sociological Review* 47:189-201.

—— and J. Mohr (1985). "Cultural Capital, Educational Attainment and Martial Selection." *American Journal of Sociology* 90:1231-1261.

Dobbs, L. (2004). *Exporting America: Why Corporate Greed Is Shipping American Jobs Overseas*. New York: Warner Business Books.

Dolan, E. (1977). *Basic Economics*. Hinsdale, IL: Dryden Press.

Domhoff, G.W. (1967). *Who Rules America?* Englewood Cliffs, NJ: Prentice-Hall.

Dorrien, G. (2004). *Imperial Designs: Neoconservatism and the New Pax Americana*. New York: Routledge.

Dowd, D.F. (1977). *The Twisted Dream: Capitalist Development in the United States Since 1776*. Cambridge, MA: Winthrop.

Dowie, M. (1979). "The Corporate Crime of the Century." *Mother Jones* Nov:23-25.

Dragulescu, A.A., and V.M. Yakovenko (2003). "Statistical Mechanics of Money, Income and Wealth: A Short Survey." *Modelling of Complex Systems, Seventh Granada Lectures, AIP Conference Proceeding*, pp. 180-183.

—— (2001a). "Exponential and Power-law Probability distributions of Wealth and Income in the United Kingdom and the United States." *Physica A* 299:213-221.

—— (2001b). "Evidence for the Exponential Distribution of Income in the USA." *The European Physics Journal B* 20:585-589.

—— (2000). "Statistical Mechanics of Money." *European Physics Journal B* 17:723-729.

Dreyfuss, R., and J. Vest (2004). "The Lie Factory," *Mother Jones*, Jan.-Feb.:34-41.

Drug Policy Foundation (1999). "Statement of Scott Ehlers, Senior Policy Analyst, Drug Policy Foundation Before Subcommittee on Criminal Justice, Drug Policy, and Human Resources Hearing on Drug Legalization, Criminalization, and Harm Reduction, June 16, 1999." Washington, DC: Drug Policy Foundation.

Du Bois, W.E.B. (1968). *The Autobiography of W. E. B. DuBois: A Soliloquy on Viewing My Life From the Last Decade of its First Century*. New York: International.

Durkheim, E. (1983). *Selected Writings of Emile Durkheim*. New York: Cambridge.

—— ([1897]1951). *Suicide: A Study in Sociology*. New York: The Free Press.

—— ([1895] 1938/1966). *The Rules of Sociological Method*. New York: The Free Press.

—— ([1893]1963/1968). *The Division of Labor in Society*. New York: The Free Press.

Dusky, L. (1996). *Still Unequal: The Shameful Truth about Women and Justice in America*. New York: Crown.

Edleman, M.J. (1971). *Politics as Symbolic Action*. Chicago, IL: Markham.

Edsall, T.B (1984). *The New Politics of Inequality*. New York: W.W. Norton.

Edwards, R. (1979). *Contested Terrain: The Transformation of the Workplace in the Twentieth Century*. New York: Anchor.

Eggen, D. (2004). "No Evidence Connecting Iraq to Al Qaeda, 9/11 Panel Says." *Washington Post*, June 16, p. A1.

Eherenreich, B. (1983). *Hearts of Men*. Garden City, NY: Anchor Press.

—— and J. Ehrenreich (1979). "The Professional-Managerial Class." In: P. Walker (ed.), *Between Labor and Capital*. Boston, MA: South End Press.

Eisendrath, C., and M. Goodman (2004). *Bush League Diplomacy: How The Neoconservatives Are Putting The World At Risk*. Amherst, NY: Prometheus Books.

Elliot, D. and D. Huizinga (1983). "Social Class and Delinquent Behavior in a National Youth Panel." *Criminology* 21(2):149-177.

Engels, F. (1983). "Crisis, Joint Stock Companies, and State Intervention." In: T. Bottomore and P. Goode (eds.), *Readings in Marxist Sociology*. Oxford, UK: Clarendon.

—— (1981). "Demoralization of the English Working Class." In: D. Greenberg (ed.), *Crime and Capitalism*. Palo Alto, CA: Mayfield.

—— ([1894]1978). *Anti-Duhring*. Moscow, SU: Progress.

—— ([1884]1968/1972). *The Origin of the Family, Private Property, and the State*. Moscow: Progress/New York: International.

—— ([1845]1973). *The Conditions of the Working Class in England*. Moscow, SU: Progress.

—— ([1844]1964). "Outlines of a Critique of Political Economy." In: D. Struik (ed.), *The Economic and Philosophic Manuscripts of 1844*. New York: International.

Ericson, R., P. Baranck and J. Chan (1991). *Visualizing Deviance*. Toronto, CAN: University of Toronto Press.

Erikson, K.T. (1966). *Wayward Puritans: A Study in the Sociology of Deviance*. New York: Wiley.

—— (1962). " Notes on the Sociology of Deviance." *Social Problems* 9:307-314.

Ermann, M.D. and W.H. Clements (1984). "The Interfaith Center on Corporate Responsibility and its Campaign Against Marketing Infant Formula in the Third World." *Social Problems* 32:185-196.

—— and R.J. Lundman (1982). *Corporate and Governmental Deviance*. New York: Oxford.

Estrich, S. (1988). *Real Rape*. Boston: Harvard University Press.

Etzioni, A. (1970). *Demonstration Democracy*. New York: Gordon and Breach.

Evans, P. (1979). *Dependent Development*. Princeton, NJ: Princeton University Press.

Everrest, L. (2004). *Oil, Power And Empire: Iraq and The U.S. Global Agenda*. Monroe, ME: Common Courage Press.

Ewen, S. (1988). *All Consuming Images: The Politics of Style in Contemporary Culture*. New York: Basic Books.

Fagin, D. and M. Lavelle (1996). *Toxic Deception*. Toronto, CAN: Birch Lane Press.

Fanon, F. ([1961]1968). *The Wretched of the Earth: The Handbook for the Black Revolution that is Changing the Shape of the World*. New York: Grove Press.

Farnworth, M., and P. Horan (1980). "Separate Justice: An Analysis of Race Differences in Court Processing." *Social Science Research* 9:381-399.

—— and M. Leiber (1989). "Strain Theory Revisited." *American Sociological Review* 54(2):263-274.

—— R.H.C. Teske and G. Thurman (1991). "Ethnic, Racial and Minority Disparity in Felony Court Processing." In: M.J. Lynch and E.B. Patterson (eds.), *Race and Criminal Justice*. Albany, NY: Harrow and Heston.

Farrell, R.A. and T.J. Morrione (1978). "Conforming to Deviance." In: R.A. Farrell and V. Swigert (eds.), *Social Deviance*. New York: J.B. Lippincott.

Farrell, R. and V. Swigert (1978a). "Prior Offense Record as a Self-Fulfilling Prophecy." *Law and Society Review* 12:437-453.

—— (1978b). "Theories Focusing on Societal Definitions." In: R.A. Farrell and V. Swigert (eds.), *Social Deviance*. New York: J.B. Lippincott.

Fawthrop, T. (2004). *Getting Away With Genocide: Cambodia's Long Struggle Against the Khmer Rouge*. London: Pluto Press.

Fenneman, E. and G. Leder (1990). *Mathematics and Gender*. New York: Teachers College Press.

Fergusen, N. (2004). *Colossus: The Price of America's Empire*. New York: Penguin Books.

Ferraro, K. (1989). "The Legal Response to Women Battering in the United States." In: J. Hanmer, J. Radford and E.A. Stanko (eds.), *Women, Policing and Male Violence*. New York: Routledge.

Ferrell, J. (1997). "Criminological Verstehen: Inside the Immediacy of Crime." *Justice Quarterly* 14(1):3-24.

—— (1996). *Crimes of Style: Urban Graffiti and the Politics of Criminality.* Boston, MA: Northeastern University Press.

—— (1995). "Urban Graffiti: Crime, Control and Resistance." *Youth and Society* 27:73-92.

—— (1992). "Making Sense of Crime." *Social Justice* 19:110-123.

—— and M. Hamm (1998). *Risky Research.* Boston, MA: Northeastern University Press.

—— and C. Sanders (eds.), (1996). *Cultural Criminology.* Boston, MA: Northeastern University Press.

—— and N.Websdale (eds.), (1999). *Making Trouble: Cultural Constructions of Crime, Deviance, and Control.* New York: Aldine.

Figart, D.M., and J. Lapidus (1998). "Will Comparative Worth Reduce Race-Based Wage Discrimination?" *The Review of Radical Political Economics* 30(3):14-24.

—— (1996). "The Impact of Comparable Worth on Earning Inequality." *Work and Occupations* 23(3):297-318.

Figueria-McDonough, J. (1984). "Feminism and Delinquency." *British Journal of Criminology* 24:325-342.

Fine, R. (1980). "The Birth of Bourgeois Punishment." *Crime and Social Justice* 14:19-26.

Firestone, S. (1971). *The Dialectics of Sex: the Case for Feminist Revolution.* New York: Bantam.

Fish, P. (2003). "Forecasters Tip Sunnier Times for US Ad Industry." http://www.smh.com.au/articles/ 1070732210668.html.

Fishman, M. and G. Cavender (eds.), (1998). *Entertaining Crime: Television Reality Programs.* New York: Aldine de Gruyter.

Fogel, D. (1979). *We Are the Living Proof the Justice Model for Corrections* (2nd ed.). Cincinnati: Anderson.

Fosdick, R. ([1920]1969). *American Police Systems.* Monclair, NJ: Patterson Smith.

Fox, J.A. (1978). *Forecasting Crime Data: An Econometric Analysis.* Lexington, MA: Lexington Books.

Fox, L. (2003). *Enron: The Rise and Fall.* New York: John Wiley.

Foucault, M. (1979). *Discipline and Punish.* New York: Vintage.

—— (1973). *The Birth of the Clinic.* New York: Vintage.

—— (1972). *The Archaeology of Knowledge.* New York: Pantheon.

—— (1970). *The Order of Things.* New York: Vintage.

—— (1965). *Madness and Civilization.* New York: Vintage.

Frank, A.G. (1975). *On Capitalist Underdevelopment*. New York: Oxford.

Frank, N. (1985). *Crimes Against Health and Safety*. Albany, NY: Harrow and Heston.

—— and M.J. Lynch (1992). *Corporate Crime, Corporate Violence: A Primer*. Albany, NY: Harrow and Heston.

Frank, R.H. and P.J. Cook (1995). *The Winner-Take-All Society: Why the Few at the Top Get So Much More than the Rest of Us*. New York: Penguin.

Frappier, J. (1985). "Above the Law: Violations of International Law by the U.S. Government from Truman to Reagan." *Crime and Social Justice* 21-22:1-36.

Fraser, S. (ed.), (1995). *The Bell Curve Wars: Race, Intelligence, and the Future of America*. New York: Basic Books, 1995.

Freeman, R. (1983). "Crime and Unemployment." In: J.Q. Wilson (ed.), *Crime and Public Policy*. San Francisco, CA: ICS Press.

French, M. (1992). *The War Against Women*. New York: Summit.

Freuchen, P. (1961). *Book of the Eskimos*. New York: Fawcett.

Freud, S. (1961). *Beyond the Pleasure Principle*. New York: Liveright.

Friedan, B. (1963). *The Feminine Mystique*. New York: Norton.

Friedman, M. (1962). *Capitalism and Freedom*. Chicago, IL: University of Chicago Press.

Friedrichs, D.O. (1996a). "White Collar Crime and the Class-Race-Gender Construct." In: M. Schwartz and D. Milovanovic (eds.), *Gender, Race and Class in Criminology*. Hamden, CT: Garland.

—— (1996b). *Trusted Criminals: White Collar Crime in Contemporary Society*. Belmont, CA: Wadsworth.

—— (1992). "White Collar Crime and the Definitional Quagmire: A Provisional Solution." *Journal of Human Justice* 3:5-21.

—— (1982). "Crime, Deviance and Criminal Justice: In Search of a Radical Humanistic Perspective." *Humanity and Society* 6(3):200-226.

—— (1980a). "Radical Criminology in the United States." In: J. Inciardi (ed.), *Radical Criminology: The Coming Crisis*. Beverly Hills, CA: Sage.

—— (1980b). "Carl Klockars vs. The 'Heavy Hitters.'" In: J. Inciardi (ed.), *Radical Criminology: The Coming Crisis*. Beverly Hills, CA: Sage.

Frum, D. and R. Perle.(2003). *An End to Evil: How to Win the War on Terror*. New York: Random House, 2003.

Fuller, L.L. (1964). *The Morality of Law*. New Haven, CT: Yale University Press.

Gagnon, V.P. (2004). *The Myth of Ethnic War: Serbia and Croatia in the 1990s*. Ithaca: NY: Cornell University Press.

Galeano, E. (1973). *The Open Veins of Latin America*. New York: Monthly Review Press.

Garfinkel, H. (1949). "Inter- and Intra-Racial Homicides." *Social Forces* 27:369-381.

Garofalo, J. (1978). "Radical Criminology and Criminal Justice: Points of Divergence and Contact." *Crime and Social Justice* 10:17-27.

Garreau, J. (1991). *Edge City: Life on the New Frontier.* New York: Doubleday.

Gelles, R. and M. Straus (1988). *Intimate Violence.* New York: Simon & Schuster.

Gellman, B. (2004) "Iraq's Arsenal Was Only On Paper." *Washington Post,* January 7, p. A01.

Georges-Abeyie, D. (1984). "The Criminal Justice System and Minorities." In: D. Georges-Abeyie (ed.), *The Criminal Justice System and Blacks.* New York: Clark Boardman.

Gerdes, L. (ed.), (1999). *Battered Women.* San Diego, CA: Greenhaven.

Gerth, H. and C.W. Mills (1964). *Character and Social Structure.* New York: Harcourt, Brace and World.

Gelsthorpe, L. (2002). "Feminism And Criminology." In: M. Maguire, R. Morgan and R. Reiner (eds.), *Oxford Handbook of Criminology.* New York: Oxford University Press.

Gibbs, J.T. (ed.), (1988). *Young, Black and Male in America.* New York: Auburn House.

Gibbs, L. (1995). *Dying from Dioxin.* Boston, MA: South End Press.

Gibson, J.W. (1994). *Warrior Dreams: Violence and Manhood in Post-Vietnam America.* New York: Hill and Wang.

—— (1989). "American Paramilitary Culture and the Reconstitution of the Vietnam War." In: G. Walsh and J. Aulich (eds.), *Vietnam Images.* London, UK: Macmillian Press.

Gilbert, D. and J. Kahl (1982). *The American Class Structure.* Homwood, IL: Dorsey.

Gillian, R. (1984). *Dialectic of Nihilism: Post-structuralism and Law.* New York: Basil Blackwell.

Gilligan, C. (1982). *In a Different Voice: Psychological Theory and Women's Development.* Cambridge, MA: Harvard University Press.

Gilman, E.A. (1995). "Childhood Cancers: Space-Time Distribution in Britain." *Journal of Epidemiology and Community Health* 49(2):158-163.

Gitlin, T. (1995). *The Twilight of Common Dreams: Why America is Wracked by Culture Wars.* New York: Metropolitan Books.

Genovese, E. (1967). *The Political Economy of Slavery.* New York: Vintage Books.

Gibson, M. (2002). *Born to Crime: Cesare Lombroso and the Origins of Biological Criminology.* Boston: Praeger Publishers.

Glantz, S., J. Slade, L.A. Bero, P. Hanauer and D.E. Barnes (1996). *The Cigarette Papers.* Berkeley, CA: University of California Press

Gleick, J. (1987). *Chaos: Making a New Science.* NY: Penguin.

Glueck, S. and E. Glueck (1935). *Five Hundred Delinquent Women.* New York: Knopf.

Gold, D., T.H. Lo and E.O. Wright (1975a). "Recent Developments in Marxist Theories of the Capitalist State, Part I." *Monthly Review* 27(5):29-43.

—— (1975b). "Recent Developments in Marxist Theories of the Capitalist State, Part II." *Monthly Review* 27(5):29-43.

Goldfarb, R. (1969). "Prisons: The Nation's Poorhouses." *The New Republic* (Nov):15-17.

Goldhagen, D. J. (1997). *Hitler's Willing Executioners: Ordinary Germans and the Holocaust* New York: Vintage Press, 1997.

Goodstein, D. (2004). *Out of Gas: The End of the Age of Oil.* New York: W.W. Norton.

Gordon, D.M. (1984). "Capitalist Development and the History of American Cities." In: W.K. Tabb and L. Sawers (eds.), *Marxism and the Metropolis: New Perspectives in Urban Political Economy.* New York: Oxford University Press.

—— (1980). "Stages of Accumulation and Long Economic Cycles." In: T.K. Hopkins and I. Wallerstein (eds.), *Processes of the World-System.* Beverly Hills, CA: Sage.

—— (1978). "Up and Down the Long Roller Coaster." In: Union for Radical Political Economics (eds.), *U.S. Capitalism in Crisis.* New York: Union for Radical Political Economics Press.

—— (1973). "Capitalism, Class and Crime in America." *Crime & Delinquency* 19:163-186.

—— (1971). "Class and the Economics of Crime." *The Review of Radical Political Economics* 3(3):51-72.

—— R. Edwards and M. Reich (1982). *Segmented Work, Divided Workers: The Historical Transformation of Labor in the United States.* New York: Cambridge University.

Göring, H. (1946). 1946 speech, quoted in J. Hillman (2004) *A Terrible Love of War.* New York: Penguin.

Gorz, A. (1979). *Ecology As Politics.* Boston: South End Press.

—— (1972). "Technical Intelligence and the Capitalist Division of Labor." *Telos* 12:27-38.

Gottfredson, M. and T. Hirschi (1990). *A General Theory of Crime.* Stanford, CA: Stanford University Press.

Gourevitch, P. (1999). *We Wish to Inform You That Tomorrow We Will be Killed With Our Families: Stories from Rwanda.* New York: Picador.

Graham, D. J., D. Campen, R. Hui, M. Spence, C. Cheetham, G. Levy, S. Shoor, and W.A Ray (2005). "Risk of Acute Myocardial Infarction and Sudden Cardiac Death in Patients Treated with Cyclo-oxygenase 2 Selective and Non-selective Non-steroidal Anti-inflammatory Drugs: Nested Case-control Study." *Lancet* 365, 945: 475-481.

Gramsci, A. (1971). *Selections from Prison Notebooks.* New York: International Publishers.

Green, L. (1996). *Policing Places with Drug Problems.* Thousand Oaks, CA: Sage.

Green, M. (1978). *The Other Government*. New York: W.W. Norton.

—— and J.F. Berry (1985). "White Collar Crime is BIG Business." *The Nation* 240:689-795.

Greenberg, D.F. (1995). "Contemporary Criminological Theory and Historical Data: The Sex Ratio of London Crime." In: F. Adler and W. Laufer (eds.), *Advances in Criminological Theory*. New Brunswick, NJ: Transaction.

—— (1993a). "The Causes of Crime." In: D.F. Greenberg (ed.), *Crime and Capitalism*. Philadelphia, PA: Temple University Press.

—— (1993b). "Marx and Engels on Crime and Punishment." In: D.F. Greenberg (ed.), *Crime and Capitalism*. Philadelphia, PA: Temple University Press.

—— (1985). "Age, Crime and Social Structure." *American Journal of Sociology* 91(1):1-21.

—— (1983a). "Donald Black's Sociology of Law: A Critique." *Law and Society Review* 17(2):337-27.

—— (1983b). "Reflections on the Justice Model Debate." *Contemporary Crises* 7(4):313-327.

—— (1983c). "Crime and Age." In: S.H. Kadish (ed.), *Encyclopedia of Crime and Justice*, vol. 1. New York: MacMillian.

—— (1981). *Crime and Capitalism*. Palo Alto, CA: Mayfield.

—— (1980). "Penal Sanctions in Poland: A Test of Alternative Models." *Social Problems* 28(2):194-204.

—— (1977a). "The Dynamics of Oscillatory Punishment Processes." *Journal of Criminal Law and Criminology* 68(4):643-651.

—— (1977b). "Socio-Economic Status and Criminal Sentences: Is There an Association?" *American Sociological Review* 42:174-175.

—— (1977c). "Delinquency and the Age Structure of Society." *Contemporary Crises* 1:189-224.

—— (1975). "On One Dimensional Marxist Criminology." *Theory and Society* 3:610-621.

—— and D. Humphries (1982). "Economic Crisis and the Justice Model: A Skeptical View." *Crime & Delinquency* 28(4):601-609.

—— and D. Humphries (1980). "The Cooptation of Fixed Sentencing Reform." *Crime & Delinquency* 26:206-225.

—— and V. West (1998). "The Persistent Significance of Race: Growth in State Prison Populations 1971-1991." Unpublished paper, Department of Sociology, New York University, New York, NY.

Greenberg, K. and J. Dratel (eds.), (2005). *The Torture Papers: The Road to Abu Ghraib*. New York: Cambridge University Press.

Greenhouse, L. (1998). "Before High Court, Chicago Defends Approach to Gangs." *New York Times,* December 10, p.A3.

Greenhouse, S. (2005). "Labor Unions Enter Social Security Debate" March 17. *New York Times* (http://www.nytimes.com/2005/03/17/business/17labor).

Gregory, D. (1971). *No More Lies: The Myth and Reality of American History.* New York: Harper and Row.

Greider, W. (1997). *One World, Ready or Not: The Manic Logic of Global Capitalism.* New York: Simon & Schuster.

Groombridge, N. (1998). "Masculinities and Crimes Against the Environment." *Theoretical Criminology* 2(2):249-67.

Grose, G. and W.B. Groves (1988). "Crime and Human Nature: A Marxist Perspective." *Contemporary Crises* 12:145-171.

Groves, W.B. (1993a). "Criminology and Epistemology." In: G.R. Newman, M.J. Lynch and D. Galaty (eds.), *Discovering Criminology.* Albany, NY: Harrow and Heston.

—— (1993b). "Criminology and Ontology." In: G.R. Newman, M.J. Lynch and D. Galaty (eds.), *Discovering Criminology.* Albany, NY: Harrow and Heston.

—— (1985). "Marxism and Positivism." *Crime and Social Justice* 23:129-150.

—— (1981). "The Sociology of Structured Choice." Paper presented at the annual meeting of the American Society of Criminology. Washington, DC.

—— and C. Corrado (1983). "Culture as Metaphysics: An Appraisal of Cultural Models." *Crime and Social Justice* 20:99-120.

—— and N. Frank (1987). "Punishment, Privilege and the Sociology of Structured Choice." In: W.B. Groves and G.R. Newman (eds.), *Punishment and Privilege.* Albany, NY: Harrow and Heston.

—— and G.R. Newman (eds.), (1987). *Punishment and Privilege.* Albany, NY: Harrow and Heston.

—— and R.J. Sampson (1987a). "Traditional Contributions to Radical Criminology." *Journal of Research in Crime and Delinquency* 24(3):181-214.

—— and R. J. Sampson (1987b). "Removing Radical Blinders on the Study of Crime." *Journal of Research in Crime and Delinquency* 24(3):181-214.

—— and M.J. Lynch (1990). "Reconciling Structural and Subjective Approaches to the Study of Crime." *Journal of Research in Crime and Delinquency* 27(4):348-375.

Gruber, J. and P. Morgan (2004). *In the Company of Men: Male Dominance and Sexual Harassment.* Boston: Northeastern University Press.

Guevara, E. (1998). *Guerrilla Warfare* (reprint ed.). Lincoln, NE: University of Nebraska Press.

Gunder-Frank, A. (1971). *Capitalism and Undevelopment in Latin American.* London, UK: Penguin Books.

Gurber, J. and L. Bjorn (1987). "Blue Collar Blues: Sexual Harassment of Women Auto Workers." *Work and Occupation* 9(3):271-298.

Gurin, G., J. Veroff and S. Feld (1960). *Americans View Their Mental Health*. New York: Basic.

Gusfield, J. (1967). "Moral Passage: The Symbolic Process in Public Designations of Deviance." *Social Problems* 15:175-188.

Gutman, R. (1993). *A Witness to Genocide*. New York: Macmillan.

Guttman, H. (1977). *Work, Culture and Society in Industrial America*. New York: New View Points.

Habermas, J. (1989). *Structural Transformation of the Public Sphere: An Inquiry into a Category of Bourgeois Society*. Cambridge, MA: MIT Press.

—— (1979). *Communication and the Evolution of Society*. Boston, MA: Beacon.

—— (1975). *Legitimation Crisis*. Boston, MA: Beacon.

Hacker, A. (1995). *Two Nations☐ Black and White, Separate, Hostile, Unequal*. New York: Ballentine.

Hagan, F. (1997). *Political Crime: Ideology and Criminality*. Boston: Allyn and Bacon.

Hagan, J. (1994). *Crime and Disrepute*. Thousand Oaks, CA: Pine Forge Press.

—— (1993). "The Social Embeddedness of Crime and Unemployment." *Criminology* 31(4):465-491.

—— and A. Celesta (1982). "Race, Class and the Perception of Criminal Justice in America." *American Journal of Sociology* 88:329-255.

—— A.R. Gillis and J. Simpson (1987). "Class in the Household: A Power-Control Theory of Gender and Delinquency." *American Journal of Sociology* 92:788-818.

—— A.R. Gillis and J. Simpson (1985). "The Class Structure of Gender and Delinquency: Toward a Power-Control Theory of Common Delinquency Behavior." *American Journal of Sociology* 90(6):1151-1178.

—— A. R. Gillis and J. Simpson (1979). "The Sexual Stratification of Social Control: A Gender Based Perspective on Crime and Delinquency." *British Journal of Criminology* 30:25-38.

—— and J. Leon (1977). "Rediscovering Delinquency: Social History, Political Ideology and the Sociology of Law." *American Sociological Review* 42(4):457-598.

—— and P. Parker (1985). "White Collar Crime and Punishment: The Class Structure and Legal Sanctioning." *American Sociological Review* 50(3):302-316.

Halberstam, D. (1986). *The Reckoning*. New York: Morrow.

Hale, C. (1989). "Economy, Punishment and Imprisonment." *Contemporary Crises* 13:327-349.

Hall, J. (1952). *Theft, Law and Society*. Indianapolis, IN: Bobbs-Merrill.

Hall, S., C. Critcher, T. Jefferson, J. Clarke and B. Roberts (1978). *Policing the Crisis: Mugging, the State and Law and Order*. London, UK: MacMillan.

Hamilton, J.T. (2000). *Channeling Violence*. Princeton, NJ: Princeton University Press.

Hamilton, V. and H. Kelman (1990). *Crimes of Obedience : Toward a Social Psychology of Authority and Responsibility*. New Haven, CT: Yale University Press.

Hancock, C.L. and A.O. Simon (eds.), (1995). *Freedom, Virtue, and the Common Good*. Mishawaka, IN: American Maritain Association.

Hardt, M. and A. Negri (2004). *Multitude: War and Democracy in the Age of Empire*. New York: Penguin.

Harries, K. and D. Cheatwood (1997). *The Geography of Execution: The Capital Punishment Quagmire in America*. Lanham, MD: Rowman & Littlefield.

Harring, S. (1983). *Policing in a Class Society: The Experience of American Cities, 1865-1915*. New Brunswick, NJ: Rutgers University Press.

—— (1982). "The Police Institution as a Class Question: Milwaukee Socialists and Police, 1900-1915." *Science and Society* 46(2):197-221.

—— (1981). "Policing in a Class Society: The Expansion of the Urban Police in the Later Nineteenth and Early Twentieth Centuries." In: D.F. Greenberg (ed.), *Crime and Capitalism*. Palo Alto, CA: Mayfield.

—— (1977). "Class Conflict and the Suppression of Tramps in Buffalo, 1892-1894." *Law and Society Review* 11(5):873-912.

—— (1976). "The Development of the Police Institution." *Crime and Social Justice* 5:54-59.

—— and L. McMullin (1975). "The Buffalo Police, 1872-1900: Labor Unrest, Political Power and the Creation of the Police Institution." *Crime and Social Justice* 4:5-14.

—— A. Platt, R. Speigelman and P. Takagi (1977). "The Management of Police Killings." *Crime and Social Justice* 8:36-43.

Harrington, M. (1976). *The Twilight of Capitalism*. New York: Simon and Schuster.

Harris, M. (1986). *Cultural Materialism*. New York: Vintage.

—— (1978). *Cannibals and Kings: The Origins of Cultures*. New York: Vintage.

Harrison, P.M., and A. J. Beck (2003). *Prisoners in 2002*. Washington, DC: Bureau of Justice Statistics. (Bulletin series, NCJ # 200248.)

Hartjen, C. (1972). "Legalism and Humanism." *Issues in Criminology* 7(1):59-69.

Hartmann, H. (1981). *Women, Work and Wages: Equal Pay for Jobs of Equal Value*. Washington, DC: National Academy Press.

Hawkins, D.F. (1997). "Which Way Toward Equality? Dilemmas and Paradoxes in Public Policies Affecting Crime and Punishment." In: C. Herring (ed.), *African Americans and the Public Agenda*. Thousand Oaks, CA: Sage.

—— (ed.), (1995). *Ethnicity, Race, and Crime: Perspectives Across Time and Place.* Albany, NY: State University of New York Press.

Hasday, J. E. (2000). "Contest and Consent: A Legal History of Marital Rape." *California Law Review* 88,5: 1373-1407.

Heinberg, R. (2003). *The Party's Over: Oil, War and the Fate of Industrial Societies.* Gabriola Island, BC: New World Publishers.

Heitlinger, A. (1979). *Women and State Socialism: Sex Inequality in the Soviet Union and Czechoslovakia.* London, UK: Macmillan.

Helmer, J. (1975). *Drugs and Minority Oppression.* New York: Seabury Press.

Hemmens, C., K. Strom and E. Schlegel (1998). "Gender Bias in the Courts: A Review of Review of the Literature." *Sociological Imagination* 35(1):22-42.

Henenway, D., T. Shinoda-Tagawa, and M. Miller (2002). "Firearm Availability and Female Homicide Victimization Rates among 25 Populous High-Income Countries." *Journal of the Amereican Medical Women's Association* 57(2):100-04.

Henkin, L. (1995). *International Law: Politics and Values.* Dordrecht, The Netherlands: Martinus Nijhoff.

Hennessy, R. and C. Ingraham (1997). "Reclaiming Anti-Capitalist Feminism." In: R. Hennessy and C. Ingraham (eds.), *Materialist Feminism and the Policy of Discourse.* New York: Routledge.

Henry, F. (1982). "Capitalism, Accumulation, and Crime." *Crime and Social Justice* 18:78-87.

Henry, J. (1965). *Culture Against Man.* New York: Vintage.

Henry, S. and D. Milovanovic (1996*). Constitutive Criminology: Beyond Postmodernism.* Thousand Oaks, CA: Sage.

—— (1994). "The Construction of Constitutive Criminology." In: D. Nelken (ed.), *The Futures of Criminology.* London, UK: Sage.

—— (1991). "Constitutive Criminology: The Maturation of Critical Theory." *Criminology* 29:293-316.

Herbert, I. (1996). "The Coca-Cola Company." In: R. Ohmann, G. Averill, M. Curtin, D. Shumway and E.G. Traube (eds.), *Making and Selling Culture.* Hanover, NH: Wesleyan University Press.

Herman, E.S. (1987). "U.S. Sponsorship of International Terrorism." *Crime and Social Justice* 27-28:1-32.

—— (1982). *The Real Terror Network.* Boston, MA: South End Press.

Hernton, C. ([1965]1988). *Sex and Racism in America.* New York: Anchor Books.

Herrnstein, R., and C. Murray (1994). *The Bell Curve: Intelligence and Class Structure in American Life.* New York: Free Press.

Hersh, S. (2004). *Chain Of Command: The Road from 9-11 to Abu Ghraib.* New York: HarperCollins.

Hill, G.D. and M.P. Atkinson (1988). "Gender, Family Control and Delinquency." *Criminology* 26(1):127-147.

Hira, R. and A. Hira (2005). *Outsourcing America: What's Behind Our National Crisis And How We Can Reclaim American Jobs.* New York: Amacom.

Hiro, D. (2004.) *Secrets And Lies: Operation "Iraqi Freedom" And After.* New York: Nation Books.

Hirsch, J. (1995). "Nation-state, international regulation and the question of democracy." *Review of International Political Economy* 2, 2:267.

Hirschi, T. (1983). "Crime and the Family." In: J.Q. Wilson (ed.), *Crime and Public Policy.* San Francisco, CA: ICS Press.

—— (1969). *The Causes of Delinquency.* Berkeley, CA: University of California Press.

—— and M. Gottfredson (1989). "The Significance of White Collar Crime for a General Theory of Crime." *Criminology* 27(2):359-371.

—— (1988). "Toward a General Theory of Crime." In: W. Buikhuisen and S. Mednick (eds.), *Explaining Criminal Behavior.* New York: Brill.

Hirst, P.Q. (1979). *On Law and Ideology.* Atlantic Fields, NJ: Humanity Press.

—— (1977). "The Marxism of the New Criminology." *British Journal of Criminology* 13(4):396-398.

—— (1975). "Radical Deviancy Theory and Marxism." In: I. Taylor, P. Walton and J. Young, (eds.), *Critical Criminology.* Boston, MA: Routledge and Kegan Paul.

—— (1972). "Marx and Engels on Law, Crime and Morality." *Economics and Society* 1:28-56.

Hittinger, R. (1987). *A Critique of the New Natural Law Theory.* Notre Dame, IN: University of Notre Dame Press.

Hobbes, T. ([1651]1968). *Leviathan.* Baltimore, MD: Penguin.

Hobsbawm, E.J. (1981). *Bandits.* New York: Pantheon.

—— (1963). *Primitive Rebels, Studies in Archaic forms of Social Movement in the 19th and 20th Centuries.* New York: Praeger.

Hobson, J.A. (1906). *The Evolution of Modern Capitalism.* London, UK: The Walter Scott Publishing Company.

Hochstetler, A.L. and N. Shover (1997). "Street Crime, Labor Surplus, and Criminal Punishment, 1980-1990." *Social Problems* 44:358-368.

Hoebel, E.A. (1973). *The Law of Primitive Man.* New York: Oxford University Press.

Hogg, R. (1982). "Imprisonment and Society Under Early British Capitalism." In: A. Platt and P. Takagi (eds.), *Punishment and Penal Discipline.* San Francisco, CA: Crime and Social Justice Associates.

Hollinger, D.A. (2005) "The One Drop Rule & The One Hate Rule." *Daedalus* 134(1):18-29.

hooks, Bell (1992). *Black Looks: Race and Representation.* Boston, MA: South End Press.

Hopkins, A. (1981). "Class Bias in the Criminal Law." *Contemporary Crises* 5(4):385-402.

Houghton, J. T., Y. Ding, D.J. Griggs, M. Noguer, P.J. van der Linden, X. Dai, K. Maskell, C.A. Johnson (eds.), (2001). *Climate Change 2001: The Scientific Basis.* Contribution of Working Group I to the third assessment report of the Inter governmental Panel on Climate Change. New York: Cambridge University Press.

Huey, J. and M.J. Lynch (1996). "The Image of Black Women in Criminology: Historical Stereotypes as Theoretical Foundation." In: M.J. Lynch and E.B. Patterson (eds.), *Justice with Prejudice.* Albany, NY: Harrow and Heston.

Huff, R. (1980). "Conflict Theory in Criminology." In: J. Inciardi (ed.), *Radical Criminology: The Coming Crisis.* Beverly Hills, CA: Sage.

Huggins, M. (1987). "U.S. Supported State Terror: A History of Police Training in Latin America." *Crime and Social Justice* 27-28:149-171.

—— (1983). *From Slavery to Vagrancy in Brazil: Crime and Social Control in the Third World.* New Brunswick, NJ: Rutgers University Press.

Hughes, R. (1987). *The Fatal Shore.* New York: Knopf.

Hulse, C. (2005). "The President's Budget: The Overview." *New York Times*, February 9: p. A18.

Human Rights Watch (2004). "Stop the Use of Child Soldiers." http://www.hrw.org/campaigns/crp/index.htm

Humphries, D. and D.F. Greenberg (1981). "The Dialectics of Crime Control." In: D.F. Greenberg (ed.), *Crime and Capitalism.* Palo Alto, CA: Mayfield.

—— and D. Wallace (1980). "Capitalist Accumulation and Urban Crime: 1950-71." *Social Problems* 28(2):180-193.

Huston, J. L. (2003). *Calculating the Value of the Union: Slavery, Property Rights, and the Economic Origins of the Civil War.* Chapel Hill: University of North Carolina Press.

Ignatieff, M. (1994). *Blood and Belonging.* New York: Farrar, Strauss and Giroux.

—— (1978). *A Just Measure of Pain: The Penitentiary in the Industrial Revolution.* New York: Pantheon.

Inciardi, J. (ed.), (1980). *Radical Criminology: The Coming Crisis.* Beverly Hills, CA: Sage.

International Commission of Jurists (1997). "Administration of the Death Penalty in the United States." *Human Rights Quarterly* 19(1):165-213.

Irwin, J. (1985). *The Jail: Managing the Underclass in American Society.* Berkeley, CA: University of California Press.

Ishay, M. (2004). *The History of Human Rights.* Berkeley, CA: University of California Press.

Issac, L. and L. Griffin (1989). "Ahistoricism in Time-Series Analyses of Historical Process: Critique, Redirection and Illustrations from U.S. Labor History." *American Sociological Review* 54:873-890.

Ivans, M. (1999). Public Presentation, ACLW Civil Libertarian of the Year Award Banquet, Tucson, Arizona, February 26.

Jacobs, D. (1980). "Marxism and the Critique of Empiricism." *Social Problems* 27(4):467-470.

—— (1979). "Inequality and Police Strength." *American Sociological Review* 44:913-924.

—— (1978a). "Inequality and the Legal Order: An Ecological Test of the Conflict Model." *Social Problems* 25(5):516-525.

—— (1978b). "Marxism and Law: Preliminary Analyses." *British Journal of Law and Society* 5(2):203-226.

—— and D. Britt (1979). "Inequality and Police Use of Deadly Force: An Empirical Assessment of the Conflict Hypothesis." *Social Problems* 26:403-411.

Jackson, G. (1994). *Soledad Brother: The Prison Letters of George Jackson*. Chicago, IL: Lawrence Hill Books.

Jackson, J. (1996). *Legal Lynching: Racism, Injustice and the Death Penalty*. New York: Marlowe.

Jackson, T. (1979). "The New Criminology is the Old Sentimentality." *Criminology* 16:516-526.

James, J. and W. Thorton (1980). "Women's Liberation and Female Delinquency." *Journal of Research in Crime and Delinquency* 20:230-244.

Jameison, K. (1994). *The Organization of Corporate Crime: The Dynamics of Antitrust Violations*. Thousand Oaks, CA: Sage.

Jankovic, I. (1982a). "Labor Market and Imprisonment." In: A. Platt and P. Takagi (eds.), *Punishment and Penal Discipline*. San Francisco, CA: Crime and Social Justice.

—— (1982b). "Social Class and Criminal Sentencing." In: A. Platt and P. Takagi (eds.), *Punishment and Penal Discipline*. San Francisco, CA: Crime and Social Justice.

—— (1977). "Labor Market and Imprisonment." *Crime and Social Justice* 8:17-31.

Jay, M. (1973). *The Dialectic Imagination*. Boston, MA: Little, Brown.

Johnson, C. (2004). *The Sorrows of Empire*. New York: Metropolitan Books.

—— (2001). *Blowback : The Costs and Consequences of American Empire*. New York: Owl Books.

Johnson, E.H. (1980). "Praxis and Radical Criminology in the United States." In: J. Inciardi (ed.), *Radical Criminology: The Coming Crisis*. Beverly Hills, CA: Sage.

Jones, T., B. MacLean and J. Young (1986). *First Inslington Crime Survey*. London, UK: Middlesex Polytechnic Centre for Criminology.

Joseph, G. (1997). "The Incompatible Menage a Trois: Marxism, Feminism and Racism." In: R. Hennessey and C. Ingraham (eds.), *Materialist Feminism*. New York: Routledge.

Josephson, M. (1934). *The Robber Barons: The Great American Capitalists, 1861-1901*. New York: Harcourt and Brace.

Jurik, N. (1985). "An Officer and a Lady: Organizational Barriers to Women as Correctional Officers in Men's Prisons." *Social Problems* 32(4):375-388.

Juston, James L. (2003). *Calculating the Value of the Union: Slavery, Property Rights, and the Economic Origins of the Civil War*.Chapel Hill, NC: University of North Carolina Press.

Kakalik, J. and S. Wildhorn (1972). *Private Policing in the United States*. National Institute of Law Enforcement (R-869/DOJ). Washington, DC: U.S. Government Printing Office.

Kallet, A. and F. J. Schlink (1933). *100,000,000 Guinea Pigs: Dangers in Everyday Foods, Drugs, and Cosmetics*. New York: Grosset and Dunlap.

Kantola, J. and H. M. Dahl (2005). "Gender and the State." *International Feminist Journal of Politics* 7(1):49-71.

Kappeler, V.E., R. Sluder and G. Alport (1994). *Forces of Deviance: Understanding the Dark Side of Policing*. Prospect Heights, IL: Waveland.

Karliner, J. (1997). *The Corporate Planet: Ecology and Politics in the Age of Globalization*. San Francisco, CA: Sierra Club.

Karst, K. (1993). *Law's Promise, Law's Expression : Visions of Power in the Politics of Race, Gender, and Religion*. New Haven, CT: Yale University Press.

Katsiaficas, G.N. (1987). *The Imagination of the New Left: A Global Analysis of 1968*. Boston, MA: South End Press.

Katz, J. (1988). *Seductions of Crime: Moral and Sensual Attractions in Doing Evil*. New York: Basic Books.

Kauzlarich, D. (1997). "Nuclear Weapons on Trial: The Battle at the International Court of Justice." *Social Pathology* 3(3):157-164.

—— (1995). "A Criminology of the Nuclear State." *Humanity and Society* 19(3):37-57.

—— and R. Kramer (1998). *Crime of the Nuclear State*. Boston, MA: Northeastern University Press.

—— and R. Kramer (1995). "The Nuclear Terrorist State." *Peace Review* 7(3/4):333-337.

—— R. Kramer, and B. Smith (1992). "Toward the Study of Governmental Crime: Nuclear Weapons, Foreign Intervention, and International Law." *Humanity and Society* 16 (1992):543-63

—— C. Mullins, and R. A. Matthews (2004). "Complicity Continuum of State Crime." *Contemporary Justice Review*. 6, 3: 241-254.

Keats, R. and J. Urry (1975). *Social Theory and Science*. London, UK: Routledge, Kegan Paul.

Keenan, G. F. (1967). *Memoirs: 1925-1960*. Boston: Atlantic Monthly Press.

Keil, T. and G.F. Vito (1995). "Race and the Death Penalty in Kentucky Murder Trials." *American Journal of Criminal Justice* 20(1):17-36.

—— (1992). "The Effects of the Furman and Gregg Decisions on Black-White Execution Ratios in the South." *Journal of Criminal Justice* 20(33):217-226.

Kendall, D. (1996). "Warner Brothers Television." In: R. Ohmann, G. Averill, M. Curtin, D. Shumway and E.G. Traube (eds.), *Making and Selling Culture*. Hanover, NH: Wesleyan University Press.

Kennedy, R.F., Jr. (2004). *Crimes Against Nature*. New York: HarperCollins.

Kennedy, R. (1997). *Race, Crime and the Law*. New York: Pantheon.

Kerner Commission (1969). *The Riot Report: A Shortened Version of the Report of the National Advisory Commission on Civil Disorders*. New York:Viking Press.

Kiernan, B. (2002). *The Pol Pot Regime: Race, Power, and Genocide in Cambodia under the Khmer Rouge, 1975-79*. New Haven:Yale University Press.

King, M.L. (1997). *Papers of Martin Luther King, Jr.* Berkeley, CA: University of California Press.

—— (1987). *The Words of Martin Luther King* (as selected by Coretta Scott King). New York: Newmarket Press.

Kinsey, R., J. Lea and J. Young (1986). *Losing the Fight Against Crime*. London, UK: Basil Blackwell.

Kitsuse, J.I. (1962). "Societal Reactions to Deviant Behavior: Problems of Theory and Method." *Social Problems* 9:247-256.

Klare, M. T. and P. Kornbluh (1989). *Low Intensity Warfare: How the USA Fights Wars Without Declaring Them*. New York: Methuen Publishing Ltd.

Klaus, P. (1994). *The Costs of Crime to Victims*. Washington, DC: Bureau of Justice Statistics.

Kleck, G. (1981). "Racial Discrimination in Criminal Sentencing." *American Sociological Review* 46:783-805.

Klein, D. (1997). "An Agenda for Reading and Writing about Women, Crime and Justice." *Social Pathology* 3(2):81-91.

—— (1982). "The Etiology of Female Crime." In: B.R. Price and N.J. Sokoloff (eds.), *The Criminal Justice System and Women*. New York: Clark Boardman.

—— (1979). "Can This Marriage Be Saved? Battery and Sheltering." *Crime and Social Justice* 12:19-33.

—— and J. Kress (1976). "Any Women's Blues: A Critical Overview of Women, Crime and the Criminal Justice System." *Crime and Social Justice* 5:34-49.

Klockars, C. (1980). "The Contemporary Crisis of Marxist Criminology." In: J. Inciardi (ed.), *Radical Criminology: The Coming Crisis*. Beverly Hills, CA: Sage.

—— (1979). "The Contemporary Crisis of Marxist Criminology." *Criminology* 16:477-494.

Knoohuizen, R. et al. (1972). *The Police and Their Use of Fatal Force in Chicago*. Chicago, IL: The Chicago Law Enforcement Study Group.

Knox, E.G. (1996). "Spatial Clustering of Childhood Cancer in Great Britain." *Journal of Epidemiology and Community Health* 50(3):313-319.

—— (1994). "Leukaemia Clusters in Childhood: Geographical Analysis in Britain." *Journal of Epidemiology and Community Health* 48(4):369-376.

—— (1992a). "Leukaemia Clusters in Great Britain, 1: Space-Time Interaction." *Journal of Epidemiology and Community Health* 46(6):566-572.

—— (1992b). "Leukaemia Clusters in Great Britain, 2: Geographic Concentrations." *Journal of Epidemiology and Community Health* 46(6):573-576.

—— and E.A. Gilman (1997). "Hazard Proximities of Childhood Cancer in Great Britain from 1953-1980." *Journal of Epidemiology and Community Health* 51:151-159.

Kobler, A. (1975a). "Police Homicides in a Democracy." *Journal of Social Issues* 31(1):167-183.

—— (1975b). "Facts and Figures on Police Killings of Civilians in the United States, 1965-1969." *Journal of Social Issues* 31(1):184-193.

Kohn, M. (1977). *Class and Conformity*. Chicago, IL: University of Chicago Press.

—— (1976). "Social Class and Parental Values: Another Confirmation of the Relationship." *American Sociological Review* 34:659-678.

—— and C. Schoolert (1969). "Class, Occupation and Orientation." *American Sociological Review* 41:538-545.

Kondratieff, N.D. (1935). "The Long Waves in Economic Life." *Review of Economic Statistics* 17:105-115.

Koppelman, A. (1996). *Antidiscrimination Law and Social Equality*. New Haven, CT: Yale University Press.

Korn, R.R. and L.W. McKorkle (1959). *Criminology and Penology*. New York: Holt, Rinehart and Winston.

Kornhauser, R. (1978). *Social Sources of Delinquency*. Chicago, IL: University of Chicago.

Korten, D.C. (1998). *Globalizing Civil Society: Reclaiming Our Right to Power*. New York: Seven Stories Press.

—— (1995). *When Corporations Rule the World*. West Hartford, CT: Kumerian Press.

Kozol, J. (1995). "Homeless in America." In: S. Ruth (ed.), *Issues in Feminism*. Mountain View, CA: Mayfield.

Kramer, R.C. (1992). "The Space Shuttle Challenger Explosion: A Case Study of State-Corporate Crime." In: K. Schlegel and D. Weisburd (eds.), *White Collar Crime Reconsidered*. Boston, MA: Northeastern University Press.

—— (1989). "Criminologists and the Social Movement Against Corporate Crime." *Social Justice* 16:146-164.

—— (1984). "Corporate Criminality: the Development of an Idea." In: E. Hochstedler (ed.), *Corporations as Criminals*. Beverly Hills, CA: Sage.

—— and R.J. Michalowski (1995). "The Iron Fist and the Velvet Tongue: Crime Control Policies in the Clinton Administration." *Social Justice* 22(2):87-101.

—— R. Michalowski and D. Kauzlarich (2002). "The Origins and Development of the Concept and Theory of State-Corporate Crime." *Crime & Delinquency* 48(2):263-282.

Kraska, P. (2001). *Militarizing the American Criminal Justice System: The Changing Roles of the Armed Forces and the Police*. Boston:Northeastern University Press.

Krisberg, B. (1975). *Power and Privilege: Toward a New Criminology*. Englewood Cliffs, NJ: Prentice-Hall.

Kressel, N. J. (2001). *Mass Hate*. Boulder, CO: Westview Press.

Krzycki, L. (1996). "Race, Popular Culture and the News." In: M.J. Lynch and E.B. Patterson (eds.), *Justice with Prejudice*. Albany, NY: Harrow and Heston.

Kuhn, T. (1970). *The Structure of Scientific Revolutions*. Chicago, IL: University of Chicago.

Ladinski, J. (1984). "The Impact of Social Background of Lawyers on Legal Practice and the Law." In: J. Bonsignore, E. Katsh, P. D'Ericco, R.M. Pipkin, S. Arons and J. Rifkin (eds.), *Before the Law*. Boston, MA: Houghton-Mifflin.

Laffargue, B. and T. Godefroy (1989). "Economic Cycles and Punishment: Unemployment and Imprisonment. A Time-Series Study: France, 1920-1985." *Contemporary Crises* 13:371-404.

LaFree, G. (1989). *Rape and Criminal Justice: The Social Construction of Sexual Assault*. Belmont, CA: Wadsworth.

—— (1985). "Official Reactions to Hispanic Defendants in the Southwest." *Journal of Research in Crime and Delinquency* 22:213-237.

—— (1980). "The Effect of Sexual Stratification by Race on Official Reactions to Rape." *American Sociological Review* 45:842-854.

Lambert, C., S. Pickering, and C. Alder (2003). *Critical Chatter: Women and Human Rights in South East Asia*. Durham, NC: Carolina Academic Press.

Lane, P. (1998). "Ecofeminism Meets Criminology." *Theoretical Criminology* 2(2):235-248.

Latouche, S. (1993). *In the Wake of the Affluent Society: An Exploration of Post Development*. Atlantic City, NJ: Zed Books.

Lauderdale, P. and G. Larson (1978). "Marxist and Organizational Approaches to Delinquency and the Sociology of Law: Crucial Problems in Testing the Perspective." *American Sociological Review* 43(6):922-925.

Lea, J. (1987). " Left Realism: A Defense." *Contemporary Crises* 11:357-370.

Lefcourt, R. (1971). *Law Against the People*. New York: Random House.

Leigh, J. P., S. Markowitz, M. Fahls and P. Landigren (2000). *Costs of Occupational Injuries and Illnesses*. Ann Arbor, MI: University of Michigan Press.

Lemert, E. ([1967]1981). *Human Deviance, Social Problems and Social Control*. Englewood Cliffs, NJ: Prentice Hall.

—— (1951). *Social Pathology*. New York: McGraw-Hill.

Leonard, E. (1982). *Women, Crime and Society*. New York: Longman.

Lessan, G. (1991). "Macro-Economic Determinants of Penal Policy: Estimating the Unemployment and Inflation Influences on Imprisonment Rate Changes in the United States, 1948-1985." *Crime, Law and Social Change* 16:177-198.

Levit, N. (1998). *The Gender Line: Men, Women and the Law*. New York: NYU Press.

Lewis, P. (1993). "Rape Was Weapon of Serbs, UN Says." *New York Times,* Oct. 20: A1.

Liazos, A. (1974). "Class Oppression and the Functions of Juvenile Justice." *The Insurgent Sociologist* 1:2-23.

Lichter, L.S. and R. Licther (1988). *Prime Time Crime*. Arlington, VA: Media Institute.

Linzer, D. and B. Gellman (2005)."Doubts on Weapons Were Dismissed." *Washington Post,* April 1, p. A1

Liska, A., J. Lawrence and M. Benson (1981). "Perspectives on the Legal Order: The Capacity for Social Control." *American Journal of Sociology* 87:413-426.

Liu, Feng (2001). *Environmental Justice Analysis: Theories, Methods and Practice*. Boca Raton, FL: Lewis Publishers.

Livingston, M.B. and D.W. Gregory (1989). *The Stripping of U.S. Treasury*. New York: Salomon Brothers Center for the Study of Financial Institutions, Leonard N. Stern School of Business, New York University.

Lizotte, A. (1978). "Extra-legal Factors in Chicago's Criminal Courts: Testing the Conflict Model of Criminal Justice." *Social Problems* 25:564-580.

—— J. Mercy and E. Monkkenon (1982). "Crime and Police Strength in an Urban Setting: Chicago, 1947-1970." In: J. Hagan (ed.), *Quantitative Criminology*. Beverly Hills, CA: Sage.

Locke, M.(2001). *Anti-Slavery in America from the Introduction of Slaves to the Prohibition of the Slave Trade: 1619-1808*. New York: Peter Smith Publishers.

Lombroso-Ferrero, G. (1972). *Criminal Man, According to the Classification of Cesare Lombroso* (reprint ed.). New York: Patterson Smith.

—— W. Ferrero (1894). *The Female Offender.* New York: Appleton.

Lowman, J. and B. Maclean (eds.), (1992). *Realist Criminology: Crime Control and Policing in the 1990s.* Toronto, CAN: University of Toronto Press.

Lubiano, W. (1992). "Black Ladies, Welfare Queens, and State Minstrels: Ideological War by Narrative Means." In: T. Morrison (ed.), *Race-ing Justice, En-Gendering Power.* New York: Pantheon.

Lukacs, G. (1985). *History and Class Consciousness.* Cambridge, MA: MIT Press.

Lynch, M.J. (2004). "Towards a Radical Ecology of Urban Violence: Integrating Medical, Epidemiological, Environmental and Criminological Research On Class, Race, Lead (Pb) and Crime." In: M. Zahn, H.Brownstein, and S. Jackson (eds.), *Violence: From Theory to Research.* Cincinnati, OH: Anderson.

—— (2000) "The Power of Oppression: Towards Understanding the History of Criminology as a Science of Oppression." *Critical Criminology* 9(1-2):144-152.

—— (1997). "Reading Radical Criminology." In: M.J. Lynch (ed.), *Radical Criminology.* Hampshire, UK: Dartmouth Press.

—— (1996). "Race, Class, Gender and Criminology: Structured Choices and the Life Course." In: M. Schwartz and D. Milovanovic (eds.), *Gender, Race and Class in Criminology.* Hamden, CT: Garland.

—— (1990). "Racial Bias and Criminal Justice: Methodological and Definitional Issues." In: B. MacLean and D. Milovanovic (eds.), *Racism, Empiricism and Criminal Justice.* Vancouver, CAN: Collective Press.

—— (1988a). "Surplus Value, Crime and Punishment." *Contemporary Crises* 12:329-344.

—— (1988b). "The Poverty of Historical Analysis in Criminology." *Social Justice* 15:173-84.

—— (1987). "Quantitative Analysis and Marxist Criminology: Some Solutions to a Dilemma in Marxist Criminology." *Crime and Social Justice* 29:110-127.

—— (1984). *Class Based Justice: A History of the Origins of Policing in Albany, NY.* Albany, NY: Michael J. Hindelang Criminal Justice Research Center.

—— and W.B. Groves (1995). "In Defense of Comparative Criminology: A Critique of General Theory and the Rational Man." In: F. Adler and W.S. Laufer (eds.), *Advances in Criminological Theory,* vol. 6. New Brunswick, NJ: Transaction.

—— and A. Lizotte (1994). "The Rate of Surplus Value and Crime: Theoretical and Empirical Examination of Marxian Economic Theory and Criminology." *Crime, Law and Social Change* 21(1):15-48.

—— M.J. Hogan and P.B. Stretesky (1999). "A Further Look at Long Cycles and Criminal Justice Legislation." *Justice Quarterly* 16(3):431-450.

—— J. Huey, B. Close, S. Nunez and C. Johnston (1992). "Cultural Literacy, Criminology, and Female Gender Issues: The Power to Exclude." *Journal of Criminal Justice Education* 3(2):183-202.

—— and L. Krzycki (1998). "Popular Culture as an Ideological Mask: Mass Produced Popular Culture, the Remaking of Popular Culture Messages and Criminal Justice Related Imagery." *Journal of Criminal Justice* 26(4):321-336.

—— D. McGurrin, and M. Fenwick (2004). "Disappearing Act: The Representation of Corporate Crime Research in Criminological Journals and Textbooks." *Journal of Criminal Justice* 32(5):389-398.

—— M. Nalla and K. Miller (1989). "Cross-Cultural Perceptions of Deviance: The Case of Bhopal." *Journal of Research in Crime and Delinquency* 26(1):7-35.

—— Newman, G.R., and W.B.Groves (1993). "Control Theory and Punishment: Control Theory as a Penal Policy." In: W.S. Laufer and F. Adler (eds.), *Advances in Theoretical Criminology*, vol. 4. New Brunswick, NJ: Transaction.

—— and E.B. Patterson (1996). "Thinking About Race and Criminal Justice: Racism, Stereotypes, Politics, Academia and the Need for Context." In: M.J. Lynch and E.B. Patterson (eds.), *Justice with Prejudice*. Albany, NY: Harrow and Heston.

—— and E.B. Patterson (1991). "Racial and Ethnic Bias in Criminal Justice: An Overview." In: M.J. Lynch and E.B. Patterson (eds.), *Race and Criminal Justice*. Albany, NY: Harrow and Heston.

—— and E.B. Patterson (1990). "Racial Discrimination in the Criminal Justice System: Evidence from Four Jurisdictions." In: B. MacLean and D. Milovanovic (eds.), *Racism, Empiricism and Criminal Justice*. Vancouver, CAN: Collective Press.

—— H. Schwendinger, and J. Schwendinger (2004). "The Empirical Status of Radical Criminology." Plenary Session paper delivered at the Annual meetings of the American Society of Criminology, November, Nashville, Tennessee.

—— and P.B. Stretesky (2003). "The Meaning of Green: Contrasting Criminological Perspectives." *Theoretical Criminology* 7(2):217-238.

—— and P. B. Stretesky (2001). "Toxic Crimes: Examining Corporate Victimization of the General Public Employing Medical and Epidemiological Evidence." *Critical Criminology* 10(3):152-172.

—— and P. B. Stretesky (2000). "Radical Criminology: Race, Class, Inequality, Crime and Justice." In: R. Paternoster and R. Bachman (eds.), *Explaining Criminals and Crime: Essays in Contemporary Criminological Theory*. Los Angeles: Roxbury.

—— and P.B. Stretesky (1998). "Marxist Criminology and Social Justice: Eclipsing Criminal Justice." In: B. Arrigo (ed.), *Justice at the Margins: The Maturation of Critical Theory in Law, Crime and Deviance*. Belmont, CA: Wadsworth.

—— Stretesky, P.B. and R. G. Burns (2004a). "Determinants of Environmental Law Violation Fines Against Oil Refineries: Race, Ethnicity, Income and Aggregation Effects." *Society and Natural Resources* 17(4):333-347.

—— Stretesky, P.B. and R. G. Burns (2004b). "Slippery Business: Race, Class and Legal Determinants of Penalties Against Oil Refineries." *Journal of Black Studies* 34(3):421-440.

—— Stretesky, P.B. and P. Hammond (2000). "Media Coverage of Chemical Crimes: Hillsborough County, Florida, 1987-1997." *The British Journal of Criminology* 40(1):112-126.

MacKinnon, K. (1989). *Toward a Feminist Theory of the State.* Cambridge, MA: Harvard University Press.

MacLean, B. (1991). "In Partial Defense of Socialist Realism." *Crime, Law and Social Change* 15:213-234.

—— and D. Milovanovic (eds.), (1990). *Racism, Empiricism and Criminal Justice.* Vancouver, CAN: Collective Press.

MacLeod, A. (1975). *A Moral Tale: Children's Fiction and American Culture, 1820-1860.* Hamden, CT: Archon Books.

MacLeod, C. (1980). *Horatio Alger, Farewell: The End of the American Dream.* New York: Seaview.

MacPherson, C.B. (1962). *The Political Theory of Possessive Individualism: Hobbes to Locke.* Oxford, UK: Clarendon Press.

Mahajan, R. (2003). *Full Spectrum Dominance: U.S. Power in Iraq and Beyond.* New York: Seven Stories Press.

Maher, L. (1997). *Sexed Work : Gender, Race, and Resistance in a Brooklyn Drug Market.* New York: Clarendon Press.

—— and K. Daly (1996). "Women in the Street-Level Drug Economy: Continuity or Change?" *Criminology* 34:465-482.

Mair, L. (1970). *Primitive Government.* London, UK: Penguin Books.

Mamdani, M. (2002). *When Victims Become Killers : Colonialism, Nativism, and the Genocide in Rwanda.* Princeton, NJ: Princeton University Press.

Mandel, E. (1980). *Long Waves of Capitalist Development: The Marxist Interpretation.* New York: Cambridge University Press.

—— (1979). *Late Capitalism.* London, UK: Unwin Brothers.

—— (1968a). *Marxist Economic Theory, Volume I.* New York: Modern Reader.

—— (1968b). *Marxist Economic Theory, Volume II.* New York: Modern Reader.

Mander, J. and E. Goldsmith (eds.), (1996). *The Case Against the Global Economy, and for a Turn Toward the Local.* San Francisco, CA: Sierra Club Books.

Manders, D. (1975). "Labelling Theory and Social Reality: A Marxist Critique." *The Insurgent Sociologist* 6(1):53-66.

Mankoff, M. (1980). "A Tower of Babel: Marxist Criminologists and their Critics." In: J. Incardi (ed.), *Radical Criminology: The Coming Crisis.* Beverly Hills, CA: Sage.

—— (1978). "On the Responsibility of Marxist Criminologists." *Contemporary Crises* 2(3):293-301.

Mann, C. (1993). *Unequal Justice: A Question of Color.* Bloomington, IN: Indiana University Press.

—— and M. Zatz (1998). *Images of Crime, Images of Color.* Los Angeles, CA: Roxbury.

Mann, M. (2003). *Incoherent Empire.* New York: Verso.

Mannheim, K. (1940). *Man and Society.* New York: Harcourt, Brace.

Manning, P. (1998). "The Death of Class, by Jan Pakulski and Malcolm Waters." *Justice Quarterly* 15(4):755-762.

Marcuse, H. (1966). *One Dimensional Man: Studies in the Ideology of Advanced Industrial Society.* Boston, MA: Beacon Press.

Marenin, O. (1982). "Parking Tickets and Class Repression." *Contemporary Crises* 6(3):241-266.

Marshall, J., D. Scott and J. Hunter (1987). *The Iran-Contra Connection: Secret Teams and Covert Operations in the Reagan Era.* Boston, MA: South End Press.

Martin, S.E. and N.C. Jurik (1996). *Doing Justice, Doing Gender.* Thousand Oaks, CA: Sage.

Marx, K. (1981). "Crime and Accumulation." In: D. Greenberg (ed.), *Crime and Capitalism.* Palo Alto, CA: Mayfield.

—— ([1867]1967a). *Capital, Volume 1.* New York: International.

—— ([1859]1982). *A Contribution to the Critique of Political Economy.* New York: International.

—— ([1847]1967b). *The Poverty of Philosophy.* New York: International.

—— ([1844]1975). "The Paris Manuscripts." In: R. Livingstone and G. Benton (eds. and translators), *Karl Marx's Early Writings.* New York: Vintage.

—— and F. Engels ([1848]1955). *The Communist Manifesto.* Arlington Heights, IL: Crofts Classics.

—— and F. Engels ([1846]1970). *The German Ideology.* New York: International.

Massey, D.S. (1995). "Getting Away with Murder: Segregation and Violent Crime in Urban America." *University of Pennsylvania Law Review* 143(5):1203-1232.

—— and N. Denton (1993). *American Apartheid: Segregation and the Making of the American Underclass.* Cambridge, MA: Harvard University Press.

—— and N. Denton (1988). "The Dimensions of Residential Segregation." *Social Forces* 67(2):281-316.

—— and N. Denton (1989). "Hypersegregation in U.S. Metropolitan Areas: Black and Hispanic Segregation Along Five Dimensions." *Demography* 26(3):373-392.

—— and A. Gross (1991). "Explaining Trends in Racial Segregation, 1970-1980." *Urban Affairs Quarterly* 27(1):13-36.

—— and Z. Hajnal (1995). "The Changing Geographic Structure of Black-White Segregation in the United States." *Social Science Quarterly* 76(3):527-543.

Matthews, R. (1987). "Taking Realist Criminology Seriously." *Contemporary Crises* 11:371-301.

Matza, D. (1968). *On Becoming Deviant.* Englewood Cliffs, NJ: Prentice Hall.

McGarrell, E.F. and T.C. Castellano (1993). "Social Structure, Crime and Politics: A Conflict Model of the Criminal Law Formation Process." In: W. Chambliss and M. Zata (eds.), *Making Law.* Bloomington, IN: Indiana University Press.

McGurrin, D., M. Fenwick and M.J. Lynch (1999). "Representing Corporate Crime: An Examination of Journal and Textbook Contents." Paper presented at the annual meeting of the Academy of Criminal Justice Sciences, Orlando, Fl, March.

McKay, N.Y. (1992). "Remembering Anita Hill and Clarence Thomas: What Really Happened When One Black Woman Spoke Out." In: T. Morrison (ed.), *Race-ing Justice, En-Gendering Power.* New York: Pantheon.

McLaughlin, G. (1975). "LEAA: A Case Study in the Development of the Social Industrial Complex." *Crime and Social Justice* 4:15-24.

Mead, G.H. ([1934]1962). *Mind, Self and Society from the Standpoint of a Social Behaviorist.* Chicago, IL: University of Chicago Press.

Meier, K. (1985). *Regulation.* New York: St. Martins Press.

Meier, R. (1976). "The New Criminology: Continuity in Criminological Theory." *Journal of Criminal Law and Criminology* 67:461-469.

Melman, S. (1985). *The Permanent War Economy: American Capitalism in Decline.* New York: Simon and Schuster.

Melossi, D. (1990). *The State of Social Control.* Cambridge, MA: Polity Press.

—— (1989). "Fifty Years Later: Punishment and Social Structure in Comparative Analysis." *Contemporary Crises* 13(4):311-326.

—— (1985). "Punishment and Social Action: Changing Vocabulary of Punitive Motive Within a Political Business Cycle." *Current Perspectives in Social Theory* 6:169-197.

—— (1982). "Punishment and Social Structure." In: A. Platt and P. Takagi (eds.), *Punishment and Penal Discipline.* San Francisco, CA: Crime and Social Justice Associates.

—— (1976). "The Penal Question in Capital." *Crime and Social Justice* 5:26-33.

—— and M. Pavarini (1980). *The Prison and the Factory.* London, UK: MacMillian.

Merton, R.K. ([1938]1979). "Social Structure and Anomie." In: J. Jacoby (ed.), *Classics in Criminology.* Oak Parks, IL: Moore.

Messerschmidt, J.W. (1997). *Crime as Structured Action: Gender, Race, Class and Crime in the Making.* Thousand Oaks, CA; Sage.

—— (1993). *Masculinities and Crime.* Lanham, MD: Rowman and Littfield.

—— (1988). "A Reply to the Schwendingers." *Social Justice* 15(1):146-160.

—— (1986). *Capitalism, Patriarchy and Crime*. Totowa, NJ: Rowman and Littlefield.

Messner, S. (1982). "Poverty, Inequality and Urban Homicide Rates." *Criminology* 20:103-114.

Messner, S. and R. Rosenfeld (1994). *Crime and the American Dream*. Belmont, CA: Wadsworth.

Michalowski, R. (1998). "International Environmental Issues." In: M. Clifford (ed.), *Environmental Crime*. Boston, MA: Aspen Publishers.

—— (1996). "Critical Criminology and the Critique of Domination: The Story of an Intellectual Movement." *Critical Criminology* 7(1):9-16.

—— (1993a). "(De)construction, Postmodernism and Social Problems: Facts, Fiction and Fantasies at the 'End of History.'" In: J.A. Holstein and G. Miller (eds.), *Reconsidering Social Constructionism*. New York: Aldine de Gruyter.

—— (1993b). "The Contradictions of Corrections." In: W. Chambliss and M. Zatz (eds.), *Making Law*. Bloomington, IN: Indiana University Press.

—— (1985). *Law, Order and Power*. New York: Random House.

—— (1983). "Crime Control in the 1980s: A Progressive Agenda." *Crime and Social Justice* 19:13-23.

—— (1979). "Violence and Values: The Criminologist's Dilemma." In: N. Kittrie and J. Susman (eds.), *Legality, Morality and Ethics in Criminal Justice*. New York: Prager.

—— (1977). "Perspective and Paradigm: Structuring Criminological Thought." In: R. Meier (ed.), *Theoretical Criminology*. Beverly Hills, CA: Sage.

—— and M. Bolander (1976). "Repression and the Criminal Justice System in Capitalist America." *Sociological Inquiry* 46:95-106.

—— and S. Carlson (1999). "Unemployment, Imprisonment and Social Structures of Accumulation: Historical Contingency in the Rusche-Kirchheimer Hypothesis." *Criminology* 37(2):217-250.

——and R. C. Kramer (eds). (2005). *State-Corporate Crime: Wrong-doing at the Intersection of Business and Government*. Piscataway, NJ: Rutgers Univerisity Press.

—— and R.C. Kramer (1998). "Globalization and Shifting Legal Spaces: An Inquiry into Transnational Corporate Crime Under The New World Order." Paper presented at the American Society of Criminology annual meeting, Washington, DC.

—— and R.C. Kramer (1987). "The Space Between the Laws: The Problem of Corporate Crime in a Transnational Context." *Social Problems* 34:34-53.

—— and M.A. Pearson (1990). "Punishment and Social Structure at the State Level: A Cross-Sectional Comparison of 1970 and 1980." *Journal of Research in Crime and Delinquency* 27:52-78.

—— and E.H. Pfuhl (1992). "Technology, Property and Law: The Case of Computer Crime." *Crime, Law and Social Change* 15:255-275.

Mickelson, R. and S.S. Smith (1995). "Education and the Struggle Against Race, Class and Gender Inequality." In: M.L Anderson and P.H. Collins (eds.), *Race, Class and Gender: An Anthology*. Belmont, CA: Wadsworth.

Middleton, J. and D. Tait (eds.), (1967). *Tribes Without Rulers*. London, UK: Routledge and Kegan Paul.

Miethe, T. (1982). "Public Consensus on Crime Seriousness: Normative Structure or Methodological Artifact?" *Criminology* 20(3-4):515-526.

—— and C.A. Moor (1985). "Socioeconomic Disparities Under Determinant Sentencing Systems." *Criminology* 23(3):337-363.

Miliband, R. (1969). *The State in Capitalist Society*. New York: Basic.

Miller, E. (1986). *Street Women*. Philadelphia, PA: Temple University Press.

Miller, J.G. (1996). *Search and Destroy: African-American Males in the Criminal Justice System*. New York: Cambridge University Press.

Miller, J. (1998). "Up It Up: Gender and the Accomplishment of Street Robbery." *Criminology* 36(1):37-65.

Miller, M. (1980). "Sinking Gradually into the Proletariate: The Emergence of the Penitentiary in the United States." *Crime and Social Justice* 13:37-43.

—— (1974). "At Hard Labor: Rediscovering the 19th Century Prison." *Issues in Criminology* 9.

Miller, S.L. (1998). *Crime Control and Women: Feminist Implications of Criminal Justice Policy*. Thousand Oaks, CA: Sage Publications.

—— and C. Burack (1993). "A Critique of Gottfredson and Hirschi's General Theory of Crime: Selective (In)Attention to Gender and Power Positions." *Women & Criminal Justice* 4:115-134.

Miller, W.B. (1958). "Lower Class Culture as a Generating Milieu of Gang Delinquency." *Journal of Social Issues* 14(3):5-19.

Mills, C.W. (1967/1969). *Power, Politics, and People*. New York: Oxford.

—— ([1962]1974. *The Marxists*. New York: Dell.

—— ([1959]1977). *The Sociological Imagination*. New York: Oxford.

—— (1956). *The Power Elite*. New York: Oxford.

Milovanovic, D. (1997). *Postmodern Criminology*. New York: Garland.

—— (1988a). *A Primer in the Sociology of Law*. Albany, NY: Harrow and Heston.

—— (1988b). *Weberian and Marxian Perspectives on Law*. Aldershot, UK: Gower.

—— (1987). "The Political Economy of Liberty and Property Interests." *Legal Studies Forum* 11(3):147-172.

—— (1981). "The Commodity Exchange Theory of Law." *Crime and Social Justice* 16:41-49.

Milton, C. et al, (1977). *Police Use of Deadly Force*. Washington, DC: Police Foundation.

Minow, M. (1997). *Not Only for Myself: Identity, Politics, and the Law.* New York: New Press.

—— (1990). *Making All the Difference: Inclusion, Exclusion and American Law.* Ithaca, NY: Cornell University Press.

Mislom, F.S. (1969). *The Historical Foundations of Common Law.* London, UK: Butterworths.

Mitchell, J. (1971). *Women's Estate.* New York: Random House.

Moffatt, M. (1989). *Coming of Age in New Jersey: College and American Culture.* New Brunswick, NJ: Rutgers University Press.

Monkkonen, E.H. (1992). "History of Urban Police." In: M. Tonry and N. Morris (eds.), *Modern Policing.* Chicago, IL: University of Chicago Press.

Morash, M. and M. Chesney-Lind (1991). "A Reformulation and Partial Test of the Power Control Theory of Delinquency." *Justice Quarterly* 8(3):347-377.

Morgan, R. (1970). *Sisterhood is Powerful: An Anthology of Writings from the Women's Liberation Movement.* New York: Random House.

Moro, J. and D. Lapierre (2002). *Five Past Midnight in Bhopal: The Epic Story of the World's Deadliest Industrial Disaster.* New York: Warner Books.

Morris, E. (2002). *Theodore Rex.* New York: The Modern Library.

Morrison, T. (ed.), (1992a). *Race-ing Justice, En-Gendering Power.* New York: Pantheon.

—— (1992b). "Friday on the Potomac." In: T. Morrison (ed.), *Race-ing Justice, En-Gendering Power.* New York: Pantheon.

Mortenson, T. G. (2002). "Shutting the College Doors: Are We Cutting off the Middle Class?" National Forum on Education Policy. Hollywood, CA.

Mugford, S.K. (1974). "Marxism and Criminology." *Sociological Quarterly* 15:591-596.

Mullins, C., D. Kauzlarich, and D.Rothe (2004). "The International Criminal Court and the Control of State Crime: Problems and Prospects" *Critical Criminology* 12:285-308.

Mundy, A. (2001). *Dispensing with the Truth.* New York: St. Martin's Press.

Myrdal, G. (1969). *Objectivity in Social Research.* New York: Pantheon.

Nader, L. (ed.), (1997). *Law and Culture in Society.* Berkeley, CA: University of California.

—— (1990). *Harmony Ideology: Justice and Control in a Zapotec Mountain Village.* Stanford, CA: Stanford University Press.

Nader, R. (1965). *Unsafe at Any Speed: The Designed in Dangers of the American Automobile.* New York: Grossman.

Naffine, N. (1987). *Female Crime: The Construction of Women in Criminology.* Boston, MA: Allen and Unwin.

Nalla, M. and C. Corley (1996). "Race and Criminal Justice: The Employment of Minorities in the Criminal Justice System." In: M.J. Lynch and E. B. Patterson (eds.), *Justice with Prejudice*. Albany, NY: Harrow and Heston.

—— M.J. Lynch and M.J. Leiber (1997). "Determinants of Police Growth in Phoenix, 1950-1988." *Justice Quarterly* 14(1):115-144.

—— and G.R. Newman (1990). *A Primer in Private Security*. Albany, NY: Harrow and Heston.

Needleman, H.L. and C. Gatsonis (1990). "Low Level Lead Exposure and the IQ of Children." *Journal of the American Medical Association* 263:673-678.

—— C. Gunnoe, A. Leviton, H. Peresie, C. Maher, and P. Barret (1979). "Deficits in Psychological and Classroom Performance of Children with Elevated Detine Lead Levels." *New England Journal of Medicine* 300:659-695.

—— C McFarland, R.B. Ness, S.E. Fienberg, M.J. Tobin (2002). "Bone Lead Levels in Adjudicated Delinquents: A Case Control Study." *Neurotoxicology and Teratology* 24,6: 711-17.

—— J. Reiss, M. Tobin, G. Biesecker, and J. Greenhouse (1996). "Bone Lead Levels and Delinquent Behavior." *Journal of the American Medical Association* 5:363-369.

—— A. Schell, D. Bellinger, A. Leviton, and E.N. Allred (1990). "The Long-Term Effects of Exposure to Low Doses of Lead in Childhood: An 11-year Follow-up Report." *New England Journal of Medicine* 322.

Neier, A. (1993) "Watching Rights." *Nation*, March 1:259.

Nettler, G. (1984). *Explaining Crime*. New York: McGraw Hill.

Newman, G. (1988). "Punishment and Social Practice." *Law and Social Inquiry* 13(2):337-357.

—— (1985). *The Punishment Response*. New York: Harrow and Heston.

—— (1976). *Comparative Deviance*. New York: Elsevier.

—— and M.J. Lynch (1987). "From Feuding to Terrorism: The Ideology of Vengeance." *Contemporary Crises* 11:223-242.

Newman, O. (1996). *Creating Defensible Space*. New York: Diane Publishing Co.

—— (1973). *Defensible Space: Crime Prevention Through Urban Design*. New York: Macmillan.

*New York Times* (1999). "The War on Drugs Retreats, Still Taking Prisoners." February 28, p. C1.

Nolan, K. J. (2004). "Pharmaceutical Companies Liable for Fraudulent Research by Subcontractors." *Drug Discovery Today* 9(4):153-154.

Novack, G. (1971). *An Introduction to the Logic of Marxism*. New York: Pathfinder.

—— (1966). *Existentialism versus Marxism*. New York: Dell.

Nye, F. (1958). *Family Relationships and Delinquent Behavior*. New York: Wiley.

Oakley, A. (1974). *Woman's Work*. New York: Vintage.

O'Connor, J. (1998). *Natural Causes: Essays in Ecological Marxism*. New York: Guilford.

—— (1992). "Murder on the Orient Express: The Political Economy of the Gulf War." *Social Justice* 19:62-75.

—— (1985). *Accumulation Crisis*. New York: Basil-Blackwell.

—— (1973). *The Fiscal Crisis of the State*. New York: St. Martin's Press.

Offe, C. (1985). *Disorganized Capitalism*. Cambridge, MA: MIT Press.

—— and V. Ronge (1975). "Theses on the Theory of the State." *New German Critique* 139-147.

Ohmann, R., G. Averill, M. Curtin, D. Shumway and E.G. Traube (eds.), (1996). *Making and Selling Culture*. Hanover, NH: Wesleyan University Press.

Ollman, B. (1978). *Alienation*. New York: Cambridge University Press.

O'Neill, S. (2003). "Justice in Ethnically Diverse Societies: A Critique of Political Alienation." *Ethnicities* 3(3):369-393.

Onwudiwe, I. (2001). *The Globalization of Terrorism*. Aldershot, UK: Ashgate.

O'Shaughnessy, N. J. (2005). Politics and Propaganda : Weapons of Mass Seduction. Ann Arbor, MI: University of Michigan Press.

Otto, D. (1997). "Rethinking the Universality of 'Human Rights' Law." *Columbia Human Rights Law Review* 29:291-46.

Painter, N.I. (1992). "Hill, Thomas and the Use of Racial Stereotypes." In: T. Morrison (ed.), *Race-ing Justice, En-Gendering Power*. New York: Pantheon.

Papp, D. (1994). *Contemporary International Relations: Frameworks for Understanding*. New York: MacMillan.

Parenti, M. (1977). *Democracy for the Few*. New York: St. Martin's Press.

Parker, R.N. and A.V. Horwitz (1986). "Unemployment, Crime and Imprisonment: A Panel Approach." *Criminology* 24:751-773.

Parks, E.L. (1976). "From Constabulary to Police Society." In: W. Chambliss and M. Mankoff (eds.), *Whose Law? What Order?* New York: Wiley.

Parsons, T. (1954). *Essays in Sociological Theory*. Glencoe, IL: Free Press.

Pashukanis, E. (1978). *Law and Marxism*. London, UK: Ink Links.

Passas, N. (1990). "Anomie and Corporate Deviance." *Contemporary Crises* 14:157-178.

Patterson, E.B. and M.J. Lynch (1991). "The Biases of Bail: Race Effects on Bail Decisions." In: M.J. Lynch and E.B. Patterson (eds.), *Race and Criminal Justice*. Albany, NY: Harrow and Heston.

—— and L. Patterson (1996). "Vice and Social Control: Predispositional Detention and the Juvenile Drug Offender." In: M.J. Lynch and E.B. Patterson (eds.), *Justice with Prejudice*. Albany, NY: Harrow and Heston.

Peak, K.J. (1999). *Community Policing and Problem Solving: Strategies and Practices.* Upper Saddle River, NJ: Prentice Hall.

Pearce, F. (1976). *Crimes of the Powerful.* London, UK: Pluto.

Pelfrey, W. (1980). "The New Criminology: Acceptance within Academe." In: J. Inciardi (ed.), *Radical Criminology: The Coming Crisis.* Beverly Hills, CA: Sage.

—— (1979). "Mainstream Criminology: More New Than Old." *Criminology* 17:323-329.

Pepinsky, H. (1987). "This Can't Be Peace: A Pessimist Looks at Punishment." In: W.B. Groves and G.R. Newman (eds.), *Punishment and Privilege.* New York: Harrow and Heston.

—— (1980). "A Radical Alternative to Radical Criminology." In: J. Inciardi (ed.), *Radical Criminology: The Coming Crisis.* Beverly Hills, CA: Sage.

—— (1978). "Communist-Anarchism as an Alternative to the Rule of Criminal Law." *Contemporary Crises* 2(3):315-327.

—— and R. Quinney (eds.), (1991). *Criminology as Peacemaking.* Bloomington, IN: Indiana University Press.

Perlow, V. (1988). *Super Profits and Crises: Modern U.S. Capitalism.* New York: International.

Perry, B. (2001). *In the Name of Hate: Understanding Hate Crimes.* New York: Routledge.

Petchesky, R.P. (1981). " At Hard Labor: Penal Confinement in Nineteenth Century America." In: D. Greenberg (ed.), *Crime and Capitalism.* Palo Alto, CA: Mayfield.

Petersilia, J. (1984). "Racial Disparity in the Criminal Justice System." In: D.G. Abeyie (ed.), *The Criminal Justice System and Blacks.* New York: Clark-Boardman.

—— (1983). *Racial Disparities in the Criminal Justice System.* Santa Monica, CA: Rand.

Peterson, F. (1938). *Strikes in the United States, 1880-1936.* Washington, DC: U.S. Government Printing Office.

Petras, J. (1987). "The Political Economy of State Terrorism." *Crime and Social Justice* 27-28:88-109.

Pfhol, S. (1985). *Images of Deviance and Social Control.* New York: McGraw-Hill.

—— (1979). "Deciding Dangerousness: Predictions of Violence as Social Control." *Crime and Social Justice* 11:28-40.

—— and A. Gordon (1986). "Criminological Displacements: A Sociological Deconstruction." *Social Problems* 33:94-113.

Pfost, D. (1987). "Reagan's Nicaragua Policy: A Case Study in Political Deviance and Crime." *Crime and Social Justice* 27-28:66-87.

Piesterse, J. (1985). "State Terrorism on a Global Scale: The Role of Israel." *Crime and Social Justice* 21-22:58-80.

Pirkle, R.A., D.J. Brody, E.W. Gunter, R.A. Kramer, D.C. Paschal, K.M. Flegal, and T.D. Matte (1994). "The Decline in Blood Lead Levels in the United States: The

National Health and Nutrition Examination Surveys (NHANES)." *Journal of the American Medical Association* 272:284-291.

Pitt, W. R. (2002). *War On Iraq*. New York: Context Books.

Piven, F.F. and R.A. Cloward (1997). *The Breaking of the American Social Compact*. New York: New Press.

—— (1977). *Poor People's Movement*. New York: Pantheon.

Platt, T. (1993a). " Rethinking Race." *Social Justice* 20(1-2):i-vii.

—— (1993b). "Beyond the Canon, with Great Difficulty." *Social Justice* 20(1-2):72-81.

—— (1993c). "Between Scorn and Longing: Frasier's Black Bourgeoisie." *Social Justice* 20(1-2):129-139.

—— (1985). "Criminology in the 1980s: Progressive Alternatives to Law and Order." *Crime and Social Justice* 21-22:191-199.

—— (1982). "Crime and Punishment in the United States: Immediate and Long-Term Reforms from a Marxist Perspective." *Crime and Social Justice* 18:38-45.

—— (1978). "Street Crime — A View from the Left." *Crime and Social Justice* 9:26-34.

—— (1974). "Prospects for a Radical Criminology in the U.S." *Crime and Social Justice* 1:2-10.

—— (1971). *The Politics of the Riot Commission*. New York: MacMillan.

—— and L. Cooper (1974). *Policing America*. Englewood Cliffs, NJ: Prentice Hall.

—— and P. Takagi (1974). *Punishment and Penal Discipline*. San Francisco, CA: Crime and Social Justice Associates.

—— and R. Pollack (1974). "Changing Lawyers." *Issues in Criminology* 9.

—— J. Frappier, G. Ray, R. Schauffler, L. Trujillo, L. Cooper, E. Currie, S. Harring with S. Bernstein, B. Bigelow, M. Klare, P. Poyner, J. Scruggs, N. Stein and M. Thayer (1982). *The Iron Fist and the Velvet Glove*. San Francisco, CA: Synthesis Press.

Pogrebin, M., M. Dodge, and P. Katsampes (2001). "The Collateral Cost of Short Term Incarceration." *Corrections Management Quarterly* 5(4):64-70.

Pollack, K. (2004). "Spies. Lies, And Weapons: What Went Wrong,." *The Atlantic Monthly*, Jan.-Feb.:78-92.

Pollak, O. (1950). *The Criminality of Women*. Philadelphia, PA: University of Pennsylvania Press.

Pollard, E.A. (1977). *Southern History of the War*. Fairfax, VA: Fairfax Press.

Pope, C. and W. Feyerherm (1990). "Minority Status and Juvenile Justice Processing: An Assessment of the Research Literature (Parts I and II)." *Criminal Justice Abstracts* June: 327-335; September: 527-542.

Popper, K. (1957). *The Poverty of Historicism*. Boston, MA: Beacon.

Porter, R. (1986). "Rape — Does it Have an Historical Meaning?" In: S. Tomaselli and R. Porter (eds.), *Rape!* New York: Basil Blackwell.

Poulantzas, N. (1978). *Politics Power and Social Classes.* London, UK: Verso.

—— (1975). *Political Power and Social Classes.* London: Verso.

Prados, J. (2004). *Hoodwinked: The Documents that Reveal How Bush Sold us a War.* New York: The New Press.

Pred, A. (1966). *The Spatial Dynamics of U.S. Industrial Growth: 1800-1914.* Cambridge, MA: MIT Press.

Preston, W. (1963). *Aliens and Dissenters: Federal Suppression of Radicals, 1903-1933.* Cambridge, MA: Harvard University Press.

Price, B.R. and N.J. Sokoloff (eds.), (1982). *The Criminal Justice System and Women.* Newbury Park, CA: Sage.

Priest, D., and W. Pincus (2004). "U.S. Almost All Wrong on Weapons." *Washington Post,* October 7, p. A 01.

Prunier, G. (1997) *The Rwanda Crisis.* New York: Columbia University Press.

Pueschel, S. M., J. G. Linakis and A. C. Anderson (eds.), (1996.) *Lead Poisoning in Childhood.* Baltimore, MD: Paul H. Brookes Publishing.

Quinney, R. (1980). *Class, State and Crime.* New York: Longman.

—— (1979). *Criminology.* Boston, MA: Little, Brown.

—— (1974a) *Criminal Justice in America.* Boston, MA: Little, Brown.

—— (1974b). *Critique of Legal Order.* Boston, MA: Little, Brown.

—— (1971). "National Commission on the Causes and Prevention of Violence." *American Sociological Review* 36:724-727.

—— (1970). *The Social Reality of Crime.* Boston, MA: Little, Brown.

Radelet, M.L. (1989). "Executions of Whites for Crimes Against Blacks: Exceptions to the Rule?" *The Sociological Quarterly* 30(4):529-544.

—— H. A. Bedau, C.E. Putnam (1994). *In Spite of Innocence: Erroneous Convictions in Capital Cases.* Boston, MA: Northeastern University Press.

Rader, M. (1979). *Marx's Interpretation of History.* New York: Oxford.

Rafter, N.H. and E.A. Stanko (eds.), (1982). *Judge, Lawyer, Victim, Thief.* Boston, MA: Northeastern University Press.

Rai, M. (2003). *Regime Unchanged: Why The War On Iraq Changed Nothing.* London: Pluto Press.

—— (2002). *War Plan Iraq: Ten Reasons Against War On Iraq.* London: Verso.

Rainwater, L. (1970). *Behind Ghetto Walls: Black Families in a Federal Slum.* Chicago, IL: Aldine.

—— (1965). *Family Design.* Chicago, IL: Aldine.

Rampton, S. and J. Stauber. (2003). *Weapons of Mass Deception: The Uses of Propaganda in Bush's War on Iraq*. New York: Jeremy P. Tarcher/Penguin.

Ratner, M. (2002). 'The United Nations Charter And The Use Of Force Against Iraq." http://www.lawyersagainstthewar.org/legalarticles/ratner.html

—— Green, J. and Olshansky, B. (2003). *Against War with Iraq*. New York: Seven Stories Press.

—— and E. Ray (2004*). Guantanamo: What the World Should Know*. White River Junction, VT: Chelsea Green Publishing Company.

Reiman, J. ([1979] 1984/1995/1998). *The Rich Get Richer and the Poor Get Prison*. Boston, MA: Allyn and Bacon.

Reinarman, C. and H.G. Levine (1997). *Crack in America: Demon Drugs and Social Justice*. Berkeley, CA: University of California Press.

Renee, Y. (1978). *The Search for Criminal Man: A Conceptual History of the Dangerous Offender*. Lexington, MA: Lexington Books.

Rhodes, D. (1989). *Justice and Gender: Sex Discrimination and the Law*. Cambridge, MA: Harvard University Press.

Ricardo, D. ([1817]1978). *The Principles of Political Economy and Taxation*. London, UK: Dent.

Rich, C.G. (2004). "Performing Racial And Ethnic Identity: Discrimination By Proxy And The Future Of Title VII." *New York University* Law *Review* 79(4):1134-1271.

Richardson, J. (1974). *Urban Police in the United States*. Port Washington, NY: Kennikat.

Rifkin, J. (1995). *The End of Work: The Decline of the Global Labor Force and the Dawn of the Post-market Era*. New York: Tarcher/Putnam.

—— (2002). *The Hydrogen Economy: The Next Great Economic Revolution*. New York: Tarcher/Putnam.

Ritter, S. (2003.) *Frontier Justice: Weapons of Mass destruction And The Bushwhacking Of America*. New York: Context Books.

Roberts, L., R. Lafta, R. Garfield, J. Khudhairi, G. Burnham (2004). "Mortality before and After the 2003 Invasion of Iraq: Cluster Sample Survey." *The Lancet* 364 (9448):1857-1864.

Roberts, P. (2004). *The End of Oil: On the Edge of a Perilous New World*. London: Bloomsbury Publishing.

Roderick, J. V. (1992). *Calculated Risks: The Toxicity and Human Health Risks of Chemicals in our Environment*. Cambridge, UK: Cambridge University Press.

Robin, G. (1963). "Justifiable Homicide by Police Officers." *Journal of Criminal Law and Criminology* 54:61-69.

Rosaldo, M. and L. Lamphere (1974). *Women, Culture and Society*. Stanford, CA: Stanford University Press.

Rosenbaum, D.P. (1994). *The Challenge of Community Policing: Testing the Promises.* Thousand Oaks, CA: Sage Publications.

Rosenfeld, R. (1987). "Review: Primer in Radical Criminology." *Journal of Criminal Law and Criminology* 78(1):201-204.

Ross, E.A. (1907). *Sin and Society.* Boston, MA: Houghton, Mifflin.

Ross, J. I. (2003). *The Dynamics of Political Crime.* Thousand Oaks, CA: Sage.

—— (2000). *Varieties of State Crime and Its Control.* Monsey, NY: Criminal Justice Press.

Rossi, P.H., E. Waite, C. Bose and R.E. Berk (1974). "The Seriousness of Crime: Normative Structure and Individual Differences." *American Sociological Review* 39:224-237.

Rotella, E.J. (1995). "Women and the American Economy." In: S. Ruth (ed.), *Issues in Feminism.* Mountain View, CA: Mayfield.

Rubin, G. (1975). "The Traffic in Women: Notes on the Political-Economy of Sex." In: E. Reiter (ed.), *Toward an Anthropology of Women.* New York: Monthly Review Press.

Rubington, E. and M.S. Weinberg (eds.), (1987). *Deviance, the Interactionist Perspective.* New York: MacMillan.

Rummel, R. (1994). *Death by Government.* New Brunswick, NJ: Transaction Press.

Rusche, G. ([1933]1982). "Labor Market and Penal Sanction." *Crime and Social Justice* 10:2-8.

—— and O. Kirchheimer ([1939]1968). *Punishment and Social Structure.* New York: Columbia.

Russell, K.K. (1998). *The Color of Crime: Racial Hoaxes, White Fear, Black Protectionism, Police Harassment, and other Macroaggressions.* New York: New York University Press.

Ruth, S. (ed.), (1995). *Issues in Feminism.* Palo Alto, CA: Mayfield.

Ryan, W. (1982). *Equality.* New York: Vintage.

Sampson, R.J. and W.B. Groves (1989). "Community Structure and Crime." *American Journal of Sociology* 94(4):774-802.

—— and J. Laub (1993). *Crime in the Making.* Cambridge, MA: Harvard University Press.

—— and J. Laub (1990). "Crime and Deviance in the Life Course." *American Sociological Review* 55:609-627.

—— and W.J. Wilson (1994). "Toward a Theory of Race, Crime and Urban Inequality." In: J. Hagan and R. Peterson (eds.), *Crime and Inequality.* Stanford, CA: Stanford University Press.

Sanday, P. (1981). "The Sociocultural Context of Rape: A Crosscultural Study." *Journal of Social Issues* 37(1):5-27.

Saro-Wiwa, K.(1992). *Genocide in Nigeria: the Ogoni Tragedy.* London: Saros International Publishers.

Sartre, J.P. (1966). "Materialism and Revolution." In: G. Novack (ed.), *Existentialism Versus Marxism.* New York: Dell.

Sassen, S.(2000). *Guests and Aliens.* New York: New Press.

Sawers, L. (1984a). "New Perspectives on the Urban Political Economy." In: W.K. Tabb and L. Sawers (eds.), *Marxism and the Metropolis: New Perspectives in Urban Political Economy.* New York: Oxford University Press.

—— (1984b). "The Political Economy of Urban Transportation: An Interpretive Essay." In: W.K. Tabb and L. Sawers (eds.), *Marxim and the Metropolis: New Perspectives in Urban Political Economy.* New York: Oxford University Press.

Schafer, Stephen (1974). *The Political Criminal: The Problems of Morality and Crime.* New York: The Free Press.

Scheff, T. (1994). *Bloody Revenge: Emotions, Nationalism, and War.* Boulder, CO: Westview Press.

Scheer, C., R. Scheer, and L. Chaudhry. (2003). *The Five Biggest Lies Bush Told Us About Iraq.* New York: Seven Stories Press and Akashic Books.

Schichor, D. (1980a). "Some Problems of Credibility in Radical Criminology." In: J. Inciardi (ed.), *Radical Criminology: The Coming Crisis.* Beverly Hills, CA: Sage.

—— (1980b). "The New Criminology: Some Critical Issues." *The British Journal of Criminology* 20(1):1-19.

Schlosser, E. (1998). "The Prison Industrial Complex." *Atlantic Monthly* (Dec.):51-77.

Schmid, A. P. (2004). "Frameworks for Conceptualizing Terrorism." *Terrorism and Political Violence.* 16, 2:197-221.

Schor, J.B. (1993). *The Overworked American.* New York: Basic Books.

Schrecker, E. (1998). *Many are the Crimes: McCarthyism in America.* Boston, MA: Little, Brown.

—— (1994). *The Age of McCarthyism: A Brief History with Documents.* Boston, MA: Bedford Books.

Schultz, W. (2003). *Tainted Legacy: 9/11 and the Ruin of Human Rights.* New York: Nation Books.

Schur, E. (1984). *Labelling Women Deviant.* New York: Random House.

—— (1980). "Can Old and New Criminologies be Reconciled?" In: J. Inciardi (ed.), *Radical Criminology: The Coming Crisis.* Beverly Hills, CA: Sage.

—— (1973). *Radical Non-Intervention.* Englewood Cliffs, NJ: Prentice Hall.

—— (1971). *Labelling Deviant Behavior.* New York: Harper and Row.

Schwartz, M.B. (1989). "The Undercutting Edge of Criminology." *The Critical Criminologist* 1(2):1-2, 5.

Schwartz, M. (1991). "Humanist Sociology and Date Rape." *Humanity and Society.* 15:304-316.

—— and W. DeKeseredy (1991). "Left Realist Criminology: Strengths and Weakness and the Feminist Critique." *Crime, Law and Social Change* 15:51-72.

—— and D.O. Friedrichs (1994). "Postmodern Thought and Criminological Discontent: New Metaphors for Understanding Violence." *Criminology* 32:221-246.

—— and D. Milovanovic (eds.), (1996). *Race, Gender and Class in Criminology.* New York: Garland.

—— (1986). *No Ivory Tower: McCarthyism and Universities.* New York: Oxford.

Schwendinger, H. and J. Schwendinger (1997). "Charting Subcultures at a Frontier of Knowledge: The Use of Sociometric Graphs to Examine Subcultures." *The British Journal of Sociology* 48(1):71-95.

—— (1993). "Giving Crime Prevention Top Priority." *Crime & Delinquency* 39:425-446.

—— (1988). "The World According to James Messerschmidt." *Social Justice* 7:4-13.

—— (1981). "The Standards of Living in Penal Institutions." In: D. Greenberg (ed.), *Crime and Capitalism.* Palo Alto, CA: Mayfield.

—— (1977). "Social Class and the Definition of Crime." *Crime and Social Justice* 7:4-13.

—— (1972). "The Continuing Debate on the Legalistic Approach to the Definition of Crime." *Issues in Criminology* 7(1):71-81.

—— (1970). "Defenders of Order or Guardians of Human Rights?" *Issues in Criminology* 5:113-146.

—— and M. J. Lynch (2002). "Critical Criminology in the United States: The Berkeley School and Theoretical Trajectories." In: R. Hogg and K. Carrington (eds.), *Critical Criminology: Issues, Debates and Challenges.* UK: Willan Publishing.

Schwendinger, J. and H. Schwendinger (1983). *Rape and Inequality.* Beverly Hills, CA: Sage.

—— (1981). "Rape, Sexual Inequality and Levels of Violence." *Crime and Social Justice* 16:3-31.

—— (1976). "Rape Victims and the False Sense of Guilt." *Crime and Social Justice* 6:4-17.

Scott, P.D. (1987). "Contragate." *Crime and Social Justice* 27-28:110-148.

Scull, A. (1977). *Decarceration.* Englewood Cliffs, NJ: Prentice-Hall.

Sellin, T. (1976). *Slavery and the Penal System.* New York: Elsevier.

—— (1968). *Forward: Punishment and Social Structure.* New York: Russell Sage.

—— (1944). *Pioneering in Penology.* Philadelphia, PA: University of Pennsylvania.

—— (1938). *Culture, Conflict and Crime.* New York: Holt, Rinehart and Winston.

—— (1935). "Race Prejudice in the Administration of Justice." *American Journal of Sociology* 41:212-217.

Shank, G. (1987a). "Contragate and Counterterrorism." *Crime and Social Justice* 27-28:i-xxvii.

—— (1987b). "Thorsten Sellin's Penology." In: A. Platt and P. Takagi (eds.), *Punishment and Penal Discipline*. San Francisco, CA: Crime and Social Justice Associates.

—— (1979). "Book Review: Michael Ignatieff, A Just Measure of Pain." *Crime and Social Justice* 11:62-66.

Shaw, C. and H. McKay (1942/1969). *Juvenile Delinquency and Urban Areas*. Chicago, IL: University of Chicago Press.

Shapiro, T.N. and M. Oliver (1998). *State of Black America*. New York: National Urban League.

Sheldon, R. (1981). "Convict Leasing: An Application of the Rusche-Kirchheimer Thesis to Penal Changes in Tennessee, 1930-1915." In: D. Greenberg (ed.), *Crime and Capitalism*. Palo Alto, CA: Mayfield.

Shi, D.E. (2001). *The Simple Life: Plain Living and High Thinking in American Culture*. Atlanta, GA: University of Georgia Press.

Short, J.F. and F. Nye (1957). "Reported Behavior as a Criterion of Deviant Behavior." *Social Problems* 5:207-213.

Shutkin, W. (2000). *The Land that Could Be: Environmentalism and Democracy in the Twenty-first century*. Cambridge, MA: MIT Press.

Silva, A.C. and V.M Yakovenko (2005). "Temporal Evolution of the 'Thermal' and 'Superthermal' Income Classes in the USA during 1983-2001." *Europhysics Letters* 69:304-309.

Silverman, M. and P.R. Lee (1974). *Pills, Profits and Politics*. Berkeley, CA: University of California Press.

Silverman, M., P. Lee and M. Lydecker (1982). *Prescription for Death: The Drugging of the Third World*. Berkeley, CA: University of California Press.

Simon, D.R. ([1995]1999). *Elite Deviance*. Boston, MA: Allyn and Bacon.

Simon, R. (1997). "Women and Crime: Two Decades Later, Another Assessment." *Social Pathology* 3(2):61-80.

—— (1975). *Women and Crime*. Lexington, MA: D.C. Heath.

Simpson, S. and L. Ellis (1995). "Doing Gender: Sorting out the Caste and Crime Conundrum." *Criminology* 33(1):47-81.

Singer, S. and M. Levine (1988). "Power-Control Theory, Gender and Delinquency." *Criminology* 26(4):627-648.

Sinha, M. M., D. Guy and A. Wollacott. (1999). *Feminisms and Internationalisms*. London: Blackwell Publishers.

Sitcoff, H. (1981). *The Struggle for Black Equality: 1954-1980*. New York: Hill and Wang.

Sklar, H. (1995). "The Upper Class and Mothers in the Hood." In: M.L. Anderson and P.H. Collins (eds.), *Race, Class and Gender: An Anthology*. Belmont, CA: Wadsworth.

Sklar, K.K. (2000). *Women's Rights Emerges within the Anti-Slavery Movement, 1830-1870*. New York: St. Martin's Press.

Sklar, M.J. (1988). *The Corporate Reconstruction of American Capitalism: 1890-1916*. New York: Cambridge University Press.

Smart, C. (1987). *Feminism and the Power of Law*. New York: Routledge.

Smith, A. ([1776]1982). *The Wealth of Nations*. New York: Penguin.

Smith, D., N. Graham and B. Adams (1991). "Minorities and the Police." In: M.J. Lynch and E.B. Patterson (eds.), *Race and Criminal Justice*. Albany, NY: Harrow and Heston.

Smith, R.J. and J.V. Grimaldi (2005). "A 3rd DeLay Trip Under Scrutiny, 1997 Russia Visit Reportedly Backed by Business Interests." *Washington Post*, April 6, p. A1.

Snider, L. (2003). "Constituting The Punishable Woman." *British Journal of Criminology*, 43(2):354-379.

Solomon, F. et al., (1980). "Civil Rights Activity and Reduction in Crime Among Negroes." *Crime and Social Justice* 13:27-37.

Solomon, N. and Erlich, R. (2003). *Target Iraq: What The News Media Didn't Tell You*. New York: Context Books.

Sommerville, W. (1968). "Double Standards in Law Enforcement with Regard to Minority Status." *Issues in Criminology* (Fall):35-63.

*Sourcebook of Criminal Justice Statistics* (2004/2002/1998). Albany, NY: Michael J. Hindelang Criminal Justice Research Center, State University of New York.

South, N. (1998). "A Green Field for Criminology? A Proposal for a Perspective." *Theoretical Criminology* 2(2):211-33.

Sparks, R. (1980). "A Critique of Marxist Criminology." In: N. Morris and M. Tonry (eds.), *Crime and Justice: An Annual Review*. Chicago, IL: University of Chicago Press.

Spiegleman, R. (1977). "Prison Psychiatry and Drugs: A Case Study." *Crime and Social Justice* 7:23-29.

Spector, M. and J.I. Kitsuse (2000). *Constructing Social Problems*. New Burnswick, NJ: Transaction Publishers.

Spitzer, S. (1983). "Marxist Perspectives in the Sociology of Law." *Annual Review of Sociology* 9:103-124.

—— (1981). "The Political Economy of Policing." In: D. Greenberg (ed.), *Crime and Capitalism*. Palo Alto, CA: Mayfield.

—— (1980). "Left Wing Criminology — An Infantile Disorder?" In: J. Inciardi (ed.), *Radical Criminology: The Coming Crisis*. Beverly Hills, CA: Sage.

—— (1979). "The Rationalization of Crime Control in Capitalist Society." *Contemporary Crises* 3:187-206.

—— (1975). "Toward a Marxian Theory of Deviance." *Social Problems* 22:638-651.

—— and A. Scull (1977a). "Social Control in Historical Perspective." In: D. Greenberg (ed.), *Corrections and Punishment*. Beverly Hills, CA: Sage.

—— and A. Scull (1979b). "Privatization and Capitalist Development: The Case of the Private Police." *Social Problems* 25:18-29.

Spohn, C., J. Gruhl and S. Welch (1987). "The Impact of Ethnicity and Gender of Defendant on the Decision to Reject or Dismiss Felony Charges." *Criminology* 25:175-191.

St. Clair, D.J. (1986). *The Motorization of American Cities*. New York: Praeger.

Stacewicz, R. (1997). *New Winter Soldiers: An Oral History of Vietnam Veterans Against the War*. New York: Twayne/Simon and Schuster.

Stanko, E. (1985). *Intimate Intrusions: Women's Experience of Male Violence*. Boston, MA: Routledge and Kegan Paul.

Stansell, C. (1992). "White Feminists and Black Realities: The Politics of Authenticity." In: T. Morrison (ed.), *Race-ing Justice, En-Gendering Power*. New York: Pantheon.

Staples, R. (1982). *Black Masculinity*. San Francisco, CA: Black Scholar Press.

Steffensmeier, D. (1981). "Crime and the Contemporary Women." In: L. Bowker (ed.), *Women and Crime in America*. New York: MacMillan.

Stein, A. and K. Plummer (1994). "'I Can't Even Think Straight:' Queer' Theory and the Missing Sexual Revolution in Sociology." *Sociological Theory* 12:178-188.

Steiner, H. and P. Alston (2000). *International Human Rights in Context Law, Politics, Morals*. New York: Oxford University Press.

Steuerle, E.C. (1996). *Privatizing Social Security: The Third Option*. Washington, DC: The Urban Institute.

Stohl, M. and G. Lopez (eds.), (1984). *The State as Terrorist*. Westport, CT: Greenwood.

Stone, C. (1975). *Where the Law Ends*. New York: Harper and Row.

Stretesky, P.B. (2003). "The distribution of air lead levels across US counties: Implications for the production of racial inequality" *Sociological Spectrum*. 23, 91-118.

—— (1999). "Testing a Broader Model of Environmental Justice." *Social Pathology* 4(2):73-85.

—— (1997a). "The Problem of Equality Revisited." *Journal of Social, Political and Economic Studies* 22:199-204.

—— (1997b). "Waste Wars: Race, Class and Toxic Waste Siting in Florida." Doctoral dissertation, Florida State University, School of Criminology and Criminal Justice, Tallahassee, FL.

—— (1996). "Environmental Equity?" *Social Pathology* 2(3):293-298.

—— and M.J. Hogan (1998). "Environmental Justice: An Analysis of Superfund Sites in Florida." *Social Problems* 45:268-287.

—— and M.J. Lynch (2004). "The Relationship Between Lead and Crime." *Journal of Health and Social Behavior.* 45(2):214-229.

—— and M. J. Lynch (2003). "Environmental Hazards and School Segregation in Hillsborough County, 1987-1999." *The Sociological Quarterly* 43(4):553-573.

—— and M. J. Lynch (2001). "The Relationship Between Lead and Homicide." *Archives of Pediatric and Adolescent Medicine.* 155(5):579-582.

—— and M.J. Lynch (1999a). "Corporate Environmental Violence and Racism." *Crime, Law and Social Change* 30(2):163-184.

—— (1999b). "Environmental Justice and the Prediction of Distance to Accidental Chemical Releases in Hillsborough County, Florida." *Social Science Quarterly* 80(4):830-846.

Steven, D. and C. O'Hare (1995). *Jailed for Freedom: American Women Win the Vote.* Troutdale, OR: NewSage Press.

Stiglitz, J. (2003). *Globalization and Its Discontents.* New York: W.W. Norton.

Sudetic, C. (1999). *Blood and Vengeance : One Family's Story of the War in Bosnia.* New York: Penguin.

Sutherland, E.H. (1983). *White Collar Crime — The Uncut Version.* (Reissue of original 1949 Dryden Press Manuscript.) New Haven, CT: Yale University Press.

—— (1949). *White Collar Crime.* New York: Holt, Rinehart and Winston.

—— (1939). *Criminology.* Philadelphia, PA: Lippincott.

Suttles, G. (1971). *The Social Order of the Slums.* Chicago, IL: University of Chicago Press.

Sweezy, P.M. (1942). *The Theory of Capitalist Development.* New York: Modern Reader.

Swett, D. (1969). "Cultural Bias in the American Legal System." *Law and Society Review* 4:79-109.

Swigert, V. and R. Farrell (1981). "Corporate Homicide." *Law and Society Review* 15:161-182.

Sykes, G. (1974). "The Rise of Critical Criminology." *Journal of Criminal Law and Criminology* 65:206-213.

Syzmanski, A. (1983). *Class Structure.* New York: Praeger.

Taguba, A. (2003). *Investigation of the 800th Military Police Brigade.* Joint Interrogation and Debriefing Center,US Military Occupation Facilities, Abu Ghurayb Prison, Iraq (http://globalsecurity.org/intell/world/iraq/abu-ghurayb-prison-abuse.htm).

Takagi, P. (1981). "Race, Crime and Social Policy." *Crime & Delinquency* 27:48-63.

—— (1979). "LEAA's Research Solicitations: Police Use of Deadly Force." *Crime and Social Justice* 11:51-61.

Tannenbaum, F. (1939). *Crime and the Community*. New York: Columbia University Press.

Tanner, M. (1996). *Privatizing Social Security*. Atlanta, GA: Georgia Policy Foundation.

Tappan, P. (1947). "Who is the Criminal?" *American Sociological Review* 12:97-102.

Taylor, I., P. Walton and J. Young (eds.), (1975). *Critical Criminology*. London, UK: Routlege and Keegan Paul.

—— (1974). "Advances towards a Critical Criminology." *Theory and Society* 1(4):441-476.

—— (1973). *The New Criminology*. New York: Harper and Row.

Thomas, J. (1991). "Racial Codes in Prison Culture: Snapshots in Black and White." In: M.J. Lynch and E.B. Patterson (eds.), *Race and Criminal Justice*. Albany, NY: Harrow and Heston.

—— and A. O'Maolchatha (1989). "Reassessing the Critical Metaphor: An Optimistic Revisionist View." *Justice Quarterly* 6(2):143-172.

Thompson, L.H. (1992). "Health Insurance: Vulnerable Payers Lose Billions to Fraud and Abuse." Report to Chairman, Subcommittee on Human Resources and Intergovernmental Operations. Washington, DC: United States General Accounting Office, (May).

Thornberry, T.P. (1973). "Race, Socioeconomic Status and Sentencing in the Juvenile Justice Process." *Journal of Criminal Law and Criminology* 64:90-98.

Tigar, M. (1984). "The Right of Property and the Law of Theft." *Texas Law Review* 62:443-475.

—— (1977). *Law and the Rise of Capitalism*. New York: Monthly Review Press.

—— (1971). *Law Against the People*. New York: Random House.

Tillman, R. (2005). *Pump and Dump*. New Brunswick, NJ: Rutgers University Press.

Tittle, C. (1995). *Control Balance: Toward a General Theory of Deviance*. Boulder, CO: Westview.

—— (1983). "Social Class and Criminal Behavior." *Social Problems* 62(3):334-357.

—— and W.J. Villemez (1978). "The Myth of Social Class and Criminality." *American Sociological Review* 43:643-656.

Toby, J. (1980). "The New Criminology is the Old Baloney." In: J. Inciardi (ed.), *Radical Criminology: The Coming Crisis*. Beverly Hills, CA: Sage.

Tombs, S. and D. Whyte (2003). "Scrutinizing the Powerful, " In: S. Tombs and D. Whyte (eds.), *Unmasking the Crimes of the Powerful*. New York: Peter Lang.

Tonry, M. (1995). *Malign Neglect: Race, Crime and Punishment in America*. New York: Oxford.

—— (1994). "Racial Politics, Racial Disparities and the War on Crime." *Crime & Delinquency* 40(4):480-492.

Topal, E. J. (2004). "Refocoxib, Merck and the FDA." *The New England Journal of Medicine* 351:27:2875-2878.

Tuchman, B.W. (1978). *A Distant Mirror: The Calamitous Fourteenth Century.* New York: Knopf.

Turk, A.T. (1982). *Political Criminality: The Defiance and Defense of Authority.* Beverly Hills, CA: Sage Publications.

—— (1980). "Analyzing Official Deviance." In: J. Inciardi (ed.), *Radical Criminology: The Coming Crisis.* Beverly Hills, CA: Sage.

—— (1977). "Class, Conflict and Criminology." *Sociological Focus* 10:209-220.

—— (1975). "Prospects and Pitfalls for Radical Criminology." *Crime and Social Justice* 4:41-52.

—— (1969). *Criminality and Legal Order.* Chicago, IL: Rand.

—— (1966). "Conflict and Criminality." *American Sociological Review* 31:338-352.

Turnbull, C. (1965). *African Pygmies.* Garden City, NY: National History Press.

United Nations General Assembly, United Nations Development Program (1999). "Resolution 51/210: Measures to Eliminate International Terrorism." New York: author.

—— (1993). Human Development Report. New York: United Nations.

U.S. Bureau of the Census. (2005*). Income, Poverty and Health Insurance Coverage in the United States, 2004.* (Current Population Reports, Consumer Income Series, P60-229). http://www.census.gov/prod/2005pubs/p60-229.pdf

—— (2004). Income, Poverty and Health Insurance Status in the United States, 2003. Washington DC: U.S. Government Printing Office.

—— (1996a). *The Dynamics of Economic Well Being. Income, 1992-1993: Moving Up and Down the Income Ladder.* Washington, DC: U.S. Government Printing Office.

—— (1996b). *The Dynamics of Economic Well Being. Poverty,1992-1993: Who Stays Poor and Who Doesn't.* Washington, DC: U.S. Government Printing Office.

—— (1993). *Statistical Abstracts of the United States.* Washington, DC: U.S. Government Printing Office.

U.S. Bureau of Labor Statistics (2004). "Median weekly earnings of full-time wage and salary workers by selected characteristics ." http://ftp.bls.gov/pub/-special.requests/lf/aat37.txt

U.S. Bureau of Labor Statistics (2004). *Highlights of Women's Earnings, in 2003.* Report # 987. http://www.bls.gov/cps/cpswom2003.pdf

U.S. Code of Federal Regulations (2005). Washington D.C.: U.S. Government Printing Office.

U.S. Congress, House of Representatives (1986). *Capital Punishment: Hearings Before the Subcommittee on Criminal Justice of the Committee on the Judiciary.* Washington, DC: U.S. Government Printing Office.

U.S. Department of Energy (2003). "21st Century Complete Guide to the National Energy Technology Lab (NETL) Fossil Fuel Research, Clean Coal Technology, Natural Gas Center, Petroleum Technology, Fossil Fuel Exploration, Supply, End-User Research." http://www.gasturbine.org/2001budgetFE.pdf

U.S. Department of Justice (2004). *Prison and Jail Inmates, Midyear, 2003.* Washington, DC: Bureau of Justice Statistics (www.ojp.usdoj.gov/bjs/pub/pdf/pjim03.pdf).

U.S. Department of Justice (1999/1998/1983). *Report to the Nation on Crime and Justice.* Washington, DC: U.S. Government Printing Office.

U.S. Department of Justice (1999). *Prisoners in 1998.* Washington, DC: Bureau of Justice Statistics.

—— (1998). *Prisoners in 1997.* Washington, DC: Bureau of Justice Statistics.

—— (1997). *Prisoners in 1996.* Washington, DC: Bureau of Justice Statistics.

—— (1996). *Prison and Jail Inmates, 1996.* Washington, DC: Bureau of Justice Statistics.

—— (1993). *Jail Inmates, 1992.* Washington, DC: Bureau of Justice Statistics.

U.S. Department of Labor (1996). *Labor Force Statistics.* http://stats.bls.gov/top20.html

U.S. Federal Bureau of Investigation (1998). *Crime in the United States.* Washington, DC: U.S. Government Printing Office.

U.S. National Commission on Criminal Justice Standards and Goals (1973) *Standards and Goals for the Administration of Justice.* Washington, DC: U.S. Government Printing Office.

U.S. National Commission on Terrorist Attacks Upon the United States (2004). *The 9/11 Commission Report* (authorized ed.). New York: W.W. Norton.

U.S. National Institute of Justice (1996). *Policing Drug Hot Spots.* U.S. Dept. of Justice, Office of Justice Programs, National Institute of Justice.

—— (2005). "Funding Opportunities, 2005." www.ojp.usdoj.gov/nij/funding.htm

U.S. Occupational Safety and Health Administration (OSHA), (1997). *Workplace Injury, Illness and Fatality Statistics.* Washington, DC: author.

U. S. Office of Budget Management (2005). *FY 2006 Budget Priorities,* Table S-1, Budget Totals. http://www.whitehouse.gov/omb/budget/fy2006/tables.html

U.S. Office of the President (1991). *Economic Report of the President Transmitted to Congress.* Washington, DC: U.S. Government Printing Office.

U.S. President's Commission on Law Enforcement and Administration of Justice (1967). *The Challenge of Crime in a Free Society.* Washington, DC: U.S. Government Printing Office.

van den Berghe, P. (1990). *State Violence and Ethnicity.* Niwot: CO: Colorado University Press.

Van Fossen, B. (1979). *The Structure of Social Inequality.* Boston, MA: Little, Brown.

Varenne, H. (1977). *Americans Together: Structured Diversity in a Midwestern Town.* New York: Columbia University Press.

Vayda, A. (1968). "Hypotheses About Functions of War." In *War: The Anthropology of Armed Conflict and Aggression,* M. Fried, M. Harris, and R. Murphy, eds. New York: Natural History Press

Veblen, T. ([1923]1964). *Absentee Ownership, and Business Enterprise in Recent Times, The Case of America.* New York: Viking Press.

—— ([1899]1948). "The Theory of the Leisure Class." In: M. Lerner (ed.), *The Portable Veblen.* New York: Viking Press.

Verderey, K. (1996). *What Was Socialism: What Comes Next.* Princeton, NJ: Princeton University Press.

Veysey, B.M. and S. Messner (1999). "Further Testing of Social Disorganization Theory: An Elaboration of Sampson and Groves' 'Community Structure and Crime.'" *Journal of Research in Crime & Delinquency* 36(2):156-174.

Vito, G.F. and T.J. Keil (1988). "Capital Sentencing in Kentucky: An Analysis of the Factors Influencing Decision Making in the Post-Gregg Period." *Journal of Criminal Law and Criminology* 79(2):483-503.

Vold, G.B. and T.J. Bernard (1979). *Theoretical Criminology.* New York: Oxford University Press.

—— T. Bernard and J. Snipes (1998). *Theoretical Criminology.* New York: Oxford University Press.

Walker, Pat (ed.), (1979). *Between Labor and Capital.* Boston, MA: South End Press.

Walker, S. (1985). *Sense and Nonsense about Crime.* Pacfic Grove, CA: Brooks-Cole.

—— C. Spohn and M. DeLone (1996). *The Color of Justice.* Belmont, CA: Wadsworth.

Wallace, D. and D. Humphries (1981). "Urban Crime and Capitalist Accumulation, 1950-1971." In: D. Greenberg (ed.), *Crime and Capitalism.* Palo Alto, CA: Mayfield.

Walmsely, R. (2003). *World Prison Population List,* (4th edition) London: United Kingdom, Home Office.

Walsh, A. (1987). "The Sexual Stratification Hypothesis and Sexual Assaults in Light of the Changing Conception of Race." *Criminology* 25(1):153-174.

Walsh, L.E. (1993). *Final Report of the Independent Counsel for Iran/Contra Matters.* Washington, DC: U.S. Court of Appeals for the District of Columbia Circuit, U.S. Government Printing Office.

Ward, B. (1979). *The Radical Economic World View.* New York: Basic.

Ward, T., and P. Green (2000). "Legitimacy, Civil Society and State Crime." *Social Justice* 27,4: 76-93.

Wargo, J. (1998). *Our Children's Toxic Legacy.* New Haven, CT: Yale University Press.

Warker, E.V.D. (1875). "The Relations of Women to Crime." *Popular Science Monthly* 8:1-16, 334-344.

Warren, R. (1978). *The Community in America.* Chicago, IL: Rand.

Warring, M. (1990). *If Women Counted: A New Feminist Economics.* San Francisco, CA: Harper.

Waxman, H. (2004). *Iraq on Record: The Bush Administration's Public Statements on Iraq.* Committee on Government Reform, Minoirty Staff, Special Investigative Division, Washington, DC: US House of Representatives.

Weber, M. (1978). *Economy and Society.* Berkeley: University of California Press.

—— ([1930]1985). *The Protestant Ethic and the Spirit of Capitalism.* (Translated by Talcott Parsons.) London, UK: Unwin Paperbacks.

—— ([1947]/1964/1977). *The Theory of Social and Economic Organization.* New York: Free Press.

Websdale, N. (2001). *Policing the Poor: From Slave Plantation to Public Housing.* Boston: Northeastern University Press.

—— (1997). *Rural Women Battering and the Justice System.* Thousand Oaks, CA: Sage.

Weeramantry, C.G. (2003). *Armageddon or Brave New World? Reflections on Hostilities in Iraq.* Ratamalan, Sri Lanka: Sarvodaya Vishva Lekha.

Weinstein, J. (2003). *The Long Detour: The History and Future of the American Left.* Boulder, CO: Westview.

Weir, D. and M. Shapiro (1982). *Circle of Poison.* San Francisco, CA: Institute for Food and Development Policy.

Weiss, J. (1976). "Liberation and Crime: The Invention of the New Female Criminal." *Crime and Social Justice* 6:17-27.

—— (1978). "The Emergence and Transformation of Private Detective Industrial Policing in the United States, 1850-1940." *Crime and Social Justice* 9:35-48.

Welch, M. (1999). *Punishment in America.* Beverly Hills: Sage.

—— (1997). "Regulating the Reproduction and Morality of Women: The Social Control of Body and Soul." *Women and Criminal Justice* 9(1):17-38.

—— (1996a). "Critical Criminology, Social Justice and an Alternative View of Incarceration." *Critical Criminology* 7(2):43-58.

—— (1996b). "Race and Social Class in the Examination of Punishment." In: M.J. Lynch and E.B Patterson (eds.), *Justice with Prejudice.* Albany, NY: Harrow and Heston.

—— (1996c). "The Immigration Crisis: Detention as an Emerging Mechanism of Social Control." *Social Justice* 23(2):169-184.

—— (1996d). *Corrections: A Critical Approach.* New York: McGraw-Hill.

—— M. Fenwick and M. Roberts (1998). "State Managers, Intellectuals and the Media." *Justice Quarterly* 15(1):232-251.

—— M. Fenwick and M. Roberts (1997). "Primary Definitions of Crime and Moral Panic." *Journal of Research in Crime and Delinquency* 34(4):474-494.

Werkentin, F., M Hofferbert and M. Bauerman (1974). "Criminology as Police Science: Or How Old is the New Criminology?" *Crime and Social Justice* 2:24-41.

West, C. and S. Fenstermaker (1995). "Doing Difference." *Gender and Society* 9(1):8-37.

—— and D.H. Zimmerman (1987). "Doing Gender." *Gender and Society* 1(2):125-151.

Westervelt, S.D. and J.A. Humphrey (eds.), (2001). *Wrongly Convicted: Perspectives on Failed Justice.* New Brunswick, NJ: Rutgers University Press.

Wheeler, S. and M.L. Rothman (1982). "The Organization as a Weapon in White Collar Crime." *Michigan Law Review* 80:1403-1427.

Wilbanks, W. (1987). *The Myth of a Racist Criminal Justice System.* Belmont, CA: Wadsworth.

Wilkins, R. (1994). *Cities after the 1960s: Where Have All the Promises Gone?.* Fairfax, VA: Institute for Conflict Analysis and Resolution, George Mason University.

Williams, W. A. (1988). *The Tragedy of American Diplomacy.* New York: W.W. Norton.

Williams. F. (1980). "Conflict Theory and Differential Processing." In: J. Inciardi (ed.), *Radical Criminology: The Coming Crisis.* Beverly Hills, CA: Sage.

Williams, W.A. (1962). *The Tragedy of American Diplomacy.* New York: Delta Books.

Willis, P. (1981). *Learning to Labor: How Working Class Kids Get Working Class Jobs.* New York: Columbia University Press.

Wilson, J.Q. and P. Cook (1985). "Unemployment and Crime." *The Public Interest* 79:3-8.

—— and R. Herrnstein (1985). *Crime and Human Nature.* New York: Simon and Schuster.

Wilson, W.J. (1996). *When Work Disappears: The World of the New Urban Poor.* New York: Alfred A. Knopf.

—— (1987). *The Truly Disadvantaged.* Chicago, IL: University of Chicago Press.

Wolfe, A. (1977). *The Limits of Legitimacy: Political Contradictions of Contemporary Capitalism.* New York: Free Press.

Wolff, E.N. (2004). *Changes in Household Wealth in the 1980s and 1990s in the U.S.* Chicago: Jerome Levy Economics Institute.

—— (1995a). "How the Pie is Sliced." *The American Prospect* 22:58-65 (http://epn.org/prospect/22/22wolf.html).

—— (1995b). *Top Heavy: A Study of the Increasing Inequality of Wealth in the United States.* New York: Twentieth Century Fund.

—— (ed.), (1987). *International Comparisons of the Distribution of Wealth.* New York: Oxford.

Wonders, N. (1996). "Determinate Sentencing: A Feminist and Postmodern Story." *Justice Quarterly* 13(4):611-648.

—— and R. J.Michalowski (2001). "A Tale of Two Cities: Tourism, Sexwork, and Globalization in Amsterdam and Havana." *Social Problems* 48(4):545-571.

—— and R.J. Michalowski (1998). "Globalization and the International Traffic in Women." Paper presented at the meetings of the American Society of Criminology, Washington, DC.

—— and R. Michalowski (1996). "Arizona Crime Survey." Flagstaff, AZ: Northern Arizona University Social Research Laboratory.

—— and F. Solop (1993). "Understanding the Emergence of Law and Public Policy." In: W. Chambliss and M. Zatz (eds.), *Making Law.* Bloomington, IN: Indiana University Press.

Wray, M. and N. Newitz (1997). *White Trash: Race and Class in America.* New York: Routledge.

Wright, E.O. (1978/1979). *Class, Crisis and the State.* London, UK: New Left Books.

—— (1973). *The Politics of Punishment.* New York: Harper and Row.

X, Malcolm (1966). *Malcolm X Speaks: Selected Speeches and Statements.* New York: Grove.

—— (1966). *The Autobiography of Malcolm X.* New York: Grove.

Yeager, M. (1979). "Unemployment and Imprisonment." *Journal of Criminal Law and Criminology* 70(4):586-588.

Young, I.S. (1990). *Justice and the Politics of Difference.* Princeton, NJ: Princeton University Press.

Young, J. (1997). "Ten Points of Realism." In: J. Young and R. Matthews (eds.), *Rethinking Criminology.* London, UK: Sage.

—— (1987). "The Task Facing a Realist Criminology." *Contemporary Crises* 11:337-356.

—— (1981). "Toward a Critical Theory of Justice." *Social Theory and Practice* 7(3):279-302.

—— (1976). "Forward: Crime of the Powerful." In: F. Pearce (ed.), *Crimes of the Powerful.* London, UK: Pluto.

—— (1975). "Working Class Criminology." In: I. Taylor, P. Walton and J. Young (eds.), *Critical Criminology.* Boston, MA: Routledge and Keegan Paul.

Young, T.R. (1996a). "Beyond Crime and Punishment: Part 1 — Beginning with Pain and Imprisonment." *Critical Criminology* 7(1):107-120.

—— (1996b). "Beyond Crime and Punishment: Part 2 — Democratic Proposals for Social Justice." *Critical Criminology* 7(2):92-107.

Zaretsky, E. (1976). *Capitalism, the Family and Personal Life.* New York: Harper & Row.

Zatz, M. (1990). "A Question of Assumptions." In: B. MacLean and D. Milovanovic (eds.), *Racism, Empiricism and Criminal Justice.* Vancouver, CAN: Collective Press.

—— (1987a). "Chicano Youth Gangs and Crime: The Creation of a Moral Panic." *Contemporary Crises* 11:129-158.

—— (1987b). "Changing Forms of Racial and Ethnic Biases in Sentencing." *Journal of Research in Crime and Delinquency* 24(1):69-92.

—— and J.H. McDonald (1993). "Structural Contradictions and Ideological Consistency: Changes in the Form and Content of Cuban Criminal Law." In: W. Chambliss and M. Zata (eds.), *Making Law.* Bloomington, IN: Indiana University Press.

Zelnick, S. (1996). "Twentieth Century Fox." In: R. Ohman, G. Averill, M. Curtin, D. Shumway and E.G. Traube (eds.), *Making and Selling Culture.* Hanover, NH: Wesleyan University Press.

Zimring, F.E. (1986). *Capital Punishment and the American Agenda.* New York: Cambridge University Press.

—— G. J. Hawkins (1973). *Deterrence: The Legal Threat in Crime Control.* Chicago: University of Chicago Press, 1973.

Zinn, H. (1995). *A People's History of the United States: 1492 to Present.* New York: Harper Perennial.

Zukav, G. (1990). *The Dancing Wu Li Masters.* New York: St. Martin's Press.

# SUBJECT INDEX

RADICAL CRIMINOLOGY (see
also: Criminology; Left Realism;
Marxism; and Justice)
contextualized explanation, 92-
93
crime and the life course, 151-
157
crime causation theories, 83-129
critical criminology and, 14 17
definition, 1, 3-5
development of, 5-14
environment and, 160-164
female criminality and, 120-125
"green" criminology (see Green
Criminology)
justice policy and, 170-172
Marx, history and, 23-25
left-realism, 292-299
Marxist methods and concepts,
21-39
overview, 17-19
policing and, 215-240
punishment, corrections and,
265-289
social capital, 144-149
strain theory and, 132-139
world systems theory, 211-212

RAPE, 127-129

RECESSIONS
crime and, 114-115

REGULATORY AGENCIES, 77-
79, 229-234

SEX DISCRIMINATION, 260-262

SOCIAL CLASS, 22-23
capitalism and, 29-30
class bias and courts, 252-255
life course and, 151-156
policing and, 224-225

production, political power and,
28-29
punishment and, 275-276
strain theory and, 134-137

SOCIAL CONSTRUCTION OF
CRIME, 80-81

STATE CRIME
genocide and, 207-210
political consciousness and, 189-
192
state and anti-state actors, 203-
207
terrorism and, 183-213

STATES
political economy, law and, 46-
58

STRAIN THEORY, 131-139

TERRORISM
Explaining terrorism, 188, 210-
213
power, labeling and, 79-80
state and anti-state actors, 203-
206
state crime and, 183-213
9/11 attacks, 192

THEORIES OF CRIME (see
Criminology)

UNEMPLOYMENT
crime and, 110-114
punishment, 282-288

WAR (see also Iraq), 188, 198-200

WHITE-COLLAR CRIME (see
Crimes of the Powerful; and
Social Class)

WORLD SYSTEMS THEORY,
211-212